ENGLISH-FRENCH
FRENCH-ENGLISH

 **BARNES & NOBLE BOOKS**
A DIVISION OF HARPER & ROW, PUBLISHERS
New York, Hagerstown, San Francisco, London

Distributed in
the U.S. by
Harper & Row, Publishers, Inc.
10 East 53rd Street
New York, N.Y. 10022

ENGLISH-FRENCH DICTIONARY

ABBREVIATIONS

adj. adjective

adv. adverb

art. article

conj. conjunction

dem. demonstrative

f. feminine

fig. figurative

impers. impersonal

inf. infinitive

int. interjection

m. masculine

pers. person

pl. plural

poss. possessive

pp. past participle

pron. pronoun

qch. quelque chose

qn. qulqu'un

rel. relative

s. substantive

sing. singular

s.o. someone

sth. something

v.a. active verb

v.a. & n. active and neuter verb

v. aux. auxiliary verb

v.n. neuter verb

* irregular verb

prep. preposition

Pronunciation

We give below a short, simple guide to French pronunciation, giving the French sounds and their description. Vowels or consonants that are equivalent to the English ones are not indicated in this list.

Letters	French key word	Description
a, à, â	la, là, bâtir	between *bag* and *bug*
ai, aî	chaise, maître	resembles *ai* in *chair*
an	dans	between the vowels of *ah* and *oh* with *n* nasalised
au	pause	as in *oh* but with no final *u*
c	a) café	before *a, o, u* pronounced as *k*
	b) ici	before *e, i, y* pronounced *s* as in *say*
ç	français	as *s* in *say*
ch	chambre	as *sh* in *she*
e	a) le, petit	as the unstressed vowel of *the, standard*
	b) derriere, mer	(in a closed syllable) as *e* in *deck*
é	été	as in *day* but with no final *i*
è, ê	père, fête	resembles the vowels in *pear* or *mare* without diphthongization
eau	eau	as in *oh* but with no final *u*
en	enfant	between *ah* and *oh* with *n* nasalized
er	donner	as in *day* but with no final
eu	jeudi, leur	closer than *earth* or *sir* pronounced with the lips pouted
g	a) rouge	before *e, i, y* pronounced as *s* in *measure, usual*
	b) grand	as *g* in *grand, good*
gn	signe	as in *new* or *lenient*
h	homme	it is never pronounced in French
i	a) ici	tenser than English short *i*
	b) mise	as *ee* in *meet*
î	île	as *ee* in *meet*
ille	fille	as in *key* with *y* at the end
in	vin	resembles the sound in *tan* pronounced through the nose
o	jour	as *s* in *usual*
jô	mot, côte	as in *oh* but with no final *u*
œ	œil	closer than *earth* pronounced with the lips pouted
oi	moi	as in *memoir* (memwaa¹)

on	non, son	between *ah and oh* with *n* nasalized
ou, où	rouge, goûter	short or long *oo* as in *foot* or
qu	quand, question	as *k* in English
r	rare	as a slightly rolled English *r*
s	a) son	usually *s* as in *say*
	b) maison	(between two vowels) *z* as in *zero*
th	thé	as *t* in English
tion	nation	always *sio* + nasal *n*
u, û	sur, sûr	no equivalent in English: round lips for *oo* and try to pronounce *ee*
un	brun	the vowel of *her*, *earth* with a nasal *n*
w	wagon	as *v* in English
x	a) deuxième	as *z* in *zero*
	b) six	as *s* in *say*
y	y	as short *i* in English

FRENCH GRAMMAR

L i a i s o n.—Final consonants are not usually pronounced, but in most cases, when a word begins with a vowel (or the mute *h*), it is linked with the last consonant of the preceding word. In such cases final *c* and *g* are pronounced as *k*, final *s* and *x* as *z*, e.g. les‿Anglais (lezanglε).

S t r e s s.—In polysyllabic words stress usually falls on the last pronounced syllable, e.g. plusieurs, le docteur, la société.

The Article

The definite article is *le* (m.), *la* (f.), *les* (m. f. pl.). *Le*, *la* are shortened to *l'* before a vowel or mute *h*.

The indefinite article is *un* (m.), *une* (f.).

The Noun

The p l u r a l is generally formed in *s*. Nouns in *s*, *x*, and *z* do not change in the plural. Nouns in *au* and *eu* form their plurals in *x*, e.g. joyau, joyaux, jeu, jeux. Nouns in *al*, form their plurals in *aux*, e.g. cheval, chevaux.

There are two *genders* in French. Nearly all nouns ending in *e* mute are feminine, except those in *isme*, *age* and *iste*. Nearly all nouns ending in a consonant or a vowel other than *e* mute are masculine, except nouns in *tion* and *té*. Nouns in *er* form their f. in *ère* e.g. *laitier, laitière*. Nouns in *en, on* form their f. in *enne, onne*, e.g. *chien, chienne, lion, lionne*. Nouns in *eur* form their 'f. in *euse* except those in *ateur* which have *atrice*, e.g. *admirateur, admiratrice*.

The Adjective

The p l u r a l is generally formed in *s*. Adjectives in *s* or *x* do not change. Those in *al* usually form their plurals in *aux*, e.g. *principal, principaux*.

The f e m i n i n e is generally formed by adding *e* to the masculine form, e.g. *élégant, élégante*. Adjectives in *f* change *f* into *ve*, e.g. *vif, vive*. Those in *x* change *x* into *se*, e.g. *heureux, heureuse*. Adj. in *er* form their f. in *ère*, e.g. *amer, amère*. Those in *el, eil, en, et, on* double the final consonant before adding *e*, e.g. *bel, belle, bon, bonne*.

C o m p a r a t i v e.— 'more . . . than' or '. . . er than' is to be translated by 'plus . . . que'; 'less . . . than' by 'moins . . . que'.

S u p e r l a t i v e.— 'the most . . .' or 'the . . . st' is to be translated by 'le plus . . .', 'la plus . . .' or 'les plus . . .'

The Pronoun

P e r s o n a l p r o n o u n s: je, tu, il, elle; nous, vous, ils, elles.—*Accusative:* me, te, le,

la; nous, vous, les. *Dative:* me, te, lui; nous, vous, leur.—

After prep.. moi, toi, lui, elle; nous, vous, eux, elles.

R e f l e x i v e p r o n o u n s: me, te, se; nous, vous, se.

P o s s e s s i v e p r o n o u n s: le mien (la mienne, les miens, les miennes), le tien (la tienne, les tiens, les tiennes), le sien (la sienne, les siens, les siennes); le nôtre (la nôtre, les nôtres), le vôtre (la vôtre, les vôtres), le leur (la leur, les leurs).

R e l a t i v e p r o n o u n s: who = qui, whom = que, whose = dont, which = qui or que, to whom = a qui.

I n t e r r o g a t i v e p r o n o u n: who, whom = qui; what = que.

The Adverb

Most French adverbs are formed by adding *ment*, to the feminine form of the corresponding adjective, e.g. *facile, facile* + *ment, heureux, heureuse* + *ment*. Those in *ant* and *ent* form their adverbs in *amment* and *emment*, respectively, e.g. *patient—patiemment*.

The Verb

We give here the conjugation of the two auxilliaries (*avoir, être*) and of the verbs in **-er, -ir,** and **-re,** giving only the principal simple forms:

avoir *Pres. Ind.* j'ai, tu as, il a, nous avons, vous avez, ils ont; *Impf.* j'avais, tu avais, il avait, nous avions, vous aviez, ils avaient; *Fut.* j'aurai, tu auras, il aura, nous aurons, vous aurez, ils auront; *Cond.* j'aurais, tu aurais, il aurait, nous aurions, vous auriez, ils auraient; *Pres. Subj.* que j'aie, que tu aies, qu'il ait, que nous ayons, que vous ayez, qu'ils aient; *Imp.* aie, ayons, ayez; *Pres. Part.* ayant; *Past. Part.* eu.

être *Pres. Ind.* je suis, tu es, il est, nous sommes, vous êtes, ils sont; *Impf.* j'étais, tu étais, il était, nous étions, vous étiez, ils étaient; *Fut.* je serai, tu seras, il sera, nous serons, vous serez, ils seront; *Cond.* je serais, tu serais, il serait, nous serions, vous seriez, ils seraient; *Pres. Subj.* que je sois, que tu sois, qu'il soit, que nous soyons, que vous soyez, qu'il soient; *Imp.* sois, soyons, soyez; *Pres. Part.* étant; *Past. Part.* été.

donner *Pres. Ind.* je donne, tu donnes, il donne, nous donnons, vous donnez, ils donnent; *Impf.* je donnais, tu donnais, il donnait, nous donnions, vous donniez, ils donnaient; *Fut.* je donnerai, tu donneras, il donnera, nous donnerons, vous donnerez, ils donneront; *Cond.* je donnerais, tu donnerais, il

donnerait, nous donnerions, vous donneriez, ils donneraient; *Pres. Subj.* que je donne, que tu donnes, qu'il donne, que nous donnions, que vous donniez, qu'ils donnent; *Imp.* donne, donnons, donnez; *Pres. Part.* donnant; *Past. Part.* donné.

finir *Pres. Ind.* je finis, tu finis, il finit, nous finissons, vous finissez, ils finissent; finis, il finit, nous finissons, vous finissez, ils finissent; *Impf.* je finissais, tu finissais, il finissait, nous finissions, vous finissiez, ils finissaient; *Fut.* je finirai, tu finiras, il finira, nous finirons, vous finirez, ils finiront; *Cond.* je finirais, tu finirais, il finirait, nous finirions, vous finiriez, ils finiraient; *Pres. Subj.* que je finisse, que tu finisses, qu'il finisse, que nous finissions, que vous finissiez, qu'ils finissent; *Imp.* finis, finissons, finissez; *Pres. Part.* finissant; *Past Part.* fini.

rendre *Pres. Ind.* je rends, tu rends, il rend, nous rendons, vous rendez, ils rendent; *Impf.* je rendais, tu rendais, il rendait, nous rendions, vous rendiez, ils rendaient; *Fut.* je rendrai, tu rendras, il rendra, nous rendrons, vous rendrez, ils rendront; *Cond.* je rendrais, tu rendrais, il rendrait, nous rendrions, vous rendriez, ils rendraient; *Pres. Subj.* que je rende, que tu rendes, qu'il rende, que nous rendions, que vous rendiez, qu'ils rendent; *Imp.* rends, rendons, rendez; *Pres. Part.* rendant; *Past. Part.* rendu.

Irregular Verbs

Verbs in *-ger* add *e* before endings in *a* and *o*. Verbs in *-eler, -eter* double the *l* or *t* before a mute *e*. Verbs having an acute *é* in the last syllable but one change for a grave *e* when the ending begins with a mute *e*. Verbs in *-yer* change *y* into *i* before a mute *e*.

In the following list of the most frequent French irregular verbs (the root verbs only) the numbers indicate the principal tenses and forms in a fixed order: **1.** Present Indicative; **2.** Imperfect; **3.** Future; **4.** Present Subjunctive; **5.** Imperative; **6.** Present Participle; **7.** Past Participle. (+ *être,* if *être* is used to form the past tenses e.g. je suis allé.)

absoudre 1. j'absous, tu absous, il absout, nous absolvons, vous absolvez, ils absolvent; **2.** j'absolvais; **3.** j'absoudrai; **4.** que j'absolve; **5.** absous, absolvons, absolvez; **6.** absolvant; **7.** absous, absoute.

acquérir 1. j'acquiers, tu acquiers, il acquiert, nous acquérons, vous acquérez, ils acquièrent; **2.** j'acquérais; **3.** j'acquerrai; **4.** que j'acquière; **5.** acquiers, acquérons, acquérez; **6.** acquérant; **7.** acquis.

aller 1. je vais, tu vas, il va, nous allons, vous allez, ils vont; **2.** j'allais; **3.** j'irai; **4.** que j'aille, que nous allions, qu'ils aillent; **5.** va, allons, allez; **6.** allant; **7.** allé (être).

assaillir 1. j'assaille, tu assailles, il assaille, nous assaillons, vous assaillez, ils assaillent; **2.** j'assaillais; **3.** j'assaillerai; **4.** que j'assaille; **5.** assaille, assaillons, assaillez; **6.** assaillant; **7.** assailli.

asseoir 1. j'assieds, tu assieds, il assied, nous asseyons, vous asseyez, ils asseyent *or* j'assois, tu assois, il assoit, nous assoyons, vous assoyez, ils assoient; **2.** j'asseyais *or* j'assoyais; **3.** j'assiérai *or* j'assoierai; **4.** que j'asseye *or* que j'assoie;

5. assieds, asseyons *or* assoyons, asseyez *or* assoyez; **6.** asseyant *or* assoyant; **7.** assis.

atteindre *as* **peindre.**

battre 1. je bats, tu bats, il bat, nous battons, vous battez, ils battent; **2.** je battais; **3.** je battrai; **4.** que je batte; **5.** bats, battons, battez; **6.** battant; **7.** battu.

boire 1. je bois, tu bois, il boit, nous buvons, vous buvez, ils boivent; **2.** je buvais; **3.** je boirai; **4.** que je boive; **5.** bois, buvons, buvez; **6.** buvant; **7.** bu.

bouillir 1. je bous, tu bous, il bout, nous bouillons, vous bouillez, ils bouillent; **2.** je bouillais; **3.** je bouillirai; **4.** que je bouille; **5.** bous, bouillons, bouillez; **6.** bouillant; **7.** bouilli.

clore 1. je clos, tu clos, il clôt; **3.** je clorai; **4.** que je close; **7.** clos.

concevoir 1. je conçois, tu conçois, il conçoit, nous concevons, vous concevez, ils conçoivent; **2.** je concevais; **3.** je concevrai; **4.** que je conçoive; **5.** conçois, concevons, concevez; **6.** concevant; **7.** conçu.

conclure 1. je conclus, tu conclus, il conclut, nous concluons, vous concluez, ils concluent; **2.** je concluais; **3.** je conclurai; **4.** que je conclue; **5.** conclus, concluons, concluez; **6.** concluant; **7.** conclu.

conduire 1. je conduis, tu conduis, il conduit, nous conduisons, vous conduisez, ils conduisent; **2.** je conduisais; **3.** je conduirai; **4.** que je conduise; **5.** conduis, conduisons, conduisez; **6.** conduisant; **7.** conduit.

connaître 1. je connais, tu connais, il connaît, nous connaissons, vous connaissez, ils connaissent; **2.** je connaissais; **3.** je connaîtrai; **4.** que je connaisse; **5.** connais, connaissons, connaissez; **6.** connaissant; **7.** connu.

conquérir *as* **acquérir.**

construire *as* **conduire.**

contraindre 1. je contrains, tu contrains, il contraint, nous contraignons, vous contraignez, ils contraignent; **2.** je contraignais; **3.** je contraindrai; **4.** que je contraigne; **5.** contrains, contraignons, contraignez; **6.** contraignant; **7.** contraint.

coudre 1. je couds, tu couds, il coud, nous cousons, vous cousez, ils cousent; **2.** je cousais; **3.** je coudrai; **4.** que je couse; **5.** couds, cousons, cousez; **6.** cousant; **7.** cousu.

courir 1. je cours, tu cours, il court, nous courons, vous courez, ils courent; **2.** je courais; **3.** je courrai; **4.** que je coure; **5.** cours, courons, courez; **6.** courant; **7.** couru.

couvrir *as* **ouvrir.**

croire 1. je crois, tu crois, il croit, nous croyons, vous croyez, ils croient; **2.** je croyais; **3.** je croirai; **4.** que je croie; **5.** crois, croyons, croyez; **6.** croyant; **7.** cru.

croître 1. je crois, tu crois, il croit, nous croissons, vous croissez, ils croissent; **2.** je croissais; **3.** je croîtrai; **4.** que je croisse; **5.** crois, croissons, croissez; **6.** croissant; **7.** crû, crue.

cueillir 1. je cueille, tu cueilles, il cueille, nous cueillons, vous cueillez, ils cueillent; **2.** je cueillais; **3.** je cueillerai; **4.** que je cueille; **6.** cueillant; **7.** cueilli.

cuire 1. je cuis, tu cuis, il cuit, nous cuisons, vous cuisez, ils cuisent; **2.** je cuisais; **3.** je cuirai; **4.** que je cuise; **5.** cuis, cuisons, cuisez; **6.** cuisant; **7.** cuit.

déchoir 1. je déchois, tu déchois, il déchoit, nous déchoyons, vous déchoyez, ils déchoient; **2.** je déchoyais; **3.** je décherrai; **4.** que je déchoie; **7.** déchu.

déconfire *as* **confire.**

découvrir *as* **ouvrir.**

déduire. détruire *as* **conduire.**

devoir 1. je dois, tu dois, il doit, nous devons, vous devez, ils doivent; **2.** je devais; **3.** je devrai; **4.** que je doive; **5.** dois, devons, devez; **6.** devant; **7. du, due.**

dire 1. je dis, tu dis, il dit, nous disons, vous dites, ils disent; **2.** je disais; **3.** je dirai; **4.** que je dise; **5.** dis, disons, dites; **6.** disant **7.** dit.

dissoudre 1. je dissous, tu dissous, il dissout, nous dissolvons, vous dissolvez, ils dissolvent; **2.** je dissolvais; **3.** je dissoudrai; **4.** que je dissolve; **5.** dissous, dissolvons, dissolvez; **6.** dissolvant; **7.** dissous, dissoute.

dormir 1. je dors, tu dors, il dort, nous dormons, vous dormez, ils dorment; **2.** je dormais; **3.** je dormirai; **4.** que je dorme; **5.** dors,

dormons, dormez; **6.** dormant; **7.** dormi.

échoir *or* **écheoir 1.** il échoit *or* il échet, ils échoient; **2.** il échoyait; **3.** il écherra, ils écherront; **4.** qu'il échoie; **6.** échéant; **7.** échu.

écrire 1. j'écris, tu écris, il écrit, nous écrivons, vous écrivez, ils écrivent; **2.** j'écrivais; **3.** j'écrirai; **4.** que j'écrive; **5.** écris, écrivons, écrivez; **6.** écrivant; **7.** écrit.

envoyer 1. j'envoie, tu envoies, il envoie, nous envoyons, vous envoyez, ils envoient; **2.** j'envoyais; **3.** j'enverrai; **4.** que j'envoie; **5.** envoie, envoyons, envoyez; **6.** envoyant; **7.** envoyé.

éteindre *as* **peindre.**

étreindre *as* **peindre.**

exclure *as* **conclure.**

faire 1. je fais, tu fais, il fait, nous faisons, vous faites, ils font; **2.** je faisais; **3.** je ferai; **4.** que je fasse; **5.** fais, faisons, faites; **6.** faisant; **7.** fait.

falloir 1. il faut; **2.** il fallait; **3.** il faudra; **4.** qu'il faille; **7.** fallu.

feindre *as* **peindre.**

frire 1. je fris, tu fris, il frit; **3.** je frirai; **5.** fris; **7.** frit.

fuir 1. je fuis, tu fuis, il fuit, nous fuyons, vous fuyez, ils fuient; **2.** je fuyais; **3.** je fuirai; **4.** que je fuie; **5.** fuis, fuyons, fuyez; **6.** fuyant; **7.** fui.

gésir 1. il gît, nous gisons,

vous gisez, ils gisent; **2.** je
gisais; **6.** gisant.

haïr 1. je hais, tu hais, il hait,
nous haïssons, vous haïssez,
ils haïssent; **2.** je haïssais;
3. je haïrai; **4.** que je
haïsse; **5.** hais, haïssons,
haïssez; **6.** haïssant, **7.** haï.

instruire *as* **conduire.**

joindre 1. je joins, tu joins, il
joint, nous joignons, vous
joignez, ils joignent; **2.** je
joignais; **3.** je joindrai; **4.**
que je joigne; **5.** joins, joignons, joignez; **6.** joignant;
7. joint.

lire 1. je lis, tu lis, il lit, nous
lisons, vous lisez, ils lisent;
2. je lisais; **3.** je lirai; **4.**
que je lise; **5.** lis, lisons,
lisez; **6.** lisant; **7.** lu.

luire *as* **nuire.**

maudire 1. je maudis, tu
maudis, il maudit, nous
maudissons, vous maudis-
sez, ils maudissent; **2.** je
maudissais; **3.** je maudirai;
4. que je maudisse; **5.**
maudis, maudissons. mau-
dissez; **6.** maudissant; **7.**
maudit.

mentir *as* **sentir.**

mettre 1. je mets, tu mets, il
met, nous mettons, vous
mettez, ils mettent; **2.** je
mettais; **3.** je mettrai; **4.**
que je mette; **5.** mets, mettons, mettez; **6.** mettant; **7.**
mis.

moudre 1. je mouds, tu
mouds, il moud, nous mou-
lons, vous moulez, ils mou-
lent; **2.** je moulais; **3.** je
moudrai; **4.** que je moule;
5. mouds, moulons, moulez;
6. moulant; **7.** moulu.

mourir 1. je meurs, tu meurs,
il meurt, nous mourons,
vous mourez, ils meurent; **2.**
je mourais; **3.** je mourrai;
4. que je meure; **5.** meurs,
mourons, mourez; **6.** mourant; **7.** mort (être.)

mouvoir 1. je meus, tu meus,
il meut, nous mouvons, vous
mouvez, ils meuvent; **2.** je
mouvais; **3.** je mouvrai; **4.**
que je meuve; **5.** meus,
mouvons, mouvez; **6.** mou-
vant; **7.** mû, mue.

naître 1. je nais, tu nais, il
nait, nous naissons, vous
naissez, ils naissent; **2.** je
naissais; **3.** je naîtrai; **4.**
que je naisse; **5.** nais, naissons, naissez; **6.** naissant;
7. né, née (être.)

nuire 1. je nuis, tu nuis, il
nuit, nous nuisons, vous
nuisez, ils nuisent; **2.** je
nuisais; **3.** je nuirai; **4.** que
je nuise; **5.** nuis, nuisons,
nuisez; **6.** nuisant; **7.** nui.

offrir *as* **ouvrir.**

ouvrir 1. j'ouvre, tu ouvres, il
ouvre, nous ouvrons, vous
ouvrez, ils ouvrent; **2.**
j'ouvrais; **3.** j'ouvrirai; **4.**
que j'ouvre; **5.** ouvre,
ouvrons, ouvrez; **6.** ouvr-
ant; **7.** ouvert.

paître 1. je pais, tu pais, il
paît, nous paissons, vous
paissez, ils paissent; **2.** je
paissais; **3.** je paîtrai; **4.**
que je paisse; **5.** pais, paissons, paissez; **6.** paissant.

paraître 1. je parais, tu parais, il paraît, nous paraissons, vous paraissez, ils paraissent; 2. je paraissais; 3. je paraîtrai; 4. que je paraisse; 5. parais, paraissons, paraissez; 6. paraissant; 7. paru.

partir 1. je pars, tu pars, il part, nous partons, vous partez, ils partent; 2. je partais; 3. je partirai; 4. que je parte; 5. pars, partons, partez; 6. partant; 7. parti (être.)

peindre 1. je peins, tu peins, il peint, nous peignons, vous peignez, ils peignent; 2. je peignais; 3. je peindrai; 4. que je peigne; 5. peins, peignons, peignez; 6. peignant; 7. peint.

plaire 1. je plais, tu plais, il plaît, nous plaisons, vous plaisez, ils plaisent; 2. je plaisais; 3. je plairai; 4. que je plaise; 5. plais, plaisons, plaisez; 6. plaisant; 7. plu.

pouvoir 1. je peux *or* je puis, tu peux, il peut, nous pouvons, vous pouvez, ils peuvent; 2. je pouvais; 3. je pourrai; 4. que je puisse; 6. pouvant; 7. pu.

prendre 1. je prends, tu prends, il prend, nous prenons, vous prenez, ils prennent; 2. je prenais; 3. je prendrai; 4. que je prenne; 5. prends, prenons, prenez; 6. prenant; 7. pris.

prescrire *as* écrire.
produire *as* conduire.
proscrire *as* écrire.

recevoir *as* concevoir.
reconstruire *as* conduire.
réduire *as* conduire.
repartir *as* partir.
reproduire *as* conduire.
résoudre 1. je résous, tu résous, il résout, nous résolvons, vous résolvez, ils résolvent; 2. je résolvais; 3. je résoudrai; 4. que je résolve; 5. résous, résolvons, résolvez; 6. résolvant; 7. résolu.

restreindre *as* peindre.

rire 1. je ris, tu ris, il rit, nous rions, vous riez, ils rient; 2. je riais; 3. je rirai; 4. que je rie; 5. ris, rions, riez; 6. riant; 7. ri.

savoir 1. je sais, tu sais, il sait, nous savons, vous savez, ils savent; 2. je savais; 3. je saurai; 4. que je sache; 5. sais, sachons, sachez; 6. sachant; 7. sus.

sentir 1. je sens, tu sens, il sent, nous sentons, vous sentez, ils sentent; 2. je sentais; 3. je sentirai; 4. que je sente; 5. sens, sentons, sentez; 6. sentant; 7. senti.

servir 1. je sers, tu sers, il sert, nous servons, vous servez, ils servent; 2. je servais; 3. je servirai; 4. que je serve; 5. sers, servons, servez; 6. servant; 7. servi.

sortir 1. je sors, tu sors, il sort, nous sortons, vous sortez, ils sortent; 2. je sortais; 3. je sortirai; 4. que je sorte; 5. sors, sortons, sortez; 6. sortant; 7. sorti (être).

souffrir as **ouvrir.**

se souvenir as **venir.**

suffire 1. je suffis, tu suffis, il suffit, nous suffisons, vous suffisez, ils suffisent; 2. je suffisais; 3. je suffirai; 4. que je suffise; 5. suffis, suffisons, suffisez; 6. suffisant; 7. suffi.

suivre 1. je suis, tu suis, il suit, nous suivons, vous suivez, ils suivent; 2. je suivais; 3. je suivrai; 4. que je suive; 5. suis, suivons, suivez; 6. suivant; 7. suivi.

surseoir 1. je sursois, tu sursois, il sursoit, nous sursoyons, vous sursoyez, ils sursoient; 2. je sursoyais; 3. je surseoirai; 4. que je sursoie; 5. sursois, sursoyons, sursoyez; 6. sursoyant; 7. sursis.

taire as **plaire.**

teindre as **peindre.**

tenir 1. je tiens, tu tiens, il tient, nous tenons, vous tenez, ils tiennent; 2. je tenais; 3. je tiendrai; 4. que je tienne; 5. tiens, tenons, tenez; 6. tenant; 7. tenu.

traduire as **conduire.**

traire 1. je trais, tu trais, il trait, nous trayons, vous trayez, ils traient; 2. je trayais; 3. je trairai; 4. que je traie; 5. trais, trayons, trayez; 6. trayant; 7. trait.

vaincre 1. je vaincs, tu vaincs, il vainc, nous vainquons, vous vainquez, ils vainquent; 2. je vainquais; 3. je vaincrai; 4. que je vainque; 5. vaincs, vainquons, vainquez; 6. vainquant; 7. vaincu.

valoir 1. je vaux, tu vaux, il vaut. nous valons, vous valez, ils valent; 2. je valais, 3. je vaudrai; 4. que je vaille; 6. valant; 7. valu.

venir 1. je viens, tu viens, il vient, nous venons, vous venez, ils viennent; 2. je venais; 3. je viendrai; 4. que je vienne; 5. viens, venons, venez; 6. venant; 7. venu (être.)

vêtir 1. je vêts, tu vêts, il vêt, nous vêtons, vous vêtez, ils vêtent; 2. je vêtais; 3. je vêtirai; 4. que je vête; 5. vêts, vêtons, vêtez; 6. vêtant; 7. vêtu.

vivre 1. je vis, tu vis, il vit, nous vivons, vous vivez, ils vivent; 2. je vivais; 3. je vivrai; 4. que je vive; 5. vis, vivons, vivez; 6. vivant; 7. vécu.

voir 1. je vois, tu vois, il voit, nous voyons, vous voyez, ils voient; 2. je voyais; 3. je verrai; 4. que je voie; 5. vois, voyons, voyez; 6. voyant; 7. vu.

vouloir 1. je veux, tu veux, il veut, nous voulons, vous voulez, ils veulent; 2. je voulais; 3. je voudrai; 4. que je veuille, que nous voulions; 5. veuille, veuillions, veuillez *or* voulez; 6. voulant; 7. voulu.

FRENCH PHRASES

Good morning. Good evening. Good-bye.
Bonjour. Bonsoir. Au revoir.

I beg your pardon. Excuse me.
Je vous demande pardon. Pardon.

How are you? Very well — and you?
Comment allez-vous? Très bien — et vous?

How do you do (delighted to meet you).
Enchanté (de faire votre connaissance) monsieur (madame, mademoiselle).

Allow me! You are very kind.
Permettez-moi! Vous etes très gentil.

It's all the same to me.
Cela m'est égal.

Your good health.
A votre santé.

Allow me to introduce you to . . .
Permettez-moi de vous présenter à . . .

It is fine (bad) weather.
Il fait beau (mauvais) temps.

You are right. You are wrong.
Vous avez raison. Vous avez tort.

It is not my fault.
Ce n'est pas ma faute.

To do one's best.
Faire son possible.

It is very annoying.
C'est très ennuyeux.

You're pulling my leg.
Vous vous moquez de moi.

So much the better (worse).
Tant mieux (pis).

He's a jolly nice fellow.
C'est un chic type.

To put one's foot in it.
Mettre les pieds dans le plat.

Things are going badly.
Rien ne va bien. Tout va mal.

I am an Englishmen (Englishwoman).
Je suis anglais (anglaise).

I cannot speak French.
Je ne parle pas français.

I am looking for . . .
Je cherche . . .

I don't understand you.
Je ne vous comprends pas.

Please speak slowly!
Parlez lentement, s'il vous plaît!

Is there anyone here who speaks English?
Y-a-t-il quelque'un qui parle anglais?

Where is the British Consulate?
Où est le consulat britannique?

It is wonderful, splendid !	C'est épatant, formidable !
No . . . Trespassers will be prosecuted.	Défense de . . . sous peine d'amende.
No entry.	Entrée interdite.
Lavatory.	Les toilettes, les lavabos, les cabinets.
What time is it?	Quelle heure est-il?
It is five past one.	Il est une heure cinq.
We are in a hurry.	Nous sommes pressés.
How long does it take to . . . ?	Combien de temps faut-il pour . . .?
This evening, tonight. Last night.	Ce soir. Hier soir.
How long have you been here?	Depuis quand êtes-vous ici?
I have been here a month.	Je suis ici depuis un mois.
Can we lunch (dine) here?	Est-ce qu'on peut déjeuner (dîner) ici?
There are four of us.	Nous sommes quatre.
We only want a snack.	Nous voudrions seulement un casse-croûte.
Please give us the menu.	Voulez-vous nous donner le menu, s'il vous plaît.

NOMBRES CARDINAUX

ET ORDINAUX

1 *one*, un.		1st *first*, premier.
2 *two*, deux.		2nd *second*, deuxième.
3 *three*, trois.		3rd *third*, troisième.
4 *four*, quatre.		4th *fourth*, quatrième.
5 *five*, cinq.		5th *fifth*, cinquième.
6 *six*, six.		6th *sixth*, sixième.
7 *seven*, sept.		7th *seventh*, septième.
8 *eight*, huit.		8th *eighth*, huitième.
9 *nine*, neuf.		9th *ninth*, neuvième.
10 *ten*, dix.		10th *tenth*, dixième.
11 *eleven*, onze.		11th *eleventh*, onzième.
12 *twelve*, douze.		12th *twelfth*, douzième.
13 *thirteen*, treize.		13th *thirteenth*, treizième.
14 *fourteen*, quatorze.		14th *fourteenth*, quatorzième.
15 *fifteen*, quinze.		15th *fifteenth*, quinzième.
16 *sixteen*, seize.		16th *sixteenth*, seizième.

A

a, an, *art.* un, -e.

abandon, *v. a.* abandonner.

abate, *v. a. & n.* diminuer; se calmer, s'apaiser.

abbey, *s.* abbaye *f.*

abbot, *s.* abbé *m.*

abbreviate, *v. a.* abréger.

abbreviation, *s.* abréviation *f.*

abdicate, *v.a. & n.* abdiquer.

abdomen, *s.* abdomen *m.*

abhor, *v. a.* détester, abhorrer.

ability, *s.* capacité *f.*, habilité *f.*

able, *adj.* capable.

aboard, *adv.* à bord.

abode, *s.* demeure *f.*

abolish, *v.a.* abolir; supprimer.

abominable, *adj.* abominable.

abound, *v.n.* abonder (de).

about, *adv. & prep.* autour (de); environ, presque; au sujet de.

above, *adv. & prep.* au-dessus (de); *(in book)* ci-dessus.

abroad, *adv.* à l'étranger.

absence, *s.* absence *f.*, éloignement *m.*

absent, *adj.* absent.

absolute, *adj.* absolu.

absolve, *v.a.* absoudre; relever de; remettre, pardonner.

absorb, *v. a.* absorber.

abstain, *v.n.* s'abstenir de.

abstract, *adj.* abstrait.

abstraction, *s.* abstraction *f.*

absurd, *adj.* absurde; ridicule.

abundance, *s.* abondance *f.*

abundant, *adj.* abondant.

abusive, *adj.* abusif; injurieux; offensant.

academic, *adj.* académique.

academy, *s.* académie *f.*

accelerate, *v.a.* accélérer; *v.n.* s'accélérer.

accent, *s.* accent *m.*

accept, *v.a.* accepter

access, *s.* accès *m.*

accessible, *adj.* accessible.

accessory, *s. & adj.* accessoire *(m.).*

accident, *s.* accident *m.*

accidental, *s.* accidentel.

accommodate, *v. a.* accommoder; loger; ~ *oneself to* s'accommoder à.

accommodation, *s.* ajustement *m.*, adaptation *f.*; commodité *f.*; logement *m.*

accompany, *v.a.* accompagner.

accomplish, *v.a.* accomplir, achever.

accomplishment, *s.* accomplissement *m.*; talent *m.*

accord, *s.* accord *m.*, consentement *m.*

according: ~ *to* selon, d'après.

accordingly, *adv.* donc; en conséquence.

account, s. compte m.; (narration) récit m.; on ~ of à cause de; on no ~ dans aucun cas; take into ~ tenir compte de; — v.n. ~ for expliquer; rendre compte de.

accuracy, s. exactitude f.

accusation, s. accusation f.

accuse, v.a. accuser; incriminer.

accustom, v.a. accoutumer (à).

ache, s. douleur f.

achieve, v.a. accomplir, achever; atteindre.

acknowledge, v.a. reconnaître; accuser réception de.

acquaint, v.a. informer (de); faire part à.

acquaintance, s. connaissance f.

acquire, v.a. acquérir.

acre, s. arpent m.

across, prep. à travers; en croix.

act, s. action f.; (law) loi f.; (theatre) acte m.; — v.n. agir; v.a. jouer.

action, s. action f.; acte m.; (war) combat m.

active, adj. actif.

activity, s. activité f.

actor, s. acteur m.

actress, s. actrice f.

actual, adj. réel.

actually, adv. en fait.

adapt, v.a. adapter.

add, v.a. ajouter; additionner.

addition, s. addition f.; in ~ to en plus de.

additional, adj. additionnel; supplémentaire.

address, s. adresse f.; — v.a. adresser.

adequate, adj. suffisant.

adjust, v.a. ajuster, régler.

administer, v.a. & n. administrer.

administration, s. administration f.

admirable, adj. admirable.

admiral, s. amiral m.

admiration, s. admiration f.

admire, v.a. admirer.

admission, s. admission f.; entrée f.

admit, v.a. admettre; laisser entrer.

adopt, v.a. adopter.

adoption, s. adoption f.

adore, v.a. adorer.

adult, adj. & s. adulte (m.f.)

advance, v. n. avancer; — s. avance f.; progrès m.

advantage, s. avantage m.

adventure, s. aventure f.

adversary, s. adversaire m.

adverse, adj. adverse.

adversity, s. adversité f.

advertise, v.a. annoncer; faire de la réclame (pour).

advertisement, s. annonce f.; réclame f.

advice, conseil m.; avis m.

advise, v.a. conseiller.

aerial, s. antenne f.

aerodrome, s. aérodrome m.

aeroplane, s. avion m.

affair, s. affaire f.

affect, *v.a.* affecter.

affection, *s.* affection *f.*

affectionate, *adj.* affectueux.

affirmative, *adj.* affirmatif; — *s.* affirmative *f.*

afford, *v.a.* donner, fournir, accorder; *can* ~ avoir les moyens de.

afraid, *adj.* effrayé; *be* ~ *of* avoir peur de.

African, *adj.* africain; — *s.* Africain, -e.

after, *prep.* & *adj.* après.

afternoon, *s.* après-midi *m.* or *f.*

afterwards, *adv.* après, ensuite.

again, *adv.* encore une fois, de nouveau.

against, *prep.* contre.

age, *s.* âge *m.*

agency, *s.* agence *f.*

agent, *s.* agent *m.*

aggression, *s.* agression *f.*

ago, *adv.* il y a.

agony, *s.* agonie *f.*

agree, *v.n.* s'accorder, être d'accord; ~ *(up-)on* convenir sur; ~ *to* consentir à; ~ *with* entrer dans les idées de.

agreeable, *adj.* agréable.

agreement, *s.* accord *m.*

agricultural, *adj.* agricole.

agriculture, *s.* agriculture *f.*

ahead, *adv.* en avant.

aid, *s.* aide *f.;* — *v.a.* aider, assister.

aim, *s.* but *m.;* objectif *m.;* visée *f.;* — *v.a.* & *n.* viser.

air, *s.* air *m.*

air-conditioning, *s.* conditionnement d'air *m.;* climatisation *f.*

aircraft, *s.* avion *m.*

air-line, *s.* ligne *f.* aérienne.

air-mail *s.* poste aérienne; *by* ~ par avion.

airport, *s.* aéroport *m.,*

alarm, *v.a.* alarmer; —*s.* alarme *f.*

alcoholic, *adj.* alcoolique.

ale, *s.* bière *(f.)* anglaise.

alike, *adj.* semblable; — *adv.* également.

alive, *adj.* vivant.

all, *pron.* *s.,* *adv.* & *adj.* tout; *not at* ~ pas du tout.

allege, *v.a.* alléguer.

alley, *s.* ruelle *f.*

allow, *v.a.* permettre; laisser; admettre.

allude, *v.n.* faire allusion.

ally, *v.a.* allier; *v.n.* s'allier; — *s.* allié, -e.

almost, *adv.* presque; à peu près.

alone, *adj.* & *adv.* seul.

along, *prep.* le long de.

aloud, *adv.* à haute voix.

already, *adv.* déjà.

also, *adv.* aussi.

altar, *s.* autel *m.*

alter, *v.a.*&*n.* changer.

alternate, *adj.* alternatif; — *v.n.* alterner.

although, *conj.* quoique; bien que.

altitude, *s.* altitude *f.,* élévation *f.*

altogether, *adv.* tout à fait; entièrement.

always, *adv.* toujours.

amaze, *v.a.* frapper d'étonnement, frapper de stupeur.

amazing, *adj.* étonnant.

ambassador, *s.* ambassadeur *m.*

ambassadress, *s.* ambassadrice *f.*

ambition, *s* ambition *f.*

ambitious, *adj.* ambitieux.

ambulance, *s.* ambulance (automobile) *f.*

amend, *v.a.* amender.

amends: *make* ~ *for* dédommager de.

American, *adj.* américain; — *s.* Américain, -e.

among, *prep.* parmi; chez.

amount, *s.* somme *f.; (total)* montant *m.;* — *v.n.* ~ *to* monter à.

ample, *adj.* ample.

amplifier, *s.* amplificateur *m.*

amuse, *v.a.* amuser; divertir.

amusement, *s.* amusement *m.;* divertissement *m.*

an *see* **a.**

analogy, *s.* analogie *f.*

analyse, *v.a.* analyser.

analysis, analyse *f.*

anarchy, *s.* anarchie *f.*

anatomy, *s.* anatomie *f.*

ancestor, *s.* ancêtre *m. f.*

anchor, *s.* ancre *f.*

ancient, *adj.* ancien; antique.

and, *conj.* et.

anecdote, *s.* anecdote *f.*

angel, *s.* ange *m.*

anger, *s.* colère, *f.*

angle, *s.* angle *m.*

angler, *s.* pêcheur *m.*

Anglican, *adj.* anglican.

angry, *adj.* fâché, irrité.

animal, *s.* animal *m. (pl.* -aux).

ankle, *s.* cheville *f.*

anniversary, *s.* anniversaire *m.*

announce, *v.a.* annoncer.

announcement, *s.* annonce.

announcer, *s.* speaker *m.*

annoy, *v.a.* ennuyer; contrarier; gêner.

annoying, *adj.* contrariant; ennuyeux.

annual, *adj.* annuel.

annul, *v.a.* annuler.

another, *pron. & adj.* un autre, une autre.

answer, *s.* réponse *f.;* — *v.a.&n.* répondre.

ant, *s.* fourmi *f.*

antelope, *s.* antilope *f.*

antibiotic, *s.* antibiotique *m.*

anticipate, *v.a.* anticiper.

antipathy, *s.* antipathie *f.*

antiquated, *adj.* vieilli.

antiquity, *s.* antiquité *f.*

anvil, *s.* enclume *f.*

anxiety, *s.* anxiété *f.*

anxious, *adj.* inquiet; désireux; *be* ~ *to* désirer faire qch.

any, *adj. & pron.* quelque; *(at all)* n'importe quoi/qui/quel; *(some, in question)* du, de la; *have you* ~? en avez vous; *not* ~ ne ... pas de; ~ *more* encore du.

anybody, *pron.* quelqu'un; *(at all)* n'importe qui.

anyhow, *adv.* n'importe comment.

anyone *see* **anybody.**

anything, *pron.* quelque chose; *(at all)* n'importe quoi.

anyway, *see* anyhow.

anywhere, *adv.* n'importe où.

apart, *adv.* à part; de côté; ~ *from* en dehors de.

apartment, *s.* logement *m.;* appartement *m.*

apologize, *v.n.* faire des excuses, s'excuser.

apology, *s.* excuse *f.*

apostle, *s.* apôtre *m.*

appalling, *adj.* épouvantable.

apparatus, *s.* appareil *m.*

apparent, *adj.* manifeste.

appeal, *s.* appel *m.;* — *v.n.* en appeler (à).

appear, *v.n.* (ap)paraître; *(seem)* sembler.

appearance, *s.* apparition *f.;* *(look)* air *m.*

appendicitis, *s.* appendicite *f.*

appendix, *s.* appendice *m.*

appetite, *s.* appétit *m.*

applaud, *v.n.* applaudir.

applause, *s.* applaudissement *m.*

apple, *s.* pomme *f.*

appliance, *s.* appareil *m.*

applicant, *s.* postulant, -e.

application, *s.* demande *f.;* *(use)* application *f.*

apply, *v.a.* appliquer; — *v.n.* avoir rapport à; ~ *for* solliciter.

appoint, *v.a.* nommer; désigner.

appointment, *s.* nomination *f.;* emploi *m.;* rendez-vous *m.*

appreciate, *v.a.* appré-cier.

appreciation, *s.* appréciation *f.*

apprehend, *v.a.* appréhender; *(understand)* comprendre.

apprentice, *s.* apprenti *m.*

approach, *s.* approche *f.;* — *v. a. & n.* (s')approcher (de).

appropriate, *adj.* approprié, convenable.

approval, *s.* approbation *f.*

approve, *v.a. & n.* a-prouver.

approximate, *adj.* approximatif.

approximation, approximation *f.*

apricot, *s.* abricot *m.*

April, *s.* avril *m.*

apron, *s.* tablier *m.*

aptitude, *s.* aptitude *f.*

Arab, *s.* Arabe *m.*

Arabian, *adj.* arabe.

arbitrary, *adj.* arbitraire.

arcade, *s.* arcade *f.*

arch, *s.* arche *f.;* arc *m.*

archaeology, *s.* archéologie *f.*

archbishop, *s.* archevêque *m.*

architect, *s.* architecte *m.*

architecture, *s.* architecture *f.*

area, *s.* surface *f.;* aire *f.*

Argentine, *adj.* argentine.

argue, *v.n.* argumenter; *v.a.* discuter.

argument, *s.* argument *m.;* discussion *f.*

arise, *v. n.* se lever; *(emerge)* surgir; *(come from)* résulter de.

aristocratic, *adj.* aristocratique.

arm[1]**,** *s.* bras *m.*

arm[2]**,** *s.(pl.)* arme(s) *f.*

armament, *s.* armement *m.*

armchair, *s.* fauteuil *m.*

armour, *s.* armure *f.*

army, *s.* armée *f.*

around, *adv. & prep.* autour (de).

arouse, *v.a.* réveiller.

arrange, *v.a.* arranger.

arrangement, *s.* arrangement *m.;* ~s mesures *f. pl.*

array, *s.* ordre *m.*

arrears, *s. pl.* arriéré *m.*

arrest, *v.a.* arrêter; — *s.* arrestation *f.*

arrival, *s.* arrivée *f.*

arrive, *v.n.* arriver.

arrow, *s.* flèche *f.*

art, *s.* art *m.*

artery, *s.* artère *f.*

article, *s.* article *m.*

artificial, *aaj.* artificiel.

artillery, *s.* artillerie *f.*

artist, *s.* artiste *m.*

artistic, *adj.* artistique.

as, *adv. & conj.* comme; *(like a)* en; *(when)* comme; ~ ... ~ aussi ... que.

ascend, *v.n.* monter.

ash(es), *s. (pl.)* cendre *f.*

ashamed, *adj.* honteux; *be* ~ *of* avoir honte de.

ashore, *adv.* à terre.

ash-tray, *s.* cendrier *m.*

Asiatic, *adj.* asiatique.

aside, *adv.* de côté.

ask, *v. a.* demander (à + qn., de + *inf.*); ~ *about* se renseigner sur; ~ *for* demander.

asleep, *adj.* endormi; *fall* ~ s'endormir.

aspect, *s.* aspect *m.; (look)* air *m.*

aspire, *v.n.* aspirer à.

ass, *s.* âne *m.*

assail, *v. a.* assaillir.

assault, *s.* assaut *m.*

assemble, *v. a.* assembler; *v.n.* s'assembler.

assembly, *s.* assemblée *f.;* ~ *hall* halle *f.* de montage; ~ *line* chaîne *f.* de montage.

assert, *v.a.* affirmer.

assess, *v.a.* cotiser.

assets, *s. pl.* actif *m.*

assign, *v. a.* assigner; céder.

assignment, *s.* cession *f.*

assist, *v.a.* aider.

assistance, *s.* aide *f.*

associate, *v.a.* associer; — *s.* associé, -e *m. f.*

association, *s.* association *f.*

assume, *v.a.* prendre; assumer; supposer.

assumption, *s.* supposition *f.*

assurance, *s.* assurance *f.*

assure, *v.a.* assurer.

astonish, *v. a.* étonner.

astonishment, *s.* étonnement *m.*

astronomy, *s.* astronomie *f.*

at, *prep. (place, time)* à; *(house, shop)* chez.

athletic, *adj.* athlétique.

athletics, *s.* athlétisme *m.*

at-home, *s.* réception *f.*

atlas, *s.* atlas *m.*

atmosphere, *s.* atmosphère *f.*

atom, *s.* atome *m.*

atomic, *adj.* atomique; ~

bomb bombe *f.* atomique; ~ *energy* énergie *f.* atomique.

attach, *v.a.* attacher.

attaché, *s.* attaché *m.;* ~ *case* petite valise *f.*

attachment, *s.* attachement *m.*

attack, *v.a.* attaquer; — *s.* attaque *f.*

attain, *v.a.* atteindre.

attainment, *s.* réalisation *f.;* connaissances *f. pl.*

attempt, *s.* tentative *f.;* — *v.a.* tenter; entreprendre.

attend, *v.a.* suivre; *(look after)* soigner; — *v.i.* faire attention à; assister.

attendance, *s.* présence *f.; (persons present)* assistance *f.*

attendant, *s.* serviteur *m.;* employé *m.;* ouvreuse *f.*

attention, *s.* attention *f.*

attitude, *s.* attitude *f.*

attorney, *s.* avoué *m.*

attract, *v.a.* attirer.

attraction, *s.* attraction *f.*

attractive, *adj.* attrayant.

attribute, *v.a.* attribuer.

auction, *s.* vente *f.*

audience, *s.* auditoire *m.*

audio-visual, *adj.* audio-visuel.

auditorium, *s.* salle *f.* (de cours).

August, *s.* août *m.*

aunt, *s.* tante *f.*

Australian, *adj.* australien — *s.* Australien, -ne *m. f.*

Austrian, *adj.* autrichien; — *s.* Autrichien, -enne *m. f.*

authentic, *adj.* authentique.

author, *s.* auteur *m.*

authority, *s.* autorité *f.*

authorize, *v.a.* autoriser.

automatic, *adj.* automatique.

autonomy, *s.* autonomie *f.*

autumn, *s.* automne *m.*

avail, *s.* be of no ~ ne servir à rien; — *v.a.* ~ *oneself of* profiter de.

available, *adj.* disponible; sous la main.

avalanche, *s.* avalanche *f.*

avenge, *v.a.* venger.

avenue, *s.* avenue *f.*

average, *s.* moyenne *f.;* — *adj.* moyen.

aversion, *s.* aversion *f.*

avoid, *v.a.* éviter.

await, *v.a.* attendre.

awake, *v. a.* éveiller; *v. n.* s'éveiller; — *adj.* éveillé.

awaken, *v.a.* éveiller.

award, *v.a.* accorder.

aware, *adj.* be ~ *of* avoir conscience de, savoir bien.

away, *adv.* (au) loin; *carry* ~ enlever; *go* ~ partir.

awful, *adj.* terrible.

awhile, *adv.* pendant quelque temps, un moment.

awkward, *adj. (pers.)* gauche; maladroit; *(things)* gênant, embarrassant.

axe, *s.* hache *f.*

axis, *s.* axe *m.*

axle, *s.* essieu *m.*

B

babble, *s.* babil *m.;* — *v.n.* babiller.

baby, *s.* bébé *m.*

baby-sitter, *s.* garde-bébé *m.*

bachelor, *s.* célibataire; *(arts)* licencié *m.*

back, *s.* dos *m.; (hand)* revers *m.; (football)* arrière *m.;* — *adj.* de derrière; arriéré; — *adv.* en arrière; *be ~* être de retour; — *v.a.* soutenir, seconder; *(bet)* parier pour; *v.n.* reculer.

background, *s.* fond *m.;* arrière-plan *m.*

backstairs, *s. pl.* escalier *m.* de service.

backward, *adj.* arriéré.

backwards, *adv.* en arrière; à reculons.

bacon, *s.* lard *m.*

bad, *adj.* mauvais.

badge, *s.* insigne *m.*

badger, *s.* blaireau *m.*

badly, *adv.* mal.

bag, *s.* sac *m.; (large)* valise *f.*

baggage, *s.* bagage *m.*

bait, *s.* amorce *f.*

bake, *v.a.* cuire; faire cuire.

baker, *s.* boulanger *m.*

bakery, *s.* boulangerie *f.*

balance, *s. (weighing, account)* balance *f.; (bank)* solde *m.: (equilibrium)* équilibre *m.;* — *v.a.* balancer; *v.n.* se balancer.

balcony, *s.* balcon *m.*

bald, *adj.* chauve; plat.

ball, *s. (games)* balle *f.* ballon *m.; (bowl)* boule *f.; (dance)* bal *m.*

ball-bearings, *s. pl.* roulement *m.* à billes.

ballet, *s.* ballet *m.*

balloon, *s.* ballon *m.*

ball(-point) pen, *s.* stylo *m.* à bille.

bamboo, *s.* bambou *m.*

banana, *s.* banane *f.*

band, *s. (people)* troupe *f.; bande f.;* orchestre *m.; (ribbon, tie)* ruban *m.;* lien *m.*

bandage, *s.* bandage *m.*

bandit, *s.* bandit *m.*

bang, *s.* coup *m.;* claquement *m.*

banish, *v.a.* bannir.

banister, *s.* rampe *f.*

bank¹, *s. (river)* rive *f.; (earth)* talus *m.*

bank², *s.* banque *f.*

bank-holiday, *s.* (jour *m.* de) fête *f.* légale.

banknote, *s.* billet *m.* (de banque).

bankruptcy, *s.* banqueroute *f.;* faillite *f.*

banner, *s.* bannière *f.*

banquet, *s.* banquet *m.*

baptism, *s.* baptême *m.*

baptize, *v.a.* baptiser.

bar, *s. (iron, tribunal, music)* barre *f.; (railway)* barrière *f.; (obstacle)* obstacle *m.; (lawyers)* barreau *m.; (counter place for drink)* comptoir *m.,* débit *m.* (de boissons), bar *m.*

barber, *s.* coiffeur *m.*

bare, *adj.* nu; *(mere)* seul.

barefoot, *adj.* nu-pieds.

barely, *adv.* à peine.

bargain, *s.* marché *m.;* — *v.n.* marchander.

bark, *s.* aboiement *m.;* — *v.n.* aboyer.

barley, *s.* orge *f.*

barmaid, *s.* demoiselle *f.* de comptoir, barmaid *f.*

barman, *s.* garçon *m.* de comptoir, barman *m.*

barn, *s.* grange *f.*

barometer, *s.* baromètre *m.*

baron, *s.* baron *m.*

baroness, *s.* baronne *f.*

barracks, *s. pl.* caserne *f.*

barrel, *s.* tonneau *m.*

barren, *adj.* stérile.

barrier, *s.* barrière *f.*

barrister, *s.* avocat *m.*

bartender *see* **barman.**

barter, *s.* échange *m.;* — *v.a.* échanger.

base, *s.* fondement *m.;* base *f.*

basement, *s.* sous-sol *m.*

bashful, *adj.* timide.

basic, *adj.* fondamental; basique.

basin, *s.* bassin *m.;* cuvette *f.*

basis, *s.* base *f.*

basket, *s.* panier *m.*

basket-ball, *s.* basket-ball *m.*

bass, *s.* basse *f.*

bat¹, *s.* chauve-souris *f.*

bat², *s.* batte *f.*

bath, *s.* bain *m.; (tub)* baignoire *f.*

bathe, *v.n.* se baigner; *v.a.* baigner.

bathing-costume, *s.* costume *m.* de bain(s).

bathroom, *s.* salle *f.* de bain.

battery, *s. (military)* batterie *f.; (electr.)* pile *f.*

battle, *s.* bataille *f.*

bay, *s.* baie *f.*

be, *v. n.* être; *(be situated)* se trouver; *there is* il y a.

beach, *s.* plage *f.*

bead, *s. (string of)* collier *m.*

beak, *s.* bec *m.*

beam, *s. (timber)* poutre *f.; (light)* rayon *m.*

bean, *s.* fève *f.*

bear¹, *s.* ours *m.*

bear², *v.a.* porter; soutenir; supporter.

beard, *s.* barbe *f.*

bearing, *s.* rapport *m.*

beast, *s.* bête *f.*

beat, *v.a.* battre; frapper; — *s.* battement *m.*

beautiful, *adj.* beau, bel, belle.

beauty, *s.* beauté *f.*

beaver, *s.* castor *m.*

because, *conj.* parce que; ~ *of* à cause de.

beckon, *v.n.* faire signe (à).

become, *v. n.* devenir.

bed, *s.* lit *m.*

bed-clothes, *s. pl.* couvertures *f. pl.*

bedroom, *s.* chambre *f.* à coucher.

bee, *s.* abeille *f.*

beech, *s.* hêtre *m.*

beef, *s.* bœuf *m.*

beef-steak, *s.* bifteck *m.*

beer, *s.* bière *f.*

beetle, *s.* scarabée *m.*

beetroot, *s.* betterave *f.*

before, *prep. (time)* avant;

(*space*) devant; — *adv.* avant; (*in front*) en avant.

beforehand, *adv.* d'avance; en avance.

beg, *v.a.* demander, prier; *v. n.* mendier; I ~ *your pardon!* excusez-moi!; pardon!

beget, *v.a.* engendrer.

beggar, *s.* mendiant, -e.

begin, *v. a. & n.* commencer.

beginner, *s.* commençant, -e *m. f.*

beginning, *s.* commencement *m.*

behalf, *s.* on ~ *of* de la part de; *in* ~ *of* en faveur de.

behave, *v.n.* se conduire.

behaviour, *s.* conduite *f.*

behind, *prep.* derrière.

Belgian, *adj.* belge; — *s.* Belge *m. f.*

belief, *s.* croyance *f.*

believe, *v.a. & n.* croire.

bell, *s.* cloche *f.*

belly, *s.* ventre *m.*

belong, *v.n.* ~ *to* appartenir à.

belongings, *s. pl.* effets *m.*; biens *m.*

below, *adv.* au-dessous; en bas; — *prep.* au-dessous de.

belt, *s.* ceinture *f.*

bench, *s.* banc *m.*; (*working*) établi *m.*

bend, *v. a.* courber; tendre fléchir; *v.n.* se courber; — *s.* courbure *f.*; (*road*) tournant *m.*

beneath *see* below.

benefit, *s.* bienfait *m.*; (*gain*) bénéfice *m.*

bent, *s.* penchant *m.*

berry, *s.* baie *f.*; (*coffee*) grain *m.*

berth, *s.* couchette *f.*; (*for ship*) mouillage *m.*

beseech, *v. a.* supplier.

beside, *prep.* auprès de, à côté de.

besides, *adv.* en outre.

best, *adj.* le meilleur; *do one's* ~ faire tout son possible (pour).

bestow, *v. a.* conférer (à).

bet, *v.a.* parier.

betray, *v. a.* trahir.

better, *adj.* meilleur; *adv.* mieux.

between, *prep.* entre.

beyond, *prep.* au delà de.

bias, *s.* biais *m.*; (*fig.*) préjugé *m.*

Bible, *s.* bible *f.*

bibliography, *s.* bibliographie *f.*

bicycle, *s.* bicyclette *f.*

big, *adj.* grand; gros.

bill, *s.* (*hotel*) note *f.*; (*restaurant*) addition *f.*; (*invoice*) facture *f.*; (*of exchange*) lettre *f.* de change; (*of fare*) carte *f.*, menu *m.*; (*poster*) affiche *f.*; (*parliament*) projet *m.* de loi.

bin, *s.* huche *f.*, coffre *m.*

bind, *v.a.* lier; (*book*) relier.

biological, *adj.* biologique.

biology, *s.* biologie *f.*

birch, *s.* bouleau *m.*

bird, *s.* oiseau *m.*

birth, *s.* naissance *f.*

birthday, *s.* anniversaire *m.*

birth-place, *s.* lieu *m.* de

naissance.

biscuit, *s.* biscuit *m.*

bishop, *s.* évêque *m.*

bit¹, *s.* morceau *m.;* *(drill)* mèche *f.; a* ~ un peu (de).

bit², *s. (horse)* mors *m.*

bite, *v. a. & n.* mordre.

bitter, *adj.* amer; mordant; *(cold)* âpre.

bitterness, *s.* amertume *f.*

black, *adj.* noir.

blackbird, *s.* merle *m.*

blackmail, *s.* chantage *m.*

blacksmith, *s.* forgeron *m.*

bladder, *s.* vessie *f.*

blade, *s.* lame *f.*

blame, *s.* blâme *m.;* – *v. a.* blâmer, accuser qn.

blameless, *adj.* innocent.

blank, *adj.* blanc; nu; — *s.* blanc *m.*

blanket, *s.* couverture *f.*

blast, *s.* rafale *f.;* coup *m.* de vent; souffle *m.;* – *v.a.* faire sauter; détruire.

blaze, *s.* flamme *f.;* – *v.n.* flamber.

bleak, *adj.* lugubre.

bleed, *v.a. & n.* saigner.

blend, *s.* mélange *m.;* – *v.a.* fondre; mêler.

bless, *v.a.* bénir.

blessing, *s.* bénédiction *f.*

blind¹, *adj.* aveugle.

blind², *s.* store *m.*

blindness, *s.* cécité *f.*

blink, *v. n.* clignoter.

bliss, *s.* félicité *f.*

blister, *s.* ampoule *f.*

block, *s.* bloc *m.;* *(wood)* billot *m.;* *(buildings)* pâté *m.;* *(traffic)* encombrement *m.*

blond *adj.* blond.

blood, *s.* sang *m.*

bloody, *adj.* sanglant.

bloom, *s.* fleur *f.;* – *v. n.* fleurir.

blossom, *s.* fleur *f.*

blot, *s.* tache *f.;* pâté *m.*

blouse, *s.* blouse *f.*

blow¹, *v. a. (trumpet)* sonner; *(glass)* souffler; ~ *out* éteindre; ~ *up* faire sauter; *v.n.* *(wind)* souffler.

blow², *s.* coup *m.*

blue, *adj.* bleu.

blunder, *s.* bévue *f.;* – *v. n.* faire une bévue

blunt, *adj.* émoussé; *(person)* brusque.

blush, *v.n.* rougir.

board, *s.* planche *f.:* *(meals)* pension *f.;* *(council)* conseil *m.;* *(paper)* carton *m.;* *(theatre)* ~s planches; ~ *and lodging* pension *f.* et chambre(s): *on* ~ *(ship)* à bord d'un navire; – *v.n.* prendre pension chez; *v.a.* monter à bord de.

boarder, *s.* pensionnaire *m. f.*

boarding-house, *s.* pension *f.*

boarding-school, *s.* pensionnat *m.*

boast, *s.* vanterie *f.;* – *v. n.* se vanter (de).

boat, *s.* bateau *m.*

body, *s.* corps *m.*

bog, *s.* marécage *m.*

boil¹, *v.a.* faire bouillir; *(cook)* faire cuire; *v. n.* bouillir.

boil², *s.* furoncle *m.*

boiler, *s.* chaudière *f.*

bold, *adj.* hardi; effronté.

boldness, *s.* hardiesse *f.*; effronterie *f.*

bolt, *s.* verrou *m.*; — *v. a.* verrouiller; *v. n.* filer.

bomb, *s.* bombe *f.*

bond, *s.* lien *m.*

bone, *s.* os *m.*; *(fish)* arête *f.*

bonnet, *s.* chapeau *m.*; bonnet *m.*; *(motor)* capot *m.*

bony, *adj.* osseux; maigre.

book, *s.* livre *m.*; — *v. a.* prendre (un billet); retenir.

bookcase, *s.* bibliothèque *f.*

booking-office, *s.* guichet *m.*

book-keeper, *s.* teneur *m.* de livres.

book-keeping, *s.* comptabilité *f.*

booklet, *s.* livret *m.*

bookseller, *s.* libraire *m.*

bookshelf, *s.* rayon *m.*

bookshop, *s.* librairie *f.*

book-stall, *s.* bibliothèque (de gare) *f.*

boot, *s.* bottine *f.*; brodequin *m.*

booth, *s.* baraque *f.*

booty, *s.* butin *m.*

border, *s.* bord *m.*; frontière *f.*

bore, *v. a.* ennuyer, raser; —*s.* raseur *m.*

boring, *adj.* ennuyeux, assommant.

born, *pp.* né; *be* ~ naître.

borrow, *v. a.* emprunter.

bosom, *s.* sein *m.*

boss, *s.* patron *m.*

botanical, *adj.* botanique.

botany, *s.* botanique *m.*

both, *pron. & adj.* l'un et l'autre; tous (les) deux; ~ ... *and* et ... et ...

bother, *v.a.* tracasser.

bottle, *s.* bouteille *f.*

bottom, *s.* bas *m.*; fond *m.*; derrière *m.*

bough, *s.* rameau *m.*

bound, *pp.* ~ *for* à destination de, en route pour.

boundary, *s.* borne *f.*

bounty, *s.* générosité *f.*

bouquet, *s.* bouquet *m.*

bow[1], *s.* arc *m.*; *(violin)* archet *m.*; *(knot)* nœud *m.*

bow[2], *v.a.* incliner; courber; *v.n.* s'incliner; se courber; — *s.* salut *m.*; *(ship)* avant *m.*

bowels, *s. pl.* entrailles *f.*

bowl, *s.* bol *m.*, jatte *f.*

box, *s.* boîte *f.*, caisse *f.*; *(horse)* stalle *f.*; *(theatre)* loge *f.*; *(on the ears)* soufflet *m.*; — *v. n.* boxer.

box-office, *s.* bureau *m.* de location.

boy, *s.* garçon *m.*; ~ *scout* boy-scout *m.*, éclaireur *m.*

bra, *s.* soutien-gorge *m.*

brace, *s.* couple *f.*; lien *m.*; ~*s* bretelles *f. pl.*

bracelet, *s.* bracelet *m.*

brain, *s.* cerveau *m.*; ~*s* cervelle *f.*

brainy, *adv.* intelligent.

brake, *s.* frein *m.*

branch, *s.* branche *f.*

brand, *s.* tison *m.*; marque *f.*; — *v.a.* marquer.

brandy, *s.* cognac *m.*

brass, *s.* cuivre jaune *m.*

brave, *adj.* brave.

brawl, *s.* querelle *f.*

bread, *s.* pain *m.*

breadth, *s.* largeur *f.*

break, *v.a.* briser, casser; *(law)* violer; *(promise)* manquer; *(news)* apprendre à; *v. n.* se casser; se briser; ~ *down* abattre; s'effondrer; *(motor)* avoir une panne; ~ *in* dresser; ~ *up* lever; — *s.* interruption *f.;* pause *f.*

break-down, *s. (motor)* panne *f.; (health)* débâcle *f.;* ~ *lorry* dépanneuse *f.*

breakfast, *s.* déjeuner *m.*

breast, *s.* poitrine *f.,* sein *m.*

breath, *s.* haleine *f.;* souffle *m.*

breathe, *v.a. & n.* respirer.

breathless, *adj.* essoufflé; sans souffle.

breeches, *s. pl.* culotte *f.*

breed, *s.* race *f.;* — *v.a.* élever.

breeze, *s.* brise *f.*

breezy, *adj.* venteux.

brew, *v.a.* brasser.

bribe, *s.* pot-de-vin *m.;* — *v.a.* corrompre.

brick, *s.* brique *f.*

bricklayer, *s.* maçon *m.*

bride, *s.* mariée *f.*

bridegroom, *s.* marié *m.*

bridge, *s.* pont *m.*

bridle, *s.* bride *f.*

brief, *adj.* bref.

briefcase, *s.* serviette *f.*

briefly, *adv.* brièvement.

briefs, *s. pl.* slip *m.*

bright, *adj.* brillant; vif; clair; éclatant.

brighten, *v.a.* faire briller; égayer.

brightness, *s.* éclat *m.*

brilliant, *s.* brillant *m.*

brim, *s.* bord *m.*

bring, *v.a.* amener; apporter; ~ *about* amener; *back* rapporter; ~ *forth* produire; ~ *up* élever.

brink, *s.* bord *m.*

brisk, *adj.* vif; actif.

bristle, *s. (brush)* poil *m.*

British, *adj.* britannique.

brittle, *adj.* cassant.

broad, *adj.* large; vaste.

broadcast, *v.a.* radiodiffuser.

broadcasting, *s.* radiodiffusion *f.*

broken, *adj.* brisé.

bronze, *s.* bronze *m.*

brooch, *s.* broche *f.*

brood, *s.* couvée *f.;* *v.n.* couver.

brook, *s.* ruisseau *m.*

broom, *s.* balai *m.*

brother, *s.* frère *m.*

brother-in-law, *s.* beau-frère *m.*

brow, *s.* sourcil *m*.

brown, *adj.* brun.

bruise, *s.* contusion *f.;* — *v.a.* meurtrir.

brush, *s.* brosse *f.;* pinceau *m.;* balai *m.;* — *v.a.* brosser; ~ *up* donner un coup de brosse à.

brutal, *adj.* brutal, cruel.

brutality, *s.* brutalité *f.*

bubble, *s.* bulle *f.;* — *v. n.* bouillonner.

buck, *s.* daim *m.*

bucket, *s.* seau *m.*

buckle, *s.* boucle *f.*

bud, *s.* bourgeon *m.*

budget, *s.* budget *m.*

buffet, *s.* soufflet *m.*

bug, *s.* punaise *f.*

build, *v.a.* bâtir; construire; sur; ~ up établir.

builder, *s.* entrepreneur *m.* de bâtiments; constructeur *m.*

building, *s.* bâtiment *m.*

bulb, *s.* bulbe *m.*; *(lamp)* ampoule *f.*

bulge, *v.n.* bomber.

bulk, *s.* masse *f.*; volume *m.*

bull, *s.* taureau *m.*

bullet, *s.* balle *f.*

bulletin, *s.* bulletin *m.*

bump, *s.* bosse *f.*; collision *f.*; coup *m.*

bumper, *s.* pare-choc *m.*

bun, *s.* brioche *f.*

bunch, *s.* bouquet *m.*; botte *f.*; grappe *f.*

bundle, *s.* botte *f.*; paquet *m.*; fagot *m.*

bunk, *s.* couchette *f.*

buoy, *s.* bouée *f.*

burden, *s.* charge *f.*; fardeau *m.*

burglar, *s.* cambrioleur *m.*

burial, *s.* enterrement *m.*

burn, *v.a. & n.* brûler.

bursary, *s.* bourse *f.*

burst, *v.n.* éclater; crever; exploser; *v.a.* faire éclater; rompre; crever; — *s.* éclat *m.*; explosion *f.*

bury, *v.a.* enterrer.

bus, *s.* autobus *m.*

bush, *s.* buisson *m.*

business, *s.* affaires *f. pl.*; profession *f.*; on ~ pour affaires; ~ *hours* heures *(f. pl.)* d'ouverture.

businessman, *s.* homme *m.* d'affaires.

bus-stop, *s.* arrêt *m.* d'autobus.

busy, *adj.* occupé, affairé.

but, *conj.* mais.

butcher, *s.* boucher *m.*; ~'s *(shop)* boucherie *f.*

butter, *s.* beurre *m.*

butterfly, *s.* papillon *m.*

buttock, *s.* fesse *f.*, derrière *m.*

button, *s.* bouton *m.*

buy, *v.a.* acheter.

buyer, *s.* acheteur *m.*

by, *prep.* par; de; ~ *Monday* d'ici à lundi.

bystander, *s.* spectateur, -trice *m. f.*

C

cab, *s.* taxi *m.*; fiacre *m.*

cabbage, *s.* chou *m.*

cabin, *s.* cabane *f.*; *(ship)* cabine *f.*

cabinet, *s.* *(politics)* cabinet *m.*

cable, *s.* câble *m.*

cablegram, *s.* câblogramme *m.*

café, *s.* café(-restaurant) *m.*

cage, *s.* cage *f.*

cake, *s.* gâteau *m.*

calculate, *v.a.&n.* calculer.

calculation, *s.* calcul *m.*

calendar, *s.* calendrier *m.*

caif, *s.* veau *m.*; *(leg)* mollet *m.*

call, *v. a. & n.* appeler; ~ *for* réclamer; ~ *on* faire visite à; — *s.*

appel *m.*; cri *m.*; *(visit)* visite *f.*

call-box, *s.* cabine *f.* téléphonique.

calm, *adj.* calme.

calorie, *s.* calorie *f.*

camel, *s.* chameau, -elle *m. f.*

camera, *s.* appareil *m.* (photographique).

camp, *s.* camp *m.*

campaign, *s.* campagne *f.*

camping, *s.* camping *m.*

can¹, *s.* broc *m.*; pot *m.*

can², *v. aux.* pouvoir; savoir.

canal, *s.* canal *m.*

canary, *s.* canari *m.*

cancel, *v.a.* annuler.

cancer, *s.* cancer *m.*

candle, *s.* chandelle *f.*; bougie *f.*

cannon, *s.* canon *m.*

canoe, e *s.* canoë *m.*

canteen, *s.* cantine *f.*

canvas, *s.* toile *f.*

cap, *s.* bonnet *m.*; casquette *f.*

capable, *adj.* capable (de).

capacity, *s.* capacité *f.*

cape, *s. (land)* cap *m.*; *(cloak)* pèlerine *f.*; cape *f.*

capital, *s. (city)* capitale *f.*; *(letter)* majuscule *f.* *(commerce)* capital *m.*

capsule, *s.* capsule *f.*

captain, *s.* capitaine *m.*

caption, *s.* sous-titre *m.*

captivate, *v.a.* captiver.

capture, *v.a.* capturer; — *s.* capture *f.*

car, *s.* voiture *f.*, auto *f.*

caravan, *s.* roulotte *f.* (de camping), cara-

vane *f.*

carbon-paper, *s.* papier *m.* carbone.

carburetter, *s.* carburateur *m.*

card, *s.* carte *f.*

cardboard, *s.* carton *m.*

cardinal, *adj. m.* cardinal *m.*

care, *s.* attention *f.*; soin *m.*; souci *m.*; ~ of aux bons soins de; take ~ of prendre soin de; — *v.n.* ~ for se soucier de; ~ to aimer.

career, *s.* carrière *f.*

careful, *adj.* soigneux.

careless, *adj.* insouciant, négligent.

caress, *v.a.* caresser.

cargo, *s.* cargaison *f.*

caricature, *s.* caricature *f.*

carnation, *s.* œillet *m.*

carpenter, *s.* charpentier *m.*

carpet, *s.* tapis *m.*

carriage, *s.* voiture *f.*; *(transport)* transport *m.*

carriage-way, *s.* chaussée *f.*

carrier, *s.* voiturier *m.*

carrot, *s.* carotte *f.*

carry, *v.a.* porter; transporter; ~ on exercer; ~ out mettre à exécution.

cart, *s.* charrette *f.*

cartridge, *s.* cartouche *f.*

carve, *v. a.& n.* sculpter; *(meat)* découper.

case, *s. (box)* étui *m.*, caisse *f.*; *(instance)* cas *m.*; cause *f.*

casement, *s.* croisée *f.*

cash, *s.* espèces *f. pl.*

cash-book, *s.* livre *m.* de caisse.

cashier, *s.* caissier, -ère *m. f.*

cash-register, *s.* caisse *f.* enregistreuse.

cask, *s.* tonneau *m.*

cast, *v.a.* jeter; *(metal)* fondre; — *s.* coup *m.*; *(theatre)* distribution *f.*

castle, *s.* château *m.*

casual, *adj.* casuel.

casualty, *s.* accident *m.*

cat, *s.* chat, -te *m. f.*

catalogue, *s.* catalogue *m.*

catastrophe, *s.* catastrophe *f.*

catch, *v.a.* saisir; attraper; *(eye)* frapper; ~ *up* rattraper; — *s.* prise *f.*; attrape *f.*

category, *s.* catégorie *f.*

cater, *v.n.* pourvoir à.

caterpillar, *s.* chenille *f.*

cathedral, *s.* cathédrale *f.*

catholic, *adj.* catholique.

catholicism, *s.* catholicisme *m.*

cattle, *s.* bétail *m.* *(pl.* bestiaux).

cauliflower, *s.* chou-fleur *m.*

cause, *s.* cause *f.*; motif *m.*; — *v.a.* causer.

caution, *s.* prudence *f.*

cautious, *adj.* prudent.

cave, *s.* caverne *f.*

cavity, *s.* cavité *f.*

cease, *v.a. & n.* cesser.

ceiling, *s.* plafond *m.*

celebrate, *v.a.* célébrer.

celebration, *s.* célébration *f.*; commémoration *f.*

celery, *s.* céleri *m.*

cell, *s.* cellule *f.*

cellar, *s.* cave *f.*

cello, *s.* violoncelle *m.*

cellophane, *s.* cellophane *f.*

cement, *s.* ciment *m.*; — *v.a.* cimenter.

cemetery, *s.* cimetière *m.*

centenary, *s.* centenaire *m.*

central, *adj.* central.

centre, *s.* centre *m.*

century, *s.* siècle *m.*

cereal, *s.* céréale *f.*

ceremony, *s.* cérémonie *f.*

certain, *adj.* certain.

certainly, *adj.* certainement; sans doute

certainty, *s.* certitude *f.*

certificate, *s.* certificat *m.*

certify, *v.a.* certifier.

chain, *s.* chaîne *f.*

chair, *s.* chaise *f.*; *(professorship)* chaire *f.*; *take the* ~ présider.

chairman, *s.* président *m.*

chalk, *s.* craie *f.*

challenge, *s.* défi *m.*; — *v.a.* défier; provoquer.

chamber, *s.* chambre *f.*; ~*s* étude *f.*; appartement *m.*

champagne, *s.* champagne *m.*

champion, *s.* champion *m.*

championship, *s.* championnat *m.*

chance, *s.* chance *f.*; *by* ~ par hasard.

chancellor, *s.* chancelier *m.*

chancery, *s.* chancellerie *f.*

change, *s.* changement *m.*; *(money)* monnaie *f.*; — *v.a.&n.* changer.

channel, *s.* canal *m.*;

m.; the English Channel la Manche.

chap, *s.* type *m.*

chapel, *s.* chapelle *f.*

chaplain, *s.* chapelain *m.*

chapter, *s.* chapitre *m.*

character *s.* caractère *m.;* *(theatre)* personnage *m.*

characteristic, *adj.* caractéristique; — *s.* trait *m.* caractéristique.

charcoal, *s.* charbon *m.* de bois

charge, *s.* charge *f.;* *(price)* prix *m.; (accusation)* accusation *f.;* — *v.a.* charger (de); *(price)* demander; faire payer; *(accuse)* accuser (de).

charity, *s.* charité *f.*

charm, *s.* charme *m.*

charming, *adj.* charmant.

chart, *s.* carte *f.* marine.

charter, *s.* charte *f.*

charwoman, *s.* femme *f.* de ménage.

chase, *v.a.* chasser; poursuivre; — *s.* chasse *f.*

chassis, *s.* châssis *m.*

chat, *s.* causette *f.;* — *v. n.* causer.

chatter, *v.n.* babiller; *(teeth)* claquer.

cheap, *adj.* bon marché.

cheat, *v.a.* tromper; tricher; — *s.* tromperie *f.;* tricherie; *(pers.)* fourbe *m.*

check, *v.a.* contrôler, vérifier; *(stop)* arrêter; — *s.* vérification *f.,* contrôle *m.*

checkmate, *s.* échec et mat *m.*

check-up, *s.* examen *m.* médical.

cheek, *s.* joue *f.*

cheeky, *adj.* impertinent.

cheer, *v.a.* réjouir, encourager; acclamer; *v.n.* ~ up reprendre sa gaieté; courage!; — *s.* joie *f.;* ~s acclamations *f.*

cheerful, *adj.* joyeux.

cheese, *s.* fromage *m.*

chemical, *adj.* chimique.

chemist, *s.* chimiste *m.;* pharmacien *m.;* ~'s *(shop)* pharmacie *f.*

chemistry, *s.* chimie *f.*

cheque, *s.* chèque *m.;* *traveller's* ~ chèque *m.* de voyage.

cheque-book, *s.* carnet *m.* de chèques.

cherish, *v. a.* soigner; *(hope)* caresser.

cherry, *s.* cerise *f.*

chess, *s.* échecs *m. pl.*

chess-board, *s.* échiquier *m.*

chest, *s.* coffre *m.; (part of body)* poitrine *f.;* ~ *of drawers* commode *f.*

chestnut, *s.* châtaigne *f.*

chew, *v.a.* mâcher.

chicken, *s.* poulet *m.*

chief, *adj.* principal; — *s.* chef *m.*

chiefly, *adv.* principalement.

child, *s.* enfant *m.f.*

childhood, *s.* enfance *f.*

childish, *adj.* enfantin.

childless, *adj.* sans enfant.

chill, *s.* coup *m.* de froid; — *v.a.* refroidir, glacer.

chilly, *adj. (weather)* frais; (un peu) froid.

chimney, *s.* cheminée *f.*

chin, *s.* menton *m.*

china, *s.* porcelaine *f.*

Chinese, *adj.* chinois; — *s.* Chinois, -e.

chip, *s.* éclat *m.;* copeau *m.;* ~s frites *f. pl.*

chirp, *v.n.* gazouiller.

chisel, *s.* ciseau *m.;* — *v.a.* ciseler.

chivalry, *s.* chevalerie *f.*

chocolate, *s.* chocolat *m.*

choice, *s.* choix *m.*

choir, *s.* chœur *m.*

choke, *v.a. & n.* étouffer.

choose, *v.a.* choisir.

chop, *s.* côtelette *f.*

chorus, *s.* chœur *m.*

Christian, *adj.* chrétien; ~ *name* prénom *m.*

Christianity, *s.* christianisme *m.*

Christmas, *s.* Noël *m.;* ~ *eve* veille *f.* de Noël.

chuckle, *v.n.* rire tout bas; — *s.* rire étouffé.

church, *s.* église *f.*

churchyard, *s.* cimetière *m.*

cider, *s.* cidre *m.*

cigar, *s.* cigare *m.*

cigarette, *s.* cigarette *f.*

cigarette-case, *s.* étui *m.* à cigarettes.

cigarette-holder, *s.* porte-cigarette *m.*

cinders, *s.pl.* cendres *f.*

cine-camera, *s.* camera *f.*

cinema, *s.* cinéma *m.*

cinerama, *s.* cinérama *m.*

circle, *s.* cercle *m.*

circuit, *s.* circuit *m.;* détour *m.;* tournée *f.*

circular, *adj.* circulaire.

circulate, *v.n.* circuler; *v.a.* faire circuler.

circulation, *s.* circulation *f.*

circumstance, *s.* circonstance *f.*

circus, *s.* cirque *m.*

cistern, *s.* citerne *f.*

citation, *s.* citation *f.*

cite, *v. a.* citer.

citizen, *s.* citoyen, -ne *m. f.,* habitant *m.*

citizenship, *s.* droit *m.* de cité.

city, *s.* ville *f.; the City* Cité *f.*

civil, *adj.* civil; *(polite)* poli; ~ *servant* fonctionnaire *m.*

civilization, *s.* civilisation *f.*

civilize, *v.a.* civiliser.

claim, *s.* demande *f.,* réclamation *f.;* droit *m.;* — *v.a.* revendiquer, réclamer.

clamp, *s.* crampon *m.*

clang, *s.* bruit *m.* métallique; — *v.n.* retentir.

clap, *s.* battement *m.;* applaudissements *m. pl.;* — *v.n.* applaudir.

clash, *v.a.* choquer; *v.n.* s'entre-choquer.

clasp, *s.* agrafe *f.;* fermoir *m.;* — *v.a.* agrafer; joindre.

class, *s.* classe *f.*

classic(al), *adj.* classique.

classify, *v.a.* classifier.

class-room, *s.* classe *f.*

clatter, *s.* bruit *m.;* fracas *m.;* — *v.n.* faire

du bruit.

clause, s. clause f., article m.

claw, s. griffe f.; serre f.; ongle m.

clay, s. glaise f.; argile f.

clean, adj. propre; blanc; pur; — v.a. nettoyer.

cleanse, v.a. nettoyer.

clear, adj. clair; — v.a. déblayer; éclaircir; v.n. s'éclaircir; ~ away en-ever; ~ out filer.

clearly, adv. clair, claire-ment; évidemment.

cleave, v.a. fendre; v.n. se fendre.

clergy, s. clergé m.

clergyman, s. ministre m.

clerk, s. employé m., commis m.

clever, adj. habile, adroit; intelligent.

client, s. client m.

cliff, s. falaise f.

climate, s. climat m.

climb, v.a. & n. grimper.

cling, v.n. ~ to se cram-ponner à.

clinic, s. clinique f.

clip, s. pince; — v.a. tondre; couper; ro-gner; (tickets) poin-conner.

cloak, s. manteau m.

cloak-room, s. consigne f.; vestiaire m.

clock, s. horloge f.; pen-dule f.; it is 10 o'clock il est dix heures.

close, v.a. (shut) fer-mer; (end) terminer; v.n. (se) fermer; se terminer; — adj. fer-mé; (narrow) étroit;

(relations) proche; in-time; — adv. tout près; — s. enclos m.; (end) fin f.

closely, adv. de près; é-troitement.

closet, s. cabinet m.; armoire f.

cloth, s. drap m.; (ta-ble) nappe f.

clothe, v.a. vêtir.

clothes, s.pl. habits m.pl.

clothing, s. vêtements m. pl.

cloud, s. nuage m.

cloudy, adj. couvert.

clover, s. trèfle m.

club, s. (stick) massue f.; (people) cercle m., club m., société f.; (cards) trèfle m.

clue, s. fil m.; (cross-word) définition f.

clumsy, adj. gauche.

cluster, s. grappe f.

clutch, v.a. empoigner; m. pour empoigner; (motor) embrayage m.

coach, s. voiture f.; wagon m.; autocar m.; (sports) entraîneur m.

coal, s. charbon m.

coal-mine, s. mine f. de houille.

coarse, adj. grossier; vul-gaire.

coast, s. côte f.

coat, s. (jacket) veston m.; (top) pardessus m., manteau m.

cock, s. coq m., mâle m.; (gun) chien m.; (tap) robinet m.

cocktail, s. cocktail m.

cocoa, s. cacao m.

cod, s. morue f.

code, *s.* code *m.*

coffee, *s.* café *m.*

coffee-pot, *s.* cafetière *f.*

coffin, *s.* cercueil *m.*

cog-wheel, *s.* roue *f.* dentée.

coil, *s.* rouleau *m.*; bobine *f.*; — *v.a.* lover; enrouler.

coin, *s.* pièce *f.*

coincidence, *s.* coïncidence *f.*

coke, *s.* coke *m.*

cold, *adj.* froid; *be ~ (pers.)* avoir froid; *(weather)* faire froid; — *s.* froid *m.*; *(in the head)* rhume *m.*; *catch a ~* s'enrhumer.

collaborate, *v. n.* collaborer.

collaborator, *s.* collaborateur, -trice *m.f.*

collapse, *v.n.* s'effondrer; *(pers.)* s'affaisser; — *s.* effondrement *m.*; *(pers.)* affaissement *m.* subit.

collar, *s.* col *m.*; collet *m.*

colleague, *s.* collègue *m. f.*

collect, *v.a.* rassembler; recueillir.

collection, *s.* collection *f.*; collecte *f.*; *(mail)* levée *f.*

college, *s.* collège *m.*

collide, *v.n.* se heurter (contre), entrer en collision.

colliery, *s.* houillère *f.*; mine *f.*

collision, *s.* collision *f.*

colon, *s.* deux points *m. pl.*

colonel, *s.* colonel *m.*

colony, *s.* colonie *f.*

colour, *s.* couleur *f.*

colourful, *adj.* coloré.

colourless, *adj.* terne, pâle.

column, *s.* colonne *f.*

comb, *s.* peigne *m.*; — *v.a.* peigner.

combat, *s.* combat *m.*

combination, *s.* combinaison *f.*

combine, *v.a.* combiner.

come, *v.n.* venir, arriver; *~ across* rencontrer; *~ back* revenir; *~ by* obtenir; passer; *~ down* descendre; *~ in* entrer; *~ off* avoir lieu; se détacher; *~ out* sortir; *~ up* monter.

comedian, *s.* comédien *m.*

comedy, *s.* comédie *f.*

comely, *adj.* avenant, bienséant.

comfort, *s.* consolation *f.*; bien-être *m.*; — *v.a.* consoler.

comfortable, *adj.* confortable; commode; *be ~* être à l'aise.

comic, *adj.* comique.

comma, *s.* virgule *f.*

command, *s.* ordre *m.*; — *v.a.* commander.

commander, *s.* commandant *m.*

commandment, *s.* commandement *m.*

commemorate, *v.a.* commémorer.

commence, *v.a.& n.* commencer.

commend, *v.a.* recommander; louer.

comment, *s.* commentaire *m.;* — *v.n.* commenter.

commentary, *s.* commentaire *m.*

commerce, *s.* commerce *m.*

commercial, *adj.* commercial; ∼ *traveller* voyageur *m.* de commerce.

commission, *s.* commission *f.;* commande *f.*

commissioner, *s.* commissaire *m.*

commit, *v.a.* committre; confier; ∼ *oneself* se compromettre.

commitment, *s.* engagement *m.*

committee, *s.* comité *m.*

commodity, *s.* marchandise *f.,* article *m.*

common, *adj.* commun.

commonwealth, *s.* the British Commonwealth commonwealth *m.*

communicate, *v. a. & n.* communiquer.

communication, *s.* communication *f.*

communication-cord, *s.* signal *m.* d'alarme.

communion, *s.* communion *f.*

communiqué, *s.* communiqué *m.*

community, *s.* communauté *f.*

compact, *s.* pacte *m.;* poudrier *m.;* — *adj.* compact; concis.

companion, *s.* compagnon, -agne *m. f.*

company, *s.* compagnie *f.;* société *f.*

comparatively, *adv.* comparativement.

compare, *v.a.* comparer

(to à, *with* avec).

comparison, *s.* comparaison *f.*

compartment, *s.* compartiment *m.*

compass, *s.* (*mariner's*) boussole *f.;* (*pair of*) ∼*es* compas *m.*

compassion, *s.* compassion *f.*

compel, *v.a.* forcer.

compete, *v.n.* faire concurrence (à); concourir.

competence, *s.* compétence *f.;* capacité *f.*

competent, *adj.* capable.

competition, *s.* concurrence *f.;* concours *m.;* compétition *f.*

competitor, *s.* concurrent *m.*

compilation, *s.* compilation *f.*

compile, *v.a.* compiler.

complain, *v.n.* se plaindre

complaint, *s.* plainte *f.;* maladie *f.;* réclamation *f.*

complement, *s.* complément *m.*

complete, *v.a.* compléter, achever; — *adj.* complet.

complicated, *adj.* compliqué.

complication, *s.* complication *f.*

compliment, *s.* compliment *m.*

comply, *v.n.* ∼ *with* se conformer à.

component, *adj. & s.* composant (*m.*).

compose, *v.a.* composer; be ∼*d of* se composer de.

composer, *s.* compositeur *m.*

composition, *s.* composition *f.*; dissertation *f.*

compound, *s. & adj.* composé (*m.*); — *v.a.* composer.

comprehend, *v.a.* comprendre.

comprehension, *s.* compréhension *f.*

compress, *v.a.* comprimer.

compromise, *s.* compromis *m.*; — *v.a.* compromettre.

compulsory, *adj.* obligatoire.

compute, *v.a.* calculer, computer.

computer, *s.* calculateur *m.* (électronique).

comrade, *s.* camarade *m.*

conceal, *v. a.* cacher.

conceit, *s.* vanité *f.*

conceive, *v.a.* concevoir.

concept, *s.* concept *m.*

concern, *v.a.* concerner; regarder; *be ~ed (in, with)* s'intéresser (à); *(about)* s'inquiéter (de); — *s.* affaire *f.*; entreprise *f.*; anxiété *f.*

concerning, *prep.* concernant.

concert, *a.* concert *m.*

concession, *s.* concession *f.*

conciliation, *s.* réconciliation *f.*

concise, *adj.* concis.

conclude, *v.a. &n.* conclure.

conclusion, *s.* conclusion *f.*; *in ~* pour conclure.

concrete, *s.* béton *m.*; — *adj.* concret.

condemn, *v.a.* condamner.

condense, *v.a.* condenser.

condition, *s.* condition *f.*; état *m.*; *on ~ that* à condition que.

conduct, *s.* conduite *f.*; *v. a.* conduire; diriger.

conductor, *s.* receveur *m.*; chef *m.* d'orchestre.

cone, *s.* cône *m.*

confederacy, *s.* confédération *f.*

confer, *v.a. & n.* conférer.

conference, *s.* conférence *f.*

confess, *v.a.* avouer; confesser.

confession, *s.* confession *f.*

confidence, *s.* confiance *f.*

confident, *adj.* confiant.

confidential, *adj .* confidentiel.

confine, *v.a.* confiner, enfermer; *be ~d to bed* être alité.

confirm, *v. a.* confirmer.

confirmation, *s.* confirmation *f.*

conflict, *s.* conflit *m.*

confound, *v. a.* confondre.

confront, *v.a.* être en face; confronter.

confuse, *v.a.* brouiller, mettre en désordre.

confusion, *s.* confusion *f.*

congratulate, *v.a.* féliciter (de).

congratulation, *s.* félicitations *f. pl.*

congregation, *s.* assemblée *f.*, congrégation *f.*

congress, *s.* congrès *m.*

conjunction, s. conjonction f.

connect, v.a. joindre, lier; associer.

connection, s. connexion f.; rapport m.; (railw.) correspondance f.

conquer, v.a. vaincre; conquérir.

conqueror, s. vainqueur m.; conquérant m.

conscience, s. conscience f.

conscious adj. be ~ (= not fainting) avoir connaissance; be ~ of avoir la conscience de.

consciousness, s. connaissance f.; conscience f.; conscient (m.).

conscript, adj. & s. conscrit (m.).

consent, s. consentement; — v.n. consentir.

consequence, s. conséquence f.

consequent, adj. conséquent.

consequently, adv. par conséquent.

conservation, s. conservation f.

consider, v.a. considérer.

considerable, adj. considérable.

considerate, adj. attentif; réfléchi.

consideration, s. considération f.; (money) rémunération f.

consign, v.a. livrer; consigner, expédier.

consignment, s. expédition f.; envoi m.

consist, v. n. ~ of se composer de, consister en.

consistent, adj. conséquent.

consolation, s. consolation f.

consonant, s. consonne f.

conspicuous, adj. en vue; frappant.

conspiracy, s. conspiration f.

conspire, v. a. & n. conspirer.

constable, s. agent m. (de police).

constant, adj. continuel; constant.

constipation, s. constipation f.

constitute, v.a. constituer.

constitution, s. constitution f.

constrain, v.a. contraindre (à).

constraint, s. contrainte f.

construct, v. a. construire.

construction, s. construction f.

consul, s. consul m.

consulate, s. consulat m.

consult, v.a. & n. consulter.

consultation, s. consultation f.; ~ room cabinet m. (de consultation).

consume, v.a. (destroy) consumer; (use up) consommer.

consumer, s. consommateur, -trice m.f.; ~ goods articles m. de grande consommation.

consumption, s. consommation f.; (disease) phtisie f., tuberculose f.

contact, s. contact m.; — v.a. entrer en relations avec.

contain, v.a. contenir.

container, s. récipient m.

contemplate, *v.a.* contempler; projeter.

contemplation, *s.* contemplation *f.*

contemporary, *adj. & s.* contemporain *(m.).*

contempt, *s.* mépris *m.*

contemptuous, *adj.* méprisant.

contend, *v.n.* lutter contre (pour).

content, *s.* contentement *m.; ~s* contenu *m.; table of ~s* table *f.* des matières; — *adj.* content.

contest, *s.* lutte *f.; (sport)* rencontre *f.*, match *m.; (dispute)* contestation *f.; — v. a.* contester.

continent, *s.* continent *m.*

continental, *adj.* continental.

continual, *adj.* continuel.

continuation, *s.* continuation *f.;* suite *f.*

continue, *v.a. & n.* continuer.

continuous, *adj.* continu.

contract, *s.* contrat *m.; — v.a.* contracter.

contractor, *s.* entrepreneur *m.*

contradiction, *s.* contradiction *f.*

contrary, *adj.* contraire; — *adv.* contrairement.

contrast, *s.* contraste *m.; — v.a.* mettre en contraste.

contribute, *v. a. & n.* contribuer.

contribution, *s.* contribution *f.;* article *m.*

contributor, *s.* contribuant *m.;* collaborateur *m.*

contrive, *v.a.* inventer.

control, *s.* autorité *f.;* maîtrise *f.;* direction *f.*, commande *f.; — v.a.* gouverner, commander, maîtriser, diriger; contrôler.

controversy, *s.* polémique *f.*, controverse *f.*

convenience, *s.* commodité *f.*, convenance *f.; public ~* cabinets *m. pl.* d'aisances.

convenient, *adj.* commode; *be ~ to s.o.* convenir à qn.

conversation, *s.* conversation *f.*

converse, *v.n.* converser; causer.

convert, *v.a.* convertir.

convey, *v.a.* transporter; transmettre; présenter.

conveyance, *s.* transport *m.;* voiture *f.*, véhicule *m.*

conveyer, *s.* porteur *m.; ~ belt* bande *f.* transporteuse.

convict, *s.* forçat *m.; — v.a.* convaincre (de), condamner.

convince, *v. a.* convaincre (de).

convoy, *s.* convoi *m.*

cook, *s.* cuisinier, -ière *m. f.; head ~* chef *m.; — v.a.* faire cuire; *v.n.* cuire.

cooking, *s.* cuisine *f.*

cool, *adj.* frais *(f.* fraîche); *(fig.)* calme; — *v.a.* rafraîchir.

co-operate, *v.n.* coopérer.

co-operation, *s.* coopération *f.*

copper, s. cuivre m.

copy, s. copie f.; exemplaire m.; numéro m. — v. a. copier.

copy-book, s. cahier m.

copyright, s. droit m. d'auteur.

coral, s. corail m.

cord, s. corde f.

cordial, adj. cordial.

cork, s. bouchon m.

corkscrew, s. tire-bouchon m.

corn, s. grain m.; grains m. pl.; (wheat) blé m.; (maize) maïs m.

corner, s. coin m.

corporal, adj. corporel; — s. caporal m.

corporation, s. corporation f.

corps, s. corps m.

corpse, s. cadavre m.

correct, adj. correct; exact; — v.a. corriger, rectifier.

correction, s. correction f.; rectification f.

correspond, v.n. correspondre; être conforme (à).

correspondence, s. correspondance f.

correspondent, s. correspondant s.

corresponding, adj. correspondant.

corridor, s. corridor m.; couloir m.

corridor-train, s. train m. à couloir.

corrupt, adj. corrompu.

cosmetics, s. pl. cosmétiques m. pl., produits m.pl. de beauté.

cosmonaut, s. cosmo-

naute m.

cost, s. coût m., frais m. pl.; prix m.; ~ of living coût de la vie; at the ~ of au prix de; — v.n. coûter.

costly, adj. coûteux.

costume, s. costume m.

cosy, adj. confortable.

cottage, s. chaumière f.

cotton, s. coton m.

couch, s. canapé m., divan m.

cough, s. toux f.; — v.n. tousser.

council, s. conseil m.

councillor, s. conseiller m.

counsel, s. conseil m.; avocat m.

count¹, s. compte m.; (title) comte m.

count², v.a. & n. compter.

countenance, s. visage m.; air m.

counter, s. comptoir m., guichet m.; jeton m.

counterfoil, s. souche f.

countersign, v.a. contresigner.

countess, s. comtesse f.

countless, adj. innombrable.

country, s. pays m.; (not town) campagne f.

countryman, s. campagnard m.

countryside, s. (les) campagnes f.pl.

countrywoman, s. paysanne f.

county, s. comté m.

couple, s. couple f.

courage, s. courage m.

courageous, adj. courageux.

course, s. cours m.; route f.; (meal) service m.; plat m.; of ~ bien entendu.

court, s. cour f.; tribunal m.; court m. (de tennis); — v.a. faire la cour à.

courteous, adj. courtois.

courtesy, s. courtoisie f.

courtship, s. cour f.

courtyard, s. cour f.

cousin, s. cousin, -e m. f.

cover, s. couverture f.; couvercle m.; (meal) couvert m.; (post) enveloppe f.; — v.a. couvrir.

cow, s. vache f.

coward, s. & adj. lâche m.

crab, s. crabe m.

crack, s. craquement m.; — v.a. faire craquer; v.n. craquer; se fêler.

cradle, s. berceau m.

craft, s. habileté f.; embarcation f.; métier m.; profession f.

craftsman, s. artisan m.

cram, v.a. fourrer; bourrer.

crane, s. grue f.

crash, s. fracas m.; débâcle; atterrissage brutal, collision; v.n, tomber avec fracas; s'écraser sur le sol.

crash-helmet, s. serretête m.

crave, v.n. ~ for désirer ardemment.

crawl, v.n. ramper; (pers.) se traîner.

crayon, s. crayon m.

craze, s. manie f.

crazy, adj. fou, toqué.

creak, s. cri m., grincement m.; — v. n. crier, grincer.

cream, s. crème f.

crease, s. (faux) pli m.

create, v.a. créer.

creation, s. création f.

creature, s. créature f.

credit, s. crédit m.; mérite m.; honneur m.; on ~ à terme: give ~ to ajouter foi à; — v.a. ajouter foi à, créditer.

creditor, s. créancier m.

creek, s. crique f.

creep, v.n. ramper; se glisser.

crew, s. équipage m.; équipe f.

crib, s. mangeoire f.; lit m. d'enfant; berceau m.

cricket, s. (game) cricket m.

crime, s. crime m.

criminal, adj. & s. criminel, -elle.

cripple, s. estropié m.

crisis, s. crise f.

crisp, adj. croquant, croustillant; (air) vif.

critic, s. critique m.

critical, adj. critique.

criticize, v.a. critiquer.

critique, s. critique f.

croak, v.n. croasser.

crochet, s. crochet m.

crop, s. récolte f.; cueillette f.

cross, s. croix f.; — v.a. croiser, traverser.

crossing, s. passage m.;

(sea) traversée *f.;* level ~ passage à ni-
veau.
cross-question, *s.* contre-
interrogatoire *m.;* —
v.a. contre-interroger.
cross-reference, *s.* renvoi *m.*
crossroad, *s.* chemin *m.*
de traverse; ~s carre-
four *m.*
cross-section, *s.* coupe *f.*
en travers.
cross-word (puzzle) *s.*
mots *m.pl.* croisés.
crouch, *v. n.* se blottir.
crow, *s.* corneille *f.*
crowd, *s.* foule *f.;* tas *m.*
crowded, *adj.* encombré,
comble.
crown, *s.* couronne *f.;* —
v.a. couronner.
crucial, *adj.* décisif.
crude, *adj.* brut; cru;
grossier.
cruel, *adj.* cruel.
cruelty, *s.* cruauté *f.*
cruet, *s.* burette *f.*
cruise, *v.n.* croiser; — *s.*
voyage *m.*
cruising, *adj.* ~ *speed*
vitesse *f.* de croisière.
crumb, *s.* mie *f.;* miette
f.
crumble, *v.a.* émietter;
v.n. s'émietter.
crusade, *s.* croisade *f.*
crush, *s.* écrasement *m.;*
cohue *f.;* — *v.a.* écraser.
crust, *s.* croûte *f.*
crutch, *s.* béquille *f.*
cry, *s.* cri *m.;* — *v.a.*
crier; ~ *down* décrier;
v.n. crier; *(weep)* pleurer.

crystal, *s.* cristal *m.*
cub, *s.* petit *m.;* *(boy
scout)* louveteau *m.*
cube, *s.* cube *m.*
cuckoo, *s.* coucou *m.*
cucumber, *s.* concombre *m.*
cue, *s.* réplique *f.*
cuff, *s.* poignet *m.,* manchette *f.*
cuff-links, *s. pl.* boutons
m.pl. de manchette.
culminate, *v.n.* se terminer.
culprit, *s.* accusé, -e *m. f.*
cultivate, *v.a.* cultiver.
cultural, *adj.* cultural.
culture, *s.* culture *f.*
cunning, *s.* ruse *f.,* finesse
f.; — *adj.* rusé.
cup, *s.* tasse *f.;* gobelet *m.*
cupboard, *s.* armoire *f.;*
placard *m.*
curate, *s.* vicaire *m.*
curb, *s.* gourmetté *f.*
curd, *s.* (lait) caillé *m.*
curdle, *v.a.* cailler; *v.n.*
se cailler.
cure, *s.* guérison *f.;* cure
f.; remède *m.;* — *v.a.*
guérir.
curiosity, *s.* curiosité *f.*
curious, *adj.* curieux.
curl, *s.* boucle *f.;* — *v.a.*
& *n.* boucler, friser; ~
up s'enrouler.
curly, *adj.* bouclé, frisé.
currant, *s. black* ~ cassis
m.; red ~ groseille *f.*
rouge.
currency, *s.* circulation
f., cours *m.;* terme *m.*
d'échéance; unité *f.*
monétaire, monnaie *f.;*
foreign ~ monnaie
étrangère.
current, *adj.* courant, en

cours; in ~ use d'usage courant; ~ events actualités f.; ~ account compte m. courant; — s. courant m.; cours m.

curse, s. malédiction f.; — v.a. maudire; v.n. blasphémer.

curtain, s. rideau m.

curve, s. courbe f.

cushion, s. coussin m.

custom, s. coutume f.; ~s douane f.; ~s duties droits m. de douane; ~s declaration déclaration f. de douane; ~s formalities la visite de la douane.

customary, adj. coutumier; accoutumé.

customer, s. client m., acheteur m.

custom-house, s. douane f.; ~ officer douanier m.

cut, v.a. couper; trancher; tailler; hacher; ~ down abattre, couper; réduire; ~ off couper; ~ out tailler; ~ up couper, débiter; — s. (knife) coup m.; (wound) coupure f.; (clothes) coupe f.; (meat) morceau m.; (in wages) réduction f.

cutlery, s. coutellerie f.

cutlet, s. côtelette f.

cutter, s. tailleur m.; coupeur m.

cycle, s. cycle m.; bicyclette f.; — v.n. pédaler.

cycling, s. cyclisme m.

cylinder, s. cylindre m.

cynic, adj. & s. cynique m.

Czech, adj. tchèque; — s. Tchèque m.

D

dad, daddy, s. papa m.

dagger, s. poignard m.

daily, adj. journalier, quotidien; — s. (journal) quotidien m.

dainty, adj. friand, délicat; gentil; — s. friandise f.

dairy, s. laiterie f.

daisy, s. marguerite f.

dam, s. barrage m.; digue f.

damage, s. dommage m.; préjudice m.; ~s dommages-intérêts m.

damn, v.a. condamner; — s. juron m.

damp, adj. humide; — s. humidité f.; — v.a. mouiller, humecter.

dance, s. danse f.; bal m.; v.n. & a. danser.

dancer, s. danseur, -euse m. f.

dancing-hall, s. salle f. de danse; dancing m.

dancing-shoes, s.pl. souliers m. de bal, escarpins m.

Dane, s. Danois, -e m. f.

danger, s. danger m.

dangerous, adj. dangereux.

Danish, adj. danois; — s. (language) danois m.

dare, v. aux. & a. oser.

daring, adj. audacieux.

dark, adj. obscur, sombre; (colour) foncé; (fig.) triste; be ~ faire som-

bre; — *s.* obscurité *f.*;
in the ~ dans l'obscurité.

darken, *v.a.* obscurcir.

darkness, *s.* obscurité *f.*

darling, *adj. & s.* chéri, -e.

darn, *v.a.* repriser.

darning, *s.* reprise *f.*

dart, *s.* dard *m.*; ~s
(game) fléchettes *f.pl.*

dash, *v.a.* lancer; flanquer (par terre); ~ *to
pieces* briser en morceaux; *v.n.* ~ *against*
se heurter contre; ~
at se précipiter sur
— *s. (with pen)* trait
m., tiret *m.*; *(vigour)*
élan *m.*, fougue *f.*;
attaque *f.* soudaine.

dash-board, *s.* tablier *m*;
tableau *m.* de bord.

data, *s. pl.* données *f.*

date[1], *s.* date *f.*; millésime *m.*; *be up to* ~
être à la page; —
v.a. & n. dater.

date[2], *s.* datte *f.*

daughter, *s.* fille *f.*

daughter-in-law, *s.* belle-fille *f.*

dawn, *s.* point *m.* du
jour; aube *f.*

day, *s.* jour *m.*; *(whole
day)* journée *f.*

daylight, *s.* jour *m.*

daytime, *s.* jour *m.*,
journée. *f.*

daze, *v.a.* étourdir;
éblouir.

dazzle, *v.c.* éblouir.

deacon, *s.* diacre *m.*

dead, *adj.* mort; *the* ~
les morts *m.pl.*

deadly, *adj.* mortel.

deaf, *adj.* sourd; ~ *and*

dumb sourd-muet.

deal, *v.a.* ~ *out* distribuer; donner; *v.n.*
~ *with* traiter qn; commercer, traiter avec qn;
traiter (d'un sujet);
~ *in* commercer de; —
s. (cards) donne *f.*;
(commerce) affaire *f.*;
a good ~, *a great* ~
beaucoup (de).

dealer, *s.* marchand *m.*
(in de).

dean, *s.* doyen *m.*

dear, *s. & adj.* cher *m.*,
chère *f.*

death, *s.* mort *f.*

debate, *s.* débat *m.*,
discussion *f.*; — *v.a.*
discuter, mettre en
discussion.

debt, *s.* dette *f.*

debtor, *s.* débiteur, -trice
m. f.

decay, *s.* décadence *f.*;
— *v.n.* tomber en
décadence; pourrir.

decease, *s.* décès *m.*;
— *v.n.* décéder.

deceit, *s.* déception *f.*;
tromperie *f.*

deceive, *v.a.* tromper;
décevoir.

December, *s.* décembre
m.

decent, *adj.* décent; assez
bon.

deception, *s.* déception *f.*

decide, *v.a.* décider.

decision, *s.* décision *f.*

decisive, *adj.* décisif.

deck, *s.* pont *m.*

deck-chair, *s.* transatlantique *f.*

declaration, *s.* déclaration
f.

declare, *v.a.* déclarer.

decline, *s.* décadence *f.*; — *v.a.* décliner; *v.n.* baisser.

decorate, *v.a.* décorer (de).

decoration, *s.* décoration *f.*

decrease, *v.a. & n.* diminuer; — *s.* diminution *f.*

decree, *s.* décret *m.*

dedicate, *v.a.* dédier.

deed, *s.* action *f.*; acte *m.*

deem, *v.a.* juger.

deep, *adj.* profond; *ten feet* ~ dix pieds de profondeur.

deer, *s.* cerf *m.*

deface, *v.a.* défigurer.

defeat, *s.* défaite *f.*; — *v.a.* vaincre.

defect, *s.* défaut *m.*

defence, *s.* défense *f.*

defend, *v.a.* défendre.

defender, *s.* défenseur *m.*

defer, *v.a.* retarder, ajourner; ~ *to* déférer à.

defiance, *s.* défi *m.*; *set at* ~ défier.

deficiency, *s.* manque *m.*

deficient, *adj.* insuffisant.

defile, *s.* défilé *m.*; — *v.n.* défiler; *v.a.* souiller.

define, *v.a.* définir.

definite, *adj.* déterminé, défini.

definition, *s.* définition *f.*

defy, *v.a.* défier; braver.

degrade, *v.a.* dégrader.

degree, *s.* degré *m.*; *(university)* grade *m.*; diplôme *m.*

delay, *s.* retard *m.*, délai *m.*; — *v.a.* retarder; différer; *v.n.* tarder.

delegate, *s.* délégué *m.*

delegation, *s.* délégation *f.*

deliberate, *adj.* délibéré; — *v.a. & n.* délibérer.

delicacy, *s.* délicatesse *f.*

delicate, *adj.* délicat.

delicious, *adj* délicieux.

delight, *v.a.* be ~ed *at* être enchanté de.

delightful, *adj.* délicieux.

delinquent, *s.* délinquant *m.*

deliver, *v.a.* *(letters)* distribuer, *(goods etc.)* livrer, *(message)* remettre; *(speech)* faire, prononcer; *(free)* délivrer; *be* ~ed *of* accoucher de.

delivery, *s.* *(letters)* distribution *f.*, *(message)* remise *f.*, *(goods)* livraison *f.*; *(speech)* prononciation *f.*, débit *m.*

delusion, *s.* illusion *f.*

demand, *s.* demande, *f.* réclamation *f.*; — *v.* a. demander, réclamer.

democracy, *s.* démocratie *f.*

democrat, *s.* démocrate *m.*

democratic, *adj.* démocratique.

demolish, *v.a.* démolir.

demonstrate, *v.a.* démontrer.

demonstration, *s.* démonstration *f.*

den, *s.* antre *m.*; repaire *m.*

denial, *s.* dénégation *f.*

denomination, *s.* dénomination *f.*; secte *f.*

denote, *v.a.* dénoter.

denounce, *v.a.* dénoncer.

dense, *adj.* dense, épais.

density, *s.* densité *f.*

dentist, s. dentiste m.
denture, s. *(artificial)* dentier m.
deny, v.a. nier.
depart, v.n. partir.
department, s. département m.
departure, s. départ m.
depend, v.n. dépendre (de); compter (sur).
dependence, s. dépendance f.
dependent, adj. dépendant.
deplore, v.a. déplorer.
deposit, s. dépôt m.; — v.a. déposer.
depot, s. dépôt m.
depression s. abattement m.
deprive, v.a. priver (de).
depth, s. profondeur f.
deputy, s. délégué m.; vice-, sous-.
derive, v.a. retirer (de); be ~d from dériver de.
descend, v.n. descendre.
descendant, s. descendant, -e m. f.
descent, s. descente f.
describe, v.a. décrire.
description, s. description f.; sorte f.
desert, s. désert m.; — v.a. déserter.
deserve, v.a. mériter.
design, s. dessein m.; projet m.; dessin m.; — v.a. dessiner.
desirable, adj. désirable.
desire, s. désir m.; — v.a. désirer.
desk, s. bureau m.
desolation, s. désolation f.
despair, s. désespoir m.; — v.n. désespérer.

despatch see dispatch.
desperate, adj. désespéré.
despise, v.a. mépriser.
despite, prep. ~ (of) en dépit de.
dessert, s. dessert m.
destination, s. destination f.
destine, v.a. destiner.
destiny, s. destin m. destinée f.
destroy, v.a. détruire.
destruction, s. destruction f.
detach, v.a. détacher.
detachment, s. détachement m.
detail, s. détail m.
detain, v.a. retenir; détenir.
detect, v.a. découvrir.
detective, s. détective m.
detention, s. détention f.
detergent, s. détergent m.
deteriorate, v.n. se détériorer.
determination, s. détermination f.
determine, v.a. & n. déterminer, décider.
detrimental, adj. préjudiciable.
develop, v.a. développer; v.n. se développer.
development, s. développement m.
deviation, s. déviation f.
device, s expédient m.; invention f.
devil, s. diable m.
devilish, adj. diabolique.
devise, v.a. combiner; tramer.
devote, v.a. consacrer.
devoted, adj. dévoué.
devotion, s. dévotion f.;

dévouement *m.*

devour, *v.a.* dévorer.

dew, *s.* rosée *f.*

diagnosis, *s.* diagnostic *m.*

diagram, *s.* diagramme *m.*

dial, *s.* cadran *m.;* — *v.a.* composer un numéro.

dialogue, *s.* dialogue *m.*

diameter, *s.* diamètre *m.*

diamond, *s.* diamant *m.; (cards)* carreau *m.*

diaper, *s.* couche *f.*

diarrhoea, *s.* diarrhée *f.*

diary, *s.* journal *m.;* agenda *m.*

dictate, *v.a.* dicter; *v.n.* ~ *to* donner des ordres à.

dictation, *s.* dictée *f.*

dictator, *s.* dictateur *m.*

dictionary, *s.* dictionnaire *m.*

die¹, *s.* dé *m.*

die², *v.n.* mourir.

Diesel engine, *s.* moteur *m.* Diesel; diesel *m.*

diet, *s.* alimentation *f.;* régime *m.*

differ, *v.n.* différer.

difference, *s.* différence *f.*

different, *adj.* différent.

difficult, *adj.* difficile.

difficulty, *s.* difficulté *f.*

diffuse, *adj.* diffus.

dig, *v.a.* bêcher.

digest, *v.a.* digérer.

digestion, *s.* digestion *f.*

dignity, *s.* dignité *f.*

diligent, *adj.* diligent.

dim, *adj.* faible, pâle, obscur.

dimension, *s.* dimension *f.*

diminish, *v. a. & n.* diminuer.

dimple, *s.* fossette *f.*

dine, *v.n.* dîner.

dining-car, *s.* wagonrestaurant *m.*

dining-hall, *s.* salle *f.* à manger; réfectoire *m.*

dining-room, *s.* salle *f.* à manger.

dinner, *s.* dîner *m.*

dinner-jacket, *s.* smoking *m.*

dip, *v.a. & n.* plonger.

diploma, *s.* diplôme *m.*

diplomacy, *s.* diplomatie *f.*

diplomat, *s.* diplomate *m.*

diplomatic, *adj.* diplomatique.

direct, *adj.* direct; — *v. a.* diriger; commander; adresser.

direction, *s.* direction *f;* instructions *f. pl.*

directly, *adv.* directement; tout de suite.

director, *s.* directeur *m.*

directory, *s.* annuaire *m.;* Bottin *m.*

dirt, *s.* saleté *f.;* boue *f.,* crotte *f.;* crasse *f.*

dirty, *adj.* sale; crotté; crasseux.

disadvantage, *s.* désavantage *m.*

disagree, *v.n.* différer; se brouiller; ne pas convenir (à).

disagreeable, *adj.* désagréable.

disappear, *v. n.* disparaître

disappearance, *s.* disparition *f.*

disappoint, *v.a.* désappointer; tromper.

disappointment, *s.* désappointement *m.*

disapprove, v.n. ~ of désapprouver qch.

disaster, s. désastre m.

disastrous, adj. désastreux.

disc see disk.

discern, v.a. discerner.

discharge, v. a. décharger; (employee) congédier; renvoyer; (prisoner) élargir; (gas) dégager; (debt) liquider; (duty) s'acquitter de; — s. décharge f.; (employee) congé m.; (prison) élargissement m.

discipline, s. discipline f.

disclose, v.a. découvrir.

discontented, adj. mécontent (de).

discourage, v. a. décourager.

discouragement, s. découragement m.

discourse, s. discours m.

discover, v.a. découvrir.

discovery, s. découverte f.

discredit, s. discrédit m.; — v.a. discréditer.

discreet, adj. discret.

discretion, s. discrétion f.; prudence f.

discuss, v.a. discuter.

discussion, s. discussion f.

disdain, v.a. dédaigner; — s. dédain m.

disease, s. maladie f.

disembark v.a. & n. débarquer.

disgrace, s. disgrâce f.; — v.a. disgracier.

disgraceful, adj. honteux.

disguise, s. déguisement; — v.a. déguiser.

disgust, s. dégoût m.; — v.a. dégoûter.

disgusting, adj. dégoûtant.

dish, s. plat m.; mets m.; wash up the ~es laver la vaisselle.

dishonest, adj. malhonnête.

dishonour, s. déshonneur m.; — v.a. déshonorer (bill) ne pas honorer.

disinfect, v.a. désinfecter.

disk, s. disque m.

dislike, s. aversion f., dégoût m.; — v.a. ne pas aimer.

dismal, adj. lugubre, sombre.

dismay, s. consternation f.

dismiss, v.a. congédier; bannir, écarter.

disobedience, s. désobéissance f.

disobedient, adj. désobéissant.

disobey, v. a. désobéir (à).

disorder, s. désordre m.

dispatch, s. expédition f.; dépêche f.

dispensary, s. pharmacie f.

dispense, v.a. dispenser; préparer; v.n. ~ with se disposer de.

disperse, v.a. disperser.

displaced, adj. ~ person personne f. déplacée.

displacement, s. déplacement m.

display, v.a. exposer; étaler; déployer; faire preuve de; — s. exposition f.; étalage m.; parade f.

displease, v.a. déplaire à

disposal, s. at s.o.'s ~ à la disposition de qn.

dispose, *v.n.* ~ *of* disposer de; vendre.

disposition, *s.* disposition *f.*

dispute, *s.* dispute *f.* discuission *f.;* — *v.a* discuter; *v. n.* se disputer.

disqualify, *v.a.* disqualifier.

dissatisfy, *v.a.* mécontenter.

dissolve, *v.a.* dissoudre; *v.n.* se dissoudre.

distance, *s.* distance *f.*

distant, *adj.* lointain; éloigné.

distil, *v. a.* & *n.* distiller.

distinct, *adj.* distinct (de); marqué.

distinction, *s.* distinction *f.*

distinguish, *v.a.* distinguer.

distract, *v.a.* distraire.

distraction, *s.* distraction *f.;* confusion *f.*

distress, *s.* détresse *f.;* — *v.a.* affliger.

distribute, *v. a.* distribuer.

distribution, *s.* distribution *f.*

district, *s.* région *f.,* contrée *f.;* district *m.*

disturb, *v.a.* troubler; déranger.

disturbance, *s.* trouble *m.,* dérangement *m.*

ditch, *s.* fossé *m.*

dive, *v.n.* plonger *(into* dans).

diver, *s.* plongeur *m.,* scaphandrier *m.*

divergent, *adj.* divergent.

diversion, *s.* déviation *f.*

divide, *v.a.* diviser.

dividend, *s.* dividende *m.*

divine, *adj.* divin.

divinity, *s.* théologie *f.*

division, *s.* division *f.*

divorce, *s.* divorce *m.;* — *v. a.* divorcer (d'avec).

dizzy, *adj.* *feel* ~ avoir le vertige.

do, *v. a.* faire; finir; ~ *away with* supprimer; ~ *up* envelopper; ~ *with* se contenter de.

dock, *s.* bassin *m.*

doctor, *s.* docteur *m.;* médecin *m.*

doctrine, *s.* doctrine *f.*

document, *s.* document *m.*

dog, *s.* chien *m.*

dogma, *s.* dogme *m.*

doll, *s.* poupée *f.*

dollar, *s.* dollar *m.*

domestic, *adj.* & *s.* domestique *(m. f.).*

domicile, *s.* domicile *m.*

dominate, *v.a.* &. *n.* dominer.

dominion, *s.* domination *f.;* ~*s* colonies *f.*

donkey, *s.* âne *m.*

doom, *s.* sentence *f.;* — *v.a.* condamner; ~*ed to* voué à.

door, *s.* porte *f.;* *(vehicle)* portière *f.*

dormitory, *s.* dortoir *m.*

dose, *s.* dose *f.*

dot, *s.* point *m.*

double, *adj.* & *s.* double *(m.).*

doubt, *s.* doute *m.;* *no* ~ sans doute; — *v.a.* & *n.* douter.

doubtful, *adj.* douteux.

doubtless, *adj.* sans doute.

dough, s. pâte f.

dove, s. colombe f.

down, adv. à bas, en bas, par en bas; be ~ with (illness) être au lit avec; fall ~ tomber à terre; go ~ aller en bas; — prep. le long de; ~ the river en aval; ~ the street plus bas dans la rue.

downhill, s. pente f.; — adv. en pente, en descendant.

downstairs, adv. en bas.

downwards, adv. en bas.

dozen, s. douzaine f.

draft, s. projet m.; (letter) minute f.; (troops) détachement m.; (drawing) esquisse f.

drag, v.a. traîner; tirer.

drain, s. égout m., canal m.; — v.a. drainer; vider.

drama, s. drame m.; théâtre m.

dramatic, adj. dramatique.

draper, s. marchand m. d'étoffes, (marchand) drapier m.; ~'s magasin m. de nouveautés.

draught, s. tirage m.; (drink) trait m.; (air) courant m. d'air.

draw, v.a. (pull) tirer, traîner; (tooth) arracher; (sketch) dessiner; ~ down baisser; ~ on tirer; ~ out prolonger; — v.n. tirer; ~ near s'approcher.

drawer, s. tiroir m.

drawing, s. dessin m.

drawing-pin, s. punaise f.

drawing-room, s. salon m.

dread, v.a. redouter.

dreadful, adj. redoutable.

dream, s. rêve m.; — v.a. &n. rêver.

dress, s. habits m.pl.; robe f.; — v.a. habiller; v.n. s'habiller; ~ a wound panser.

dress-circle, s. (premier) balcon m.

dressing-gown, s. (woman) peignoir m., (man) robe f. de chambre.

dressmaker, s. couturière f.

drift, v.n. flotter; dériver; — s. dérive f.; amoncellement m.

drill, s. foret m.; (soldiers) exercice m.

drink, s. boisson f.; — v.a. boire.

drip, v.n. dégoutter.

drive, v.a. conduire; ~ in (nail) enfoncer; v.n. conduire; aller en voiture.

driver, s. (engine) mécanicien m.; (bus) conducteur m.; (car) chauffeur m.

driving, s. conduite f.; ~ licence permis m. de conduire.

drop, s. goutte f.; — v.a. laisser tomber; abandonner; v.n. (dé)goutter; ~ in entrer en passant.

drown, v.a. noyer; v.n. se noyer.

drug, s. drogue f.

druggist, s. droguiste m.

drum, s. tambour m.

drunk, adj. ivre.

dry, *adj.* sec, sèche; aride; tari; — *v.a.* sécher.

dry-clean, *v.a.* nettoyer à sec.

dual, *adj.* double.

dub, *v.a.* doubler.

duchess, *s.* duchesse *f.*

duck, *s.* cane *f.*; canard *m.*

due, *adj.* (proper) dû; (owing) exigible; échéant, payable; in ∼ form en bonne et due forme; in ∼ time en temps voulu; ∼ to causé par, par suite de; the train is ∼ at le train arrive à; — *s.* dû *m.*; droit *m.*

duke, *s.* duc *m.*

dull, *adj.* borné; ennuyeux; (colour) terne; (weather, sad) triste.

dumb, *adj.* muet.

dummy, *s.* mannequin *m.*; (cards) mort *m.*

dung, *s.* fumier *m.*

dupe, *s.* dupe *f.*; — *v.a.* duper.

duplicate, *s.* duplicata *m.*; — *adj.* en double; *v.a.* faire en double.

during, *adv.* pendant, au cours de.

dusk, *s.* crépuscule *m.*

dust, *s.* poussière *f.*

dustbin, *s.* poubelle *f.*

dusty, *adj.* poussiéreux, poudreux.

Dutch, *adj.* hollandais.

Dutchman, *s.* Hollandais *m.*

duty, *s.* devoir *m.*; (customs) droit *m.*; (task) tâche *f.*, fonction(s) *f.(pl.)*; be on ∼ être de service.

duty-free, *adj.* exempt de droits, en franchise.

dwarf, *s.* nain, -e *m. f.*

dwell, *v.n.* habiter; ∼ (up)on s'appesantir sur.

dwelling, *s.* habitation *f.*

dwelling-house *s.* maison *f.* d'habitation.

dwindle, *v.n.* diminuer.

dye, *s.* teinte *f.*, teinture *f.*; — *v.a.* teindre.

dynasty, *s.* dynastie *f.*

E

each, *pron.* chacun, -e; ∼ other l'un l'autre; — *adj.* chaque.

eager, *adj.* ardent.

eagle, *s.* aigle *m.*

ear, *s.* oreille *f.*

earl, *s.* comte *m.*

early, *adv.* de bonne heure — *adj.* précoce; premier.

earn, *v. a.* gagner; mériter

earnest, *adj.* sérieux.

earnings, *s.pl.* salaire *m.*

earth, *s.* terre *f.*

earthenware, *s.* poterie *f.*

earthquake, *s.* tremblement *m.* de terre.

ease, *s.* aise *f.*; repos *m.*; at one's ∼ à son aise; with ∼ avec facilité.

east, *s.* est *m.*; — *adj.* d'est, de l'est; — *adv.* à l'est (de).

Easter, *s.* Pâques *m. pl.*

eastern, *adj.* (de l')est, oriental.

eastwards, *adv.* vers l'est.

easy, *adj.* facile.

easy-chair, *s.* fauteuil *m.*

easy-going, *adj.* nonchalant.

eat, *v.a.* manger; ~ *up* finir; dévorer.

ebb, *s.* reflux *m.*

ecclesiastic, *adj.* & *s.* ecclésiastique *(m.).*

economic, *adj.* économique.

economical, *adj.* économe.

economics, *s.* économie *f.* politique.

economize, *v.n.* faire des économes.

economy, *s.* économie *f.*

ecstasy, *s.* extase *f.*

edge, *s.* tranchant *m.*, fil *m.*; bord *m.*

edition, *s.* édition *f.*

editor, *s.* rédacteur *m.*

editorial, *s.* article *m.* de fond.

educate, *v.a.* élever.

education, *s.* éducation *f.*

effect, *s.* effet *m.*

effective, *adj.* efficace; effectif.

efficiency, *s.* efficacité *f.*

efficient, *adj.* capable.

effort, *s.* effort *m.*

egg, *s.* œuf *m.*; *boiled* ~ œuf à la coque; *fried* ~ œuf sur le plat.

Egyptian, *adj.* égyptien; — *s.* Egyptien, -enne *m. f.*

eight, *adj.* & *s.* huit.

eighteen, *adj.* & *s.* dix-huit.

eighteenth, *adj.* dix-huitième.

eighth, *adj.* huitième.

eighty, *adj.* & *s.* quatre-vingt(s).

either, *pron.* & *adj.* l'un ou l'autre; chacun; chaque; ~ ... *or* ou ... ou.

elaborate, *v.a.* élaborer; — *adj.* minutieux.

elastic, *adj.* élastique.

elbow, *s.* coude *m.*

elderly, *adj.* d'un certain âge.

elect, *v.a.* choisir; élire.

election, *s.* élection *f.*

electric(al), *adj.* électrique; ~al *engineer* (ingénieur) électricien *m.*

electricity, *s.* électricité *f.*

electron, *s.* électron *m.*

electronic, *adj.* électronique.

elegance, *s.* élégance *f.*

elegant, *adj.* élégant.

element, *s.* élément *m.*

elementary, *adj.* élémentaire.

elephant, *s.* éléphant *m.*

elevate, *v.a.* élever.

eleven, *adj.* & *s.* onze.

eleventh, *adj.* onzième.

elm, *s.* orme *m.*

else, *adj.* autre; *anything* ~, *madam?* encore quelque chose, Madame?; — *adv. or* ~ ou bien, autrement.

elsewhere, *adv.* ailleurs.

embankment, *s.* remblai *m.*

embark, *v.a.* embarquer; *v.n.* s'embarquer.

embarrass, *v.a.* embarrasser.

embassy, *s.* ambassade *f.*

embrace, *v.a.* embrasser.

embroidery, broderie *f.*

emerge, *v.n.* émerger; apparaître.

emergency, *s.* circonstance *f.* critique; *in case of* ~ en cas d'accident or d'urgence; ~ *exit* sortie *f.* de secours.

emigrant, *s.* émigrant, -e *m. f.*

emigrate, *v.n.* émigrer.

emigration, *s.* émigration *f.*

eminent, *adj.* éminent.

emit, *v.a.* émettre.

emotion, *s.* émotion *f.*

emphasis, *s.* accent *m.*, force *f.*; *lay* ~ *on* appuyer sur.

emphasize, *v. a.* appuyer sur.

empire, *s.* empire *m.*

employ, *v.a.* employer.

employee, *s.* employé *m.*

employer, *s.* employeur *m.*

employment, *s.* emploi *m.*

empty, *adj.* vide.

enable, *v. a.* rendre capable.

enclose, *v.a.* entourer (de); joindre (à une lettre).

encounter, *v.a.* affronter; rencontrer.

encourage, *v.a.* encourager.

encouragement, *s.* encouragement *m.*

encyclopaedia, *s.* encyclopédie *f.*

end, *s.* bout *m.*; fin *f.*; — *v.a.&n.* finir; ~ *in* finir en.

endeavour, *s.* effort *m.*; — *v. n.* s'efforcer (à or de).

ending, *s.* terminaison *f.*; fin *f.*

endless, *adj.* sans fin.

endorse, *v.a.* endosser.

endorsement, *s.* endossement *m.*

endow, *v.a.* doter (de).

endure, *v.a.* supporter, endurer.

enemy, *s.* ennemi, -e *m. f.*

energetic, *adj.* énergique.

energy, *s.* énergie *f.*

enforce, *v.a.* imposer; *(law)* faire exécuter.

engage, *v.a.* engager; fiancer; *be* ~*d* être occupé; être fiancé(e).

engagement, *s.* engagement *m.*; fiançailles *f. pl.*

engine, *s.* machine *f.*

engine-driver, *s.* mécanicien *m.*

engineer, *s.* ingénieur *m.*

English, *adj.* anglais.

Englishman, *s.* Anglais *m.*

Englishwomen, *s.* Anglaise *f.*

enjoy, *v. a.* jouir de; trouver bon; ~ *oneself* s'amuser.

enjoyment, *s.* jouissance *f.*

enlarge, *v.a.* agrandir.

enlist, *v.a.* enrôler.

enormous, *adj.* énorme.

enough, *adj.* & *adv.* assez (de).

enquire *see* inquire.

enrage, *v.a.* exaspérer.

enrol(l), *v.a.* enrôler.

ensign, *s. (flag)* drapeau *m.*, pavillon *m.*; *(pers.)* porte-drapeau *m.*

ensue, *v.n.* s'ensuivre.

enter, *v.a.* entrer (dans);

(in list) inscrire.

enterprise, *s.* entreprise *f.*

entertain, *v.a.* amuser; recevoir; avoir (une opinion).

entertainment, *s.* divertissement *m.;* amusement *m.;* hospitalité *f.*

enthusiasm, *s.* enthousiasme. *m.*

enthusiastic, *adj.* enthousiaste.

entire, *adj.* entier.

entirely, *adv.* entièrement.

entitle, *v.a.* be ∼d to avoir droit à.

entrance, *s.* entrée *f.;* ∼ *examination* examen d'entrée *m.*

entreat, *v.a.* supplier.

entry, *s.* entrée *f.;* inscription *f.*

enumerate, *v.a.* énumérer.

envelope, *s.* enveloppe *f.*

envious, *adj.* envieux (de).

environment, *s.* milieu *m.*

envy, *s.* envie *f.;* — *v.a.* envier.

epidemic, *s.* épidémie *f.*

equal, *adj.* égal.

equality, *s.* égalité *f.*

equation, *s.* équation *f.*

equip, *v.a.* équiper.

equipment, *s.* équipement *m.*

erase *v.a.* effacer.

erect, *adj.* droit ; — *v.a.* dresser; ériger.

err, *v.n.* errer.

error, *s.* erreur *f.*

escalator, *s.* escalator *m.,* escalier *m.* roulant.

escape, *v. n.* (s')échapper;

— *s.* fuite *f.*

escort, *s.* escorte *f.;* — *v.a.* escorter.

essay, *s.* essai *m.,* composition *f.*

essential, *adj.* essentiel.

establish, *v.a.* établir.

establishment, *s.* établissement *m.*

estate, *s.* propriété *f.;* biens *m. pl.*

esteem, *s.* estime *f.;* — *v.a.* estimer.

estimate, *s.* estimation *f.;* évaulation *f.;* — *v.a.* estimer.

eternal, *adj.* éternel.

eucharist, *s.* eucharistie *f.*

European, *adj.* européen.

evacuate, *v.a.* évacuer.

even, *adj.* uni; égal; pair; — *adv.* même; ∼ *if* même si.

evening, *s.* soir *m.;* *(party)* soirée *f.*

event, *s.* événement *m.*

eventual, *adj.* éventuel.

ever, *adv.* toujours; *(any time)* jamais.

evermore, *adv.* toujours.

every, *adj. (all)* tous; *(each)* chaque; ∼ *day* tous les jours.

everybody, *pron.* tout le monde.

everyday, *adj.* de tous les jours.

everyone *see* everybody.

everything, *pron.* tout *m.*

everywhere, *adv.* partout.

evidence, *s.* évidence *f.*

evident, *adj.* évident.

evil, *s.* mal *m.;* — *adj.* mauvais.

evolution, *s.* évolution *f.*

ewe, brebis *f.*

exact, *adj.* exact.

exactly, *adv.* exactement.

exaggerate, *v.a.* exagérer.

exaggeration, *s.* exagération *f.*

examination, *s.* examen *m.*

examine, *v.a.* examiner; vérifier; *(customs)* visiter.

example, *s.* example *m.*; *for* ~ par exemple.

excavation, *s.* fouille *f.*

exceedingly, *adv.* excessivement.

excel, *v. a.* surpasser; *v. n.* exceller à.

excellent, *adj.* excellent.

except, *v.a.* excepter; — *prep.* excepté; sauf; ~ *for* exception faite pour.

exception, *s.* exception *f.*

exceptional, *adj.* exceptionnel.

excess, *s.* excès *m.*; ~ *luggage* excédent *m.* de bagages.

excessive, *adj.* excessif.

exchange, *s.* échange *m.*; *(telephone)* bureau central *m.*; *foreign* ~ change *m.*; — *v.a.* échanger.

excite, *v.a.* exciter.

excitement, *s.* excitation *f.*

exclaim, *v.n.* s'écrier.

exclamation, *s.* exclamation *f.*

exclude, *v.a.* exclure.

exclusive, *adj.* exclusif.

excursion, *s.* excursion *f.*

excuse, *s.* excuse *f.*; — *v.a.* excuser.

execute, *v.a.* exécuter.

execution, *s.* exécution *f.*

executive, *adj. & s.* exécutif *m.*; agent *m.* d'exécution.

exempt, *adj.* exempt (de); *v.a.* exempter (de).

exercise, *s.* exercice *m.*; — *v.a.* exercer.

exertion, *s.* effort *m.*

exhaust, *v.a.* épuiser.

exhaust-pipe, *s.* tuyau *m.* d'échappement.

exhibit, *v. a.* présenter, exhiber; exposer.

exhibition, *s.* exhibition *f.*; exposition *f.*

exist, *v.n.* exister.

existence, *s.* existence *f.*

exit, *s.* sortie *f.*

expand, *v.a.* étendre; dilater.

expansion, *s.* expansion *f.*

expect, *v.a.* attendre, s'attendre à; *(think)* croire.

expedient, *s.* expédient *m.*

expedition, *s.* expédition *f.*

expel, *v.a.* expulser.

expense, *s.* dépense *f.*

expensive, *adj.* coûteux, cher.

experience, *s.* expérience *f.*; — *v.a.* éprouver.

experiment, *s.* expérience *f.*; — *v.n.* faire des expériences, expérimenter.

experimental, *adj.* expérimental.

expert, *s.* expert *m.*

expire, *v.n.* expirer.

explain, *v.a.* expliquer.

explanation, *s.* explication *f.*

exploration, *s.* exploration.

explore, *v.a.* explorer.

explosion, s. explosion f.

export, s. exportation f.;
~**s** articles m.pl. d'exportation; — v.a. exporter.

exporter, s. exportateur m.

expose, v.a. exposer.

exposure, s. exposition f.; révélation f.

express, adj. exprès; formel; exact; ~ *letter* lettre f. par exprès; — s. *(train)* express m.; — v.a. exprimer.

expression, s. expression f.

exquisite, adj. exquis.

extend, v.a. étendre; prolonger.

extension, s. extension f.; prolongation f.

extensive, adj. étendu, vaste.

extent, s. étendue f.

extinguish, v.a. éteindre.

extra, adj. supplémentaire.

extract, s. extrait m.; — v.a. extraire.

extraordinary, adj. extraordinaire.

extravagant, adj. extravagant.

extreme, adj. & s. extrême (m.).

extremely, adv. extrêmement.

extremity, s. extrémité f.

eye, s. œil m.

eyebrow, s. sourcil m.

eyelid, s. paupière f.

eyepiece, s. oculaire m.

F

fable, s. fable f.

fabric, s. tissu m.; textile m.

face, s. visage m.; face f.; figure f.; in ~ of devant; — v.a. affronter, faire face à, braver.

facility, s. facilité f.

fact, s. fait m.; in ~ de fait; en effet.

factor, s. facteur m.; élément m.

factory, s. fabrique f.; usine f.

faculty, s. faculté f.

fade, v.n. se faner; ~ away s'évanouir.

fail, v.n. manquer (de); *(not succeed)* échouer, *(in an exam)* être refusé.

failure, s. insuccès m.

faint, v.n. s'évanouir.

fair, adj. beau; bel, belle; *(hair)* blond; *(just)* juste; *(weather)* clair; ~ play jeu loyal m.

fairly, adv. assez bien.

faith, s. foi f.

faithful, adj. fidèle.

falcon, s. faucon m.

fall, v.n. tomber; baisser; ~ back on avoir recours à; ~ in s'effondrer; ~ off se déprécier; ~ under être compris dans; — s. chute f.; baisse f.

false, adj. faux; artificiel.

falter, v.n. hésiter.

fame, s. réputation f.; renommée f.

familiar, adj. familier, intime (avec).

family, s. famille f.

famous, adj. célèbre, fameux.

fan[1], s. éventail m.; ventilateur m.

fan[2], s. passionné, -e m. f., fervent m.

fancy, s. fantaisie f., imagination f.

fantastic, adj. fantastique; fantasque.

far, adv. loin; ~ off au loin; as ~ as autant que; by ~ de beaucoup; how ~ is it? à quelle distance est-ce?; — adj. lointain.

fare, s. prix de (la) place m.; (taxi) prix de la course m.; (food) chère f.

farewell, s. adieu m.; bid ~ to dire adieu à.

farm, s. ferme f.

farmer, s. fermier m.

farming, s. agriculture f.

farmyard, s. cour f. de ferme.

farther, adv. plus loin (que).

fashion, s. mode f.; manière f.

fashionable, adj. élégant.

fast, adj. vite, rapide; be ~ (clock) avancer; — adv. vite.

fasten, v.a. attacher.

fastener, s. attache f.; agrafe f.; zip ~ fermeture éclair f.

fat, adj. gros, gras; — s. gras m.; graisse f.

fatal, adj. fatal.

fate, s. destin m., sort m.

father, s. père m.

father-in-law, s. beau-père m.

fatigue, s. fatigue f.

fault, s. défaut m.; faute f.

faultless, adj. sans faute.

faulty, adj. défectueux.

favour, s. faveur f.; in ~ of en faveur de; do a ~ rendre un service (à).

favourable, adj. favorable.

favourite, adj. favori.

fear, s. crainte f.; — v.a. & n. craindre.

fearful, adj. affreux, effrayant.

feast, s. fête f.; festin m.

feat, s. exploit m.

feather, s. plume f.

feature, s. trait m.; caractéristique f.; ~ film le grand film.

February, s. février m.

federal, adj. fédéral.

federation, s. fédération f.

fee, s. honoraires m. pl.; (school) ~s frais m. pl.

feeble, adj. faible.

feed, v. a. nourrir; paître.

feel, v.n.&a. (se) sentir; éprouver, ressentir, (with hand) toucher; tâter; ~ cold avoir froid.

feeling, s. sentiment m.

fellow, s. camarade m.; compagnon m.; garçon m.; (of a society) membre m.; (university) agrégé m.

fellowship, s. camaraderie f.; communauté f.

female, adj. féminin; (animal) femelle; — s. femme f.; femelle f.

feminine, adj. féminin.

fence, s. clôture f.; palissade f.; — v.a. enclore; v. n. faire de l'escrime.

fencing, s. escrime f.

fender, s. pare-choc(s) m.

ferry, s. (passage m. en) bac m.

ferry-boat, s. bac m.

fertile, adj. fertile.

fertilize, v.a. fertiliser.

festival, s. festival m.

fetch, v.a. aller chercher; apporter.

feudal, adj. féodal.

fever, s. fièvre f.

few, pron. & adj. peu (de); a ~ quelques- -(uns).

fiancé, -e, s. fiancé, -e m. f.

fibre, s. fibre f.

fiction, s. fiction f.; (novels) romans m. pl.

field, s. champ m.; (sport) terrain m.

fierce, adj. cruel, violent, féroce.

fiery, adj. de feu; ardent.

fifteen, adj. & s. quinze (m.).

fifteenth, adj. quinzième.

fifth, adj. cinquième; cinq.

fiftieth, adj. cinquan- tième.

fifty, adj. & s. cinquante (m.).

fig, s. figue f.

fight, s. combat m.; lutte f.

fighter, s. combattant m.; avion m. de chas- se.

figure, s. figure f.; (a- rithm.) chiffre m.

file[1], s. (tool) lime f.; — .a. limer.

file[2], s. classeur m., dossier

m.; liasse f.; (people) file f.; — v.a. classer; enregistrer.

filing-cabinet, s. carton- nier m., fichier m.

fill, v.a. remplir; occuper; ~ in, up remplir.

film, s. (photo) pellicule f.; (cinema) film m.

filter, s. filtre m.; — v.a. filtrer.

filthy, adj. sale; (fig.) obscène.

fin, s. nageoire f.

final, adj. final.

finally, adv. enfin.

finance, s. finance f.

financial, adj. financier.

find, v.a. trouver; ~ out inventer, découvrir.

fine[1], s. (penalty) amende f.; — v.a. mettre à l'amende.

fine[2], adj. fin; beau.

finger, s. doigt m.; first ~ index m.

finger-print, s. empreinte f. digitale.

finish, v. a. finir; ter- miner.

Finnish, adj. finlandais.

fir, s. sapin m.

fire, s. feu m.; on ~ en feu; — v.a. mettre feu à; (gun) tirer; v.n. tirer.

fire-arm, s. arme f. à feu.

fire-brigade, s. les pom- piers m. pl.

fire-engine, s. pompe f. à incendie.

fire-escape, s. escalier m. de sauvetage.

fireplace, s. cheminée f.

fire-station, s. poste m.

d'incendie.

fireworks, s.pl. feu m. d'artifice.

firm[1], s. maison f. (de commerce).

firm[2], adj. ferme.

firmament, s. firmament m.

firmness, s. fermeté f.

first, adj. premier; — adv. premièrement; d'abord; (railway) en première; at ~ d'abord.

firstly, adv. premièrement.

first-rate, adj. de premier ordre.

fish, s. poisson m.; — v. a. & n. pêcher.

fisher(man), s. pêcheur m.

fishmonger, s. poissonnier m.

fist, s. poing m.

fit[1], s. attaque f.; accès m.

fit[2], adj. convenable, bon, propre; en état (de), capable (de).

five, adj. & s. cinq (m.).

fix, v.a. fixer; ~ up arranger.

flag, s. drapeau m.; (navy) pavillon m.

flagrant, adj. flagrant.

flake, s. flocon m.

flame, s. flamme f.

flannel, s. flanelle f.

flap, s. coup m., tape f.

flare, v.n. flamboyer.

flash, s. éclair m.; — v.n. jeter des éclairs, étinceler.

flashlight, s. flash (électronique) m.

flat[1], adj. plat; insipide; (positive) formel, net;

— s. plat m.; (music) bémol m.

flat[2], s. appartement m.; étage m.

flatter, v.a. flatter.

flattery, s. flatterie f.

flavour, s. saveur f., goût m., arome m.

flax, s. lin m.

flea, s. puce f.

flee, v.a. & n. fuir, se sauver.

fleece, s. toison f.

fleet, s. flotte f.

flesh, s. chair f.; viande f.

flexible, adj. flexible.

flight, s. vol m. (birds, stairs) volée f.; (fleeing) fuite f.

flimsy, adj. ténu; fragile; frivole.

fling, v.a. jeter.

flirt, s. coquette f.; — v.n. flirter.

float, v.n. flotter; v.a. faire flotter.

flock, s. troupeau m., troupe f.

flood, s. inondation f.; (tide) flux m.; — v.a. inonder.

flood-light, v.a. illuminer par projecteurs.

floor, s. plancher m., parquet m.; (storey) étage m.

flour, s. farine f.

flourish, v.n. fleurir; prospérer.

flow, v.n. couler, s'écouler; — s. flux m.; cours m.

flower, s. fleur f.

flower-bed, s. plate-bande f.

flu, s. grippe f.

flue, *s.* tuyau *m.*

fluent, *adj.* facile, coulant.

fluid, *adj.* & *s.* fluide *(m.).*

fluorescent, *adj.* ~ *lamp* tube *m.* fluorescent.

flush, *v.a.* inonder; nettoyer avec une chasse d'eau; *v. n.* rougir.

flute, *s.* flûte *f.*

flutter, *s.* voltigement *m.;* — *v. a.* agiter; *v. n.* voltiger.

fly¹, *s.* mouche *f.*

fly², *v.n.* voler; prendre l'avion (pour).

foam, *s.* écume *f.;* *(beer)* mousse *f.*

focus, *s.* foyer *m.*

fodder, *s.* fourrage *m.*

fog, *s.* brouillard *m.*

foil¹, *s.* feuille *f.;* tain *m.*

foil², *s.* *(fencing)* fleuret *m.*

fold, *s.* pli *m.;* — *v.a.* plier; envelopper; *(arms)* croiser; ~ *up* replier.

folding, *adj.* pliant.

foliage, *s.* feuillage *m.*

folk, *s.* gens *m. pl.*

follow, *v.a.* suivre; accompagner; *v.n.* suivre; s'ensuivre; *as* ~s comme suit.

follower, *s.* suivant *m.,* compagnon *m.,* partisan *m.*

following, *adj.* suivant; *the* ~ ce qui suit.

folly, *s.* sottise *f.*

fond, *adj.* be ~ *of* aimer.

food, *s.* nourriture *f.,* aliments *m. pl.*

fool, *s.* sot *m.*

foolish, *adj.* sot; fou.

foot, *s.* pied *m.;* *on* ~ à pied.

football, *s.* football *m.;* ballon *m.*

foot-brake, *s.* frein *m.* à pied

foot-note, *s.* note *f.* (au bas de la page).

footstep, *s.* pas *m.*

for¹, *prep.* pour; *(in exchange for)* contre; *(because of)* à cause de; *(time)* pendant; *(in spite of)* malgré.

for², *conj.* car.

forbid, *v.a.* défendre; interdire.

force, *s.* force *f.;* violence *f.;* — *v.a.* forcer.

forearm, *s.* avant-bras *m.*

forecast, *s.* prévision *f.;* — *v.a.* prévoir.

forefinger, *s.* index *m.*

foreground, *s.* premier plan *m.*

forehead, *s.* front *m.*

foreign, *adj.* étranger.

foreigner, *s.* étranger, -ère *m. f.*

foremost, *adj.* premier; — *adv. first and* ~ tout d'abord.

foresee, *v.a.* prévoir.

forest, *s.* forêt *f.*

foretell, *v.a.* prédire.

foreword, *s.* avant-propos *m.*

orge, *v.a.* forger.

forgery, *s.* contrefaçon *f.;* faux *m.*

forget, *v.a.* oublier.

forgetful, *adj.* oublieux.

forgive, *v.a.* pardonner.

fork, *s.* fourchette *f.;* *(hay)* fourche *f.*

form, *s.* forme *f.; (bench)* banc *m.; (class)* classe *f.; (paper)* formule *f.;* ~ *of government* régime *m.; —* *v.a.* former.

formal, *adj.* formel.

formality, *s.* formalité *f.*

former, *pron.* le premier, la première; celui-là, celle-là; — *adj.* premier, -ère; précédent.

formerly, *adv.* autrefois.

formula, *s.* formule *f.*

forsake, *v. a.* abandonner.

fortieth, *adj.* quarantième.

fortification, *s.* fortification *f.*

fortify, *v.a.* fortifier.

fortnight, *s.* quinze jours *m. pl.*

fortress, *s.* forte sse *f.*

fortunate, *adj.* ureux.

fortunately *ud* heureusement.

fortune, *s.* fortune *f.*

forty, *adj. & s.* quarante *(m.)*.

forward, *adv.* en avant; *go* ~ (s')avancer; — *adj.* avancé; — *v.a.* faire suivre; expédier.

forwarding, *s.* expédition *f.;* ~ *agency* entreprise *f.* de transport.

forwards, *adv.* en avant.

foul, *adj.* sale; impure; *(language)* ordurier.

found, *v. a.* fonder.

foundation, *s.* fondation *f.*

founder, *s.* fondateur *m.*

fountain, *s.* fontaine *f.*

fountain-pen, *s.* stylo-(graphe) *m.*

four, *adj. & s.* quatre *(m.)*.

fourteen, *adj. & s.* qua-torze *(m.)*.

fourth, *adj.* quatrième; quatre.

fowl, *s.* poule *f.*

fox, *s.* renard *m.*

fraction, *s.* fraction *f.*

fracture, *s.* fracture *f.*

fragile, *adj.* fragile.

fragment, *s.* fragment *m.*

fragrant, *adj.* parfumé.

frame, *s. (picture)* cadre *m.; (structure)* charpente *f.; (window)* châssis *m.*

framework, *s.* charpente *f.*

frank, *adj.* franc.

frankness, *s.* franchise *f.*

fraud, *s.* fraude *f.*

free, *adj.* libre; ~ *of, from* exempt de.

freedom, *s.* liberté *f.*

freely, *adv.* librement; gratis.

freeze, *v.a.* geler.

freight, *s.* fret *m.*

French, *adj.* français; — *s. (language)* le français; *the* ~ les Français *m. pl.*

French-bean(s), *s. (pl.)* haricots *m.pl.* verts.

Frenchman, *s.* Français *m.*

Frenchwoman, *s.* Française *f.*

frequent, *adj.* fréquent; — *v. a.* fréquenter.

frequently, *adv.* fréquemment.

fresh, *adj.* frais, fraîche; nouveau, nouvel, -elle.

friar, *s.* moine *m.*

fricassee, *s.* fricassée *f.*

friction, *s.* friction *f.*

Friday, *s.* vendredi *m.*

fridge, *s.* frigo *m.*

friend, s. ami, -e m. f.
friendly, adj. aimable;
ami; amical.
friendship, s. amitié f.
fright, s. peur f.; take ~
prendre peur.
frighten, v.a. effrayer.
frightful, adj. affreux;
effrayant.
frock, s. robe f.
frog, s. grenouille f.
frolic, s. ébats m. pl.; —
v.n. folâtrer, gambader.
from, prep. (place) de;
(time) depuis; (separa-
tion) de, à; (change) de.
front, s. front m.; devant
m.; façade f.; in ~ of
en face de, en avant de;
— adj. de devant.
front-door, s. porte f.
d'entrée.
frontier, s. frontière f.
frost, s. gelée f.
frosty, adj. de gelée; fig.
froid.
frown, v.a. & n. froncer
les sourcils.
frozen, adj. gelé.
fruit, s. fruit m.
fruitful, adj. fructueux.
fruit-tree, s. arbre fruitier
m.
frustrate, v.a. déjouer;
décevoir; contrecarres.
fry, v. a. & n. (faire) frire.
frying-pan, s. poêle (à
frire) f.
fuel, s. combustible m.
fulfil, v.a. accomplir.
full, adj. plein; complet;
~ name les nom et
prénoms m. pl.; ~ stop
point m.
full-time, adj. de toute la
journée.

fully, adv. pleinement.
fume, s. fumée f.
fun, s. amusement m.;
for ~ pour rire.
function, s. fonction f.
fund, s. fonds m.
fundamental, adj. fondamental.
funeral, s. funérailles f. pl.
funnel, s. entonnoir m.;
(steamer) cheminée f.
funny, adj. drôle.
fur, s. fourrure f.
fur-coat, s. manteau m.
de fourrure.
furious. adj. furieux.
furnace, s. fourneau m.
furnish, v. a. pourvoir (de);
fournir; meubler (de).
furniture, s. meubles m.
pl., ameublement m.;
piece of ~ meuble m.
furrier, s. fourreur m.
furrow, s. sillon m.
further, adv. plus loin;
(any longer) davanta-
ge; — adj. ultérieur;
autre; plus lointain;
supplémentaire, nou-
veau.
furthermore, adv. en
outre, de plus.
fury, s. fureur f.; (pers.)
furie f.
fuss, s. embarras m.;
bruit m.; make a ~
faire des embarras; —
v. n. faire des embarras;
~ about faire l'affairé.
future, s. avenir m.;
(gramm.) futur m.; in
the ~ à l'avenir; — adj.
futur.

G

gain, s. gain m.; — v.a.

gagner.

gait, s. allure f.

gala, s. gala m.

gale, s. grand vent m.

gall, s. bile f.; fiel m; amertume f.

gallant, adj. brave; galant.

gallery, s. galerie f.

gallon, s. gallon m.

gallop, s. galop m.; — v.n. galoper.

gamble, v. n. jouer; — s. jeu m.

game, s. jeu m.; partie f.; (animal) gibier m.

gamekeeper, s. garde-chasse m.

gang, s. bande f.; équipe f.

gangway, s. passage m.

gaol see jail.

gap, s. trou m.; brèche f.; vide m.

gape, v.n. bâiller; stand gaping gober des mouches; ~ at regarder bouche bée.

garage, s. garage m.

garden, s. jardin m.

gardener, s. jardinier m.

garlic, s. ail m.

garment, s. vêtement m.

garnish, s. garniture f.; — v.a. garnir.

garter, s. jarretière f.

gas, s. gaz m.

gasp, s. soupir m.

gas-works, s. pl. usine f. à gaz.

gate, s. porte f.

gateway, s. portail m.

gather, v.a. réunir; amasser; cueillir; (understand) conclure; v.n. s'assembler.

gathering, s. rassemblement m.; abcès m.

gauge, s. jauge f.; calibre m.; indicateur m.; — v.a. jauger; calibrer.

gauze, s. gaze f.

gay, adj. gai.

gear, s. attirail m., appareil m.; (motorcar) vitesse f.

gear-box, s. boîte f. des vitesses.

gear-lever, s. levier m. des vitesses.

general, adj. général; — s. général m. (pl. généraux).

generation, s. génération f.

generator, s. générateur m.

generosity, s. générosité f.

generous, adj. généreux.

genial, adj. doux, douce; bienfaisant.

genius s. génie m.

gentle, adj. doux, douce.

gentleman, s. gentleman m.

genuine, adj. authentique; vrai.

geographical, adj. géographique.

geography, s. géographie f

geology, s. géologie f.

geometric(al), adj. géométrique.

geometry, s. géométrie f.

germ, s. germe m.

German, adj. allemand; — s. Allemand, -e m.f.

gesticulate, v.n. gesticuler.

gesture, s. geste m.

get, v.a. obtenir, procurer, trouver, recevoir; — v.n. arriver; (become) devenir; ~ at parvenir (à); ~ in entrer;

~ off partir; ~ on prospérer; *(agree)* s'accorder (avec); ~ out of sortir (de); ~ over surmonter; *(illness)* se remettre; ~ up se lever.

geyser, *s.* chauffe-bain *m.*

ghost, *s.* esprit *m.*; revenant *m.*, fantôme *m.*

giant, *s.* géant *m.*

gift, *s.* don *m.*

gifted, *adj.* bien doué.

gills, *s. pl.* ouïes *f.*

gin, *s.* genièvre *m.*; gin *m.*

giraffe, *s.* girafe *f.*

girdle, *s.* ceinture *f.*; — *v.a.* ceinturer.

girl, *s.* jeune fille *f.*

give, *v. a.* donner; ~ up renoncer à; livrer; *v.n.* ~ in céder (à).

glacier, *s.* glacier *m.*

glad, *adj.* heureux; content; joyeux.

gladness, *s.* joie *f.*

glance, *s.* coup *m.* d'œil,; — *v. n.* ~ *at* jeter un regard sur.

glare, *s.* lumière *f.* éblouissante; clinquant *m.*; — *v.n.* briller d'un éclat éblouissant.

glass, *s.* verre *m.*; *(pane)* vitre *f.*; ~*es* lunettes *f. pl.*

glazier, *s.* vitrier *m.*

gleam, *s.* lueur *f.*; — *v. n.* luire.

glide, *v. n.* glisser; planer.

glider, *s.* planeur *m.*

glimmer, *s.* lueur *f.*; — *v.n.* jeter une lueur faible.

glimpse, *s.* coup *m.* d'œil (rapide).

glitter, *v.n.* étinceler.

globe, *s.* globe *m.*

gloomy, *adj.* sombre.

glorious, *adj.* glorieux.

glory, *s.* gloire *f.*

glove, *s.* gant *m.*

glow, *v.n.* luire rouge; *(joy)* rayonner; *(coal)* être rouge; — *s.* chaleur *f.*; lumière *f.*; *fig.* ardeur *f.*

glue, *s.* colle (forte) *f.*; — *v.a.* coller.

gnat, *s.* cousin *m.*; moustique *f.*

gnaw, *v.a. & n.* ronger.

go, *v. n.* aller; ~ *away* s'en aller; ~ *back* retourner; ~ *back on one's word* reprendre sa parole; ~ *down* descendre; baisser; ~ *in for* s'occuper de, s'adonner à, faire (de); ~ *into* entrer dans; ~ *off* s'en aller; ~ *on* continuer; *(happen)* se passer; ~ *out* sortir; ~ *over*, *through* traverser; *(read)* parcourir; ~*up* monter; ~ *with* accompagner; ~ *without* se passer de; *let* ~ lâcher prise.

goal, *s.* but *m.*

goalkeeper, *s.* gardien (de but) *m.*

goat, *s.* bouc *f.*, chèvre *f.*

God, *s.* Dieu *m.*

god-child, *s.* filleul, -e *m. f.*

godfather, *s.* parrain *m.*

godmother, *s.* marraine *f.*

goggles, *s. pl.* bésicles *f.*

gold, *s.* or *m.*

golden, *adj.* d'or, en **or**.

golf, s. golf m.

good, adj. bon; ~ evening! bonsoir!; ~ morning! bonjour!; be so ~ as to avoir la bonté de; make ~ remplir; indemniser de; — s. bien m.; ~s marchandise f.; ~s station gare f. de marchandises; ~s train train m. de marchandises.

good-bye, int. & s. adieu (m.).

good-looking, adj. de belle mine, beau.

goodness, s. bonté f.

good-tempered, adj. de caractère facile, de bonne humeur.

goodwill, s. bonne volonté f.

goose, s. oie f.

gooseberry, s. groseille f. à maquereau.

gospel, s. évangile m.

gossip, s. bavardage m.; raconter m., cancan m.; (pers.) compère m.; commère f.; — v.n. bavarder.

Gothic, adj. gothique.

govern, v.a. & n. gouverner.

governess, s. gouvernante f.

government, s. gouvernement m.

governor, s. gouverneur m.

gown, s. robe f.

grace, s. grâce f.

graceful, adj. gracieux.

gracious, adj. gracieux.

grade, s. grade m.; classe f.

gradual, adj. graduel.

graduate, s. gradué, -e m. f.; — v.a. graduer; v.n. prendre ses diplômes.

grain, s. grain m.

grammar, s. grammaire f.

grammar-school, s. lycée m., collège m.

grammatical, adj. grammatical.

gram(me), s. gramme m.

gramophone, s. gramophone m., phonographe m.

gramophone-record, s. disque m.

grand, adj. grand; magnifique; ~ stand tribune f.

grandchild, s. petit-fils m., petite-fille f. (pl. petits-enfants m.)

granddaughter, s. petite-fille f.

grandfather, s. grand-père m.

grandmother, s. grand'mère f.

grandson, s. petit-fils m.

granite, s. granit m.

granny, s. grand'maman f.

grant, v.a. accorder, concéder; accéder; ~ that admettre que; — s. don m., concession f.; subside m.

grape, s. grain m. de raisin; bunch of ~s grappe f. de raisin.

grape-fruit, s. pamplemousse f.

graph, s. graphique m., courbe f.

graphic, adj. graphique.

grasp, v.a. saisir; comprendre; — s. prise f., étreinte f.

grass, s. herbe f.; gazon m.

grasshopper, s. sauterelle f.

grate, s. grille f.; — v.a. râper; faire grincer; v.n. grincer.

grateful, adj. reconnaissant (à).

gratitude, s. reconnaissance f.

grave[1], s. tombe f., tombeau m.

grave[2], adj. grave.

gravel, s. gravier m.

gravy, s. jus m.

gray, adj. gris.

graze, v.n. paître.

grease, s. graisse f.; — v.a. graisser.

great, adj. grand; a ~ many beaucoup (de).

greatly, adj. très; beaucoup.

greatness, s. grandeur f.

greed, s. avidité f.

greedy, adj. avide.

Greek, adj. grec, grecque; — s. Grec m., Grecque f.

green, adj. vert.

greengrocer, s. fruitier, -ère m. f.

greenhouse, s. serre f.

greet, v.a. saluer.

greeting, s. salutation f.

grey, adj. gris.

grief, s. chagrin m.

grieve, v.a. affliger; v.n. s'affliger.

grill, s. gril m.; — v.a. griller.

grim, adj. sévère, menaçant, sinistre.

grin, v.n. grimacer; ~ at faire des grimaces à; — s. rire m.; grimace f.

grind, v.a. moudre.

grinder, s. (tooth) molaire f.

grindstone, s. meule f.

grip, s. étreinte f.; prise f.; — v.a. saisir, étreindre.

groan, v. n. gémir; — s. gémissement m.

grocer, s. épicier, -ère m. f.; ~'s (shop) épicerie f.

grocery, s. épicerie f.

groove, s. rainure f.

gross, adj. gros; grossier; (weight) brut.

ground, s. terre f.; terrain m.; (reason) raison f.; ~s jardins m. pl.; — v.a. fonder.

group, s. groupe m.

grow, v.a. cultiver; v.n. (pers.) grandir; (plant) croître; (become) devenir.

growl, s. grondement m.; — v.n. gronder.

grown-up, s. grande personne f.

growth, s. croissance f.; culture f.; récolte f.

grudge, s. rancune f.; — v.a. donner à contre-cœur à.

grumble, v.n. grommeler; — s. grognement m.

grunt, s. grognement m.; — v.n. grogner.

guarantee, s. garantie f.; (pers.) garant, -e m. f.; — v.a. garantir.

guard, s. garde f.; (train) conducteur m.; — v.a. garder; v.n. ~ against se garder.

guardian, *s.* gardien, -enne *m. f.*

guess, *v.a. & n.* deviner; conjecturer; — *s.* conjecture *f.*

guest, *s.* invité *m.,* convive *m.;* hôte, -esse *m. f.*

guide, *s.* guide *m.; — v. a.* guider.

guide-book, *s.* guide *m.*

guilt, *s.* culpabilité *f.*

guilty, *adj.* coupable (de).

guitar, *s.* guitare *f.*

gulf, *s.* golfe *m.*

gull, *s.* mouette *f.*

gullet, *s.* gosier *m.*

gum¹, *s.* gomme *f.;* — *v.a.* gommer.

gum², *s. (teeth)* gencive *f.*

gun, *s.* fusil *m.;* canon *m.*

gush, *v.i.* jaillir; — *s.* jaillissement *m.*

gutter, *s. (street)* ruisseau *m.*

gymnasium, *s.* gymnase *m.*

gymnastics, *s.* gymnastique *f.*

H

haberdashery, *s.* mercerie *f.*

habit, *s.* habitude *f.*

hail, *s.* grêle *f.;* — *v.n.* grêler.

hair, *s. (single)* cheveu *m.; (whole)* cheveux *m. pl.; (animal)* poil *m.*

hairdresser, *s.* coiffeur, -euse *m. f.*

half, *s.* moitié *f.;* demi *m.;* — *adj.* demi; ∼ **an**

hour une demi-heure *f.*

half-time, *s.* mi-temps *m.*

half-way, *adv.* à mi-chemin; à moitié chemin; à mi-distance.

hall, *s. (grande)* salle *f.; (college)* réfectoire *m.; (house)* vestibule *m.; (hotel)* hall *m.*

halt, *s.* halte *f.; v.a.* faire arrêter; *v.n.* faire halte; boiter.

ham, *s.* jambon *m.*

hammer, *s.* marteau *m.*

hand, *s.* main *f.; (pers.)* ouvrier *m.; (clock)* aiguille *f.; on the one* ∼ *...on the other* ∼ *...on the one* ∼ *part ...* d'autre part.

handbag, *s.* sac (à main) *m.*

handbook, *s.* manuel *m.*

handkerchief, *s.* mouchoir *m.*

handle, *s.* manche *m.,* anse *f.;* poignée *f.;* bras *m.;* — *v.a.* manier; traiter.

hand-made, *adj.* fait à la main.

handsome, *adj.* joli.

handwriting, *s.* écriture *f.*

handy, *adj. (pers.)* adroit; *(thing)* commode.

hang, *v.a.* pendre; *(with tapestry)* tendre; ∼ **up** accrocher; *v. n.* pendre; dépendre (de).

hanger, *s.* crochet *m.;* cintre *m.*

happen, *v.n.* arriver; se trouver; *I* ∼**ed to be present** je me trouvais là par hasard.

happiness, *s.* bonheur *m.*

happy, *adj.* heureux.

harbour, *s.* port *m.*

hard, *adj.* dur; difficile; sévère; ~ up gêné; — *adv.* durement; *work* ~ travailler dur.

hardly, *adv.* à peine.

hardware, *s.* quincaillerie *f.*

hare, *s.* lièvre *m.*

harm, *s.* mal *m.*; tort *m.*; *do* ~ *to* nuire à.

harmful, *adj.* nuisible.

harmless, *adj.* inoffensif.

harmony, *s.* harmonie *f.*

harness, *s.* harnais *m.*

harp, *s.* harpe *f.*

harsh, *adj.* revêche; âpre; rigoureux.

hart, *s.* cerf *m.*

harvest, *s.* moisson *f.*; *(crop)* récolte *f.*

haste, *s.* hâte *f.*; *make* ~ se dépêcher.

hasten, *v.a.* hâter; *v. n.* se dépêcher.

hasty, *adj.* précipité.

hat, *s.* chapeau *m.*

hate, *v: a.* haïr; — *s.* haine *f.*

hateful, *adj.* odieux.

hatred, *s.* haine *f.*

haul, *v.a.* traîner; haler; — *s.* traction *f.*

haulage, *s.* roulage *m.*; frais *m.pl.* de roulage.

haunch, *s.* hanche *f.*

haunt, *v.a.* fréquenter; hanter.

have, *v.a.* avoir; *(food)* prendre; ~ *to* il faut que, il faut (+ *inf.*); *had rather* préférer (+ *inf.*); ~ *on (clothes)* porter.

haversack, *s.* havresac *m.*

hawk, *s.* faucon *m.*

hay, *s.* foin *m.*

hazard, *s.* hasard *m.*

hazy, *adj.* brumeux; *(fig.)* vague.

he, *pron.* il, *(alone)* lui; ~ *who* celui qui.

head, *s.* tête *f.*; *chief)* chef *m.*: *(river)* source *f.*; — *v.a.* être en tête de; — *adj.* principal.

headache, *s.* mal *m.* de tête.

heading, *s.* en-tête *m.*

headlight, *s.* phare *m.*, projecteur *m.*

headline, *s.* manchette *f.*

headmaster, *s.* directeur *m.*

headquarters, *s. pl.* quartier *m.* général.

heal, *v.a.* guérir; *v.n.* se guérir.

health, *s.* santé *f.*

healthy, *adj.* bien portant; sain.

heap, *s.* amas *m.*, tas *m.*; — *v.a.* ~ *up* entasser.

hear, *v.a.* entendre; *(listen to)* écouter; *v. n.* entendre; ~ *from* recevoir une lettre de; ~ *of* avoir des nouvelles de; entendre parler de.

heart, *s.* cœur *m.*; *by* ~ par cœur.

hearth, *s.* foyer *m.*

hearty, *adj.* cordial.

heat, *s.* chaleur *f.*; *(anger)* colère *f.*; — *v.a.&n.* chauffer.

heating, *s.* chauffage *m.*

heave, *v.a.* lever; pousser; jeter; *v.n.* se soulever.

heaven, *s.* ciel *m.*

heavy, *adj.* pesant; lourd.

hedge, *s.* haie *f.*

hedgehog, s. hérisson m.

heed, s. attention f.; *take ~ to* faire attention à.

heedless, adj. insouciant; inattentif.

heel, s. talon m.

height, s. hauteur f.

heir, s. héritier m.

heiress, s. héritière f.

helicopter, s. hélicoptère m.

hell, s. enfer m.

hello, int. allô!

helm, s. barre (du gouvernail) f.

helmet, s. casque m.

help, v.a. aider; secourir; *~ oneself* se servir; — s. aide f.

helpful, adj. (pers.) serviable; (thing) utile.

helping, s. portion f.

helpless, adj. sans secours.

hem, s. ourlet m.; bord m.

hen, s. poule f.

hence, adv. (place, time) d'ici; (reason) de là.

her, pron. (acc.) la; (dat.) lui; (alone) elle.

herb, s. herbe f.

herd, s. troupeau m.

here, adv. ici; *from ~* d'ici; *look ~!* dites donc!; *~ he is!* le voici!

heritage, s. héritage m.

hermit, s. ermite m.

hero, s. héros m.

heroic, adj. héroïque.

heroine, s. héroïne f.

herring, s. hareng m.

hers, pron. à elle; le sien, la sienne, les siens, les siennes.

herself, pron. elle-même; (reflex.) se.

hesitate, v.n. hésiter.

hew, v.a. couper.

hiccough, hiccup, s. hoquet m.

hide, v.a. cacher; v.n. se cacher.

hideous, adj. hideux; horrible.

high, adj. haut; (speed) grand; (price) élevé; — adv. haut.

highness, s. altesse f.

highroad, highway, s. grande route f.

hike, v.n. faire du tourisme à pied.

hiker, s. touriste f., randonneur, -euse (à pied) m. f.

hill, s. colline f.

hilly, adj. montueux.

him, pron. (acc.) le; (dat.) lui; (alone) lui.

himself, pron. lui-même; (reflex.) se; *by ~* tout seul.

hinder, v.a. empêcher.

hindrance, s. empêchement m.

hinge, s. gond m.; charnière f.; — v.n. tourner sur.

hint, s. allusion f.; avis m.; — v.n. *~ at* faire allusion à.

hip, s. hanche f.

hire, s. louage m.; *for ~* à louer; — v.a. & n. louer.

his, pron. son, sa; ses.

hiss, s. sifflement m.; — v.a. & n. siffler.

historic(al), adj. historique.

history, s. histoire f.

hit, v.a. frapper; atteindre; trouver; —

s. coup *m.*; succès *m.*

hitch-hike, *v.n.* faire de l'auto-stop.

hive, *s.* ruche *f.*

hoard, *s.* magot *m.*, amas *m.*; — *v. a.* thésauriser; entasser.

hoarse, *adj.* rauque.

hobby, *s.* dada *m.*

hockey, *s.* hockey *m.*

hoe, *s.* houe *f.*

hog, *s.* porc *m.*

hoist, *v.a.* hisser; —*s.* monte-charge *m.*

hold, *v.a.* tenir; retenir; maintenir; contenir; *(consider)* tenir (pour); ~ **back** retenir; ~ **out** tendre; offrir ; ~ **that** soutenir que; — *v.n.* tenir; *(be true)* être vrai; ~ **on** ne pas lâcher prise; ~ **out** durer.

holder, *s.* possesseur *m.*

hole, *s.* trou *m.*

holiday, *s.* fête *f.*, jour *m.* férié; *(holidays)* vacances *f. pl.*, congé *m.*; *be on* être en congé, en vacance(s).

hollow, *adj.* reux, -euse; *fig.* faux, fausse.

holy, *adj.* saint; bénit.

home, *s.* foyer *m.*, demeure *f.*; *at* ~ chez soi, à la maison; — *adv.* chez soi; *come, go* ~ rentrer; — *adj.* domestique; de l'intérieur.

homeless, *adj.* sans asile.

homely, *adj.* simple; modeste.

homesickness, *s.* mal du pays *m.*

homeward, *adv.* vers la maison; ~ **bound** en retour.

honest, *adj.* honnête.

honesty, *s.* honnêteté *f.*

honey, *s.* miel *m.*

honeymoon, *s.* lune *f.* de miel.

honour, *s.* honneur *m.*; — *v.a.* honorer.

hood, *s.* capuchon *m.*; capeline *f.*; *(motor)* capote *f.*

hoof, *s.* sabot *m.*

hook, *s.* crochet *m.*, croc *m.*; *(fishing)* hameçon *m.*

hoop, *s.* cercle *m.*

hoot, *v.a.* huer; *v.n.* corner; — *s.* huée *f.*

hooter, *s.* sirène *f.*; corne *f.*, trompe *f.*

hop, *v.n.* sautiller.

hope, *s.* espérance *f.*; espoir *m.*; — *v.n.* espérer.

hopeful, *adj.* plein d'espoir.

hopeless, *adj.* sans espoir

horizon, *s.* horizon *m.*

horizontal, *adj.* horizontal.

horn, *s.* corne *f.*; trompe *f.*

horrible, *adj.* affreux, -euse.

horse, *s.* cheval *m.* *(pl.* chevaux).

horseback: *on* ~ à cheval.

horseman, *s.* cavalier *m.*

horse-race, *s.* course *f.* de chevaux.

horseshoe, *s.* fer *m.* à cheval.

hose, *s.* bas *m. pl.*

hospitable, *adj.* hospitalier.

hospital, *s.* hôpital *m.*

hospitality, *s.* hospitalité *f.*

host, *s.* hôte *m.*

hostel, *s.* pension *f.* pour étudiants, hôtellerie *f.*

hostess, *s.* hôtesse *f.*

hostile, *adj.* hostile (à).

hostility, *s.* hostilité *f.*

hot, *adj.* chaud.

hotel, *s.* hôtel *m.*

hour, *s.* heure *f.*

house, *s.* maison *f.*; *(theatre)* salle *f.*

household, *s.* ménage *m.*

housekeeper, *s.* gouvernante *f.*

housekeeping, *s.* ménage *m.*

housewife, *s.* ménagère *f.*

housework, *s.* travaux *(m. pl.)* domestiques; do the ~ faire le ménage.

how, *adv.* comment; ~ many, much? combien de?; ~ long? combien de temps?; ~ are you? comment allez-vous?

however, *adv.* de quelque manière que...; toutefois, cependant.

howl, *v. a. & n.* hurler; — *s.* hurlement *m.*

hue, *s.* couleur *f.*; cri *m.*

hug, *v.a.* serrer dans les bras.

huge, *adj.* énorme.

hullo, *int.* holà; allô!

hum, *v. n.* bourdonner; — *s.* bourdonnement *m.*

human, *adj.* humain.

humanity, *s.* humanité *f.*

humble, *adj.* humble.

humorous, *adj.* amusant; humoristique; drôle.

humour, *s.* humour *m.*; be in a ~ to être d'humeur à.

hundred, *s.* cent *m.*

hundredth, *adj.* centième.

hundredweight, *s.* quintal *m.*

Hungarian, *adj.* hongrois; — *s.* Hongrois, -e *m. f.*

hunger, *s.* faim *f.*; — *v.n.* avoir faim.

hungry, *adj.* affamé; be ~ avoir faim.

hunt, *v.a. & n.* chasser; *(with hounds)* chasser à courre; — *s.* chasse (à courre) *f.*

hunter, *s.* chasseur *m.*

hurl, *v.a.* jeter; lancer.

hurry, *s.* hâte; be in a ~ to être pressé de; — *v.n.* se presser; ~ up! pressez-vous!; *v.a.* presser, hâter.

hurt, *v.a.* faire mal à; blesser; *(feelings)* froisser.

husband, *s.* mari *m.*

hush, *int.* chut!; — *s.* calme *m.*; — *v.a.* calmer.

husk, *s.* cosse *f.*; glume *f.*; — *v. a.* écosser, monder.

hut, *s.* cabane *f.*

hydrogen, *s.* hydrogène *m.*

hygiene, *s.* hygiène *f.*

hymn, *s.* hymne *m.*

hyphen, *s.* trait d'union *m.*

hypnotize, *v.a.* hypnotiser.

hypocrisy, *s.* hypocrisie *f.*

hysterical, *adj.* hystérique.

I

I, *pron.* je; moi.

ice, s. glace f.

ice-cream, s. glace f.

icy, adj. glacial.

idea, s. idée f.

ideal, adj. & s. idéal (m.).

identical, adj. identique.

identity, s. identité f.; ~ card carte f. d'identité.

idle, adj. désœuvré;(lazy) paresseux; — v.a. ~ away perdre.

idleness, s. oisiveté f.; paresse f.

if, conj. si; as ~ comme si.

ignition, s. ignition f.; (motor) allumage m.

ignorant, adj. ignorant; be ~ of ignorer.

ignore, v.a. refuser de connaître.

ill, adj. malade; (bad) mauvais; be taken ~ tomber malade; ~ luck malheur m.; — adv. ~ mal; — s. mal m.

illegal, adj. illégal.

illegitimate, adj. illégitime.

illicit, adj. illicite.

illness, s. maladie f.

illusion, s. illusion f.

illustrate, v.a. illustrer.

illustration, s. illustration f.; exemple m.

image, s. image f.

imagination, s. imagination f.

imagine, v. a. imaginer; se figurer.

imitate, v.a. imiter.

immediate, adj. immédiat.

immense, adj. immense.

immigrant, adj. & s. immigrant, -e (m. f.).

immigrate, v. n. immigrer

immigration, s. immigration f.

immoral, adj. immoral.

immortal, adj. immortel.

impatience, s. impatience f.

impatient, adj. impatient.

impediment, s. obstacle m.

impel, v.a. forcer; pousser.

imperfect, adj. & s. imparfait (m.).

imperial, adj. impérial.

impertinent, adj. impertinent.

implement, s. outil m., ustensile m.

implication, s. implication f.

implore, v.a. implorer.

imply, v.a. impliquer; donner à entendre.

import, v.a. importer; (mean) signifier; — s. (usu. pl.) importation(s) f.

importance, s. importance f.

important, adj. important.

importer, s. importateur m.

impose, v.a. imposer (à).

impossibility, s. impossibilité f.

impossible, adj. impossible.

impression, s. impression f.

imprison, v.a. emprisonner.

imprisonment, s. emprisonnement.

improbable, adj. improbable.

improper, adj. impropre;

inconvenant.
improve, *v.a.* améliorer;
perfectionner; *v.n.* s'a-
méliorer.
improvement, *s.* améliora-
tion *f.*; progrès *m.*
impulse, *s.* impulsion *f.*
in, *prep.* dans; en; à; ~
the morning le matin;
~ *the evening* le soir; ~
time à temps; ~ *spring*
au printemps.
inadequate, *adj.* insuffisant.
incapable, *adj.* incapable
(de).
incense, *s.* encens *m.*
inch, *s.* pouce *m.*
incident, *s.* incident *m.*
incidental, *adj.* fortuit;
incidental.
incline, *v.a. & n.* incliner.
include, *v.a.* comprendre;
renfermer.
inclusive, *adj.* inclusif; ~
of y compris.
income, *s.* revenu *m.*
income-tax, *s.* impôt *m.*
sur (le) revenu.
incompatible, *adj.* incompatible.
incompetent, *adj.* incompétent.
inconsistent, *adj.* inconséquent.
inconvenient, *adj.* incommode, gênant.
increase, *v.a.&n.*
augmenter; — *s.* augmen-
tation *f.*
incredible, *adj.* incroyable.
incur, *v. a.* contracter; en-
courir; s'attirer.
incurable, *adj.* incurable.
indebted, *adj.* endetté.

indeed, *adv.* de fait; vraiment.
independence, *s.* indépen
dance *f.*
independent, *adj.* indépen-
dant.
index, *s.* index *m.*; *(on
dial)* aiguille *f.*; *(math.)*
exposant *m.*; ~ *finger*
index *m.*
Indian, *adj.* indien; des
Indes; ~ *corn* maïs *m.*
— *s.* Indien, -enne *m. f.*
india-rubber, *s.* gomme *f.*
indicate, *v.a.* indiquer.
indicator, *s.* indicateur *m.*
indifference, *s.* indifféren-
ce *f.*
indifferent, *adj.* indifférent (à).
indigestion, *s.* indigestion
f.
indignant, *adj.* indigné.
indirect, *adj.* indirect.
indiscreet, *adj.* indiscret.
indiscretion, *s.* indiscrétion *f.*; imprudence *f.*
indispensable, *adj.* indispensable.
individual, *adj.* individuel;
— *s.* individu *m.*
indoor, *adj.* d'intérieur.
indoors, *adv.* à la maison;
stay ~ ne pas sortir.
induce, *v.a.* persuader;
(cause) occasionner.
inducement, *s.* encouragement *m.* ~s attraits
m. pl.
indulge, *v. a.* se livrer (à);
caresser; *v.n.* ~ *in*
s'abandonner à; se lais-
ser aller à.
indulgence, *s.* indulgence
f.; laisser-aller *m.*
industrial, *adj.* industriel.

industrious, *adj.* travailleur.

industry, *s.* industrie *f.*

inefficient, *adj.* incapable; inefficace.

inestimable, *adj.* inestimable.

inevitable, *adj.* inévitable.

inexpensive, *adj.* peu coûteux, peu cher, bon marché.

inexperienced, *adj.* inexpérimenté.

inexplicable, *adj.* inexplicable.

infallible, *adj.* infaillible.

infamous, *adj.* infâme.

infant, *s.* enfant *m. f.*

infantry, *s.* infanterie *f.*

infant-school, *s.* école *f.* maternelle.

infection, *s.* infection *f.*

infer, *v.a.* conclure, déduire.

inferior, *adj.* inférieur.

infinitive, *s.* infinitif *m.*

infirm, *adj.* infirm.

infirmary, *s.* infirmerie *f.*

inflame, *v.a.* enflammer

inflammable, *adj.* inflammable.

inflate, *v.a.* gonfler.

inflexion, *s.* inflexion *f.*

inflict, *v.a.* infliger; imposer à.

influence, *s.* influence *f.*; — *v.a.* influencer.

influenza, *s.* grippe *f.*

inform, *v.a.* informer.

informal, *adj.* sans cérémonie.

information, *s.* information *f.*; renseignements *m. pl.*

ingenious, *adj.* ingénieux.

ingenuity, *s.* ingéniosité *f.*

ingredient, *s.* ingrédient *m.*

inhabit, *v.a.* habiter.

inhabitant, *s.* habitant *m.*

inherit, *v.a. & n.* hériter (de).

inheritance, *s.* héritage *m.*

initial, *s.* initiale *f.*

initiative, *s.* initiative *f.*

injection, *s.* injection *f.*

injure, *v.a.* nuire à; blesser.

injury, *s.* préjudice *m.*; dommage *m.*; blessure *f.*

injustice, *s.* injustice *f.*

ink, *s.* encre *f.*

inland, *s. & adj.* intérieur (*m.*).

inn, *s.* auberge *f.*; taverne *f.*

inner, *adj.* intérieur.

innocence, *s.* innocence *f.*

innocent, *adj.* innocent.

innumerable, *adj.* innombrable.

inoculate, *v.a.* inoculer.

inquire, *v.n.* ~ *about* s'enquérir, se renseigner sur; ~ *after* demander après, demander des nouvelles de.

inquiry, *s.* demande *f.*; recherche *f.*; *make inquiries about* s'informer de; ~ *office* bureau *m.* des renseignements.

insane, *adj.* fou, fol, folle.

inscription, *s.* inscription *f.*

insect, *s.* insecte *m.*

insecure, *adj.* peu sûr, mal assuré.

insensible, *adj.* sans connaissance; insensible.

inseparable, *adj.* inséparable.

insert, *v. a.* insérer (dans).
inside, *s. & adj.* intérieur *(m.);* — *adv.* à l'intérieur.
insignificant, *adj.* insignifiant.
insist, *v.n.* insister *(on* sur).
insistence, *s.* insistance *f.*
inspect, *v.a.* inspecter.
inspection, *s.* inspection *f.*
inspector, *s.* inspecteur *m.*
inspiration, *s.* inspiration *f.*
inspire, *v.a.* inspirer.
install. *v.a.* installer.
instalment, *s.* fraction *f.,* acompte *m.*
instance, *s.* exemple *m.;* cas *m.; for ~* par exemple.
instant, *adj.* urgent; — *s.* instant *m.*
instead, *adv. ~ of* au lieu de.
instinct, *s.* instinct *m.*
institute, *s.* institut *m.;* — *v.a.* instituer.
institution, *s.* institution *f.*
instruct, *v. a.* instruire.
instruction, *s.* instruction *f.*
instructive, *adj.* instructif.
instrument, *s.* instrument *m.*
instrumental, *adj.* instrumental.
insufficiency, *s.* insuffisance *f.*
insufficient, *adj.* insuffisant.
insult, *s.* insulte *f.;* — *v.a.* insulter.
insurance, *s.* assurance *f.*
insure, *v. a.* (faire) assurer.
integral, *adj.* intégral; —

s. intégrale *f.*
integrity, *s.* intégrité *f.*
intellectual, *adj.* intellectuel.
intelligence, *s.* intelligence *f.; (information)* renseignements *m.pl.*
intelligent, *adj.* intelligent.
intend, *v. a.* avoir l'intention de (faire qch.), se proposer de: destiner qn., qch. (à); vouloir dire.
intense, *adj.* intense.
intensity, *s.* intensité *f.*
intent, *s.* intention *f.;* — *adj. ~ on* absorbé dans.
intention, *s.* intention *f.*
intercontinental, *adj.* intercontinental.
interest, *s.* intérêt *m.;* — *v.a.* intéresser.
interesting, *adj.* intéressant.
interfere, *v. n.* intervenir; *~ with* gêner; se mêler de.
interior, *adj. & s.* intérieur *(m.).*
intermediate, *adj.* intermédiaire.
intermission, *s.* interruption *f.,* pause *f.*
internal, *adj.* interne; intérieur.
international, *adj.* international.
interpret, *v.a.* interpréter.
interpretation, *s.* interprétation *f.*
interpreter, *s.* interprète *m.*
interrogation, *s.* interrogation *f.*
interrupt, *v.a.* interrompre.
interruption, *s.* interrup-

tion *f.*

interval, *s.* intervalle *m.*

intervention, *s.* intervention *f.*

interview, entrevue *f.;* interview *m. f.*

intimate, *adj.* intime.

into, *prep.* dans; en.

intolerable, *adj.* intolérable.

introduce, *v.a.* introduire; *(pers.)* présenter.

introduction, *s.* introduction *f.; (pers.)* présentation *f.*

invade, *v.a.* envahir.

invalid¹, *s.* malade *m. f.*

invalid², *adj.* invalide.

invasion, *s.* invasion *f.*

invent, *v.a.* inventer.

invention, *s.* invention *f.*

inverted, *adj.* ~ *commas* guillemets *m.*

invest, *v.a.* *(money)* placer.

investigate, *v.a.* rechercher.

investigation, *s.* investigation *f.*

investment, *s.* placement *m.*

invisible, *adj.* invisible.

invitation, *s.* invitation *f.*

invite, *v.a.* inviter.

invoice, *s.* facture *f.*

involuntary, *adj.* involontaire.

involve, *v.a.* envelopper (dans); impliquer (dans); entraîner.

inward, *adj.* intérieur; interne.

inwards, *adv.* intérieurement; en dedans.

Irish, *adj.* irlandais

iron, *s.* fer *m.* — *v.a.* repasser.

ironical, *adj.* ironique.

ironware, *s.* quincaillerie *f.*

ironworks, *s.* ferronnerie *f.*

irony, *s.* ironie *f.*

irregular, *adj.* irrégulier.

irrelevant, *adj.* non pertinent; hors de la question; inapplicable (à).

irresolute, *adj.* irrésolu.

irritate, *v.a.* irriter.

island, *s.* île *f.; (street)* refuge *m.*

isle, *s.* île *f.*

isolate, *v.a.* isoler.

isotope, *s.* isotope *m.*

issue, *s.* *(way out)* sortie *f.; (end)* issue *f.,* fin *f.,* résultat *m.; (publication)* publication *f.,* édition, *(paper)* numéro *m., (money)* émission *f.; — v. a.* émettre; publier.

it, *pron.* il, elle; *(acc.)* le, la; *of it* en; *to* ~ y.

Italian, *adj.* italien; — *s.* Italien, -enne *m.f.*

itch, *s.* démangeaison *f.; — v.n.* démanger.

itchy, *adj.* galeux.

item, *s.* article *m.,* détail *m.*

its, *pron.* son, sa, *pl.* ses.

itself, *pron.* lui-même, elle-même; se; *(emphatic)* même.

ivory, *s.* ivoire *m.*

ivy, *s.* lierre *m.*

J

jack, *s.* *(cards)* valet *m.;*

(lifting) cric *m.*, lève-auto *m.*

jackal, *s.* chacal *m.*

jacket, *s.* veston *m.*

jail, *s.* prison *f.*

jam¹, *s.* confiture *f.*

jam², *v.a.* serrer; coincer; encombrer; — *s.* encombrement *m.*

January, *s.* janvier *m.*

Japanese, *adj.* japonais.

jar, *s.* jarre *f.;* bocal *m.*

javelin, *s.* javeline *f.*

jaw, *s.* mâchoire *f.*

jealous, *adj.* jaloux.

jealousy, *s.* jalousie *f.*

jelly, *s.* gelée *f.*

jerk, *s.* saccade *f.;* secousse *f.*

jersey, *s.* jersey *m.*

jet, *s.* jet *m.; (gas)* bec *m.;* ~ *plane* avion *m.* à réaction.

Jew, *s.* Juif *m.*

jewel, *s.* bijou *m.*

jeweller, *s.* bijoutier *m.;* ~'s *shop* bijouterie *f.*

jewellery, *s.* bijouterie *f.*

jib, *s.* foc *m.*

job, *s.* tâche *f.;* travail *m. (pl. -aux);* emploi *m.; odd* ~s petits travaux *m.*

join, *v.a.* joindre; unir; se joindre (à); *v.n.* se joindre; s'unir; ~ *in* prendre part à.

joiner, *s.* menuisier *m.*

joint, *s.* joint *m.;* articulation *f.; (meat)* gros morceau *m.;* — *adj.* commun; indivis; co-; ~*-stock company* société *f.* par actions.

joke, *s.* plaisanterie *f.*

jolly, *adj.* joyeux; jovial.

journal, *s.* journal *m. (pl. -aux).*

journalist, *s.* journaliste *m.*

journey, *s.* voyage *m.*

joy, *s.* joie *f.*

joyful, *adj.* joyeux.

judge, *s.* juge *m.;* — *v.a.&n.* juger.

judg(e)ment, *s.* jugement *m.*

jug, *s.* cruche *f.;* pot *m.*

juggler, *s.* jongleur *m.*

Jugoslav, *adj.* yougoslave.

juice, *s.* jus *m.*

July, *s.* juillet *m.*

jump, *s.* saut *m.;* — *v.n. & a.* sauter.

junction, *s.* jonction *f.; (gare f. d')*embranchement. *m.*

June, *s.* juin *m.*

jungle, *s.* jungle *f.*

junior, *adj.* jeune.

jury, *s.* jury *m.*

juryman, *s.* juré *m.*

just, *adj.* juste; — *adv. (exactly)* juste; *(barely)* à peine; ~ *now* il n'y a qu'un instant; ~ *so* précisément.

justice, *s.* justice *f.*

justification, *s.* justification *f.*

justify, *v.a.* justifier.

jut, *v.n.* ~ *out* faire saillie.

juvenile, *adj.* juvénile; d'enfants.

K

kangaro, *s.* kangourou *m.*

keel, *s.* quille *f.*

keen, *adj.* aigu; tranchant; *(mind)* pénétrant; *be* ~ *on* être enthousiaste de, avoir la passion de.

keep, *v.a.* tenir; garder; maintenir; observer; ~ *back* retenir; ~ *up* soutenir; — *v. n.* rester; ~ *on* continuer à.

keeper, *s.* gardien *m.*

kerb, *s.* bordure *f.*

kernel, *s.* amande *f.*

kettle, *s.* bouilloire *f.*

key, *s.* clé *f.*; *(piano)* touche *f.*; *(music)* ton *m.*

keyboard, *s.* clavier *m.*

kick, *v.a.* donner un coup de pied (à); *v.n.* ruer; — *s.* coup *m.* de pied.

kid, *s.* chevreau *m.*; *(child)* gosse *m. f.*

kidney, *s.* rein *m.*; *(food)* rognon *m.*

kill, *v.a. & n.* tuer; abattre.

kilogram(me), *s.* kilogramme *m.*

kilometre, *s.* kilomètre *m.*

kind, *adj.* bon; bienveillant; aimable.

kindle, *v.a.* allumer; exciter; enflammer; *v.n.* s'enflammer.

kindly, *adj.* bon; doux.

kindness, *s.* bonté *f.*; bienveillance *f.*

kindred, *s.* parenté *f.*; parents *m.pl.*

king, *s.* roi *m.*

kingdom, *s.* royaume *m.*

kinsman, *s.* parent *m.*

kiss, *s.* baiser *m.*; *v.a.* embrasser; baiser.

kit, *s.* fourniment *m.*

kitchen, *s.* cuisine *f.*

kite, *s.* cerf-volant *m.*

kitten, *s.* petit chat *m.*

knapsack, *s.* havresac *m.*

knee, *s.* genou *m.* (pl. -x).

kneel, *v.n.* s'agenouiller; ~ *down* se mettre à genoux.

knife, *s.* couteau *m.*

knight, *s.* chevalier *m.*; *(chess)* cavalier *m.*

knit, *v. a.* tricoter; *(brow)* froncer.

knob, *s.* bosse *f.*; bouton *m.*

knock, *s.* coup *m.*; — *v.a. & n.* frapper; ~ *down* renverser.

knocker, *s.* marteau *m.*

knot, *s.* nœud *m.*; — *v.a.* nouer; *v.n.* se nouer.

know, *v.a.* savoir; connaître; reconnaître; ~*n for* connu pour; — *v.n.* savoir; ~ *of* avoir connaissance de; *let* ~ prévenir.

knowledge, *s.* connaissance *f.*; *(acquired)* savoir *m.*

knuckle, *s.* articulation *f.* de doigt.

L

label, *s.* étiquette *f.*; — *v.a.* étiqueter.

laboratory, *s.* laboratoire *m.*

labour, *s.* travail *m.*; ~ *(e)xchange* bureau *m.* de placement; — *v.n.* travailler.

labourer, *s.* travailleur *m.*

lace, *s.* dentelle *f.*

lack, s. manque; — v.a. & n. ~ (for) manquer (de).

lad, s. jeune garçon m.

ladder, s. échelle f.

lading, s. chargement m.

ladle, s. louche f.

lady, s. dame f.; young ~ jeune dame f.; demoiselle f., jeune fille f.

lag, v.n. ~ behind rester en arrière.

lake, s. lac m.

lamb, s. agneau m.

lame, adj. boiteux.

lamp, s. lampe f.

lamp-shade, s. abat-jour m.

land, s. (not sea) terre f.; (country) pays m.; — v.n. & a. débarquer; (plane) atterrir.

landing, s. débarquement m.; (plane) atterrissage m.

landing-strip, s. piste f. d'atterrissage.

landlady, s. propriétaire f.; aubergiste f.

landlord, s. propriétaire m.; aubergiste m.

landscape, s. paysage m.

lane, s. ruelle f.; chemin m.

language, s. langue f.; (expression) langage m.

lap¹, s. genoux m. pl.; (coat) pan m.; (sports) tour (de piste) m.

lap², v. a. envelopper (de); laper.

lapse, s. faute f.; chute f.; lapsus m.; (time) laps m.; — v.n. retomber (dans); (time)

s'écouler; (fail) faire un faux pas.

lard, s. saindoux m.

larder, s. dépense f.

large, adj. gros, grand; considérable; at ~ en liberté, en général.

lark, s. alouette f.

last, adj. dernier; — adv. dernièrement, en dernier lieu; — v.n. durer.

lasting, adj. durable.

latch, s. loquet m.

latch-key, s. clef f. de porte.

late, adj. tardif; be ~ être en retard; — adv. tard; ~r on par la suite; plus tard.

lately, adv. dernièrement, récemment.

latest, adj. récent, le dernier; at (the) ~ au plus tard.

lathe, s. tour m.

lather, s. mousse f.

Latin, adj. latin; s. latin m.

latter, adj. dernier; the ~ ce dernier; celui-ci, celle-ci, ceux-ci.

laugh, v.n. rire (at de); — s. rire m.

laughter, s. rire m.

launch, v.a. lancer.

launching, adj. ~ site rampe f. à fusées.

laundry, s. buanderie f., blanchisserie f.

lavatory, s. lavabo m. cabinet m. de toilette.

lavish, adj. prodigue (de). — v.a. prodiguer.

law, s. loi f.; droit m.

law-court, s. cour f. de justice, tribunal m.

lawful, adj. légal; permis; légitime.

lawn, s. pelouse f.

lawn-mower, s. tondeuse f.

lawsuit, s. procès m.

lawyer, s. homme m. de loi avoué m.; avocat m.

lay, v.a. coucher, poser, étendre; ~ aside, by mettre de côté; (money) réserver; ~ down poser; ~ on appliquer; be laid up être alité.

lay-by, s. refuge m., garage m.

layer, s. couche f.

lazy, adj. paresseux.

lead¹, s. (metal) plomb m.

lead², v.a. & n. mener, conduire; ~ the way montrer le chemin.

leader, s. conducteur m.; (newspaper) éditorial m.

leadership, s. conduite f.; direction f.

leaf, s. feuille f.; (book) feuillet m.; page f.

leak, s. fuite f.; voie d'eau f.; — v.n. fuir.

lean, adj. maigre.

leap, v. n. & a. sauter; — s. saut m.

learn, v.a. & n. apprendre.

learning, s. savoir m., science f.

leash, s. laisse f.

least, adj. le plus petit; le moindre; — adv. le moins; — s. moins m.; at ~ au moins, à tout le moins; not in the ~ pas le moins du monde.

leatner, s. cuir m.

leave, v. a. laisser; quitter; be left rester; — s. permission f.; congé m.; on ~ en congé.

lecture, s. conférence f. (on sur); — v.n. faire des conférences.

lecturer, s. conférencier m.; (univ.) professeur m. (de faculté).

left, adj. & s. gauche (f.).

left-luggage office, s. consigne f.

leg, s. jambe f.; patte f.

legal, adj. légal.

legislature, s. législature f.

legitimate, adj. légitime.

leisure, s. loisir m.; be at ~ être de loisir.

lemon, s. citron m.

lemonade, s. limonade f.

lend, v.a. prêter.

length, s. longueur f.; (time) durée f.

lengthen, v.a. allonger; prolonger.

lens, s. lentille f.

leopard, s. léopard m.

less, adj. moindre; moins de; — adv. moins; ~ than moins de.

lessen, v.a. & n. diminuer.

lesson, s. leçon f.

lest, conj. de peur que.

let, v.a. laisser, permettre à; (house) louer; ~ me go laisse-moi aller; ~ down laisser tomber (à); ~ in laisser entrer.

letter, s. lettre f.; ~s belles-lettres f. pl.

lettuce, s. laitue f.

level, s. niveau m.; — adj. uni; plat; horizontal;

— v.a. niveler; pointer.
lever, s. levier m.
levy, s. levée f.; — v.a. lever.
lexicon, s. lexique m.
liability, s. responsabilité f.; *liabilities* passif m.
liable, adj. responsable (de); sujet (à).
liar, s. menteur, m.
liberal, adj. libéral; généreux.
liberty, s. liberté f.
librarian, s. bibliothécaire m. f.
library, s. bibliothèque f.
licence, s. permission f.; permis m., patente f.; *(excess of liberty)* licence f.
license, v.a. accorder un permis (à).
lick, v.a. lécher.
lid, s. couvercle m.
lie¹, s. mensonge m.; — v.n.&a. mentir.
lie², v.n. être couché; *(dead)* reposer; *(be situated)* se trouver; ~ *down* se coucher; *it ~s with you* cela dépend de vous.
lieutenant, s. lieutenant m.
life, s. vie f.
life-insurance, s. assurance f. sur la vie.
lifeless, adj. inanimé.
lift, v.a. lever; *fig.* élever; ~ *up* soulever; — s. *(apparatus)* ascenseur m.; *give s. o. a* ~ faire monter qn *(dans sa voiture).*
light¹, s. lumière f.; éclairage f.; jour m.; lampe

f.; *(fire)* feu m.; *come to* ~ se révéler; — v. a. allumer; éclairer; v.n. s'éclairer; — adj. clair; éclairé.
light², adj. léger; *make* ~ *of* faire peu de cas de.
lighten¹, v.a. éclairer; v.n. faire des éclairs.
lighten², v.a. alléger.
lighter, s. briquet m.
lighthouse, s. phare m.
lighting, s. éclairage m.
lightning, s. éclair m.
like¹, adj. semblable, pareil, ressemblant; — prep. comme.
like², v.a. aimer; *I should* ~ *to* je voudrais + inf.
likely, adv. probable.
likeness, s. ressemblance f.; portrait m.
lily, s. lis m.
limb, s. membre m.
limit, s. limite f.; v.a. limiter.
limited, adj. ~ *liability company* société anonyme f.
line, s. ligne f.; *(poetry)* vers m.; *railw.)* voie f.; — v.a. *(garment)* doubler; v.n. ~ *up* s'aligner; faire la queue.
linen, s. toile f.; ligne m.
lining, s. doublure f.
link, s. chaînon m., *fig.* lien m.; — v.a. lier; unir.
lion, s lion m.
lip, s. lèvre f.
lipstick, s. rouge m. à lèvres.
liquid, adj.. & s. liquide (m.).

list, s. liste f.; — v.a. enregistrer.

listen, v.n. (also ~ in) écouter.

listener, s. auditeur, -trice m. f.

literary, adj. littéraire.

literature, s. littérature f.

litter, s. litière f.

little, adj. petit; peu de.

live, v.n. vivre; (reside) habiter, demeurer; ~ on vivre de.

lively, adv. vivant, gai.

liver, s. foie m.

living-room, s. salle f. de séjour.

load, s. charge f.; fardeau m.; — v.a. charger.

loaf, s. pain m.

loan, s. prêt m.; emprunt m.

loathe, v.a. détester.

lobby, s. couloir m., vestibule m.

lobster, s. homard m.

local, adj. local.

location, s. emplacement m.; situation f.

lock¹, s. serrure f.

lock², s. (hair) boucle f.

locksmith, s. serrurier m.

lodger, s. locataire m. f.

lodging, s. logement m. furnished ~s garni m.

log, s. bûche f.; bille f.

logical, adj. logique.

loin, s. (pork) longe f.; (beef) aloyau m.; rein m.

lonely, adj. solitaire.

long¹, adj. long; a ~ time (since) depuis longtemps; be ~ in être long à; — adv. longtemps; how ~? combien de temps?; ~ ago il y a longtemps.

long², v.n. ~ for désirer qch., soupirer après.

long-distance, adj. à (longue) distance.

long-play(ing), adj. ~ record microsillon m.

look, v. n. & a. regarder; ~ after soigner; ~ at regarder; ~ back regarder en arrière; ~ for chercher; ~ into examiner; ~ out être sur ses gardes, int. gare!; ~ over parcourir; ~ up chercher; — s. regard m.; air m.; aspect m.

looking-glass, s. miroir m.

loom, s. métier m. de tisserand.

loop, s. boucle .

loose, adj. lâche; délié, détaché; vague.

loosen, v.a. desserrer.

lord, s. maître m.; seigneur m.

lorry, s. camion m.

lose, v.a. & n. perdre.

loss, s. perte f.

lot, s. sort m.; (portion) partage m.; a ~ of beaucoup de.

lottery, s. loterie f.

loud, adj. fort; bruyant.

loud-speaker, s. haut-parleur m.

lounge, s. (grand) vestibule m.; foyer m., hall m.; — v.n. flâner.

lounge-suit, s. complet veston m.

love, s. amour m.; — v.a. aimer.

lovely, *adj.* beau, bel, belle; charmant.

lover, *s.* amoureux *m.*; amant *m.*

low, *adj. & adv.* bas.

lower, *adj.* inférieur; *(deck)* premier (pont); — *v.a.* baisser; *(flags, sails)* amener.

loyal, *adj.* loyal; fidèle.

loyalty, *s.* loyauté *f.*

lubricate, *v.a.* lubrifier.

luck, *s.* chance *f.*; bad ~ malchance *f.*

lucky, *adj.* heureux.

luggage, *s.* bagages *m. pl.*

luggage-van, *s.* fourgon *m.* (aux bagages).

lump, *s.* morceau *m.*

lunch, *s.* déjeuner *m.*; — *v.n.* déjeuner.

lung, *s.* poumon *m.*

lute, *s.* luth *m.*

luxurious, *adj.* luxueux.

luxury, *s.* luxe *m.*

lyre, *s.* lyre *f.*

lyric, *adj.* lyrique.

M

machine, *s.* machine *f.*

machinery, *s.* machines *f.pl.*; *fig.* mécanisme *m.*

mackintosh, *s.* imperméable *m.*

mad, *adj.* fou, fol, folle.

madam, *s.* madame *f.*

magazine, *s.* revue *f.*; *(rifle)* magasin *m.*

magic, *adj.* magique.

magistrate, *s.* magistrat *m.*

magnet, *s.* aimant *m.*

magnetic, *adj.* magnétique.

magnificent, *adj.* magnifique.

maid, *s.* (jeune) fille *f.*; bonne *f.*

mail, *s.* courrier *m.*

mail-boat, *s.* paquebot-poste *m.*

mail-van, *s.* wagon-poste *m.*

main, *adj.* principal.

mainland, *s.* terre *f.* ferme.

mainly, *adv.* principalement.

mains, *s.* secteur (de courant) *m.*

maintain, *v.a.* maintenir; soutenir.

maintenance, *s.* entretien *m.*

majesty, *s.* majesté *f.*

major, *s.* commandant *m.*; — *adj.* majeur.

majority, *s.* majorité *f.*; plupart *f.*

make, *v.a. & n.* faire; rendre; ~ away with détruire; ~ for se diriger vers; ~ off décamper; ~ out comprendre; prouver; ~ over céder; ~ up *(list)* dresser; *(invent)* inventer; ~ up for compenser; — *s.* forme *f.*, fabrication *f.*

male, *adj.* mâle; masculin; — *s.* mâle *m.*

malice, *s.* méchanceté *f.*

man, *s.* homme *m.*

manage, *v. a.* conduire, diriger, gérer, gouverner; I shall ~ it j'en viendrai à bout.

management, s. direction f.; gérance f.

manager, s. directeur m.; gérant m.

manicure, s. manicure n. f.

manifest, adj. manifeste; – v.a. manifester.

manipulate, v.a. manipuler.

manner, s. manière f.; air m.; ∼s manières f. pl.; (morals) mœurs f. pl.

manœuvre, s. manœuvre f.; – v.a. faire manœuvrer.

manor, s. manoir m.

manual, adj. & s. manuel (m.).

manufacture, s. manufacture f.; – v.a. fabriquer.

manufacturer, s. manufacturier m.; fabricant m.

manure, s. fumier m.

manuscript, s. manuscrit m.

many, adj. beaucoup de.

map, s. carte f. géographique.

marble, s. marbre m.

march, s. marche f.; – v.n. marcher.

March, s. mars m.

mare, s. jument f.

margarine, s. margarine f.

marine, s. marine f.; – adj. marin; maritime.

mariner, s. marin m.

mark, s. marque f.; (aim) but m.; (school) point m.; (coin) marc m.; – v.a. marquer;

souligner.

market, s. marché m.

market-price, s. prix m. courant.

marmalade, s. marmelade f. (d'oranges).

marriage, s. mariage m.

married, adj. marié.

marry, v.a. épouser; v. n. (get married) se marier.

marsh, s. marais m.

marshal, s. maréchal m.; – v.a. ranger; conduire.

martial, adj. martial.

martyr, s. martyr m.

marvel, s. merveille f.; – v.n. s'étonner (de).

marvellous, adj. merveilleux.

masculine, adj. mâle; masculin.

mask, s. masque m.

mason, s. maçon m.

mass¹, s. masse f.; majorité f.

mass², s. (eccles.) messe f.

mast, s. mât m.

master, s. maître m.; – v. a. maîtriser

mat, s. (door) paillasson m.; (table) dessous de plat, m.

match¹, s. égal, -e m.f., pareil, -le m. f., mariage m.; (pers.) parti m.; (sport) match m.; – v.a. assortir; v.n. s'assortir.

match², s. allumette f.

mate, s. camarade m.; (birds) mâle m., femelle f.; (chess) mat m.; (ship) second m.; – v.a. marier (à); v.n.

s'accoupler.

material, *s.* matière *f.;*
— *adj.* matériel.

maternal, *adj.* maternel.

mathematical, *adj.* mathématique.

mathematics, *s.* mathé-
matiques *f. pl.*

matinée, *s.* matinée *f.*

matron, *s.* mère de famille, *f.; (hospital)*
infirmière-en-chef *f.;*
surveillante *f.*

matter, *s.* matière *f.;* affaire *f.;* sujet *m.;* chose
f.; as a ~ of fact en
fait; *what is the* ~?
qu'est-ce qu'il y a?; —
v.n. importer; *it does
not* ~ n'importe.

mattress, *s.* matelas *m.;*
spring ~ sommier *m.,*
matelas *m.* à ressort.

mature, *adj.* mûr; — *v.a.*
& *n.* mûrir.

maturity, *s.* maturité *f.*

May, *s.* mai *m.*

may, *v. aux.* pouvoir; ~
I? vous permettez?

maybe, *adv.* peut-être.

mayor, *s.* maire *m.*

me, *pron.* (acc.) me;
(alone, with prep.) moi.

meadow, *s.* pré *m.*

meal, *s.* repas *m.*

mean¹, *s.* moyen terme,
m.; (math.) moyenne
f.; ~s moyens *m. pl.,*
(way to do) moyen *m.;*
by ~s of au moyen de:
by all ~s mais certaine-
ment; *by no* ~s en
aucune façon; — *adj.*
moyen.

mean², *v.a.* *(signify)*
vouloir dire, signifier;

(wish) vouloir (faire),
avoir l'intention (de);
destiner; *what does that
word* ~? que signifie
ce mot?; *what do you*
~ *by that*? qu'entendez-
vous par là?

mean³, *adj.* misérable,
pauvre; bas, vil; la-
dre.

meaning, *s.* intention *f.;*
sens *m.*

meantime, -while, *adv.*
(in the ~) dans l'in-
tervalle, pendant ce
temps-là.

measure, *s.* mesure *f.;* —
v.a. mesurer.

meat, *s.* viande *f.; (food)*
nourriture *f.*

mechanic, *s.* artisan *m.,*
mécanicien *m.*

mechanical, *adj.* mécanique.

mechanics, *s.* mécanique
f.

mechanism, *s.* mécanisme
m.

mechanize, *v.a.* mécaniser.

medal, *s.* médaille *f.*

medical, *adj.* médical;
~ *student* étudiant *m.*
en médicine.

medicine, *s.* médecine *f.*

meditate, *v.a. & n.* méditer.

medium, *s.* moyen terme
m.; milieu *m.;* — *adj.*
moyen.

meet, *v.a.* rencontrer
(qn.), se rencontrer
avec (qn.); *(face)* af-
fronter; *(expenses)*
faire face à; ~ *sy at
the station* aller recevoir

qn. à la gare; — *v. n.* se rencontrer; ~ *with* rencontrer; éprouver.

meeting, *s.* rencontre *f.;* réunion *f.*

mellow, *adj.* mûr; moelleux.

melody, *s.* mélodie *f.*

melon, *s.* melon *m.*

melt, *v.a.* fondre.

member, *s.* membre *m.*

memorial, *s.* monument *m.; mémorial m.*

memory, *s.* mémoire *f.;* souvenir *m.*

mend, *v. a.* raccommoder; réparer; corriger.

mental, *adj.* mental.

mention, *v. a.* mentionner; citer; *don't* ~ *it* il n'y a pas de quoi.

merchandise, *s.* marchandise *f.*

merchant, *s.* négociant *m.;* commerçant *m.*

merciful, *adj.* miséricordieux.

mercy, *s.* pitié *f.;* miséricorde *f.*

mere, *adj.* seul.

merely, *adv.* purement; simplement.

merit, mérite *m.;* — *v.a.* mériter.

merry, *adj.* gai.

mess, *s.* gâchis *m.; make a* ~ *of* gâcher.

message, *s.* message *m.*

messenger, *s.* messager *m.*

metal, *s.* métal *m.*

meteorology, *s.* météorologie *f.*

method, *s.* méthode *f.*

metre, *s.* mètre *m.*

microphone, *s.* micro-

phone *m.*

microscope, *s.* microscope *m.*

middle, *s.* milieu *m.;* — *adj.* du milieu; moyen.

midnight, *s.* minuit *m.*

might, *s.* force *f.;* puissance *f.*

mighty, *adj.* fort; puissant

migrate, *v.n.* émigrer.

mild, *adj.* doux; bénin.

mile, *s.* mille *m.*

mileage, *s.* parcours *m.; (expense)* prix *m.* par mille.

military, *adj.* militaire.

milk, *s.* lait *m.*

milkman, *s.* laitier *m.*

mill, *s.* moulin *m.;* fabrique *f.*

miller, *s.* meunier *m.*

milliner, *s.* modiste *f.*

million, *s.* million *m.*

mince, *s.* hachis *m.;* — *v.a.* hacher.

mind, *s.* esprit *m.; (remembrance)* souvenir *m.; (opinion)* pensée *f.,* avis *m.; change one's* ~ changer d'avis; *make up one's* ~ *to* se décider à, se résigner à; — *v.a.* faire attention à, prendre garde à; écouter; *(look after)* garder; *(trouble about)* s'inquiéter de; *do you* ~ *my smoking?* est-ce que cela vous gêne que je fume?; *I don't* ~ cela m'est égal; *never* ~ ça ne fait rien.

mine[1]**,** *s.* mine *f.;* — *v.a.* miner.

mine[2]**,** *pron.* à moi; le mien.

miner, s. mineur m.

mineral, adj. & s. minéral (m.).

minister, s. ministre m.

ministry, s. ministère m.

minor, adj. mineur.

minority, s. minorité.

mint, s. Hôtel m. de la Monnaie; (plant) menthe f.

minus, adj. en moins; — adv. moins.

minute, s. minute f.; petit moment, m.; ~ hand grande aiguille f.

miracle, s. miracle m.

mirror, s. miroir m.

miscarry, v.n. avorter.

miscellaneous, adv. divers.

mischief, s. mal m.; méchanceté f.

miser, s. avare m.

miserable, adj. misérable; malheureux.

misery, s. misère f.

misfortune, s. malheur m.

miss¹, v.a. manquer; ne pas entendre; ne pas voir; s'apercevoir de l'absence (de); ~ out omettre; be ~ing manquer.

miss², s. mademoiselle f.

missile, s. projectile m.

mission, s. mission f.

missionary, s. missionnaire m. f.

mist, s. brouillard m., brume f.

mistake, s. erreur f., méprise f.; faute f.; — v.a. se tromper de; ~ for prendre pour; be ~n se tromper.

mistress, s. maîtresse f.

(de maison).

mistrust, s. méfiance f.

misty, adj. brumeux.

misunderstand, v. a. comprendre mal.

mitten, s. mitaine f.

mix, v.a. mêler; mélanger; be ~ed up in être mêlé à.

mixture, s. mélange m.; mixture f.

moan, v.n. gémir; — s. gémissement m.

mob, s. foule f., populace f.

mobilization, s. mobilisation f.

mobilize, v.a. mobiliser.

mock, s. moquerie f.; — adj. faux; — v.a. railler.

mockery, s. moquerie f.

model, s. modèle m.

moderate, adj. modéré; — v.a. modérer.

moderation, s. modération f.

modern, adj. moderne.

modest, adj. modeste.

modesty s. modestie f.

modify, v.a. modifier.

moist, adj. moite, humide.

moisten, v.a. humecter.

moisture, s. humidité f.

molecule, s. molécule f.

moment, s. moment m.

momentary, adj. momentané.

monarch, s. monarque m.

monarchy, s. monarchie f.

Monday, s. lundi m.

money, s. argent m.; monnaie f.

money-order, s. mandat m.

monk, *s.* moine *m.*

monkey, *s.* singe *m.*

monopolize, *v.a.* monopoliser.

monopoly, *s.* monopole *m.*

monotonous, *adj.* monotone.

monstrous, *adj.* monstrueux.

month, *s.* mois *m.*

monthly, *adj.* mensuel; — *adv.* mensuellement.

monument, *s.* monument *m.*

monumental, *adj.* monumental.

mood, *s.* humeur *f.;* mode *m.*

moon, *s.* lune *f.*

moonlight, *s.* clair *m.* de lune

moor, *s.* bruyère *f.*

mop, balai *m.:* — *v.a.* (also ~ up) éponger, essuyer.

moral, *s.* morale *f.;* ~*s* moeurs *f. pl.;* — *adj.* moral; de morale.

more, *adj. & pron.* plus de; davantage de; ~ *than* plus que; *some* ~ en ... davantage; *no* ~ n'en ... pas davantage, ne ... plus; — *adv.* plus; davantage; ~ *and* de plus en plus.

moreover, *adv.* de plus.

morning, *s.* matin *m.;* *in the* ~ le matin; — *adj.* du matin.

mortal, *adj. & s.* mortel (*m., f.*).

mortality, *s.* mortalité *f.*

mortgage, *s.* hypothèque *f.;* — *v. a.* hypothéquer.

mosquito, *s.* moustique *f.*

moss, *s.* mousse *f.*

most, *adj. & pron.* le plus (de); la plupart (de); *at the* ~ tout au plus; ~ *people* la plupart des gens; *make the* ~ *of* tirer le meilleur parti de; — *adv.* très, fort, bien.

mostly, *adv.* pour la plupart; principalement; la plupart du temps.

motel, *s.* motel *m.*

moth, *s.* mite *f.*

mother, *s.* mère *f.*

mother-in-law, *s.* belle-mère *f.*

mother-tongue, *s.* langue *f.* maternelle.

motion, *s.* mouvement *m.;* signe *m.; (proposal)* motion *f.*

motionless, *adj.* immobile.

motive, *s.* motif *m.*

motor, *s.* moteur *m.*

motor-bus, *s.* autobus *m.*

motor-car, *s.* auto(mobile) *f.*

motor-coach, *s.* autocar *m.*

motor-cycle, *s.* motocyclette *f.*

motor-scooter, *s.* scooter *m.*

motorway,, *s.* autoroute *f.*

mould, *s.* moule *m.;* — *v.a.* mouler.

mount, *s.* mont *m.;* — *v.a. & n.* monter.

mountain, *s.* montagne *f.*

mountaineering, *s.* alpinisme *m.*

mountainous, *adj.* montagneux.

mourn, *v. n. & a.* pleurer, (se) lamenter.

mouse, *s.* souris *f.*

moustache, *s.* moustache *f.*

mouth, *s.* bouche *f.;* *(beast)* gueule *f.*

move, *s.* mouvement *m.;* *(chess)* coup *m.;* — *v.a.* remuer; déplacer; *(goods)* transporter; *(affect)* émouvoir; *(motion)* proposer ~ *house (also:* ~*)* déménager; — *v.n.* se mouvoir, se déplacer; s'avancer; *(chess)* jouer; ~ *forward* s'avancer; ~ *in* emménager; ~ *out* déménager; ~ *on* avancer; *int.* circulez!

movement, *s.* mouvement *m.*

mow, *v.a.* faucher; tondre.

mower, *s.* faucheur *m.;* faucheuse (à moteur) *f.*

much, *adj. & pron.* beaucoup; — *adv.* beaucoup; très; *too* ~ trop.

mud, *s.* boue *f.*

muddle, *s.* fouillis *m.;* — *v.a.* embrouiller.

muddy, *adj.* boueux.

mug, *s.* timbale *f.*

mule, *s.* mulet *m.,* mule *f.*

multiple, *adj.* multiple.

multiplication, *s.* multiplication *f.*

multiply, *v.a.* multiplier.

multitude, *s.* multitude *f.*

municipal, *adj.* municipal.

murder, *s.* meurtre *m.*

murderer, *s.* meurtrier *m.*

murmur, *s.* murmure *m.*

muscle, *s.* muscle *m.*

museum, *s.* musée *m.*

mushroom, *s.* champignon *m.*

music, *s.* musique *f.*

musical, *adj.* musical; ~ *instrument* instrument *m.* de musique.

music-hall, *s.* café *m.* concert.

musician, *s.* musicien, -enne *m. f.*

must, *v. aux.* il faut que; devoir.

mustard, *s.* moutarde *f.*

mute, *adj.* muet.

mutter, *s.* murmure *m.;* — *v. n.* murmurer.

mutton, *s.* mouton *m.*

mutual, *adj.* mutuel.

my, *pron.* mon, ma; mes *(pl.).*

myself, *pron.* moi-même; *by* ~ seul.

mysterious, *adj.* mystérieux.

mystery, *s.* mystère *m.*

mystic, *adj.* mystique.

myth, *s.* mythe *m.*

N

nail, *s.* *(to hammer)* clou *m.; (on fingers)* ongle *m.;* — *v.a.* clouer.

nail-brush, *s.* brosse *f.* à ongles.

naked, *adj.* nu; dénudé.

name, *s.* nom *m.;* — *v.a.* nommer; désigner.

namely, *adv.* savoir.

nap, *s.* somme *m.*

napkin, *s.* serviette *f.;* *(infant)* couche *f.*

narrate, *v. a.* raconter.

narrow, *adj.* étroit.

nation, *s.* nation *f.*

national, *adj.* national.

nationality, *s.* nationalité *f.*

nationalize, *v.a.* nationaliser.

native, *adj. & s.* natif, -ive *(m. f.).*

natural, *adj.* naturel.

naturalize, *v.a.* naturaliser.

nature, *s.* nature *f.*

naughty, *adj.* méchant.

naval, *adj.* naval.

navigate, *v.n.* naviguer.

navigator, *s.* navigateur *m.*

navy, *s.* marine *f.*

near, *adv.* près, proche; — *prep.* près de, auprès de; — *adj.* proche.

nearly, *adv.* *(almost)* presque.

neat, *adj.* propre; élégant.

necessary, *adj.* nécessaire.

necessity, *s.* néccesité *f.*

neck, *s.* cou *m.*

necklace, *s.* collier *m.*

necktie, *s.* cravate *f.*

need, *s.* besoin; — *v.a.* avoir besoin (de); demander.

needle, *s.* aiguille *f.*

needless, *adj.* inutile.

needy, *adj.* nécessiteux.

negative, *adj.* négatif; — *s.* négative *f.;* *(photo)* cliché *m.;* *in the* ~ négativement.

neglect, *v. a.* négliger (de).

negligence, *s.* négligence *f.*

negotiation, *s.* négociation *f.*

negro, -ess *s.* nègre *m.,* négresse *f.*

neighbour, *s.* voisin, -e *m. f.*

neighbourhood, *s.* voisinage *m.*

neither, *pron. & adj.* ni l'un ni l'autre.

nephew, *s.* neveu *m.*

nerve, *s.* nerf *m.*

nervous, *adj.* nerveux.

nest, *s.* nid *m.*

net¹, *s.* filet *m.*

net², *adj.* net.

network, *s.* réseau *m.*

neutral, *adj.* neutre.

never, *adj.* (ne . . .) jamais.

nevertheless, *adv.* néanmoins.

new, *adj.* neuf, neuve; nouveau, -el, -elle; *New Year* Nouvel An.

news, *s.* nouvelle *f.*

newspaper, *s.* journal *m.*

next, *adj.* le plus proche; prochain, suivant; ~ *door to* à côté de; *adv.* ensuite, après; — *prep.* ~ *to* à côté de.

nice, *adj.* agréable, bon; gentil.

niece, *s.* nièce *f.*

night, *s.* nuit *f.;* soir *m.;* *by* ~ de nuit; *good* ~*!* bonne nuit!

nightingale, *s.* rossignol *m.*

nine, *adj. & s.* neuf *(m.).*

nineteen, *adj. & s.* dix-neuf (m.).

ninety, adj. & s. quatre-
-vingt-dix (m.).

ninth, adj. neuvième;
neuf.

nip, v.a. pincer.

nitrogen, s. azote m.

no, adj. ne ... pas (de),
ne ... aucun.

noble, adj. noble.

nobleman, s. gentilhomme
m.

nobody, no one, pron.
personne ne (+ verb).

noise, s. bruit m.

noisy, adj. bruyant.

none, pron. ne ... aucun;
personne ne (+ verb.).

nonsense, s. bêtise; m. no
~ de bêtises.

non-smoker, s. compartiment m. pour non-
fumeurs.

non-stop, adj. & adv.
sans arrêt; sans escale.

noon, s. midi m.

nor, conj. ni; (and ...
not) et ne ... pas,
non plus.

normal, adj. normal.

north, s. nord m.; — adj.
du nord.

north-east, adj. & s.
nord-est m.

northern, adj. du nord.

north-west, adj. & s.
nord-ouest m.

nose, s. nez m.

nostril, s. narine f.

not, adv. ne ... pas, ne
... point.

notable, adj. notable.

note, s. note f.; (letter
and money) billet m.;
(tone) ton m.; — v.a.
noter; remarquer.

note-book, s. carnet m.

noted, adj. distingué.

nothing, pron. rien; ne ...
rien.

notice, s. avis m.; attention f.; connaissance
f.; take ~ of faire
attention à.

notify, v.a. avertir, noti-
fier.

notion, s. idée f.

noun, s. nom m.

nourish, v.a. nourrir.

novel, s. roman m.

novelist, s. romancier m.

novelty, s. nouveauté f.

November, s. novembre m.

now, adv. maintenant.

nowadays, adv. de nos
jours.

nowhere, adv. ne ... nulle
part.

nuclear, adj. nucléaire; ~
energy énergie f. nu-
cléaire; ~ physics
physique f. nucléaire;
~ power station centrale
f. nucléaire.

nuisance, s. (pers.) peste
f.; (thing) ennui m.

number, s. nombre m.,
numéro m.

number-plate, s. plaque
f. matricule.

numerous, adj. nom-
breux.

nun, s. religieuse f.

nurse, s. nourrice f.,
bonne (d'enfant) f.;
(hospital) infirmier,
-ère m. f.; — v.a.
(suckle) allaiter; (the
sick) soigner.

nursery, s. chambre f. des
enfants.

nut, s. noix f., noisette f.

nylon, s. nylon m.; ∼ *stockings* (or ∼s) bas nylons m. pl.

O

oak, s. chêne m.
oar, s. rame f.
oat(s) s. (pl). avoine f.
oath, s. serment m.
obedience, s. obéissance f.
obedient, adj. obéissant.
obey, v.a. & n. obéir (à)·
object, s. objet m.; but m.; (gramm.) régime m.; — v.a. objecter; v.n. s'opposer (à).
objection, s. objection f.
objective, adj. &. s. objectif (m.).
obligation, s. obligation f.
oblige, v.a. obliger.
obscure, adj. obscur.
observation, s. observation f.
observe, v.a.& n. observer.
obstacle, s. obstacle m.
obstinate, adj. obstiné.
obtain, v.a. obtenir.
obvious, adj. évident.
occasion, s. occasion f.
occasional adj. occasionnel.
occasionally, adv. de temps en temps.
occupation, s. occupation f.
occupy, v.a. occuper; ∼ oneself with s'occuper de.
occur, v.n. arriver; se trouver; it ∼red to me il m'est venu à l'idée que.
occurrence, s. événement m.

ocean, s. océan m.
October, s. octobre m.
odd, adj. impair; dépareillé, déparié; (strange) non usuel, bizarre.
odds, s. pl. avantage m.; chances f. pl.
of, prep.
off, adv. à ... de distance; be ∼ s'en aller; be well ∼ être à l'aise; — prep; de.
offence, s offense f.
offend, v. a. & n. offenser.
offensive, s. offensive f.
offer, s. o.fre f.; — v.a. offrir.
office, s. bureau m.; (of pers.) charge f.; fonction f.
officer, s. officer m.; (police) agent m.
official, adj. officiel; — s. fonctionnaire m. f.
often, adv. souvent.
oil, s. huile f.; pétrole m.
ointment, s. onguent m.
old, adj. vieux, -eil, -eille; âgé; ancien; how ∼ are you? quel âge avez-vous?; ∼ age vieillesse f.; grow ∼ vieillir.
old-fashioned, adj. à l'ancienne mode.
omission, s. omission f.
omit, v.a. omettre (de).
on, prep. sur; (prep. omitted with days etc.); ∼ Monday lundi; ∼ time à la minute.
once, adv. une fois; autrefois; at ∼ tout de suite.
one, adj. & s. un, une; — pron. (∼, ∼s omitted if

preceded by adj.); (people, they) on; this ~ celui-ci; that ~ celui-là; ~'s son, sa, ses; which ~? lequel ...?

oneself, pron, soi-même; by ~ tout seul.

onion, s. oignon m.

onlooker, s. spectateur, -trice m. f.

open, adj. ouvert; découvert; public; franc; — v.a. ouvrir; v.n. s'ouvrir.

opening, s. ouverture f.

opera, s. opéra m.

operate, v.a. & n. opérer; ~ on opérer (qn).

operating-theatre, s. salle f. d'opération.

operation, s. opération f.

operative, adj. actif.

opinion, s. opinion f.; in my ~ à mon avis.

opponent, s. adversaire m.

opportunity, s. occasion f.

oppose, v.a. s'opposer à; ~d to opposé à.

opposition, s. opposition f.

optional, adj. facultatif.

or, conj. ou; whether ... ~ ou ... ou.

oral, adj. oral.

orange, s. orange f.

orchard, s. verger m.

orchestra, s. orchestre m.

order, s. ordre m.; (commerce) commande f.; (ruling) règlement m.; — v.a. ordonner; (goods) commander.

order-form, s. bon m. commande.

ordinary, adj. ordinaire m.

ore, s. minerai m.

organ, s. organe m.; (music) orgue m.

organic, adj. organique.

organization, s. organisation f

organize, v.a. organiser.

oriental, adj. oriental.

origin, s. origine f.

original, adj. original.

ornament, s. ornement m.; — v.a. orner.

ornamental, adj. ornemental.

orphan, adj. & s. orphelin, -e (m. f.).

other, adj. & pron. autre.

otherwise, adv. autrement.

ought, v. aux. devoir.

ounce, s. once f.

our, adj. notre, (pl.) nos.

ours, pron. le, la nôtre; les nôtres.

ourself, pron. nous(-mêmes); ourselves nous(-mêmes); by ourselves seul, -s.

out, adv. dehors; — prep. ~ of hors de.

outdoors, adv. dehors, en plein air.

outfit, s. trousseau m.

outing, s. excursion f.

outline, s. contour m.; aperçu m.; — v.a. esquisser.

outlive, v.a. survivre à.

outlook, s. perspective f.

output, s. production f.

outrageous, adj. outrageant; atroce.

outset, s. début m.; at the ~ dès le commencement.

outside, *adv.* au dehors; — *prep.* en dehors de; — *adj.* du dehors; — *s.* extérieur.

outskirts, *s. pl.* banlieue *f.*; lisière *f.*

outstanding, *adj.* non réglé, à payer; saillant; éminent.

outward, *adj.* extérieur.

outwards, *adv.* à l'extérieur, en dehors.

oven, *s.* four *m.*

over, *prep.* au-dessus de; *(motion)* par dessus; *(superior)* sur; *(more than)* plus de; *(across)* par; — *adv.* *(more)* davantage; *(finished)* fini, passé; *(too)* trop.

overcoat, *s.* pardessus *m.*

overcome, *v.a.* surmonter; vaincre.

overcrowded, *adj.* surpeuplé.

overdo, *v.a.* faire trop cuire; exagérer.

overexpose, *v.a.* surexposer.

overflow, *s.* débordement *m.*; — *v.a.* inonder; *v.n.* déborder.

overlook, *v.a.* *(look on to)* avoir vue sur; *(neglect)* négliger; *(superintend)* surveiller.

overpower, *v.a.* accabler; subjuguer.

oversea, *adj.* d'outre-mer; ~s *(adv.)* outre-mer.

oversight, *s.* inadvertence *f.*

overtake, *v.a.* rattraper; surprendre (par).

overthrow, *s.* renverse-

ment *m.*; — *v.a.* renverser.

overtime, *s.* heures *f. pl.* supplémentaires.

overwhelming, *adj.* accablant.

owe, *v.a.* devoir (à); être redevable (à).

owing, *adj.* ~ to à cause de.

owl, *s.* hibou *m.*

own, *adj.* propre; *of my* ~ à moi; — *v.a.* posséder.

owner, *s.* propriétaire *m. f.*

ox, *s.* bœuf *m.*

oxygen, *s.* oxygène *m.*

oyster, *s.* huître *f.*

P

pace, *s.* pas *m.*; *v.a.* arpenter; *v.n.* aller au pas.

pack, *s.* paquet; *(cards)* jeu *m.*; *(wool)* balle; *(hounds)* meute *f.*; — *v.a.* emballer; faire; ~ off expédier.

package, *s.* colis *m.*; paquet *m.*

packet, *s.* paquet *m.*

pact, *s.* pacte *m.*

pad, *s.* bourrelet *m.*; tampon *m.*; bloc *m.*; *blotting* ~ buvard *m.*

paddle, *v.n.* pagayer.

page, *s.* page *f.*

pail, *s.* seau *m.*

pain, *s.* douleur *f.*; *take* ~s se donner de la peine.

painful, *adj.* douloureux.

paint, *s.* peinture *f.*; — *v. a.* peindre.

painter, s. peintre m.

painting, s. peinture f.

pair, s. paire f.; couple m.

palace, s. palais m.

palate, s. palais m.

pale, adj. pâle; grow ~ pâlir.

palm, s. palme f.

pan, s. poêle f.

pane, s. vitre f.

panel, s. panneau m.

panorama, s. panorama m.

pansy, s. pensée f.

pantry, s. office f.

pants, s.pl. caleçon m.; pantalon m.

paper, s. papier m.; (newspaper) journal m.; (essay) étude f.; (exam) composition f.

parade, s. parade f.; — v.n. parader.

paraffin, s. pétrole m.

paragraph, s. paragraphe m.

parallel, s. (line) parallèle f.; (comparison) parallèle m.; — adj. parallèle.

paralysis, s. paralysie f.

parcel, s. paquet m.

pardon, s. pardon m.; I beg your ~ je vous demande pardon; (I beg your) ~? comment (dites-vous)?, pardon?; — v.a. pardonner.

parents, s. pl. père m. et mère f., parents.

parish, s. paroisse f.

Parisian, adj. parisien; — s. Parisien, -enne m.f.

park, s. parc m.; (car) (parc de) stationnement m.; — v.a. garer; stationner; no ~ing stationnement interdit.

parliament, s. parlement m.

parliamentary, adj. parlementaire.

parlour, s. petit salon m.

parrot, s. perroquet m.

part, s. part f.; partie f.; (theatre) rôle m.; (region) région f.; on my ~ de ma part; take ~ in prendre part à; — v.a. diviser; séparer; v.n. se diviser; (pers.) se séparer (de).

partial, adj. (unfair) partial; (incomplete) partiel.

participant, s. participant m.

participate, v.n. ~ in prendre part à.

participation, s. participation f.

participle, s. participe m.

particular, adj. particulier; — s. détail m.

partly, adv. en partie.

partner, s. associé, -e m. f.; partenaire m. f.

partridge, s. perdrix f.

party, s. parti m.; partie f.; groupe m.; réception f., soirée f.

pass, v.a. passer; dépasser; surpasser; (law) voter; (resolution) prendre (à); (exam) être reçu (à); — v. n. passer; — s. défilé m.; laisser-passer m.

passage, s. passage m.; couloir m.

passenger, s. voyageur,

-euse *m. f.*; passager, -ère *m. f.*
passer-by, *s.* passant *m.*
passion, *s.* passion *f.*
passionate, *adj.* passionné.
passive, *adj. & s.* passif *(m.).*
passport, *s.* passeport *m.*
past, *adj.* passé; dernier; — *s.* passé *m.*
paste, *s.* pâte *f.*
pastime, *s.* passe-temps *m*
pastry, *s.* pâtisserie *f.*
patch, *s.* pièce *f.*
patent, *s.* brevet *m.* d'invention.
path, -way, *s.* sentier *m.*
patience, *s.* patience *f.*
patient, *s.* malade *m. f.*; — *adj.* patient.
patriot, *s.* patriote *m. f.*
patrol, *s.* patrouille; — *v.n.* aller en patrouille.
patron, *s.* patron *m.*; client *m.*
pattern, *s.* modèle *m.*
pause, *s.* pause *f.*; — *v.n.* faire une pause.
pave, *v.a.* paver.
pavement, *s.* trottoir *m.*
pavilion, *s.* pavillon *m.*
paw, *s.* patte *f.*
pay, *v.a.* payer; *(visit)* faire; ~ *off* acquitter; *v.n.* payer; — *s.* paye *f.*, salaire *m.*
payable, *adj.* payable (à).
payment, *s.* payement *m.*
pea, *s.* pois *m.*
peace, *s.* paix *f.*
peaceful, *adj.* paisible.
peach, *s.* pêche *f.*
peacock, *s.* paon *m.*
peak, *s.* pic *m.*, cime *f.*
pear, *s.* poire *f.*
pearl, *s.* perle *f.*

peasant, *s.* paysan, -anne *m. f.*
pebble, *s.* caillou *m.*
peck, *s.* coup *m.* de bec.
peculiar, *adj.* particulier.
pedestrian, *s.* piéton *m.*
peel, *s.* pelure *f.*; — *v.a.* peler.
peer, *s.* pair *m.*
peg, *s.* pince *f.*; piquet *m.*
pen, *s.* stylo *m.*
penalty, *s.* peine *f.*
pencil, *s.* crayon *m.*
penicillin, *s.* pénicilline *f.*
penknife, *s.* canif *m.*
penny, *s.* penny *m.*
pension, *s.* pension *f.*
people, *s.* peuple *m.*; gens *m. pl.* [*f.* with *adj.* before it]; famille *f.*
pepper, *s.* poivre *m.*
per, *prep.* par; ~ *cent* pour cent.
perceive, *v.a.* percevoir.
perch, *s.* perchoir *m.*; — *v.n.* se percher.
perfect, *adj.* parfait; — *v.a.* rendre parfait; achever.
perform, *v.a.* accomplir, exécuter.
performance, *s.* représentation *f.*
perfume, *s.* parfum *m.*
perhaps, *adv.* peut-être.
peril, *s.* péril *m.*
period, *s.* période *f.*
periodical, *s.* périodique *m.*
perish, *v.n.* périr.
perishable, *adj.* périssable.
permanent, *adj.* permanent.
permission, *s.* permission

f.

permit, *s.* permis *m.;* — *v.a.* permettre.

persecution, *s.* persécution *f.*

Persian, *adj.* persan.

persist, *v.n.* persister.

person, *s.* personne *f.*

personal, *adj.* personnel.

personality, *s.* personnalité *f.*

perspiration, *s.* transpiration *f.*

persuade, *v.a.* convaincre (de), persuader.

pertain, *v.n.* appartenir (à).

pet, *s.* enfant *m.f.* gâté, -e; — *adj.* favori; ~ *dog* chien *m.* familier.

petrol, *s.* essence *f.*

petroleum, *s.* pétrole *m.*

petticoat, *s.* jupon *m.*

phase, *s.* phase *f.*

pheasant, *s.* faisan, -e *m. f.*

phenomenon, *s.* phénomène *m.*

philosopher, *s.* philosophe *m.*

philosophy, *s.* philosophie *f.*

phone, *s.* téléphone *m.;* — *v.a. & n.* téléphoner.

photo(graph), *s.* photographie *f.* — *v.a.* photographier.

phrase, *s.* phrase *f.*

physical, *adj.* physique.

physician, *s.* médecin *m.*

physicist, *s.* physicien *m.*

physics, *s.* physique *f.*

pianist, *s.* pianiste *m.f.*

piano, *s.* piano *m.*

pick, *v.a.* cueillir; picoter; *(teeth)* curer; *(bone)*

ronger; *(choose)* choisir; ~ *out* choisir; ~ *up* ramasser; prendre.

pickle, *s.* marinade *f.* ~*s* pickles *m.*

picnic, *s.* pique-nique *m.*

picture, *s.* tableau *m.;* portrait *m.;* film *m.;* ~*s* cinéma *m.*

pie, *s.* pâté *m.*

piece, *s.* morceau *m.;* partie *f.;* pièce *f.;* ~ *of news* nouvelle *f.;* ~ *of work* ouvrage *m.*

pier, *s.* jetée *f.*

pierce, *v.a.* percer.

pig, *s.* cochon *m.*

pigeon, *s.* pigeon *m.*

pile[1], *s.* tas *m.;* — *v.a.* (also ~ *up*) entasser, amasser.

pile[2], *s.* pieu *m.*, pilot *m.*

pill, *s.* pillule *f.*

pillar, *s.* pilier *m.*

pillar-box, *s.* boîte *f.* aux lettres.

pillow, *s.* oreiller *m.*

pilot, *s.* pilote *m.*

pin, *s.* épingle *f.*

pinch, *v.a.* pincer.

pine, *s.* pin *m.*

pineapple, *s.* ananas *m.*

pink, *adj. & s.* rose (*m.*).

pint, *s.* pinte *f.*

pious, *adj.* pieux.

pipe, *s.* tuyau *m.; (smoking)* pipe *f.*

pistol, *s.* pistolet *m.*

pit, *s.* fosse *f.;* creux *m.; (theatre)* parterre *m.*

pitch, *s.* degré *m.;* ton *m.;* *v.a. (tent)* dresser; *(camp)* asseoir.

pity, *s.* pitié *f.;* dommage *m.*

place, *s.* lieu *m.*, endroit *m.*; place *f.*; emploi *m.*; – *v.a.* mettre.

plain, *adj.* uni; simple; évident; ordinaire.

plait, *s.* tresse *f.*

plan, *s.* plan *m.*; projet *m.*; – *v.a.* faire le plan (de).

plane, *s.* plan *m.*; *(tool)* rabot *m.*; *(aero-)* avion *m.*; – *v.a.* raboter.

planet, *s.* planète *f.*

plank, *s.* planche *f.*

plant, *s.* plante *f.*; *(works)* usine *f.*, fabrique *f.*; – *v.a.* planter.

plantation, *s.* plantation *f.*

plaster, *s.* (em)plâtre *m.*

plastic, *adj.* plastique; ~s plastiques *m. pl.*

plate, *s.* plaque *f.*; planche *f.*; *(china)* assiette *f.*; *(silver)* vaisselle *f.*

platform, *s.* quai *m.*

platinum, *s.* platine *m.*

platter, *s.* plat *m.*

play, *s.* jeu *m.*; pièce *f.* de théâtre; – *v.a. & n.* jouer.

player, *s.* joueur, -euse *m. f.*

playground, *s.* cour *f.* de récréation.

plea, *s.* excuse *f.*; défense *f.*

plead, *v.a. & n.* plaider

pleasant, *adj.* agréable.

please, *v.a. & n.* plaire (à); be ~ed with, to être content de; as you ~ comme vous voulez; if you ~ s'il vous plaît.

pleasure, *s.* plaisir *m.*

pledge, *s.* gage *m.*; – *v.a.* mettre en gage.

plenty, *s.* abondance *f.*; ~ of quantité de, beaucoup de.

plot, *s.* *(land)* terrain *m.*; *(story)* intrigue *f.*; *(conspiracy)* complot *m.*; *v. n.* conspirer.

plough, *s.* charrue *f.*; – *v.a. & n.* labourer.

plug, *s.* tampon *m.*; prise *f.* de courant; – *v.a.* tamponner.

plum, *s.* prune *f.*

plume, *s.* plume *f.*; plumet *m.*

plunder, *v.a.* piller; – *s.* pillage *m.*

plunge, *v.a. & n.* plonger; – *s.* plongeon *m.*

plural, *s. & adj.* pluriel *(m.)*.

plus, *prep.* plus.

ply, *v.a.* manier; s'appliquer (à); *v.n.* faire le service (entre).

pocket, *s.* poche *f.*

pocket-book, *s.* carnet *m.*; portefeuille *m.*

poem, *s.* poème *m.*

poet, *s.* poète *m.*

poetic(al), *adj.* poétique

poetry, *s.* poésie *f.*

point, *s.* point *m.*; pointe *f.*; – *v.a. & n.* ~ out montrer du doigt; faire valoir (un fait); ~ to indiquer.

poison, *s.* poison *m.*; *v.a.* empoisonner.

poisonous, *adj.* vénéneux.

pole, *s.* pôle *m.*

Pole, *s.* Polonais, -e *m. f.*

police, s. police f.
policeman, **-officer**, s. agent (de police) m.
police-station, s. poste (de police) m.
policy, s. politique f.; *(insurance)* police f.
polish, s. poli m.; *fig.* politesse f.; — v. a. polir.
Polish, adj. polonais.
polite, adj. poli.
political, adj. politique.
politician, s. politique m.; politicien m.
politics, s. politique f.
poll, s. vote m.; liste f. (électorale); scrutin m.
pool[1], s. mare f.
pool[2], s. pool m.
poor, adj. pauvre; *(bad)* mauvais.
pope, s. pape m.
popular, adj. populaire.
popularity, s. popularité f.
population, s. population f.
pork, s. porc m.; ~ butcher charcutier m.
port, s. port m.; *(ship)* bâbord m.
portable, adj. portatif.
porter, s. portier m.; *(railw.)* porteur m.
portfolio, s. serviette f.
portion, s. portion f.; — v.a. partager.
portrait, s. portrait m.
Portuguese, adj. portugais; — s. Portugais, -e m. f.
position, s. position f.
positive, adj. & s. positif *(m.)*.
possess, v.a. posséder.

possession, s. possession f.
possibility, s. possibilité f.
possible, adj. possible.
post[1], s. poteau m.; — v.a. afficher, placarder.
post[2], s. poste f.; courrier m. — v.a. mettre à la poste.
postage, s. port m., affranchissement; ~ paid port payé.
postal, adj. postal; ~ order mandat (de poste) m.
poster, s. affiche f.
post-free, adj. franco.
postman, s. facteur m.
post(-)office, s. bureau m. de poste
postpone, v.a. remettre.
postscript, s. post-scriptum m.
pot, s. pot m.
potato, s. pomme f. de terre.
pottery, s. poterie f.
pouch, s. blague f.
poultry, s. volaille f.
pound, s. livre f.
pour, v.a. verser.
pouring, adj. torrentiel.
poverty, s. pauvreté f.
powder, s. poudre f.
power, s. pouvoir m.; puissance f.; force f.
powerful, adj. puissant.
power-plant, **-station**, s. centrale f. électrique.
practical, adv. pratique.
practice, s. pratique f.; exercise m.
practise, v.a. pratiquer, exercer; étudier.
praise, s. louange f.; — v.a. louer.
pray, v.a. & n. prier.

prayer, s. prière f.

preach, v.a. & n. prêcher.

preacher, s. prédicateur m.

precede, v.a. précéder.

preceding, adj. précédent.

precious, adj. précieux.

precision, s. précision f.

predecessor, s. prédécesseur m.

predict, v.a. prédire.

prefabricated, adj. préfabriqué.

preface, s. préface f.

prefer, v.a. préférer (to à), aimer mieux.

preferable, adj. préférable (à).

preference, s. préférence f.

pregnant, adj. enceinte.

prejudice, s. préjugé m.

preliminary, adj. préliminaire.

premature, adj. prématuré.

premier, s. premier ministre m., (in France) président m. du conseil.

premises, s. pl. lieux m. pl.; local m., immeuble m.

premium, s. prime f.

preparation, s. préparation f.

prepare, v.a. préparer, apprêter; — v.n. se préparer.

preposition, s. préposition f.

Presbyterian, adj. presbytérien.

prescribe, v.a. prescrire, ordonner; v.n. ~ for faire une ordonnance pour.

prescription, s. prescription f.; (medical) ordonnance f.

presence, s. présence f.

present[1], adj. présent; actuel; — s. présent m.; at ~ à présent.

present[2], s. (gift) cadeau m., présent m.; — v.a. présenter; donner.

presently, adv. tout à l'heure.

preserve, v.a. préserver; (fruits) conserver; — s. confiture f.; conserve f.

president, s. président m.

press, s. presse f.; — v.a. presser; serrer.

pressure, s. pression f.

presume, v.a. présumer.

presumption, s. présomption f.

pretend, v.a. & n. feindre, faire semblant; prétendre (à).

pretention, s. prétension f.

pretty, adj. joli.

prevail, v.n. prévaloir; prédominer.

prevent, v.a. empêcher.

prevention, s. empêchement m.

previous, adj. antérieur (à).

prey, s. proie f.

price, s. prix m.; cours m.

price-list, s. prix-courant m., tarif m.

prick, v.a. piquer; — s. piqûre f.

pride, s. orgueil m.

priest, s. prêtre m.

primary, *adj.* primaire.
prime, *adj.* ~ *minister*
see **premier.**
primitive, *adj.* primitif.
prince, *s.* prince *m.*
princess, *s.* princesse *f.*
principal, *adj.* principal;
— *s.* directeur *m.*,
patron, -ne *m.f.*, principal *m.*
principle, *s.* principe *m*
print, *s.* empreinte *f.*;
impression *f.*; *out of* ~
épuisé; — *v.a.* im-
primer; faire une em-
preinte (sur); *(photo)*
tirer; ~*ed matter* im-
primés *m. pl.*
printing-office, *s.* imprimerie *f.*
prison, *s.* prison *f.*
prisoner, *s.* prisonnier,
-ère *m. f.*
private, *adj.* particulier;
personel; privé.
privilege, *s.* privilège *m.*
prize, *s.* prix *m.*
probability, *s.* probabilité *f.*
probable, *adj.* probable.
probably, *adv.* probablement.
problem, *s.* problème *m.*
procedure, *s.* procédé *m.*
proceed, *v.n.* aller (à);
se mettre (à); avan-
cer; passer (à); pro-
céder; ~ *with* conti-
nuer.
process, *s.* développement *m.;* méthode *f.*,
procédé *m.;* — *v.n.*
aller en procession.
procession, *s.* cortège *m.*;
procession *f.*
proclaim, *v. a.* proclamer.

proclamation, *s.* proclamation *s.*
produce, *v.a.* produire.
producer, *s.* producteur,
-trice *m. f.*
product, *s.* produit *m.*
production, *s.* production
f.
profess, *v.a.* professer, déclarer.
profession, *s.* profession *f.*
professional, *adj.* professionnel; de profession.
professor, *s.* professeur *m.*
profit, *s.* profit *m.;*
v.n. ~ *by* profiter de.
profitable, *adj.* profitable.
profound, *adj.* profond.
programme, *s.* programme *m.*
progress, *s.* progrès *m.;*
marche *f.;* — *v.n.*
s'avancer, faire des
progrès.
prohibit, *v.a.* défendre.
prohibition, *s.* prohibition *f.*, défense *f.*
project, *s.* projet *m.;*
— *v.a.* projeter; *v.n.*
saillir.
projector, *s.* projecteur
m.
prolong, *v.a.* prolonger.
prominent, *adj.* (pro)émi-
nent.
promise, *s.* promesse *f.;*
— *v.a.* promettre.
promote, *v.a.* donner de
l'avancement (à); en-
courager.
promotion, *s.* promotion
f., avancement *m.*
prompt, *adj.* prompt; —
v.a. *(rheatre)* souffler;
inspirer.
pronoun, *s.* pronom *m.*

pronounce, *v.a.* prononcer.

pronunciation, *s.* prononciation *f.*

proof, *s.* preuve *f.*; épreuve *f.*

propeller, *s.* hélice *f.*

proper, *adj.* propre; convenable.

property, *s.* propriété *f.*

prophet, *s.* prophète *m.*

proportion, *s.* proportion *f.*

propose, *v.a.* proposer.

proposition, **proposal**, *s.* proposition *f.*

prose, *s.* prose *f.*

prospect, *s.* prospective *f.*

prospectus, *s.* prospectus *m.*

prosper, *v.n.* prospérer.

prosperity, *s.* prospérité *f.*

prosperous, *adj.* prospère.

protest, *s.* protestation *f.*; protêt *m.*; — *v.a.* protester.

Protestant, *adj. & s.* protestant, -e (*m. f.*).

proud, *adj.* fier, -ère.

prove, *v.a.* prouver; éprouver.

proverb, *s.* proverbe *m.*

provide, *v.a.* pourvoi de; fournir de; *v.n.* ~ *for* pourvoir à; ~*d that* pourvu que.

providence, *s.* prévoyance *f.*

province, *s.* province *f.*

provincial, *adj.* provincial.

provision, *s.* provision *f.*

provoke, *v. a.* provoquer (à).

prudent, *adj.* prudent.

psalm, *s.* psaume *m.*

psychological, *adj.* psychologique.

psychology, *s.* psychologie *f.*

public, *adj. & s.* public *m.*

publication, *s.* publication *f.*

publicity, *s.* publicité *f.*

publish, *v.a.* publier.

publisher, *s.* éditeur *m.*

pudding, *s.* pouding *m.*

pull, *v.a.* tirer; ~ *down* démolir; ~ *out* arracher; ~ *up* arrêter; *v. n.* tirer; ~ *through* s'en tirer; — *s.* traction *f.*, tirage *f.*

pulpit, *s.* chaire *f.*

pulse, *s.* pouls *m.*

pump, *s.* pompe *f.*; — *v. a.* pomper.

punch¹, *s.* poinçon *m.*; — *v.a.* poinçonner, percer.

punch², *s.* punch *m.*

punctual, *adj.* ponctuel.

puncture, *s.* piqûre *f.*; (*tyre*) crevaison *f.*; — *v.a.& n.* crever.

punish, *v.a.* punir.

punishment,, *s.* punition *f.*

pupil¹, *s.* élève *m. f.*

pupil², *s.* (*eye*) pupille *f.*

puppy, *s.* petit chien *m.*

purchase, *s.* achat *m.*; — *v.a.* acheter.

pure, *adj.* pur.

purge, *v.a.* purger.

purify, *v.a.* purifier.

purity, *s.* pureté *f.*

purpose, *s.* but *m.*

purse, *s.* porte-monnaie

m., bourse *f.*

pursue, *v.a.* (pour)suivre.

pursuit, *s.* poursuite *f.*

push, *v.a. & n.* pousser; ~ *back* repousser; ~ *on* faire avancer; pousser (jusqu'à); — *s.* poussé *f.*; allant *m.*

puss, *s.* minet *m.*

put, *v.a.* mettre; *(express)* dire; ~ *back* remettre; ~ *down* déposer; attribuer; inscrire; ~ *off* remettre; ôter; ~ *on* mettre; ~ *out* tendre; éteindre; ~ *up* ouvrir; loger; ~ *up with* s'accommoder.

puzzle, *v.a.* embarrasser.

pyjamas, *s. pl.* pyjama *m.*

pyramid, *s.* pyramide *f.*

Q

quadrangle, *s.* quadrilatère *m.*; cour *f.*

quake, *v.n.* trembler.

qualification, *s.* qualification *f.*; compétence *f.*

qualify, *v.a.* qualifier; *v.n.* ~ *for* passer l'examen de

quality, *s.* qualité *f.*

quantity, *s.* quantité *f.*

quarrel, *s.* querelle *f.*; brouille *f.*; — *v.n.* se brouiller; ~ *with* se quereller avec.

quarter, *s.* quartier *m.*; quart *m.*; ~s quartiers *m.pl.*

quartet(te), *s.* quatuor *m.*

quay, *s.* quai *m.*

queen, *s.* reine *f.*; *(cards)* dame *f.*

queer, *adj.* bizarre.

quench, *v.a.* éteindre.

question, *s.* question *f.*; — *v.a.* interroger.

queue, *s.* queue *f.*; — *v.n.* ~ *up* faire (la) queue.

quick, *adj.* prompt, rapide; vif.

quick(ly), *adv.* vite.

quiet, *adj.* tranquille; calme; *be* ~ se taire.

quilt, *s.* courtepointe *f.*

quit, *v.a.* quitter.

quite, *adv.* tout à fait.

quiver, *v.n.* trembler.

quiz, *s.* mystification *f.*; persifleur *m.*; *v.a.* railler.

quotation, *s.* citation *f.*

quote, *v.a.* citer.

R

rabbi, *s.* rabbin *m.*

rabbit, *s.* lapin, -e *m. f.*

race[1], *s.* course *f.*; — *v.n.* faire la course; courir; lutter de vitesse.

race[2], *s.* race *f.*

rack, *s.* râtelier *m.*

racket, *s.* raquette *f.*

radiate, *v.n.* rayonner, irradier; *v.a.* dégager.

radiator, *s.* radiateur *m.*

radical, *adj.* radical.

radio, *s.* radio *f.*

radioactive, *adj.* radioactif.

radish, *s.* radis *m.*

rag, *s.* chiffon *m.*

rage, *s.* rage *f.*

raid, *s.* razzia *f.*, rafle *f.*; raid *m.*

rail, *s.* barre *f.*, rampe *f.*; rail *m.*; by ~ par chemin de fer.

railway, *s.* chemin *m.* de fer.

rain, *s.* pluie *f.*; — *v.n.* pleuvoir.

rainy, *adj.* pluvieux.

raise, *v.a.* lever, élever; soulever; *(plants)* faire pousser, cultiver.

rake, *s.* râteau *m.*

rally, *v.n.* se rallier; — *s.* ralliement *m.*

ramify, *v.n.* ramifier.

random, *s.* at ~ par hasard.

range, *s.* rangée *f.*; *(mountains)* chaîne *f.*; *(extent)* étendue *f.*; *(kitchen)* fourneau *m.*; — *v.a.* ranger.

rank, *s.* rang *m.*; grade *m.*

ransom, *s.* rançon *f.*; — *v.a.* payer rançon pour.

rap, *s.* tape *f.*; coup *m.*; — *v.a.* frapper.

rapid, *adj.* rapide.

rare, *adj.* rare.

rascal, *s.* coquin *m.*

rash, *adj.* téméraire; inconsidéré.

raspberry, *s.* framboise *f.*

rat, *s.* rat *m.*

rate, *s.* taux *m.*, cours *m.*, tarif *m.*; *(speed)* vitesse *f.*, allure *f.*; *(tax)* taxe *f.*; at the ~ of à la vitesse de;

at any ~ en tout cas, quoi qu'il en soit; — *v.a.* estimer; taxer.

rather, *adv.* plutôt; un peu.

ratify, *v.a.* ratifier.

ration, *s.* ration *f.*

rational, *adj.* raisonnable.

rattle, *s.* bruit *m.*; — *v.n.* faire du bruit.

raven, *s.* corbeau *m.*

raw, *adj.* cru; ~ material matière *f.* première.

ray, *s.* rayon *m.*

razor, *s.* rasoir *m.*; safety ~ rasoir de sûreté; electric ~ rasoir électrique.

razor-blade, *s.* lame *f.* de rasoir.

reach, *v.a.* arriver (à); atteindre; *v. n.* atteindre; parvenir (à); — *s.* étendue *f.*; portée *f.*; within ~ à portée.

react, *v.n.* réagir.

reaction, *s.* réaction *f.*

reactor, *s.* réacteur *m.*

read, *v.a.* lire; étudier; ~ for *(exam)* préparer.

reader, *s.* lecteur, -trice *m. f.*

reading, *s.* lecture *f.*

ready, *adj.* prêt (à); prompt (à); près (de); get ~ (se) préparer.

real, *adj.* réel; véritable.

reality, *s.* réalité *f.*

realization, *s.* réalisation *f.*

realize, *v.a.* réaliser.

really, *adv.* vraiment.

realm, *s.* royaume *m.*; *fig.* domaine *m.*

reap, *v.a. & n.* moissonner.

reaper, *s.* moissonneur *m.*

rear, *adj.* de derrière; — *s.* arrière *m.*; queue *f.*; — *v.a.* élever; *v. n.* se cabrer.

reason, *s.* raison *f.*; — *v. a. & n.* raisonner.

reasonable, *adj.* raisonnable.

reasoning, *s.* raisonnement *m.*

rebellion, *s.* rébellion *f.*

rebuke, *s.* réprimande *f.*; — *v.a.* réprimander.

recall, *v.a.* rappeler; *(remember)* se rappeler.

receipt, *s.* reçu *m.*, quittance *f.*; recette *f.*

receive, *v.a.* recevoir.

receiver, *s.* destinataire *m. f.*; *(phone, wireless)* écouteur *m.*, récepteur *m.*, poste *m.*

recent, *adj.* récent.

recently, *adv.* récemment.

reception, *s.* réception *f.*

receptionist, *s.* portier *m.* d'auberge; employé à la réception.

recipe, *s.* recette *f.*

recital, *s.* récit *m.*; récital *m.*

recite, *v.a. & n.* réciter.

reckless, *adj.* insouciant.

reckon, *v.a.* compter.

recognize, *v.a.* reconnaître.

recollect, *v. a.* se rappeler.

recommend, *v.a.* recommander.

recommendation, *s.* recommandation *f.*

reconcile, *v. a.* réconcilier.

record, *s.* rapport *m.* officiel; souvenir *m.*; mention *f.*; archives *f. pl.*; *(gramophone)* disque *m.*; *(sport)* record *m.*; — *v.a.* enregistrer; rapporter.

recount, *v.a.* raconter.

recover, *v.a.* recouvrer; *v.n.* se remettre.

recreation, *s.* récréation *f.*

recruit, *s.* recrue *f.*; — *v.a.* recruter.

rectangle, *s.* rectangle *m.*

rector, *s.* recteur *m.*; curé *m.*

recur, *v. n.* revenir.

red, *adj.* rouge; roux.

redress, *v.n.* réparer; redresser.

reduce, *v.a.* réduire.

reduction, *s.* réduction *f.*

reed, *s.* roseau *m.*

reef, *s.* ris *m.*; récif *m.*

reel, *s.* dévidoir *m.*; bobine *f.*; — *v.n.* tourner.

refer, *v.a.* référer; renvoyer; *v.n.* ~ *to* se rapporter à, s'en rapporter à, se référer à.

referee, *s.* arbitre *m.*; *v.a.* arbitrer.

reference, *s.* renvoi *m.*, référence *f.*; rapport *m.*; allusion *f.*; *with* ~ *to* à propos de; *have* ~ *to* se rapporter à.

refill, *s.* recharge *f.*

reflect, *v.a.* réfléchir; *v.n.* méditer (sur).

reflection, *s.* réflexion

f.; image f.

reform, *s.* réforme *f.*; — *v.a.* réformer.

Reformation, *s.* Réforme *f.*

refrain, *v.n.* ~ *from* se retenir de.

refresh, *v.a.* refraîchir.

refreshment, *s.* rafraîchissement *m.*; ~ *room* buffet *m.*

refrigerator, *s.* réfrigérateur *m.*

refuge, *s.* refuge *m.*; *take* ~ se réfugier.

refugee, *s.* réfugié, -e *m. f.*

refusal, refus *m.*

refuse, *v.a.* refuser.

refute, *v.a.* réfuter.

regain, *v.a.* reconquérir; regagner; reprendre.

regard, *s.* égard *m.*; *with* ~ *to* à l'égard de; *kind (est)* ~s meilleurs amitiés *f. pl.*; — *v.a.* regarder; tenir compte (de); considérer.

regent, *s.* régent *m.*

regime, *s.* régime *m.*

regiment, *s.* régiment *m.*

region, *s.* région *f.*

register, *v. a.* enregistrer.

regret, *v.a.* regretter; — *s.* regret *m.*

regular, *adj.* régulier.

regulate, *v.a.* régler.

regulation, *s.* ordonnance *f.*; réglementation *f.*

rehearsal, *s.* répétition *f.*

rehearse, *v.a.* répéter.

reign, *s.* règne *m.*; — *v. a.* régner.

rein, *s.* rêne *f.*

reject, *v.a.* rejeter; refuser.

relate, *v.a.* raconter; *be* ~*ed to* être apparenté à; *v.n.* ~ *to* se rapporter à; *relating to* relatif à.

relation, *s.* relation *f.*, rapport *m.* (à); *(relative)* parent, -e *m. f.*

relative, *s.* parent, -e *m. f.*; — *adj.* relatif; ~ *to* au sujet de.

relax, *v.n.* se relâcher; *v. a.* relâcher.

relay, *s.* relais *m.*

release, *s.* délivrance *f.*; — *v.a.* libérer; décharger (de).

reliable, *adj.* digne de confiance.

relic, *s.* relique *f.*

relief[1], *s.* délivrance *f.*; soulagement *m.*; secours *m.*

relief[2], *s.* relief *m.*

relieve, *v.a.* soulager; secourir; délivrer.

religion, *s.* religion *f.*

religious, *adj.* religieux.

rely, *v.n.* ~ *upon* compter sur.

remain, *v.n.* rester.

remark, *s.* remarque *f.*; — *v.a.* remarquer; *v.n.* faire une remarque.

remarkable, *adj.* remarquable.

remedy, *s.* remède *m.*

remember, *v.a.* se souvenir (de), se rappeler.

remembrance, *s.* souvenir *m.*

remind, *v. a.* ~ *of* rappeler (à), faire souvenir (de).

remit, *v.a.* remettre.

remittance, *s.* remise *f.*

remorse, *s.* remords *m.*

remote, *adj.* reculé.

removal, *s.* déménagement *m.; enlèvement; (dismissal)* renvoi *m.*

remove, *v.a.* déménager; enlever; *(dismiss)* renvoyer; *(from school)* retirer; *v.n.* déménager; s'en aller.

Renaissance, *s.* Renaissance *f.*

render, *v.a.* rendre.

renew, *v.a.* renouveler.

renounce, *v.a.* renoncer (à); dénoncer; répudier.

rent, *s. (house)* loyer *m.; — v.a.* louer.

repair, *s.* réparation *f.; — v.a.* réparer.

repay, *v.a.* rembourser.

repeat, *v.a.* répéter.

repentance, *s.* repentir *m.*

repetition, *s.* répétition *f.*

replace, *v.a.* replacer.

reply, *s.* réponse *f.; — v.a. & n.* répondre.

report, *s.* rapport *m.,* compte *m.* rendu; bruit *m.; bulletin m.; — v.a.* rapporter; rendre compte (de).

reporter, *s.* reporter *m.*

represent, *v.a.* représenter.

representation, *s.* représentation *f.*

representative, *s.* représentant *m.*

reproach, *s.* reproche *m.*

reproduce, *v.a.* reproduire.

reproduction, *s.* reproduction *f.*

reprove, *v.a.* réprimander.

republic, *s.* république *f.*

repulsion *s.* répulsion *f.*

repulsive, *adj.* repoussant.

reputation, repute, *s.* réputation *f.*

request, *s.* requête *f.; — v.a.* demander.

require, *v. a.* demander; exiger.

requirement, *s.* besoin *m.; exigence f.*

rescue, *s.* délivrance *f.; secours m.; — v.a.* délivrer; secourir.

research, *s.* recherche *f.*

resemble, *v.a.* ressembler (à).

resent, *v.a.* être froissé (de); ressentir.

reserve, *s.* réserve *f.; — v.a.* réserver.

reside, *v.n.* résider.

residence, *s.* résidence *f.*

resident, *s.* habitant *m.; — adj.* résidant.

resign, *v.a.* résigner, se démettre (de); *v.n.* donner sa démission.

resignation, *s.* résignation *f.; démission f.*

resist, *v. a.* résister (à).

resistance, *s.* résistance *f.*

resolution, *s.* résolution *f.*

resolve, *v.a.* résoudre; *v.n.* se résoudre (à), se décider (à faire).

resort, *s.* recours *m.; ressource f.; — v.n. ~ to* avoir recours à.

resource, *s.* ressource *f.*

respect, *s.* respect *m.; rapport m.; in this ~* sous ce rapport; *with ~ to* concernant ...;

— *v.a.* respecter.

respectful, *adj.* respectueux.

respective, *adj.* respectif.

respond, *v.n.* répondre.

response, *s.* réponse *f.*

responsibility, *s.* responsabilité *f.*

responsible, *adj.* responsable (de).

rest[1], *s.* reste *m.; the ~* les autres.

rest[2], *s.* repos *m.; pause f.;* — *v.n.* se reposer.

restaurant, *s.* restaurant *m.*

restless, *adj.* sans repos; inquiet; agité.

restoration, *s.* restauration *f.*

restore, *v.a.* restaurer.

restrain, *v.a.* retenir; *~ from* empêcher de.

restraint, *s.* contrainte *f.;* retenue *f.*

restrict, *v.a.* restreindre.

restriction, *s.* restriction *f.*

result, *s.* résultat *m.;* — *v.n. ~ from* résulter de; *~ in* avoir pour résultat.

resume, *v.a.* reprendre.

retain, *v.a.* retenir.

retire, *v.n.* se retirer.

retreat, *s.* retraite *f.*

return, *v.n.* revenir, retourner; *v.a.* rendre; renvoyer; *(answer)* faire; — *s.* retour *m;* renvoi *m.; ~ ticket* billet *m.* d'aller et retour.

reveal, *v.a.* révéler.

revenge, *s.* vengeance *f.;* — *v.a.* venger.

revenue, *s.* revenu *m.*

reverend, *adj.* révérend.

reverse, *adj.* inverse; — *s.* revers *m.*

review, *s.* revue *f.; (of book)* compte *m.* rendu, critique *f.;* — *v.a.* revoir; *(book)* faire la critique (d'un livre).

revision, *s.* révision *f.*

revolt, *s.* révolte *f.*

revolution, *s.* révolution *f.; (motor)* tour *m.*

reward, *s.* récompense *f.;* — *v.a.* récompenser.

rheumatism, *s.* rhumatisme *m.*

rhyme, *s.* rime *f.*

rhythm, *s.* rythme *m.*

rib, *s.* côte *f.*

rice, *s.* riz *m.*

rich, *adj.* riche.

rid, *v.a. get ~ of* se débarrasser de.

riddle, *s.* énigme *f.*

ride, *v.n.* monter; aller à cheval *or* à bicyclette; *(bus)* voyager; aller (en autobus); *v.a.* monter; — *s.* promenade *f.*

ridge, *s.* crête *f.*

ridiculous, *adj.* ridicule.

rifle, *s.* fusil *m.*

right, *adj.* droit; correct, exact; juste, bon; bien; *~ side* endroit *m.; be ~* avoir raison; *that's ~* c'est ça; — *s.* droit *m.; (opposed to left)* droite *f.;* — *adv.* droit; bien; *(very)* très.

rim, *s.* bord *m.*

ring[1], *s.* anneau *m.; cercle m.; (sport)* ring *m.;*

ring[2], *v.n. & a.* sonner;

~ up appeler (au téléphone); — s. son m.; coup m. de sonnette; there is a ~ at the door on sonne (à la porte).

rinse, v.a. rinser.

riot, s. émeute f.

rip, v.a. déchirer; ~ up arracher; v.n. aller à toute vitesse.

ripe, adj. mûr.

rise, v. n. se lever; (revolt) se soulever; (prices) hausser; (originate) naître (de); — s. montée f.; (salary) augmentation f.; give ~ to donner lieu à.

risk, s. risque m.; — v.a. risquer.

rival, adj. & s. rival, -e (m. f.); — v.a. rivaliser (avec).

rivalry, s. rivalité f.

river, s. fleuve m., rivière f.

road, s. route f., chemin m.

road-map, s. carte f. routière. f.

roar, s. rugissement m.; — v.n. rugir; hurler.

roast, v.a. & n. rôtir; — s. rôti m.

rob, v.a. voler.

robber, s. voleur m.

robbery, s. vol m.

robe, s. robe f.

robin, s. rouge-gorge m.

rock, s. rocher m., roc m.

rocket, s. fusée f.

rocky, adj. rocheux.

rod, s. baguette f.

rogue, s. coquin, -e m. f.

roll, s. rouleau m.; liste

f.; — v. a. rouler.

roller-towel, s. essuie-mains m. à rouleau.

Roman, adj. romain; — s. Romain, -e m. f.

romantic, adj. romanesque; romantique.

roof, s. toit m.

room, s. chambre f.; salle f.; (space) place f.

root, s. racine f.; source f.

rope, s. corde f.

rose, s. rose f.

rotten, adj. pourri, carié.

rough, adj. rude; grossier; brut; (sea) gros.

roughly, adv. approximativement.

round, adj. rond; — adv. de tour, en rond, autour; hand ~ faire circuler; go ~ tourner; turn ~ tourner, se retourner; — prep. autour de; — s. rond m., cercle m.; tournée f.; tour m.

rouse, v.a. réveiller.

route, s. route f.

routine, s. routine f.

row[1], s. rang m., rangée f.; ligne f.

row[2], v.n. ramer; v.a. faire aller (à la rame); — s. promenade f. en canot.

row[3], s. chahut m., vacarme m., querelle f.; réprimande f.

royal, adj. royal.

rub, v.a. frotter.

rubber, s. caoutchouc m.

rubbish, s. décombres m. pl.; ordure(s) f. (pl) immondices f. pl.

ruby, *s.* rubis *m.*

rudder, *s.* gouvernail *m.*

rude, *adj.* rude.

ruffian, *s.* bandit *m.*

ruffle, *s.* ride *f.;* — *v.a.* rider; ébouriffer.

rug, *s.* couverture *f.;* tapis *m.*

ruin, *s.* ruine *f.;* — *v. a.* ruiner.

rule, *s.* autorité *f.;* règle *f.; (of the road)* code *m.; as a ~* générale-ment; — *v.a.* gouver-ner; régler; guider; *~ out* exclure.

ruler, *s.* gouverneur *m.,* souverain *m.; (for lines)* règle *f.*

rum, *s.* rhum *m.*

Rumanian, *adj.* rou-main; — *s.* Roumain, -e *m. f.*

rumour, *s.* rumeur *f.*

run, *v.n.* courir; fuir, se sauver; *(flow)* couler; *(veh.)* marcher, faire le service; *(engine)* fonctionner; *(play in theatre)* se jouer; *v.a.* faire fonctionner; met-tre en service; faire marcher, faire aller; *~ after* courir après; *~ away* s'enfuir; *~ down* descendre en cou-rant; *(health)* s'affai-blir; *~ in (motor)* roder; *~ into* heurter, rencontrer; *~ off* s'en-fuir; s'écouler; *~ out* se terminer; *~ over* passer dessus; *~ up (debts)* entasser; — *s.* course *f.;* voyage *m.*

runner, *s.* coureur, -euse

runway, *s.* piste (d'envol) *f.*

rupture, *s.* rupture *f.*

rural, *adj.* rural.

rush, *v.n.* se précipi-ter, se jeter; *v.a.* en-traîner à toute vitesse; — *s.* ruée *f.,* hâte *f.; ~ hours* heures *f.pl.* d'affluence, coup *m.* de feu.

Russian, *adj.* russe; — *s.* Russe *m. f.*

rust, *s.* rouille *f.*

rustic, *adj.* rustique.

rustle, *s.* bruissement *m.*

rye, *s.* seigle *m.*

S

sabre, *s.* sabre *m.*

sack, *s.* sac *m.*

sacrament, *s.* sacrement *m.*

sacrifice, *s.* sacrifice *m.*

sad, *adj.* triste.

saddle, *s.* selle *f.*

sadness, *s.* tristesse *f.*

safe, *adj.* sûr, en sûreté. sans danger; — *s.* coffre-fort *m.*

safely, *adv.* sain et sauf; en sûreté.

safety, *s.* sûreté *f.*

sail, *s.* voile *f.;* — *v.n.* faire voile, naviguer.

sailor, *s.* marin *m.,* ma-telot *m.*

saint, *s.* saint, -e *m. f.*

sake: *for the ~ of* pour l'amour de.

salad, *s.* salade *f.*

salary, *s.* traitement *m.,* appointements *m. pl.*

sale, *s.* vente *f.; (auction)* vente *f.* aux enchères.

salesman, *s.* vendeur *m.*

saleswoman, *s.* vendeuse *f.*

salmon, *s.* saumon *m.*

saloon, *s.* salon *m.;* ∼ **bar** bar *m.*

salt, *s.* sel *m.*

salt-cellar, *s.* salière *f.*

salvation, *s.* salut *m.*

same, *adj. & pron.* même.

sanatorium, *s.* sanatorium *m.*

sanction, *s.* sanction *f.;* – *v.a.* sanctionner.

sand, *s.* sable *m.; the* ∼**s** la plage.

sandal, *s.* sandale *f.*

sandwich, *s.* sandwich *m.*

sanitary, *adj.* sanitaire.

sarcastic, *adj.* sarcastique.

sardine, *s.* sardine *f.*

Satan, *s.* Satan *m.*

satellite, *s.* satellite *m.*

satire, *s.* satire *f.*

satisfaction, *s.* satisfaction *f.*

satisfactory, *adj.* satisfaisant.

satisfy, *v.a.* satisfaire.

Saturday, *s.* samedi *m.*

sauce, *s.* sauce *f.*

sausage, *s.* saucisse *f.*

save, *v. a.* sauver; *(spare)* épargner, gagner; *v.n.* économiser.

savings-bank, *s.* caisse *f.* d'épargne.

Saviour, *s.* Sauveur *m.*

saw, *s.* scie *f.;* – *v.a. & n.* scier.

say, *v. a.* dire; *that is to* ∼ c'est-à-dire.

scale¹, *s.* plateau (de balance) *m.; (pair of)*

∼s balance *f.;* – *v. a.* peser.

scale², *s.* échelle *f.; (music)* gamme *f.*

scale³, *s. (fish)* écaille *f.*

scanty, *adj.* maigre.

scar, *s.* cicatrice *f.*

scarce, *adj.* rare.

scarcely, *adv.* à peine.

scare, *s.* panique *f.;* – *v.a.* effrayer.

scarf, *s.* écharpe *f.,* foulard *m.*

scarlet, *adj.* écarlate.

scatter, *v.a.* disperser; éparpiller; dissiper.

scene, *s.* scène *f.; behind the* ∼**s** dans les coulisses.

scenery, *s.* paysage *m.; (theatre)* décor *m.*

scent, *s.* odeur *f.;* parfum *m.; (dog)* flair *m.*

schedule, *s.* liste *f.;* cédule *f.*

scheme, *s.* plan *m.;* projet *m.*

scholar, *s. (child)* écolier, -ère *m.f.; (learned)* savant *m.*

scholarship, *s.* bourse *f.*

school, *s.* école *f.;* classe *f.*

schoolboy, -girl, *s.* écolier, -ère *m. f.*

schoolmaster, *s.* instituteur *m.,* maître *m.* d'école.; *(secondary)* professeur *m.*

schoolmistress, *s.* maîtresse *f.* d'école; *(secondary)* professeur *m.*

schoolroom, *s.* (salle de) classe *f.*

science, *s.* science *f.*

scientific, *adj.* scientifique.

scientist, *s.* savant *m.*

scissors, *s. pl.* ciseaux *m. pl.*

scold, *v.a.* gronder.

scoop, *s.* écope *f.*

scooter, *s.* scooter *m.*

scope, *s.* portée *f.;* envergure *f.;* carrière *f.*

scorch, *v.a.* roussir, brûler.

score, *s.* entaille *f.; (sum)* compte *m.; (games)* points *m. pl.,* marque *f.,* score *m.; (twenty)* vingtaine *f.; (music)* partition *f.* — *v.a.* marquer; ~ *out* rayer.

scorn, *s.* mépris *m.*

Scotch, Scottish, Scots, *adj.* écossais.

Scotsman, *s.* Écossais *m.*

scout, *s.* éclaireur *m.*

scrambled: ~ *eggs* œufs *m. pl.* brouillés.

scrap, *s.* morceau *m.;* bout *m.*

scrape, *v.a.* gratter; râcler; ~ *off* décrotter.

scratch, *v.a.* gratter; égratigner; *v. n.* griffer gratter; — *s.* égratignure *f.; m.* coup d'ongle.

scream, *v.n.* & *a.* crier; — *s.* cri *m.*

screen, *s.* écran *m.*

screw, *s.* vis *f.*

scrub, *v.a.* frotter; nettoyer à la brosse.

scrupulous, *adj.* scrupuleux.

sculptor, *s.* sculpteur *m.*

sculpture, *s.* sculpture *f.;* — *v.a.* sculpter.

scythe, *s.* faux *f.*

sea, *s.* mer *f.; by* ~ par (voie de) mer.

seal[1]**,** *s. (animal)* phoque *m.*

seal[2]**,** *s.* sceau *m.;* — *v.a.* sceller; cacheter.

seam, *s.* couture *f.*

seaport, *s.* port *m.* de mer.

search, *v.a.* chercher; — *s.* recherche *f.*

search-light, *s.* projecteur *m.*

seasickness, *s.* mal *m.* de mer.

seaside, *s.* bord *m.* de la mer.

season, *s.* saison *f.*

seat, *s.* siège *m.;* — *v.a.* asseoir; placer.

second, *adj.* second; deux; deuxième; — *s.* seconde *f.*

secondary, *adj.* secondaire; ~ *school* école *f.* secondaire.

second-hand, *adj.* de seconde main, d'occasion.

secret, *adj.* & *s.* secret *(m.).*

secretary, *s.* secrétaire *m. f.*

section, *s.* section *f.*

secular, *adj.* séculier.

secure, *adj.* en sûreté, sûr; — *v.a.* mettre en sûreté; obtenir; fixer.

security, *s.* sécurité *f.;* caution *f.;* sûreté *f.;* *securities* valeurs *f. pl.; social* ~ sécurité sociale.

sediment, *s.* sédiment *m.*

see, *v.a.* voir; *(under-*

stand) comprendre;
(make sure) s'assurer;
(accompany) accompagner; ~ *about* s'occuper de; ~ *out* accompagner jusqu'à la porte;
~ *through* voir à travers, pénétrer; mener à bonne fin; ~ *to* veiller à, s'occuper de.

seed, *s.* semence *f.*; graine *f.*

seek, *v.a.* chercher.

seem, *v.n.* sembler, paraître.

seize, *v.a.* saisir; prendre.

seldom, *adv.* rarement.

select, *v.a.* choisir.

selection, *s.* choix *m.*

self, *s.* moi *m.*

self-conscious, *adj.* gêné.

self-control, *s.* maîtrise *f.* de soi-même.

selfish, *adj.* égoïste.

selfishness, *s.* égoïsme *m.*

self-respect, *s.* respect *m.* de soi.

self-service, *adj.* ~ *restaurant* restaurant à libre service.

sell, *v.a.* vendre; ~ *out* vendre tout son stock; *v. n.* se vendre.

seller, *s.* vendeur, -euse *m. f.*

semaphore, *s.* sémaphore *m.*

semicolon, *s.* point (et) virgule *m.*

senate, *s.* sénat *m.*

senator, *s.* sénateur *m.*

send, *v.a.* envoyer; *(money)* remettre; ~ *back* renvoyer; ~ *for* envoyer chercher; ~

forth exha er; ~ *off* expédier; ~ *on* faire suivre; ~ *out* lancer.

sender, *s.* expéditeur, -trice *m. f.*

sense, *s.* sens *m.*

senseless, *adj.* insensé; sans connaissance.

sensibility, *s.* sensibilité *f.*

sensible, *adj.* sensible; sensé, raisonnable.

sensitive, *adj.* sensible.

sensual, *adj.* sensuel.

sentence, *s.* jugement *m.*; sentence *f.*; phrase *f.*; — *v. a.* condamner.

sentiment, *s.* sentiment *m.*

sentry, *s.* sentinelle *f.*

separate, *adj.* séparé; à part; ~ *v.a.* séparer; *v.n.* se séparer.

separation, *s.* séparation *f.*

September, *s.* septembre *m.*

serenade, *s.* sérénade *f.*

sergeant, *s.* sergent *m.*

series, *s.* série *f.*

serious, *adj.* sérieux.

sermon, *s.* sermon *m.*

servant, *s.* serviteur, -vante *m. f.*; domestique *m. f.*

serve, *v. a. & n.* servir.

service, *s.* service *m.*; utilité *f.*

service-station, *s.* station-service *f.*

session, *s.* séance *f.*, session *f.*

set, *v.a.* mettre, placer; *(limb)* remettre; *(fashion)* donner; *(jewels)* monter; *(watch)* régler; *(problem)* donner; *(appoint)* fixer; *(trap)* tendre; — *v.n. (sun)* se coucher; — ~ about se mettre à; ~ aside mettre de côté; ~ down déposer; noter; ~ forth exposer; ~ in commencer; ~ off, out partir; ~ on pousser (à); ~ up dresser; établir; ~ up for se donner pour. — s ensemble m., assortiment m., collection f.; (tea) service m.; (radio) poste m.; (ornaments) garniture f.; (tennis) set m.; (gang) bande f.; ~ of furniture ameublement m.; ~ of false teeth dentier m.

setting, s. mise f., pose f.; montage m.; installation f.; coucher m.

settle, v. a. fixer; arranger; régler, payer; décider, résoudre; v.n. s'établir; se poser (sur); se décider à; ~ down s'établir.

settlement, s. colonie f.

seven, adj. & s. sept.

seventeen, adj. dix-sept.

seventh, adj. septième.

seventy, adj. & s. soixante-dix.

several, adj. plusieurs; différent.

severe, adj. sévère.

sew, v.a. coudre.

sewing-machine, s. machine f. à coudre.

sex, s. sexe m.

sexual, adj. sexuel.

shabby, adj. usé, râpé.

shade, s. ombre f.; ombrage m.; — v.a. ombrager.

shadow, s. ombre f.

shady, adj. ombreux.

shaft, s. bois m.; trait m.; flèche f.; arbre m.

shake, v.a. secouer; ébranler; (hands) serrer; v.n. trembler; s'ébranler; — s. secousse f.

shaky, adj. tremblant; branlant; cassé; faible.

shall (future see Grammar); (command) vouloir; (duty) devoir.

shallow, adj. peu profond.

shame, s. honte f.

shameless, adj. éhonté; honteux.

shampoo, s. shampooing m.

shank, s. jambe f.

shape, s. forme f.; — v. a. façonner; former; diriger; v.n. se développer; promettre.

shapeless, adj. sans forme.

share, s. part f.; action f.; have a ~ in contribuer (à); go ~s (in) partager; — v. a. & n. partager.

shareholder, s. actionnaire m. f.

sharp, adj. tranchant; aigu; aigre; piquant; perçant; — s. (music) dièse m.; — adv. net; 9.0 = 9 heures précises.

sharpen, v.a. aiguiser; tailler.

shatter, v.a. fracasser; déranger.

shave, v.a. raser; v.n. se raser.

shawl, s. châle m.

she, pron. elle.

shear, v.a. tondre; cou-

per; — s. (pair of) ~s
cisailles f. pl.

sheath, s. étui; fourreau
m.

shed, v.a. verser; (light)
répandre.

sheep, s. mouton m.

sheer, adj. pur; perpendi-
culaire.

sheet, s. drap m.; (paper)
feuille f.; ~ iron tôle f.

shelf, s. rayon m.

shell, s. (egg, nut) coque
f.; (peas) cosse f.

shelter, s. abri m.; take ~
s'abriter; — v.a. abri-
ter (de); v. n. se mettre
à l'abri (de).

shepherd, s. berger.

shield, s. bouclier m.; écu
m.

shift, s. changement m.;
(work) équipe f.;
make ~ to s'arranger
(de); — v. n. & a. chan-
ger de place.

shine, v. n. briller; rayonner (de); the sun is shining il fait du soleil.

ship, s. vaisseau m., navire
m.; — v. a. embarquer.

shipping, s. embarquement m.; navires m. pl.;
~ company compagnie
f. de navigation.

shipping-agent, s. agent
maritime, m.; (goods)
expéditeur m.

shipwreck, s. naufrage
m.; — v.a. be ~ed
faire naufrage.

shipyard, s. chantier m. de
construction.

shirt, s. chemise f.

shiver, v.n. frissonner;
(cold) grelotter;

shock, s. choc m.; coup
m.; — v.a. choquer;
frapper d'horreur.

shocking, adj. affreux;
choquant.

shoe, s. soulier m.

shoeblack, s. décrotteur
m., cireur m.

shoe-lace, s. lacet m.

shoemaker, s. cordon-
nier m.

shoot, v.a. tirer, fusiller;
lancer; décharger;
(game) chasser; (plant)
pousser; (rays) darder;
(film) tourner; v.n.
tirer; se précipiter, se
lancer; (plant) pousser;
(pain) élancer.

shooting, s. tir m., fusillade f.; (game) chasse
f.; — adj. (pain) lan-
cinant.

shop, s. boutique f.,
magasin m.; — v.n. go
~ping faire des achats
or emplettes.

shop-assistant, s. commis
m.; demoiselle f., ven-
deur, -euse m. f.

shopkeeper, s. marchand,
-e m. f.; commerçant,
-e m. f.

shore, s. rivage m.; rive f.

short, adj. court; petit;
bref, brève; (lacking)
de manque; — adv.
be ~ of manquer de.

shorten, v. a. & n. raccourcir; abréger.

shorthand, s. sténographie f.

shortly, adv. sous peu;
bientôt; brièvement.

shot, s. coup m.; trait m.;
(bullet) balle f., (can-

non) boulet m.

shoulder, s. épaule f.

shout, s. cri m.; – v. a. & n. crier.

shove, v.a. pousser.

shovel, s. pelle f.

show, v.a. montrer; indiquer; manifester; exposer; expliquer; v.n. se montrer; ~ in faire entrer; ~ off étaler; faire ressortir; se donner des airs; ~ out reconduire; ~ up ressortir; – s. blant m.; spectacle m.; parade f.; exposition f.

shower, s. averse f.; – v.a. faire pleuvoir.

shower-bath, s. douche f.

shrill, adj. aigre; aigu, -ë.

shrine, s. châsse f.; lieu saint m.

shrink, v.a. & n. rétrécir; reculer.

shroud, s. linceul m.

shrub, s. arbrisseau m., arbuste m.

shrug, s. haussement m. d'épaules; – v.a. hausser.

shudder, s. frisson m.; – v. n. frissonner (de).

shut, v.a. fermer; (also ~ in) enfermer; ~ off couper; ~ up fermer; se taire.

shutter, s. volet m.

shy, adj. timide.

sick, adj. malade; be ~ vomir; be ~ of être dégoûté de; fall ~ tomber malade.

sickle, s. faucille f.

sickly, adj. maladif; malsain.

sickness, s. maladie f.

side, s. côte m.; bord m.; (team) équipe f.

siege, s. siège m.

sieve, s. crible m.

sift, v.a. cribler.

sigh, s. soupir m.; – v. n. soupirer.

sight, s. vue f.; spectacle m.; ~s curiosités f. pl.

sightseeing: go ~ visiter les curiosités.

sign, s. signe m.; enseigne f.; – v. a. & n. signer; ~ on engager.

signal, s signal m.; – v.a. signaler; v.n.faire des signaux.

signature, s. signature f.

significant, adj. significatif.

signify, v.a. signifier; v.n. importer.

signpost, s. poteau m. indicateur.

silence, s. silence m.

silent, adj. silencieux; muet.

silk, s. soie f.

silly, adj. sot.

silver, s. argent m.; – adj. d'argent; argenté.

similar, adj. semblable.

simple, adj. simple.

simultaneous, adj. simultané.

sin, s. péché m.; – v.n. pécher.

since, adv. & prep. depuis; – conj. depuis que; (because) puisque.

sincere, adj. sincère.

sinew, s. tendon m.

sinful, adj. pécheur.

sing, v. a. & n. chanter.

singer, s. chanteur, -euse m. f.; cantatrice f.

single, adj. simple; seul; célibataire; particulier; ~ **ticket** billet m. d'aller.

singular, s. singulier m.; — adj. remarquable; singulier.

sink, v. n. tomber au fond, sombrer; s'enfoncer; baisser; v. a. enfoncer; faire baisser; foncer; couler; — s. évier m.

sinner, s. pécheur, -eresse m. f.

sir, s. monsieur m.; Sir m.

sister, s. sœur f.; (nurse) infirmière f.

sister-in-law, s. belle-sœur f.

sit, v.n. s'asseoir; être assis; rester; ~ **down** s'asseoir; se mettre (à); ~ **for (exam)** se présenter à; ~ **up** se dresser; (at night) veiller.

site, s. emplacement m.; terrain m.; site m.

sitting-room, s. petit salon m.

situation, s. situation f.; (employment) position f.; emploi m.

six, adj. & s. six (m.).

sixteen, adj. & s. seize (m.).

sixth, adj. sixième; six.

sixty, adj. & s. soixante.

size, s. grandeur f., mesure f.; (shoes etc.) pointure f.; numéro m., taille f.; (pers.) taille f.

skate, v.n. patiner.

skating, s. patinage m.

sketch, s. croquis m.; es-

quisse f.; — v.a. esquisser.

ski, s. ski m.

skid, v.n. déraper.

skier, s. skieur m.

skiff, s. esquif m.

skilful, adj. adroit.

skill, s. adresse f.

skim, v.a. écrémer.

skin, s. peau f.; — v.a. écorcher; peler.

skip, v. a. & n. sauter.

skirt, s. jupe f.

skull, s. crâne m.

sky, s. ciel m. (pl. cieux).

slack, adj. lâche; négligent.

slacken, v.a. ralentir; relâcher; v.n. se relâcher; diminuer.

slacks, s. pl. pantalon m.

slander, s. calomnie f.; — v.a. calomnier.

slant, s. biais m.; — v. a. faire pencher; v. n. être en pente.

slap, s. claque f.; soufflet m.; — v. a. claquer; souffleter.

slate, s. ardoise f.

slaughter, s. massacre m.

slave, s. esclave m. f.

sledge, s. traîneau m.

sleep, s. sommeil m.; go to ~ s'endormir; — v. a. & n. dormir.

sleeping-car, s. wagon-lit m.

sleepy, adj. somnolent; be ~ avoir sommeil.

sleeve, s. manche f.

slender, adj. mince, faible.

slice, s. tranche f.

slide, s. glissade f.; (photo) diapositive f.

slight, adj. mince; léger.

slim, *adj.* mince, svelte.
sling, *s.* fronde *f.*
slip, *v.n.* glisser; se glisser (dans); *v.a.* filer; pousser, glisser; ~ *off* ôter; ~ *on* mettre; ~ *out* s'esquiver; — *s.* glissade *f.; (mistake)* faux pas *m.; (paper)* fiche *f.; (underwear)* combinaison *f.*
slipper, *s.* pantoufle *f.*
slope, *s.* biais *m.;* pente *f.; — v. n.* incliner.
slot, *s.* fente *f.*
slow, *adj.* lent; *(clock)* en retard; *(dull)* peu intelligent; ~ *to* lent à; — *v.n. & a.* ~ *down* ralentir.
slumber, *s.* sommeil *m.;* — *v.n.* sommeiller.
slump, *s.* débâcle *f.; (in trade)* mévente *f.;* dépression *f.*
sly, *adj.* rusé.
small, *adj.* petit; faible; peu important; menu.
smart, *adj. (clever)* habile, débrouillard; *(witty)* spirituel; *(dress, pers.)* élégant, chic, pimpant; *(society)* élégant.
smash, *v. a.* briser; *fig.* écraser; — *s.* fracas *m.;* collision *f.*
smear, *v.a.* enduire; — *s.* tache *f.*
smell, *s.* odorat *m.;* odeur *f.; — v. a. & n.* sentir; ~ *out* flairer.
smile, *s.* sourire *m.;* — *v.n.* sourire (at à).
smoke, *s.* fumée *f.;* — *v.a. & n.* fumer.

smooth, *adj.* lisse; uni; doux, -ce; *(sea)* calme; — *v.a.* aplanir; lisser.
smuggle, *v.a.* ~ *in* faire passer en contrebande; *v.n.* faire la contrebande.
smuggler, *s.* contrebandier *m.*
snack, *s.* morceau (sur le pouce) *m.; have a* ~ casser la croûte.
snail, *s.* colimaçon *m.*
snake, *s.* serpent *m.*
snap, *s.* fermoir *m.;* coup *m.* de dents; claquement *m.; (photo)* instantané *m.; — v. a.* faire claquer; fermer; ~ *at* happer; ~ *off* casser.
snapshot, *s.* instantané *m.*
snatch, *s.* action de saisir, *f.; (in trade)* fragment *m.; — v. a.* saisir; ~ *at* saisir au vol.
sneeze, *v. n.* éternuer; — *s.* éternuement *m.*
sniff, *v.a.&n.* renifler.
snore, *v. n.* ronfler.
snow, *s.* neige *f.; — v.n.* neiger.
snug, *adj.* commode.
so, *adv.* ainsi; si; donc; ~ *that* de sorte que; afin que.
soak, *v.n.* tremper.
soap, *s.* savon *m.*
soar, *v.n.* prendre son essor; *fig.* s'élancer.
sob, *v.n.* sangloter; — *s.* sanglot.
sober, *adj.* sobre; sensé;
social, *adj.* social.
socialism, *s.* socialisme *m.*
society, *s.* société *f.*
sock, *s.* chaussette *f.*

socket, *s.* cavité *f.; (electric)* prise *f.* de contact.

soda-water, *s.* eau *f.* de Seltz.

sofa, *s.* canapé *m.*

soft, *adj.* mou, mol molle; doux, -ce.

soil, *s.* terroir; *(stain)* tache; — *v. a.* souiller.

soldier, *s.* soldat *m.*

sole¹, *s.* plante *f.;* semelle *f.; (fish)* sole *f.*

sole², *adj.* seul.

solicit, *v. a.* solliciter.

solicitor, *s.* avoué *m.* solicitor *m.*

solidarity, *s.* solidarité *f.*

solitude, *s.* solitude *f.*

solution, *s.* solution *f.*

solve, *v.a.* résoudre.

some, *adj.* quelque; de; — *pron.* quelques-uns; les uns; en *(+ verb)* — *adv.* environ.

somebody, -one, *pron.* quelqu'un.

somehow, *adv.* d'une façon quelconque; *∼ or other* d'une façon ou d'une autre.

something, *s. & pron.* quelque chose *m.*

sometime, *adv.* quelque jour, autrefois.

sometimes, *adv.* quelquefois, parfois.

somewhere, *adv.* quelque part.

son, *s.* fils *m.*

song, *s.* chanson *f.*

son-in-law, *s.* gendre *m.*

soon, *adv.* bientôt.

sore, *adj.* douloureux; *have a ∼ ...* avoir mal à ...; — *s.* plaie *f.*

sorrow, *s.* douleur *f.*

sorry, *adj.* be *∼ for* regretter; *∼!* pardon!

sort, *s.* sorte *f.;* genre *m.;* type *m.; ∼ of* une espèce de.

soul, *s.* âme *f.*

sound¹, *s.* son *m.;* bruit *m.;* — *v. n.* sonner; — *v.a.* sonner; sonder; *(physician)* ausculter.

sound², *adj.* sain; solide; droit; profond; en bon état.

soup, *s.* potage *m.;(clear)* consommé *m.; (thick)* soupe *f.*

sour, *adj.* aigre; acide; *(milk)* tourné.

source, *s.* source *f.*

south, *s.* sud *m.,* midi *m.;* — *adj.* sud; du sud; — *adv.* vers le sud.

southeast, *adj. & s.* sud-est *(m.);* — *adv.* vers le sud-est.

southern, *adj.* du sud.

southwest, *adj. & s.* sud-ouest *(m.);* — *adv.* vers le sud-ouest.

sovereign, *s.* souverain, -e *m. f.*

sow¹, *v. a. & n.* semer (de).

sow², *s.* truie *f.*

space, *s.* espace *m.*

space-craft, -ship, -vehicle, *s.* astronef *m.*

space-flight, *s.* navigation *f.* astronautique.

spaceman, *s.* cosmonaute *m.,* astronaute *m.*

spade, *s.* bêche *f.; (cards)* pique *m.*

span, *s.* empan *m.;* ouverture; — *v.a.* traverser; couvrir.

Spaniard, *s.* Espagnol, -e.

Spanish, *adj. & s.* espagnol *(m.).*

spanner, *s.* clef *f.*

spare, *adj.* maigre; disponible; de réserve; ~ *parts* pièces de rechange *f. pl.;* ~ *time* loisir *m.;* — *v.a.* épargner; économiser; *(evade)* éviter.

spark, *s.* étincelle *f.*

sparrow, *s.* moineau *m.*

speak, *v.n.* parler; *v.a.* dire; ~ *out* parler hardiment; ~ *up* parler plus haut; ... ~*ing* ici ...

spear, *s.* lance *f.*

special, *adj.* spécial.

specialist, *s.* spécialiste *m. f.*

specific, *adj.* spécifique.

specify, *v.a.* spécifier.

speck, *s.* grain *m.;* tache *f.*

spectacles, *s. pl.* lunettes *f.*

spectacular, *adj.* impressionnant.

spectator, *s.* spectateur, -trice *m. f.*

speech, *s.* parole *f.;* langage *m.; (address)* discours *m.*

speed, *s.* vitesse *f.*

speedy, *adj.* rapide; prompt.

spell[1], *v.a. & n.* épeler; orthographier, écrire; *how is it spelt?* comment cela s'écrit-il?

spell[2], *s.* période *f.;* tour *m.*

spelling, *s.* ortographe *f.*

spend, *v.a.* dépenser; *(time)* passer; *v.n.* dépenser.

sphere, *s.* sphère *f.*

spice, *s.* épice *f.*

spider, *s.* araignée *f.*

spill, *v.a.* répandre; renverser.

spin, *v.a. & n.* filer; faire tourner.

spinach, *s.* épinards *m. pl.*

spine, *s.* épine (dorsale) *f.*

spinster, *s.* vieille fille *f.;* célibataire *f.*

spiral, *adj.* en spirale.

spire, *s.* flèche *f.*

spirit, *s.* esprit *m.;* âme *f.;* spectre *m.;* caractère *m.,* cœur *m.;* ~*s* spiritueux *m. pl.*

spiritual, *adj.* spirituel.

spit, *s.* crachat *m.;* — *v. a. & n.* cracher.

spite, *s.* dépit *m.; in* ~ *of* malgré.

splash, *s.* éclaboussement *m.;* — *v. a. & n.* éclabousser (de).

spleen, *s.* rate *f.*

splendid, *adj.* splendide.

splinter, *s.* éclat *m.; (bone)* esquille *f.*

split, *v. a.* fendre; (also ~ *up)* partager; *v.n.* se fendre; se diviser.

spoil, *v.a.* gâter; dépouiller (de); endommager; *v.n.* se gâter.

sponge, *s.* éponge *f.*

spontaneous, *adj.* spontané.

spoon, *s.* cuiller *f.*

spoonful, *s.* cuillerée *f.*

sport, *s.* sport *m.;* amusements *m. pl.*

sportsman, *s.* sportsman *m.*

spot, *s.* tache *f.; (place)* endroit *m.;* — *v.a.* tacher; reconnaître.

spout, *s.* gouttière *f.;* bec

m.; — *v.a.* lancer.

sprain, *v.a.* donner une entorse (à).

spray, *s.* embrun *m.;* vaporisateur *m.;* atomiseur *m.;* — *v.a.* vaporiser, atomiser; arroser.

spread, *v.a.* étendre; répandre; *(cloth)* mettre; *(cover)* couvrir; *(news)* faire circuler; *v.n.* s'étendre; — *s.* propagation *f.;* étendue *f.*

spring[1], *s.* printemps *m.*

spring[2], *v.n.* sauter; pousser; jaillir; provenir (de), descendre (de), naître (de); ~ *up* se lever vite; jaillir; — *s.* saut *m.; (watch etc.)* ressort *m.*

sprinkle, *v.a.* répandre; asperger (de), arroser.

sprout, *v. & n.* germer; pousser; — *s.* pousse *f.; Brussels* ~s choux *m. pl.* de Bruxelles

spur, *s.* éperon *m.,* aiguillon *m.;* — *v. a.* éperonner; ~ *on* pousser à.

spy, *s.* espion, -onne *m. f.;* — *v.n.* espionner.

squander, *v. a.* gaspiller.

square, *s.* carré *m.; (town)* place *f.;* — *adj.* carré; honnête.

squeeze, *v.a.* serrer; presser.

squint, *v.n.* loucher; — *s.* strabisme *m.*

squire, *s.* écuyer *m.;* châtelain *m.*

squirrel, *s.* écureuil *m.*

stability, *s.* stabilité *f.*

stable, *s.* écurie *f.;* — *adj.*

stable.

stack, *s.* pile *f.;* meule *f.*

stadium, *s.* stade *m.*

staff, *s.* état-major *m.;* bâton *m.;* hampe *f.; (institution)* personnel *m.;* ~ *officer* officier d'état-major *m.*

stag, *s.* cerf *m.*

stage, *s.* scène *f.; (drama)* théâtre *m.; (period)* période *f.; (platform)* estrade *f.;* — *v.a.* mettre en scène.

stagger, *v.n.* chanceler; *v.a.* bouleverser.

stain, *s.* tache *f.;* — *v.a.* tacher; salir.

stair, *s.* marche; ~s escalier *m.*

staircase, *s.* escalier *m.*

stake, *s.* pieu *m.; at* ~ en jeu; — *v.a.* garnir de pieux; mettre au jeu; jouer.

stale, *adj.* rassis.

stall, *s.* stalle *f.;* fauteuil *m.; (books)* kiosque *m.* à journaux.

stammer, *v. n.* bégayer.

stamp, *s.* timbre-poste *m.;* estampe *f.;* contrôle *m.;* empreinte *f.;* — *v.a.* timbrer; estamper; contrôler.

stand, *v.n.* être debout, se tenir debout, se soutenir; *(be situated)* se trouver; *(remain)* rester; ~ *out* ressortir; ~ *up* se lever; — *s.* position *f.; (vehicles)* station *f.; (stall)* étalage *m.;* stand *m.*

standard, *s.* étendard *m.;* étalon *m.;* niveau *m.;*

— *adj.* régulateur; au titre; *(authors)* classique.

star, *s.* étoile *f.*

stare, *v.n.* (also ~ at) regarder fixement.

start, *v.n.* partir; commencer; *v. a.* faire partir; faire lever; commencer; lancer; — *s.* commencement *m.;* départ *m.*

starve, *v.n.* mourir de faim; *v. a.* faire mourir de faim.

state, *s.* état *m.;* — *v. a.* affirmer; porter; déclarer.

statement, *s.* déclaration *f.*

statesman, *s.* homme *m.* d'état.

station, *s.* poste *m.;* endroit *m.; (railway)* gare *f.; (police)* poste *m.* de police.

stationer, *s.* papetier *m.;* ~'s shop papeterie *f.*

statistic(al), *adj.* statistique.

statistics, *s.* statistique *f.*

statue, *s.* statue *f.*

statute, *s.* statut *m.;* ordonnance *f.*

stay, *v.n.* rester; être installé; ~ away rester absent; ~ up veiller.

steady, *adj.* ferme; soutenu; *(pers.)* rangé; — *int.* attention!

steak, *s.* tranche *f.;* bifteck *m.*

steal, *v.a.* voler.

steam, *s.* vapeur *f.*

steamboat, *s.* bateau *m.* à vapeur.

steam-engine, *s.* locomotive *f.*

steel, *s.* acier *m.*

steep, *adj.* raide, escarpé.

steeple, *s.* clocher *m.*

steer, *v.a.* gouverner; diriger.

steering-gear, *s.* appareil *m.* de direction.

steering-wheel, *s.* volant *m.*

stem, *s.* tige *f.;* queue *f.*

step, *s.* pas *m.; (stair)* marche *f.; (ladder)* échelon *m.;* take ~s faire des démarches; — *v.n.* faire un pas; marcher; aller, venir; ~ in entrer.

stepmother, *s.* belle-mère *f.*

stereotype, *s.* cliché *m.*

sterile, *adj.* stérile.

stern, *s.* arrière *m.* — *adj.* sévère.

stew, *s.* ragoût *m.; (fruit)* compote *f.;* — *v.a. (meat)* faire un ragout de; *(fruit)* faire une compote de.

steward, *s.* régisseur *m.;* steward *m.*

stewardess, *s.* hôtesse *f.* de l'air.

stick, *s.* bâton *m.*, canne *f.*, petite branche *f.;* — *v.a.* coller; *v.n.* se coller; ~ on attacher; ~ to rester fidèle à.

sticky, *adj.* gluant.

stiff, *adj.* raide; dur.

still, *adj.* calme — *adv.* toujours; encore; cependant.

sting, *s.* aiguillon *m.;* — *v.a.* & *n.* piquer.

stink, *v.n.* puer; — *s.* puanteur *f.*

stipulate, *v.a.* stipuler.

stir, *v.a.* remuer; exciter; *v.n.* remuer; bouger; — *s.* remuement *m.*

stirrup, *s.* étrier *m.*

stitch, *s.* point *m.;* — *v.a.* & *n.* coudre.

stock, *s.* marchandises *f. pl.;* provision *f.; (tree)* tronc *m.; (cattle)* bestiaux *m. pl.; (finance)* valeurs *f. pl.; Stock Exchange* Bourse *f.*

stockholder, *s.* actionnaire *m. f.*

stocking, *s.* bas *m.*

stomach, *s.* estomac *m.*

stone, *s.* pierre; *(fruit)* noyau *m.;* — *v.a.* lapider.

stony, *adj.* pierreux.

stool, *s.* tabouret *m.,* escabeau *m.*

stop, *v.a.* arrêter; empêcher (de); *(teeth)* plomber; retenir suspendre; *v.n.* s'arrêter; cesser; — *s.* halte *f.;* arrêt *m.; (organ)* jeu *m.; (sign)* signe de ponctuation, *m.*

store, *s.* provision *f.;* ∼*s* grand magasin *m.;* — *v.a.* emmagasiner.

stork, *s.* cigogne *f.*

storm, *s.* orage *m.*

story[1], *s.* histoire *f.*

story[2], *s.* étage *m.*

stout, *adj.* fort; intrépide.

stove, *s.* poêle *m.;* fourneau *m.*

straight, *adj.* droit; honnête; d'aplomb; — *adv.* juste; droit.

straighten, *v.a.* (re)dresser; *v.n.* se redresser.

strain, *s.* effort *m.;* tension *f.;* — *v. a.* tendre; *(filter)* passer; *(muscle)* forcer.

strange, *adj.* étrange(r).

stranger, *s.* étranger -ère *m. f.*

strap, *s.* courroie *f.*

straw, *s.* paille *f.*

strawberry, *s.* fraise *f.*

stray, *adj.* égaré; — *v. n.* errer.

streak, *s.* raie *f.;* bande *f.*

stream, *s.* courant *m.;* — *v.n.* couler, ruisseler.

street, *s.* rue *f.*

strength, *s.* force *f.*

strengthen, *v.a.* fortifier.

stress, *s.* force *f.; (grammar)* accent *m.*

stretch, *s.* effort *m.;* étendue *f.;* — *v.a.* étendre; élargir.

stretcher, *s.* brancard *m.*

strew, *v.a.* semer.

strict, *adj.* strict.

stride, *s.* enjambée *f.;* grand pas *m.;* — *v. n.* enjamber.

strike, *v.a.* frapper; *(blow)* asséner; *(work)* cesser; *v.n.* frapper; *(clock)* sonner; *(workers)* se mettre en grève — *s.* grève *f.; be on* ∼ être en grève.

striking, *adj.* frappant.

string, *s.* ficelle *f.;* corde *f.*

strip, *s.* bande *f.;* bout

m.; — v. a. déshabiller; *v.n.* se déshabiller.

stripe, *s.* bande *f.*

strip-lighting, *s.* éclairage *m.* par luminescent.

strive, *v. n.* s'efforcer (de).

stroke, *s.* coup *m.; (swimming)* brasse *f.; (pen)* trait *m.*

strong, *adj.* fort; vigoureux; puissant; solide.

structure, *s.* structure *f.*

struggle, *v.n.* lutter (avec); faire de grands efforts (pour); — *s.* lutte *f.;* mêlée *f.*

stub, *s.* souche *f.;* bout *m.*

stubborn, *adj.* obstiné.

stud, *s.* bouton *m.*

student, *s.* étudiant, -e *m. f.*

studio, *s.* atelier *m.*

study, *s.* étude *f.;* cabinet *m.* de travail — *v. a. & n.* étudier.

stuff, *s.* étoffe *f.;* materiaux *m.pl.; — v.a.* remplir; fourrer.

stumble, *v.n.* trébucher; ~ *(up)on* tomber sur; — *s.* faux pas *m.*

stump, *s.* souche *f.; — v.a.* estomper.

stupid, *adj.* stupide.

style, *s.* style *m.*

subject, *s.* sujet, -te *m. f.; — adj.* ~ *to* sujet à; — *v.a.* assujettir (à).

submarine, *s.* sous-marin *m.*

submission, *s.* soumission *f.*

submit, *v.a.* soumettre.

subordinate, *adj. & s.* subordonné; — *v.a.*

subordonner.

subscribe, *v.a. & n.* (~ *to*) souscrire (à); s'abonner (à).

subscriber, *s.* souscripteur *m.;* abonné; -e souscripteur *m.;* abonné, -e *m. f.*

subscription, *s.* souscription *f.;* abonnement *m.*

subsequent, *adj.* subséquent.

subsequently, *adv.* par la suite.

subsidy, *s.* subside *m.*

subsist, *v. n.* exister; subsister (de).

subsistence, *s.* subsistance *f.*

substance, *s.* substance *f.*

substantial, *adj.* substantiel.

substantive, *s.* substantif *m.*

substitute, *v.a.* substituer *(for* à).

substitution, *s.* substitution *f.*

subtle, *adj.* subtil.

subtract, *v.a.* soustraire.

subtraction, *s.* soustraction *f.*

suburb, *s.* faubourg *m.;* ~s banlieue *f.*

subway, *s.* souterrain *m.;* métro *m.*

succeed, *v.a.* succéder (à); *v.n. (be successful)* réussir (à); faire ses affaires; ~ *to* succéder à.

success, *s.* succès *m.*

successful, *adj.* heureux, *(exam)* reçu.

succession, *s.* succession *f.*

successive, *adj.* successif.
such, *adj.* tel, -le; ~ *and* ~ tel(le) ou tel(le); — *pron.* ~ *as* ceux, celles.
suck, *v. a. & n.* sucer; — *s. give* ~ *to* allaiter.
sudden, *adj.* soudain.
suddenly, *adv.* soudain.
suet, *s.* graisse *f.* de rognon.
suffer, *v. a. & n.* souffrir.
sufficient, *adj.* suffisant.
sufficiently, *adv.* suffisamment.
sugar, *s.* sucre *m.*
suggest, *v.a.* suggérer; proposer.
suggestion, *s.* suggestion *f.*
suicide, *s.* suicide *m.*
suit, *s. (clothes)* complet *m.; (cards)* couleur *f.; (law)* procès *m.; (request)* requête *f.;* — *v.a.* convenir (à); adapter (à); *v.n.* convenir (à); aller (avec).
suitable, *adj.* convenable; ~ *for* adapté à.
suitcase, *s.* mallette *f.,* valise *f.*
sum, *s.* somme *f.;* ~ *total* somme totale, *f.;* — *v.a.* ~ *up* résumer.
summary, *s.* résumé *m.*
summer, *s.* été *m.*
summon, *v.a.* convoquer; appeler.
sun, *s.* soleil *m.*
Sunday, *s.* dimanche *m.*
sunny, *adj.* ensoleillé; exposé au soleil.
sunrise, *s.* lever *m.* du soleil.

sunset, *s.* coucher *m.* du soleil.
sunshine, *s.* soleil *m.*
sunstroke, *s.* coup *m.* de soleil.
superannuate, *v. a.* mettre à la retraite.
superficial, *adj.* superficiel.
superfluous, *adj.* superflu.
superior, *s. & adj.* supérieur *(m.).*
supermarket, *s.* supermarché *m.*
supersonic, *adj.* supersonique.
superstition, *s.* superstition *f.*
superstitious, *adj.* superstitieux.
supervise, *v.a.* surveiller.
supervision, *s.* surveillance *f.*
supper, *s.* souper *m.*
supplement, *s.* supplément *m.; — v.a.* suppléer (à).
supplementary, *adj.* supplémentaire.
supply, *s.* provision *f.;* approvisionnement *m.;* ~ *and demand* l'offre et la demande; — *v.a.* fourner (de); suppléer.
support, *s.* appui *m.;* support *m.; — v.a.* supporter; soutenir; appuyer.
suppose, *v.a.* supposer.
supposition, *s.* supposition *f.*
suppress, *v.a.* supprimer.
suppression, *s.* suppression *f.;* répression *f.*
supreme, *adj.* suprême.

sure, *adj.* sûr; *be ~ to* ne pas manquer de; *make ~ that* s'assurer que.

surely, *adv.* sûrement.

surface, *s.* surface *f.*

surgeon, *s.* chirurgien *m.*

surgery, *s.* chirurgie *f.*

surname, *s.* nom *m.* de famille.

surpass, *v.a.* surpasser.

surprise, *s.* surprise *f.;* — *v.a.* surprendre.

surprising, *adj.* surprenant.

surrender, *s.* abandon *m.;* reddition *f.;* — *v.a.* rendre; renoncer; *v.n.* se rendre.

surround, *v.a.* entourer (de).

surroundings, *s. pl.* environs *m. pl.;* entourage *m.*

survey, *s.* vue *f.;* examen *m.;* — *v.a.* contempler, regarder; examiner; expertiser.

survive, *v. n. & a.* survivre (à).

suspect, *adj. & s.* suspect, -e *(m. f.);* — *v. a. & n.* soupçonner.

suspenders, *s. pl.* jarretelles *f. pl.*

suspicion, *s.* soupçon *m.*

suspicious, *adj.* soupçonneux; suspect.

swallow¹, *s.* hirondelle *f.*

swallow², *v. a.* avaler; gober.

swan, *s.* cygne *m.*

swarm, *s.* essaim *m.;* foule *f.;* — *v.n.* essaimer; s'assembler en foule.

swear, *v.a.* jurer; prêter; *v.n.* jurer.

sweat, *s.* sueur *f.;* — *v.a.* exploiter; *v.n.* suer.

Swede, *s.* Suédois, -e *m. f.*

Swedish, *adj. & s.* suédois *(m.).*

sweep, *v.a.* balayer; *(chimney)* ramoner; — *s.* coup *m.* de balai; courbe *f.;* grand geste *m.;* *(pers.)* ramoneur *m.*

sweet, *adj.* doux; *(pers.)* gentil; — *s.* bonbon *m.;* entremets *m.*

sweetheart, *s. (pers.)* bien-aimé, -ée *m. f.;* ~! mon amour!, ma chérie!

swell, *v.n.* (s')enfler; se gonfler; grossir; *v.a.* gonfler; bouffir; — *s.* houle *f.;* élévation *f.*

swim, *v. n.* nager; aller à la nage; flotter; *v.a.* nager; — *s. have a ~* aller nager.

swimmer, *s.* nageur, -euse *m. f.*

swimming-pool, *s.* piscine *f.*

swine, *s.* cochon *m.*

swing, *s.* va-et-vient *m.;* rythme *m.;* *(for children)* escarpolette *f.* balançoire *f.;* — *v.a.* balancer; *v. n.* osciller; se balancer.

Swiss, *adj.* suisse; — *s.* Suisse *m. f.*

switch, *s.* badine *f.;* aiguille *f.;* interrupteur *m.,* commutateur *m.;* — *v.a.* cingler; aiguiller; couper; ~ *off* couper (le courant);

~ *on* donner (le courant), tourner (le bouton).

sword, *s.* épée *f.*; sabre *m.*

syllable, *s.* syllabe *f.*

symbol, *s.* symbole *m.*

symmetrical, *adj* symétrique.

symmetry, *s.* symétrie *f.*

sympathy, *s.* sympathie *f.*

symphony, *s.* symphonie *f.*

synagogue, *s.* synagogue *f.*

synthetic, *adj.* synthétique.

syringe, *s.* seringue *f.*

syrup, *s.* sirop *m.*

system, *s.* système *m.*

systematic(al), *adj.* systématique.

T

table, *s.* table *f.*; *clear the* ~ desservir; *lay the* ~ mettre le couvert.

table-cloth, *s.* nappe *f.*

table-spoon, *s.* cuiller *f.* à soupe.

tablet, *s.* tablette *f.*

tack, *s.* broquette *f.*, petit clou *m.*

tackle, *s.* attirail *m.*; apparaux *m. pl.*; — *v.a.* saisir à bras le corps; *(problem)* essayer de résoudre.

tact, *s.* tact *m.*

tag, *s.* ferret *m.*; étiquette (volante) *f.*; bout *m.*

tail, *s.* queue *f.*

tailor, *s.* tailleur *m.*

take, *v.a.* prendre; *(carry)* porter; *(walk)* faire; ~ *after* ressembler à; ~ *away* enlever; ~ *down* descendre, *(write)* prendre (par écrit); ~ *in (paper)* s'abonner à; ~ *off* ôter; *(v.n.)* prendre son élan; ~ *on* se charger de; ~ *to* se mettre à; ~ *up* ramasser, relever.

tale, *s.* conte *m.*, histoire *f.*

talent, *s.* talent *m.*

talk, *v.a. & n.* parler *(about, of* de); ~*ing of* à propos de; — *s.* conversation *f.*; causerie *f.*

tall, *adj.* grand; *how* ~ *is he?* quelle est sa taille?

tame, *adj.* apprivoisé.

tan, *s.* tan *m.*

tank, *s.* réservoir *m.*; char *m.* d'assaut.

t ankard, *s.* chope *f.*

tap, *s.* robinet *m.*; *(blow)* tape *f.*; petit coup *m.*; — *v.a.* mettre en perce; *(strike)* frapper légèrement, taper.

tape, *s.* ruban *m.* (de coton).

tape-recorder, *s.* magnétophone *m.*

tapestry, *s.* tapisserie *f.*

target, *s.* cible *f.*

tariff, *s.* tarif *m.*

tart, *s.* tarte *f.*

task, *s.* tâche *f.*; *(school)* devoir *m.*

taste, *s.* goût *m.*

tasteless, *adj.* sans saveur.

tasty, *adj.* savoureux,

de bon goût.

tatter, s. lambeau m.

tavern, s. taverne f.

tax, s. impôt m.; ~ *free* exempt d'impôts.

taxi, s. taxi m.

tea, s. thé m.

teach, v.a. enseigner, instruire; *(how to)* apprendre (à).

teacher, s. instituteur, -trice m. f.; professeur m. f.

teaching, s. enseignement m.

team, s. équipe f.

tea-pot, s. théière f.

tear[1], s. *(eye)* larme f.

tear[2], v.a. déchirer; ~ *away, down, out* arracher; ~ *up* déchirer; — s. déchirure f.

tease, v.a. taquiner.

tea-spoon, s. cuiller f. à thé.

technical, adj. technique.

technique, s. technique f.

technology, s. technologie f.

tedious, adj. ennuyeux.

teenager, s. adolescent, -e m. f.

telecast, v.a. téléviser.

telegram, s. télégramme m.

telegraph, s. télégraphe m.

telephone, s. téléphone m.; — v.a. & n. téléphoner *(to* à).

telescope, s. télescope m.; réfracteur m.; — v.a. télescoper.

televise, v.a. téléviser.

television, s. télévision f.

television-set, s. appareil m. de TV, téléviseur m.

telex, s. télex m.

tell, v.a. dire; raconter; distinguer; ~ *s.o. to do sth.* enjoindre, dire à qn de faire qch.

temper, s. colère f.; tempérament m.

temperature, s. température f.

temporary, adj. temporaire.

tempt, v.a. tenter.

ten, adj. & s. dix *(m.).*

tenant, s. locataire m. f.

tend, v.n. tendre (à).

tendency, s. tendance f.

tender[1], v.a. offrir; ~ *for* soumissionner; — s. soumission f.

tender[2], adj. tendre.

tennis, s. tennis m.

tension, s. tension f.

tent, s. tente f.

tenth, adj. dixième; dix.

term, s. terme m.; *(school)* trimestre m.; *be on good* ~s être bien (avec); — v.a. appeler.

terminate, v.a. terminer; vn. se terminer.

terminus, s, *(gare* f.) terminus m.

terrace, s. terrasse f.

terrible, adj. terrible.

territory, s. territoire m.

test, s. épreuve f.; examen m.; *(school)* composition f., *(oral)* épreuve f.; orale — v.a. mettre à l'épreuve.

testify, v.a. affirmer.

testimony, s. témoignage m.

text, *s.* texte *m.*

text-book, *s.* manuel *m.*

textile, *s.* textile *m.*

than, *conj.* que; *(with numbers)* de.

thank, *v.a.* remercier; ~ you merci; — *s.* ~s remerciements *m. pl.;* merci.

thankful, *adj.* reconnaissant.

that[1], *adj.* ce, cet, cette' ces; — *pron.* celui, celle, ceux; cela; ~'s it c'est cela.

that[2], *conj.* que.

the, *art.* le, la, les; ce, cet, cette; ces.

theatre, *s.* théâtre *m.*

their, *pron.* leur, leurs.

theirs, *pron.* le leur, la leur, les leurs; à eux, à elles.

them, *pron.* les; leur; eux, elles.

theme, *s.* thème *m.;* sujet *m.*

themselves, *pron.* se; eux-mêmes, elles-mêmes.

then, *adv.* alors; *(after that)* puis; *(consequently)* donc.

theology, *s.* théologie *f.*

theoretical, *adj.* théorique.

theory, *s.* théorie *f.*

there, *adv.* là; *(with verb)* y; ~ is, are il y a.

therefore *adv.* donc.

thermometer, *s.* thermomètre *m.*

thermos, *s.* thermos *f.*

they, *pron.* ils, elles; ~ say on dit

thick, *adj.* épais.

thief, *s.* voleur, -euse *m. f.*

thigh, *s.* cuisse *f.*

thimble, *s.* dé *m.*

thin, *adj.* mince; maigre; *fig.* pauvre.

thing, *s.* chose *f.;* ~s effets *m. pl.*

think, *v.a.* croire; concevoir; *v.n.* croire; penser *(about, of* à); ~ out élaborer; ~ over réfléchir à, penser.

third, *adj.* troisième; trois; — *s.* tiers *m.*

thirsty, *adj.* altéré; *be* ~ avoir soif.

thirteen, *adj. & s.* treize *(m.).*

thirty, *adj. & s.* trente *(m.).*

this, *pl.* these, *pron.* cela, — *adj.* ceci; ce, cet, cette; ces.

thorn, *s.* épine *f.*

thorough, *adj.* profond, complet; consommé.

thoroughfare, *s.* artère *f.* principal, grande rue *f.; no* ~ rue barrée, passage interdit.

thoroughly, *adv.* tout à fait, à fond.

though, *conj.* quoique, bien que; — *adv.* tout de même.

thought, *s.* pensée *f.;* idée *f.; (care)* souci *m.*

thoughtful, *adj.* pensif; attentif.

thoughtless, *adj.* étourdi; insouciant.

thousand, *s. & adj.* mille *(m.)*

thrash, *v.a.* battre.

thread, *s.* fil *m.; — v. a.*

enfiler.

threat, *s.* menace *f.*

threaten, *v. a. & n.* mena-cer (de).

three, *adj. & s.* trois *(m.).*

threshold, *s.* seuil *m.*

thrifty, *adj.* économe.

thrill, *s.* tressaillement *m.;* — *v. a.* be ~ed with frissonner de.

thrive, *v. n.* prospérer.

throat, *s.* gorge *f.*

throne, *s.* tône *m.*

through, *prep.* à travers; au travers de; par; par suite de; pendant; — *adv.* d'un bout à l'autre; be ~ with avoir fini qch.; — *adj.* direct.

throughout, *prep. & adv.* d'un bout à l'autre.

throw, *v.a.* jeter; ~ away jeter, dissiper; ~ down renverser; jeter à terre; ~ off se débarrasser de; ôter; ~ out rejecter; ~ over abandonner; — *s.* jet *m.*

thrust, *v.a.* fourrer, pousser; enforcer; — *s.* poussée *f.;* botte *f.*

thumb, *s.* pouce *m.*

thunder, *s.* tonnerre *m.;* — *v.n.* tonner.

Thursday, *s.* jeudi *m.*

thus, *adv.* ainsi.

ticket, *s.* billet *m.;* éti-quette *f.*

ticket-collector, *s.* con-trôleur *m.*

tide, *s.* marée *f.;* courant *m.*

tidy, *adj.* propre; bien rangé; *(pers.)* ordonné; — *v.a.* (also ~ up)

mettre en ordre.

tie, *v.a.* attacher; lier; nouer; ~ down lier; ~ up attacher; — *s.* lien *m.;* cravate *f.;* *(sport)* partie *f.* égale.

tiger, *s.* tigre, -esse *m. f.*

tight, *adj.* serré; tendu.

tighten, *v.a.* serrer.

tile, *s.* tuile *f.*

till, *prep.* jusqu'à; — *conj.* jusqu'à ce que.

tilt, *s.* inclinaison *f.;* — *v. n.* s'incliner, pen-cher; *v.a.* pencher.

time, *s.* temps *m.;* mo-ment *m.; (clock)* heure *f.;* *(occasions)* fois; at ~s de temps en temps; by the ~ that avant que; for the ~ being actuellement; what ~ is it? quelle

heure est-il?; have a good ~ s'amuser bien; keep good ~ marcher bien.

timely, *adj.* opportun.

timetable, *s.* horaire *m.;* indicateur *m.; (school)* emploi *m.* du temps.

tin, *s.* étain *m.; (conser-ve)* boîte *f.* (en fer blanc).

tinned, *adj.* en boîte; conservé.

tint, *s.* teinte *f.*

tiny, *adj.* tout petit.

tip¹, *s.* bout *m.;* — *v.a.* renverser; *v.n.* (also ~ over) se renverser.

tip², *s. (money)* pourboi-re *m.;* — *v.a.* don-ner un pourboire (à).

tire¹, tyre, *s.* pneu(mati-que) *m.*

tire², *v.a.* fatiguer; *v.n.* se fatiguer.

tired, *adj.* be ~ of être las de.

tissue, *s.* tissu *m.*

tissue-paper, *s.* papier *m.* de soie.

title, *s.* titre *m.*

to, *prep.* à; vers; en, ce soir.

toast, *s.* rôtie *f.*; *(bread, drink)* toast *m.*; — *v.a.* rôtir.

tobacco, *s.* tabac *m.*

tobacconist, *s.* marchand *m.* de tabac; ~'s débit *m.* de tabac.

today, *adv.* aujourd'hui.

toe, *s.* orteil *m.*, doigt *m.* du pied.

together, *adv.* ensemble; en même temps.

toil, *s.* travail *m.*; — *v.n.* travailler.

toilet, *s.* toilette *f.*

toilet-paper, *s.* papier *m.* hygiénique.

tomato, *s.* tomate *f.*

tomb, *s.* tombeau *m.*

tomorrow, *adv.* demain.

ton, *s.* tonne *f.*

tone, *s.* ton *m.*

tongs, *s. pl.* pincettes *f. pl.*; pince *f.*

tongue, *s.* langue *f.*

tonight, *adv.* cette nuit; ce soir.

tonsil, *s.* amygdale *f.*

too, *adv.* trop; *(also)* aussi.

tool, *s.* outil *m.*; instrument *m.*

tooth, *s.* dent *f.*

toothache, *s.* mal *m.* de dents.

toothbrush, *s.* brosse *f.* à dents.

toothpaste, *s.* pâte *f.* dentifrice.

top, *s.* sommet *m.*, faîte *m.*; dessus *m.*; couvercle *m.*; tête *f.*; premier, -ère *m. f.*; — *v.a.* couronner; dépasser.

topic, *s.* sujet *m.*; ~s of the day actualités *f. pl.*

torch, *s.* torche *f.*

tortoise, *s.* tortue *f.*

toss, *s.* mouvement *m.*; — *v.a.* jeter; lancer en l'air; ballotter; ~ up lancer en l'air.

total, *adj. & s.* total *(m.)*.

totter, *v.n.* chanceler.

touch, *s.* toucher *m.*; attouchement *m.*; touche *f.*; légère *f.* attaque; — *v.a.* toucher.

tough, *adj.* dur; robuste; rude.

tour, *s.* voyage *m.*; tour *m.*; tournée *f.*; — *v.n.* voyager.

tourism, *s.* tourisme *m.*

tourist, *s.* touriste *m.*

tournament, *s.* tournoi *m.*

tow, *s.* étoupe *f.*; remorque *f.*; — *v.a.* remorquer.

toward(s), *prep.* vers; envers; pour.

towel, *s.* essuie-main(s) *m.*, serviette *f.*

tower, *s.* tour *f.*

town, *s.* ville *f.*

town-hall, *s.* hôtel *m.* de ville.

toy, *s.* jouet *m.*; — *v.n.* jouer (avec).

trace, *s.* trace *f.*; trait *m.*; — *v.a.* tracer; ~ back remonter à.

track, *s.* traces *f. pl.;* sentier *m.; (railw.)* voie *f.; (running)* piste *f.*

tractor, *s.* tracteur *m.*

trade, *s.* commerce *m.; (occupation)* métier *m.; v.n.* commercer; **~** *in* faire le commerce de.

trade-mark, *s.* marque *f.* de fabrique.

tradesman, *s.* commerçant *m.*

trade(s)-union, *s.* syndicat *m.*

tradition, *s.* tradition *f.*

traditional, *adj.* traditionnel.

traffic, *s.* trafic *m.;* circulation *f.;* **~** *lights* feux *m.pl.* de signalisation.

tragedy, *s.* tragédie *f.*

tragic(al), *adj.* tragique.

trail, *s.* trace *f.;* — *v.a. & n.* traîner.

train, *s.* train *m.; (series)* suite *f.;* — *v.a.* entraîner; former.

trainer, *s.* entraîneur *m.*

traitor, *s.* traître *m.*

tram, *s.* tramway *m.*

tramp, *v.n.* aller à pied; — *s.* bruit *m.* de pas; *(pers.)* chemineau *m.*

transaction, *s.* transaction *f.*

transfer, *s.* transport *m.;* — *v.a.* transférer.

transform, *v.a.* transformer (en).

transfusion, *s.* transfusion *f.*

transgress, *v.a.* transgresser; *v.n.* pécher.

transistor, *s.* transistor *m.*

transit, *s.* transit *m.; in* **~** en cours de route.

translate, *v.a.* traduire.

translation, *s.* traduction *f.*

translator, *s.* traducteur, -trice *m. f.*

transmission, *s.* transmission *f.*

transmit, *v.a.* transmettre, émettre.

transmitter, *s.* *(poste)* émetteur *m.*

transparency, *s.* diapositive *f.*

transport, *s.* transport *m.;* — *v.a.* transporter.

trap, *s.* piège *m.*

trash, *s.* rebut *m.;* niaiseries *f. pl.*

travel, *v.n.* voyager; — *s.* voyage *m.*

traveller, *s.* voyageur, -euse *m. f.*

tray, *s.* plateau *m.*

treachery, *s.* trahison *f.*

tread, *s.* pas *m.;* — *v.n. & a.* marcher (sur).

treasure, *s.* trésor *m.*

treasury, *s.* trésor *m.;* trésorerie *f.*

treat, *v.a.* traiter.

treatment, *s.* traitement *m.*

treaty, *s.* traité *m.*

tree, *s.* arbre *m.*

tremble, *v.n.* trembler.

tremendous, *adj.* terrible; immense.

trench, *s.* tranchée *f.*

trend, *s.* tendance *f.*

trespass, *v.n.* envahir sans autorisation; **~**

against offenser; ~ *on* abuser de; — *s.* offense *f.*

trial, *s.* essai *m.;* épreuve *f.; (law)* procès *m.*

tribe, *s.* tribu *f.*

tribute, *s.* tribut *m.*

trick, *s.* ruse *f.;* tour *m.;* truc *m.;* — *v.a.* duper.

trifle, *s.* bagatelle *f.;* *a* ~ un peu; — *v.n.* ~ *with* traiter légèrement.

trim, *s.* état *m.;* tenue *f.;* — *adj.* bien tenu; — *v.a.* arranger; garnir, orner; dresser.

trip, *s.* excursion *f.;* voyage *m.;* — *v.a.* ~ *up* faire trébucher.

triumph, *s.* triomphe *m.;* — *v.n.* triompher.

triumphant, *adj.* triomphant.

trolley, *s.* fardier *m.,* diable *m.;* trolley *m.*

trolley-bus, *s.* trolleybus *m.*

troop, *s.* troupe *f.*

trophy, *s.* trophée *m.*

tropic(al), *adj.* tropique.

tropics, *s. pl.* tropiques *m. pl.*

trot, *s.* trot *m.;* — *v.n.* trotter.

trouble, *s.* affliction *f.;* malheur *m.;* dérangement *m.;* difficulté *f.;* — *v.a.* inquiéter; déranger; affliger.

troublesome, *adj.* ennuyeux.

trousers, *s. pl.* pantalon *m.*

trout, *s* truite *f.*

truck, *s.* wagon *m.*

true, *aaj.* vrai; exact; fidèle; *come* ~ se réaliser.

truly, *adv.* vraiment.

trumpet, *s.* trompette *f.;* — *v. a.* proclamer.

trunk, *s.* melle *f. (tree)* tronc *m.*

trunk-call, *s.* appel *m.* interurbain.

trust, *s.* confiance *f.;* espoir *m.;* dépôt *m.;* trust *m.;* — *v.a.* se confier (à); faire crédit (à); *v.n.* espérer; compter sur.

truth, *s.* vérité *f.*

try, *v.a.* essayer, éprouver; *(law)* mettre en jugement; ~ *on* essayer; — *s.* essai *m.*

tub, *s.* bac *m.; (bath)* tub *m.*

tube, *s.* tube *m.;* tuyau *m.;* métro *m.*

Tuesday, *s.* mardi *m.*

tug, *s.* effort *m.;* — *v.a.* tirer; remorquer.

tug-boat, *s.* (bateau) remorqueur *m.*

tuition, *s.* enseignenient *m.*

tumble, *v. n.* tomber.

tumour, *s.* tumeur *f.*

tune, *s.* air *m.;* accord *m.;* harmonie *f.; in* ~ d'accord; *out of* ~ faux; — *v.a.&n.* accorder; ~ *in to* mettre sur; ~ *up* régler; s'accorder.

tunnel, *s.* tunnel *m.*

turbine, *s.* turbine *f.*

turbo-jet: ~ *engine* turboréacteur *m.*

turbo-prop, *s.* turbopropulseur *m.*

turkey, *s.* dindon, din-
de *m. f.*

Turkish, *adj.* turc, -que;
— *s.* Turc, -que *m. f.;*
(lang.) turc *m.*

turn, *v.a.* tourner, détourner; diriger; *v.n.*
tourner; se diriger; de-
venir; avoir recours (à);
~ *about* (se) tourner;
~ *back* retourner; ~
down plier, baisser;
repousser; ~ *upside
down* renverser; ~ *in*
se coucher; ~ *off* fer-
mer, serrer; éteindre;
~ *on* ouvrir; allumer;
~ *over* (se) renverser;
~ *up* arriver, appa-
raître — *s.* tour *m.;* détour *m.; (mind, style)*
tournure *f.; (tide)*
changement *m.*

turning, *s.* tournant *m.*

turnip, *s.* navet *m.*

turnover, *s.* chiffre *m.*
d'affaires.

turret, *s.* tourelle f.

turtle, *s.* tortue f.

tutor, *s.* précepteur *m.;*
— *v.a.* instruire.

twelfth, *adj.* douzième;
douze.

twelve, *adj. & s.* douze
(m.).

twentieth, *adj.* vingtième.

twenty, *adj. & s.* vingt
(m.).

twice, *adv.* deux fois.

twig, *s.* brindille f.

twin, *adj. & s.* jumeau
(m.), jumelle *(f.).*

twist, *s. (road)* coude *f.;*
torsion *f.: — v. a.*
tordre; dénaturer; *v.n.*
s'entortiller.

twitter, *v.n.* gazouiller.

two, *adj. & s.* deux *(m.).*

type, *s.* type *m.;* caractère
m.; — v.a. taper (à
la machine).

type-script, *s.* manuscrit
m. dactylographié.

typewriter, *s.* machine
à écrire, *f.*

typical, *adj.* typique.

typist, *s.* dactilo(graphe)
m. f.

tyre *see* **tire.**

U

udder, *s.* mamelle *f.*

ugly, *adj.* laid.

ulcer, *s.* ulcère *m.*

ultimate, *adj.* final, dernier.

umbrella, *s.* parapluie *m.*

umpire, *s.* arbitre *m. f.*

unable, *adj.* incapable;
~ *to* impuissant à
faire qch.; dans l'im-
possibilité de.

unaccustomed, *adj.* inaccoutumé, peu habitué
(à).

unaided, *adj.* sans aide.

unanimous, *adj.* unanime.

unassisted, *adj.* sans aide.

unaware: *be* ~ *of* ignorer.

unbearable, *adj.* insupportable.

uncertain, *adj.* incertain.

uncertainty, *s.* incerti-
tude *f.*

unchangeable, *adj.* im-
muable.

uncle, *s.* oncle *m.*

uncomfortable, *adj.* peu
confortable.

uncommon, *adj.* rare; extraordinaire.

unconditional, *adj.* sans conditions.

unconscious, *adj.* sans connaissance; ~ *of* sans conscience de.

uncover, *v. a.* découvrir.

undamaged, *adj.* non endommagé.

undefined, *adj.* non défini.

undeniable, *adj.* incontestable.

under, *prep* sous; au-dessous de; dans.

undercarriage, *s.* châssis *m.*, train (d'atterrissage) *m.*

underclothes, *s. pl.* vêtements *m. pl.* de dessous.

underdeveloped, *adj.* sous-développe.

underdone, *adj.* pas assez cuit, saignant.

undergo, *v.a.* subir.

undergraduate, *s.* étudiant, -e (non diplomé) *m. f.*

underground, *s.* métro-(politain) *m.*

underline, *v.a.* souligner.

undermine, *v.a.* miner.

underneath, *prep.* & *adv.* au-dessous (de).

undersigned, *adj.* & *s.* soussigné, -e *(m. f.).*

understand, *v.a.&n.* comprendre; *it is understood that* il est convenu que.

understanding, *s.* entendement *m.;* intelligence *f.*

undertake, *v.a.* entre-

prenøre; ~ *to* se charger de, s'engager à.

undertaking, *s.* entreprise *f.*

underwear, *s.* vêtements *m.pl.* de dessous.

undesirable, *adj.* peu désirable.

undo, *v.a.* défaire.

undress, *v. n.* se déshabiller.

undue, *adj.* indu.

uneasy, *adj.* inquiet; mal à l'aise; incommode.

uneducated, *adj.* sans instruction.

unemployed, *adj.* & *s.* sans travail; *the* ~ les chômeurs *m.*

unemployment, *s.* chômage *m.*

unequal, *adj.* inégal.

uneven, *adj.* inégal; impair.

unexpected, *adj.* inattendu; soudain.

unfair, *adj.* injuste; déloyal.

unfavorable, *adj.* défavorable.

unfortunate, *adj.* malheureux.

unfortunately, *adv.* malheureusement.

unhappy, *adj.* malheureux.

unhealthy, *adj.* maladif; *(place)* insalubre.

uninhabited, *adj.* inhabité.

uninteresting, *adj.* peu intéressant, sans intérêt.

union, *s.* union *f.*

unique, *adj.* unique.

unit, *s.* unité *f.; (motor)*

bloc *m.*

unite, *v.a.* unir; *v.n.* s'unir.

unity, *s.* unité *f.;* harmonie *f.*

universal, *adj.* universel.

university, *s.* université *f.*

unjust, *adj.* injuste.

unkind, *adj.* dur; peu aimable.

unknown, *adj.* inconnu.

unless, *conj.* à moins que... ne; à moins de.

unlike, *adj.* dissemblable.

unload, *v.a.* décharger.

unlock, *v.a.* ouvrir.

unmarried, *adj.* célibataire.

unnatural, *adj.* non naturel, dénaturé.

unnecessary, *adj.* inutile.

unnoticed, *adj.* inaperçu.

unoccupied, *adj.* inoccupé; libre; non occupe.

unpack, *v.a.* déballer.

unpaid, *adj.* impayé.

unparalleled, *adj.* incomparable.

unpleasant, *adj.* désagréable.

unprecedented, *adj.* sans exemple. *or.* précédent.

unprejudiced, *adj.* sans préjugés, impartial.

unprepared, *adj.* non préparé; *be* ~ *for* ne pas s'attendre à qch.

unprofitable, *adj.* peu profitable.

unpromising, *adj.* qui s'annonce mal; peu prometteur.

unqualified, *adj.* non qualifié; sans restriction.

unreal, *adj.* irréel.

unreasonable, *adj.* déraisonnable.

unsatisfactory, *adj.* peu satisfaisant.

unseen, *adj.* invisible; inaperçu.

unsettled, *adj.* non réglé; *(in mind)* indécis; incertain.

unskilled, *adj.* non spécialisé.

unsolved, *adj.* non résolu.

unspeakable, *adj.* inexprimable.

unsteady, *adj.* tremblant; peu fixe; chancelant; inconstant.

unsuccessful, *adj.* malheureux; infructueux.

unsuitable, *adj.* inconvenant; peu propre (à).

untidy, *adj.* sans ordre, malpropre; en désordre.

until, *prep.* jusqu'à; — *conj.* jusqu'à ce que; avant que.

unto, *prep.* jusqu'à.

unusual, *adj.* rare, peu commun.

unwell, *adj.* indisposé; souffrant.

unwilling, *adj.* peu disposé (à).

unworthy, *adj.* indigne.

unyielding, *adj.* inflexible.

up, *adv.* en montant, vers le haut; (en) haut; *go* ~ monter; *be* ~ *in* être fort en; *what's* ~? qu'est-ce qu'il y a?; — *prep.* vers le haut de; en haut; *be* ~ *adj.* montant.

uphill, *adj.* montant; — *adv. go* ~ monter.

uphold, *v.a.* soutenir; appuyer.

upholsterer, *s.* tapissier *m.*

upon, *prep* sur.

upper, *adj.* supérieur; *(deck)* deuxième; *the ~ classes* les hautes classes.

upright, *adj.* droit; honnête.

upset, *v.a.* renverser; *fig.* troubler, bouleverser; — *adj.* renversé; *fig.* dérangé; *be ~* être indisposé.

upside do·n, *adv.* sens dessus dessous.

upstairs, *adv.* en haut; *go ~* monter (l'escalier).

up-to-date, *adj* moderne, à la mode.

upwards, *adv.* en haut, vers le haut, en montant.

urge, *v.a.* prier instamment (de); recommander instamment; pousser en avant.

urgent, *adj.* urgent; pressant.

us, *pron.* nous.

usage, *s.* usage *m.*

use, *v.a.* se servir de; traiter; faire usage (de); consommer; *~ up* user; consommer; *~d to* habitué à; *get ~d to* s'habituer à; — *s.* usage *m.;* emploi *m.;* utilité *f.;* *be of ~* être utile (à); *(of) no ~* inutile; *out of ~* hors d'usage *or* de service.

useful, *adj.* utile (à).

useless, *adj.* inutile.

usher, *s.* *(court)* (huissier) audiencier *m.*

usherette, *s.* *(theatre)* ouvreuse *f.*

usual, *adj.* usuel.

usually, *adv.* ordinairement.

utensil, *s.* ustensile *m.*

utility, *s.* utilité *f.*

utilize, *v.a.* utiliser.

utmost, *adj.* extrême; le plus grand; — *s.* le plus; tout son possible.

utter¹, *adj.* le plus grand; absolu.

utter², *v.a.* dire, prononcer; pousser.

utterance, *s.* prononciation. *f.;* expression *f.;* parole *f.*

V

vacancy, *s.* vacance *f.*

vacant, *adj.* vacant; vide; sans expression.

vacation, *s.* vacances *f. pl.*

vaccinate, *v.a.* vacciner.

vaccination, *s.* vaccination *s.*

vacuum-cleaner, *s.* aspirateur *m.*

vague, *adj.* vague.

vain, *adj.* vain; vaniteux; *in ~* en vain.

valid, *adj.* valide.

validity, *s.* validité *f.*

valley, *s.* vallée *f.*

valuable, *adj.* de valeur.

value, *s.* valeur *f.;* — *v.a.* évaluer; priser.

valve, *s.* soupape *f.;*

lampe *f.*, tube *m.*

van, *s.* fourgon *m.*; camion *m.* de livraison; wagon *m.*

vanish, *v.n.* disparaître; (also ~ *away*) s'évanouir.

vanity, *s.* vanité *f.*

variety, *s.* variété *f.*

various, *adj.* divers.

varnish, *s.* vernis *m.*

vary, *v.a. & n.* varier.

vase, *s.* vase *m.*

vast, *adj.* vaste.

vault, *s.* voûte *f.*; cave *f.*, caveau *m.*

veal, *s.* veau *m.*

vegetable, *s.* légume *m.*

vehicle, *s.* véhicule *m.*

veil, *s.* voile *m.*

vein, *s.* veine *f.*

velvet, *s.* velours *m.*

venison, *s.* venaison *f.*

vent, *s.* ouverture *f.*; *give* ~ *to* donner libre cours à.

ventilation, *s.* ventilation *f.*

ventilator, *s.* ventilateur *m.*

venture, *s.* risque *m.*; hasard *m.*; — *v.a.* risquer; hasarder; *v.n.* ~ (*up*)on se hasarder à, se risquer à.

verb, *s.* verbe *m.*

verdict, *s.* décision *f.*, verdict *m.*

verge, *s.* bord *m.*

verify, *v.a.* vérifier.

verse, *s.* vers *m.*; strophe *f.*

version, *s.* version *f.*

vertical, *adj.* vertical.

very, *adv.* très; ~ *good*

très bien; — *adj.* vrai; même.

vessel, *s.* vaisseau *m.*

vest, *s.* gilet *m.*; chemise *f.* américaine.

vestry, *s.* sacristie *f.*; assemblée *f.*

veterinary, *adj.* ~ *surgeon* vétérinaire *m.*

veto, *s.* véto *m.*; — *v.a.* mettre son véto (à).

vex, *v.a.* vexer.

vibrate, *v.n.* vibrer, osciller.

vibration, *s.* vibration *f.*

vicar, *s.* curé *m.*

vice-, *prefix* vice-.

vicinity, *s.* voisinage *m.*

victim, *s.* victime *f.*

victorious, *adj.* victorieux.

victory, *s.* victoire *f.*

victuals, *s. pl.* victuailles *f. pl.*

view, *s.* vue *f.*; *on* ~ exposé; *have in* ~ se proposer (de); *with a* ~ *to* en vue de; *point of* ~ point *m.* de vue; — *v.a.* voir; regarder; envisager.

viewer, *s.* spectateur, -trice *m. f.*

vigorous, *adj.* vigoureux.

vigour, *s.* vigueur *f.*

village, *s.* village *m.*

villain, *s.* scélérat *m.*

vine, *s.* vigne *f.*

vinegar, *s.* vinaigre *m.*

vineyard, *s.* vignoble *m.*

vintage, *s.* vendange *f.*

violate, *v.a.* violer.

violation, *s.* violation *f.*

violence, *s.* violence *f.*

violent, *adj.* violent.

violet, *s.* violette *f.*; (*colour*) violet *m.*; —

adj. violet.

violin, *s.* violon *m.*

violinist, *s.* violoniste *m. f.*

violoncellist, *s.* violoncelliste *m.*

violoncello, *s.* violoncelle *m.*

virgin, *s.* vierge *f.*

virtue, *s.* vertu *f.*

visa, visé, *s.* visa *m.*

visibility, *s.* visibilité *f.*

visible, *adj.* visible.

vision, *s.* vision *f.*, vue *f.*

visit, *s.* visite *f.*; séjour *m.*; *be on a* ~ *to* être en visite chez; — *v.a.* visiter.

visitor, *s.* visiteur, -euse *m. f.*

vital, *adj.* vital.

vitamin, *s.* vitamine *f.*

vocabulary, *s.* vocabulaire *m.*

vocation, *s.* vocation *f.*

voice, *s.* voix *f.*; — *v. a.* exprimer.

voltage, *s.* voltage *m.*

volume, *s.* volume *m.*

voluntary, *adj.* volontaire.

volunteer, *s.* volontaire *m.*; — *v.n.* s'engager (pour).

vomit, *v.a. & n.* vomir.

vote, *s.* voix; — *v.a. & n.* voter (sur).

voucher, *s.* pièce *f.* de dépense ; pièce *f.* de recette; bon *m.*

vo v, *s.* vœu *m.*; — *v. a.* vouer; jurer; *v. n.* faire un v u; jurer.

vowel, *s.* voyelle *f.*

voyage, *s.* voyage *m.*; — *v. n.* voyager (par mer).

vulgar, *adj.* vulgaire.

W

wade, *v.a.* passer à gué.

wafer, *s.* gaufrette *f.*; hostie *f.*

wag, *v.a.* hocher; *(tail)* agiter; *v.n.* s'agiter.

wage(s), *s.* — *(pl.)* salaire *m.*, gages *m. pl.*; — *v.a.* ~ *war* faire la guerre.

wag(g)on, *s.* wagon *m.*

waist, *s.* taille *f.*

waistcoat, *s.* gilet *m.*

wait, *v. a. & n.* attendre *(for* qn, qch).

waiter, *s.* garçon *m.* (de restaurant); *head* ~ premier garçon *m.*, maître *m.* d'hôtel.

waiting-room, *s.* salle *f.* d'attente.

wake, *v.a.* (also ~ *up*) réveiller; *v.n.* (also ~ *up)* s'éveiller.

waken, *v.a.* éveiller; *v.n.* s'éveiller.

walk, *s.* marche *f.*; promenade *f.*; *(path)* allée *f.*; *go for a* ~ faire une promenade; — *v.n.* aller à pied; marcher; *(pleasure)* se promener; ~ *off* s'en aller; ~ *out* sortir.

wall, *s.* mur *m.*

wallet, *s.* portefeuille *m.*

walnut, *s.* noyer *m.*; *(fruit)* noix *f.*

waltz, *s.* valse *f.*

wander, *v.n.* errer; s'égarer (de); divaguer.

want, s. besoin m.; manque m.; for ~ of faute de; — v.a. avoir besoin (de); manquer (de); vouloir; demander; v. n. faire défaut; be ~ing in manquer de.

war, s. guerre f.

ward, s. pupille m. f.; (hospital) salle f.

warden, s. gouverneur m.; directeur m.

warder, s. gardien, -enne m. f.

wardrobe, s. armoire f.

ware, s. marchandise(s) f. (pl.); article m.

warehouse, s. magasin m.; dépôt m.

warm, adj. chaud; be ~ avoir chaud; — v.a. chauffer; ~ up réchauffer; v.n. se chauffer.

warmth, s. chaleur f.

warn, v.a. avertir; prévenir; mettre sur ses gardes (contre).

warning, s. avertissement m.; avis m.

warrant, s. autorisation f.; mandat m.; — v. a. garantir; justifier.

wash, v.a. laver; v.n. se laver; ~ away effacer; ~ up the dishes faire la vaisselle; — s. lavage m.; lotion f.; toilette f.; lessive f.

wash-basin, s. cuvette f. (de lavabo).

washing-machine, s. machine f. à laver.

wasp, s. guêpe f.

waste, s. désert m.,

(money) gaspillage m.; (energy) déperdition f.; (loss) perte f.; déchets m. pl.; ~ of time perte de temps f.; — adj. inculte; de rebut; ~ paper papier m. de rebut; — v.a. gaspiller; perdre; ravager.

watch, s. garde f.; gardien m., garde m.; (to indicate time) montre f.; — v. a. veiller, garder; observer; regarder; v.n. veiller; ~ out! ouvrez l'œil!

watch-maker, s. horloger m.

water, s. eau f.

water-closet, s. cabinet m.

waterfall, s. chute f. d'eau

watering-place, s. station f. balnéaire; ville f. d'eaux.

waterproof, adj. imperméable; — s. caoutchouc m.

wave, s. vague f.; onde f.; — v.a. agiter; (hair) onduler; v. n. flotter; onduler.

wave-length, s. longueur f. d'onde.

waver, v.n. vaciller.

wax, s. cire f.

way, s. chemin m., route f.; distance f.; côte m.; (means) moyen m.; façon f., manière f.; which ~? de quel côté?; it's a long ~ to il y a loin pour aller (à); on the ~ chemin faisant; ~ in entrée f.; ~ out sortie

f.; out of the ~ retiré;
extraordinaire; *this* ~
de ce côté-ci, par ici;
by ~ *of* par; *by the* ~
à propos; *in a* ~ à
certains égards; *give* ~
to céder à.

we, *pron.* nous.

weak, *adj.* faible.

weakness, *s.* faiblesse *f.*

wealth, *s.* richesse *f.;*
profusion *f.*

wealthy, *adj.* riche.

weapon, *s.* arme *f.*

wear, *v.a.* porter; ~ *away,*
down, out (s')user; ~ *off*
(s')effacer; — *s.* usage
m.; usure f.

weary, *adj.* las, fatigué.

weather, *s.* temps *m.*

weather-forecast, *s.* prévisions *f. pl.* du temps;
bulletin *m.* météorolo-
gique.

weave, *v. a.* tisser.

web, *s.* tissu *m.; (spider)*
toile *f.*

wedding, *s.* mariage *m.*

wedding-ring, *s.* alliance
f., anneau *m.* de ma-
riage.

wedge, *s.* coin *m.; —*
v.a. coincer; caler.

Wednesday, *s.* mercredi
m.

weed, *s.* mauvaise herbe
f.; — *v.a.* sarcler.

week, *s.* semaine *f.*

week-day, *s.* jour *m.*
de semaine; *on* ~*s* en
semaine.

week-end, *s.* fin *f.* de
semaine, week-end *m.*

weekly, *adj.* de la semaine; hebdomadaire; —
s. (journal) hebdoma-

daire *m.*

weep, *v.n.* pleurer.

weigh, *v.a. & n.* peser;
~ *down* faire pencher,
surcharger, accabler.

weight, *s.* poids *m.;*
put on ~ prendre du
corps.

welcome, *adj.* bienvenu;
~*!* soyez le bienvenu!
— *s.* accueil *m.; — v.a.*
souhaiter la bien-
venue (à); accueillir
(avec plaisir).

well[1], *adv.* bien; ~, ~*!*
allons, allons!; — *adj.*
bien (portant).

well[2], *s.* puits *m.*

well-being, bien-être *m.*

well-informed, *adj.* bien
informé, renseigné.

well-to-do, *adj.* aisé; *be* ~
être dans l'aisance

west, *s.* ouest *m.*

western, *adj.* de l'ouest.

westward, *adv.* vers l'ouest.

wet, *adj.* mouillé, humide; pluvieux; ~
through trempé jus-
qu'aux os; — *v.a.*
mouiller; tremper.

whale, *s.* baleine *f.*

what, *rel. pron.* ce qui,
ce que; — *interrog.*
pron. qu'est-ce qui,
que; — *int.* quoi!

wheat, *s.* blé *m.,* froment
m.

wheel, *s.* roue *f.; (steer-*
ing) volant *m.*

when, *adv. & conj.* quand.

whenever, *adv.* toutes les
fois que.

where, *adv.* où.

whereas, *conj.* tandis que;

vu que.

wherever, *adv.* partout où.

whether, *conj.* soit que; *(if)* si; ~ *or not* ... qu'il en soit ainsi ou non...

which, *(interrogative) adj.* quel, quelle; *pron.* lequel; *(relative) adj.* lequel, laquelle; *pron.* qui, que, lequel.

while, *conj.* pendant que; *(whereas)* tandis que; *(as long as)* tant que; — *s.* temps *m.*; *be worth* ~ *to* cela vaut la peine de; — *v.a.* ~ *away* faire passer.

whip, *s.* fouet.

whisk, *v.a.* fouetter; — *s.* époussette *f.*; *(eggs)* fouet à œufs, *m.*

whisper, *s.* chuchotement *m.*; murmure *m.*; *v.a.* dire à l'oreille; *v.n.* chuchoter; murmurer.

whistle, *s.* sifflet *m.*; — *v.a.* & *n.* siffler.

white, *adj.* blanc, blanche; pâle.

Whit Sunday, dimanche *m.* de la Pentecôte.

who, *pron.* qui.

whole, *s.* tout *m.*; totalité *f.*; *on the* ~ à tout prendre; — *adj.* tout le, toute la; entier, -ère.

wholesale, *adj.* & *adv.* en gros.

wholesome, *adj.* sain.

wholly, *adv.* entièrement.

whom, *pron.* que; lequel; *interrog.* qui?, qui est-ce que?

whose, *pron.* dont; *interrog.* de qui?

why, *adv.* pourquoi.

wicked, *adj.* méchant.

wide, *adj.* large; étendue; *6 feet* ~ *6* pieds de largeur.

widow, *s.* veuve *f.*

widower, *s.* veuf *m.*

width, *s.* largeur *f.*

wife, *s.* femme *f.*

wild, *adj.* sauvage; déréglé; impétueux; frénétique.

wilful, *adj.* volontaire.

will, *s.* volonté *f.*; intention *f.*; testament *m.*; *at* ~ à volonté; *of one's own free* ~ de plein gré; — *v.n.* & *aux.* vouloir; *(future tense unexpressed, see grammar).*

willing, *adj.* bien disposé; *be* ~ vouloir bien.

willingly, *adv.* volontiers.

win, *v. a.* & *n.* gagner.

winch, *s.* manivelle *f.*

wind¹, *s.* vent *m.*; souffle *m.*

wind², *v. a.* enrouler; dévider; ~ *up (clock)* remonter; *fig.* liquider; *v.n.* tourner, serpenter; s'enrouler.

window, *s.* fenêtre *f.*; *(car)* glace *f.*

windscreen, *s.* pare-brise *m.*

windy, *adj.* venteux.

wine, *s.* vin *m.*

wing, *s.* aile *f.*; vol *m.*; *take* ~ s'envoler.

wink, *s.* clin d'œil, *m.*; — *v.a.* clignoter.

winner, *s.* gagnant *m.*

winter, *s.* hiver *m.*

wipe, *v.a.* essuyer; ~ *out* effacer; ~ *s.* coup *m.* de torchon.

wire, *s.* fil *m.* (de fer); télégramme *m.; live* ~ fil *m.* en charge; — *v.a.* & *n.* télégraphier.

wireless, *s.* T.S.F.; télégraphie sans fil; ~ *set* poste *m.* (de T.S.F.).

wise, *adj.* sage; prudent.

wish, *s.* désir *m.;* ~*es* vœux *m.* pl.; — *v.a.* désirer (de); souhaiter; *(should like)* vouloir *(in conditional).*

wit, *s.* esprit *m.; (pers.)* bel esprit *m.*

witch, *s.* sorcière *f.*

with, *prep.* avec; *(at)* chez.

withdraw, *v.n.* se retirer; *v.a.* retirer.

within, *adv.* dedans; — *prep. (time)* en; *(place)* dans; à.

without, *prep.* sans; *(place)* en dehors de.

witness, *s.* témoignage *m.; (pers.)* témoin *m.;* — *v.a.* être témoin de; *(attest)* témoigner; *(document)* signer (à).

witty, *adj.* spirituel.

wizard, *s.* sorcier *m.*

wolf, *s.* loup, louve *m.* f.

woman, *s.* femme *f.*

womb, *s.* matrice *f.; fig.* sein *m.*

wonder, *s.* étonnement *m.; (a thing)* merveille *f.;* — *v.n.* ~ *at*

être étonné de; *(curious)* se demander; *I* ~ je me le demande.

wonderful, *adj.* étonnant.

wood, *s.* bois *m.*

wooden, *adj.* de bois.

woodman, *s.* bûcheron *m.*

wool, *s.* laine *f.*

woollen, *adj.* de laine.

word, *s.* mot *m.; (utterance)* parole *f.; (term)* terme *m.; (information* avis *m.; upon my* ~! ma parole!; *have a* ~ *with* avoir deux mots avec.

work, *s.* travail *m.; (achievement)* ouvrage *m.;* ~ *(of art)* œuvre *f.* d'art; ~*s (of s.o.)* œuvres *f.*pl., *(factory)* usine *f.; set to* ~ se mettre à l'œuvre; — *v.a.* faire travailler; *(wood)* ouvrager; *v.n.* travailler; *(operate)* fonctionner, marcher.

worker, *s.* travailleur, -euse *m.* f., ouvrier, -ère *m.* f.

workman, *s.* ouvrier *m.*

workshop, *s.* atelier *m.*

world, *s.* monde *m.*

world-war, *s.* guerre *f.* mondiale.

world-wide, *adj.* universel; mondial.

worm, *s.* ver *m.*

worry, *s.* ennui *m.*, tracas *m.;* — *v.a.* tracasser; importuner; *v. n.* se tracasser (de), se tourmenter; *don't* ~! soyez tranquille!

worse, *adj.* pire, plus mauvais; *grow ~* empirer; — *adv.* pis.

worship, *s.* culte *m.*; — *v.a. & n.* adorer.

worst, *adj.* le, la pire; le, la plus malade; — *adv.* le plus mal; — *s.* pis *m.*

worth, *s.* valeur *f.*; — *adj.* be *~* valoir; *is it ~ while?* cela (en) vaut-il la peine?; *it is not ~ the trouble* cela ne vaut pas la peine.

worthless, *adj.* sans valeur, indigne.

worthy, *adj.* digne.

wound, *s.* blessure *f.*

wounded, *adj.* blessé; *the ~* les blessés.

wrap, *s.* *(garment)* peignoir *m.*; *v.a. ~ up* envelopper; *fig.* être absorbé *(in* dans).

wrapper, *s.* toile d'emballage *f.*; *(book)* bande *f.*

wreck, *s.* naufrage *m.*; navire *m.* naufragé; *fig.* ruine *f.*; *v.a.* ruiner; *be ~ed* faire naufrage; être naufragé.

wrench, *s.* torsion *f.*; *(tool)* clef (à écrous) *f.*; — *v.a.* tordre; *(ankle)* fouler.

wrestle, *v.n.* lutter (avec).

wrestler, *s.* lutteur *m.*

wrestling, *s.* lutte *f.*

wring, *v.a.* tordre.

wrinkle, *s.* ride *f.*; *(crease)* faux pli *m.*; — *v.a.* rider.

wrist, *s.* poignet *m.*

writ, *s.* exploit *m.*

write, *v.a. & n.* écrire; *~ down* noter; *~ off* amortir; *~ out* transcrire.

writer, *s.* écrivain *m.*

writing, *s.* écriture *f.*; écrit *m.*; *in ~* par écrit.

writing-desk, *s.* bureau *m.*

wrong, *adj.* incorrect, faux; *be ~* avoir tort; se tromper (de); *take the ~ train* se tromper de train; *it is the ~ book* ce n'est pas le livre qu'il faut.

X

Xmas, *s.* Noël *m.*

x-ray, *adj.* *~ treatment* radiothérapie *f.*; *~ photograph* radiograph e *f.*

Y

yacht, *s.* yacht *m.*

yard, *s.* yard *m.*; cour *f.*

yarn, *s.* fil *m*; histoire *f.*

yawn, *s.* bâillement *m.*; — *v.n.* bâiller.

year, *s.* an *m.*; année *f.*

yearly, *adv.* annuellement.

yearn, *v.n.* *~ for* soupirer après.

yeast, *s.* levure *f.*

yell, *v. n.* hurler.

yellow, *adj.* jaune.

yes, *adv.* oui; *(after negation)* si.

yesterday, *adv.* hier.

yet, *adv.* encore; *not* ~ pas encore; *as* ~ jusqu'à présent; — *conj.* néanmoins.

yield, *v.a.* produire; accorder; rendre; *v.n.* céder (à); fléchir.

yoke, *s.* joug *m.*

yolk, *s.* jaune *m.*

you, *pron.* tu; vous.

young, *adj.* jeune; *(animal)* petit; ~er plus jeune. cadet.

your, *adj.* votre, *(pl.)* vos.

yours, *pron.* à vous; le, la vôtre, les vôtres.

yourself, *pron.* vous-même, -*s.*

youth, *s.* jeunesse *f.;* *(pers.)* jeune homme *m.*

youth-hostel, *s.* auberge *f.* de la jeunesse.

Z

zeal, *s.* zèle *m.*

zealous, *adj.* zélé.

zero, *s.* zéro *m.*

zest, *s.* enthousiasme *m.;* goût *m.*

zigzag, *s.* zigzag *m.;* — *adv.* en zigzag.

zinc, *s.* zinc *m.*

zipper, *s.* fermeture éclair. *f.*

zone, *s.* zone *f.*

zoo, *s.* zoo *m.*

zoology, *s.* zoologie *f.*

FRENCH - ENGLISH
DICTIONARY

LES SONS DE L'ANGLAIS

I. Consonnes. La plupart des consonnes se prononcent à peu près comme en français. Il faut cependant faire attention:

1. Au **th**, qui se produit en appliquant la langue contre les alvéoles des dents d'en haut en expirant fortement, tantôt sans vibration des cordes vocales (comme dans **thin**, mince); tantôt avec vibration (comme dans **this**, ce, ceci);

2. à l'**r**. Au commencement d'un mot, ce son est roulé; au milieu, il est plutôt grasseyé; tandis qu'à la fin il est muet, à moins d'être suivi d'un mot commençant par une voyelle. Dans ce cas il se rattache à cette voyelle, et reprend la valeur roulée;

3. au **g**, qui au début d'un mot est tantôt dur (comme dans **get**, obtenir), tantôt doux (comme dans **general**, général), où il a la valeur du **g** français précédé d'un **d**.

II. Voyelles. Les sons de la plupart des voyelles se retrouvent également en français, mais ce ne sont pas toujours les mêmes lettres qui les représentent.

Le **a** de **pas** se retrouve dans **ask**, demander, etc.

Le **a** de **patte** est le premier son de la diphtongue **ai**, qui s'entend dans **mine**, le mien; de la diphtongue **aou** qui s'entend dans **down**, en bas.

La voyelle de **man**, homme, a la valeur de l'**a** faubourien de **Clamart**.

La voyelle de **cut**, couper, est entre l'**a** et l'**é** français.

La voyelle **i** a deux sons: tantôt long, comme dans **machine**, machine (même valeur qu'en français); tantôt bref, comme dans **it**, il, où il est plus bref que l'**i** d'**ami**.

Le son bref de l'**e** anglais est celui de l'**e** de **livret**. Il s'entend dans **get**, obtenir; et dans la diphtongue de **day**, jour (où il est suivi de l'**i** bref). Le son long est celui de l'**é** français, mais il est toujours suivi d'un **e** muet, comme dans **where**, où (qui peut se figurer par les lettres **wée**).

Le son de l'**e** muet est très fréquent en anglais, surtout dans les syllabes non accentuées (comme dans **ago**, il y a, où l'**a** se prononce ainsi) et à la fin d'un mot (comme dans **father**, père). Ce même son, prolongé (comme dans **heu, heu** français), s'entend dans **bird**, oiseau. L'**e** muet fait partie, on l'a vu, de la diphtongue de **where**, où; et aussi de la diphtongue de **beer**, bière (qui peut se figurer par **bie**), et de **poor**, pauvre (qui peut se figurer par **poue**).

L'**o** anglais a trois valeurs. Il est tantôt bref, comme dans **box**, boîte (comme l'**o** de **note**); tantôt long, comme dans le son de l'**a** de **all** (où il a presque la valeur de l'**ô** de **dôme**); et tantôt il fait partie de la diphtongue qui s'entend dans **no**, non, où il a presque la valeur de l'**e** muet suivi d'un son qui peut se figurer par **ou**. Le son bref s'entend aussi dans la diphtongue de **boy**, garçon.

L'**u** anglais a deux valeurs. Il est tantôt bref (exactement comme l'**ou** de **bout**) et s'entend dans **put**, mettre; tantôt long (comme l'**ou** de **cours**), et s'entend dans **shoe**, soulier. (L'on a vu déjà qu'il fait partie de la diphtongue de **poor**, pauvre).

NOMS

Abyssinie, *s. f.* Abyssinia.
Adriatique, *s. f.* Adriatic.
Afrique, *s. f.* Africa.
Albanie, *s. f.* Albania.
Alexandre, *s. m.* Alexander.
Alexandrie, *s. f.* Alexandria.
Alger, *s. m.* Algiers.
Algérie, *s.f.* Algeria, Algiers.
Allemagne, *s. f.* Germany.
(les) Alpes, *s. f. pl.* The Alps.
Amérique, *s. f.* America; *l'~ du Nord, du Sud* North America, South America.
Angleterre, *s. f.* England.
(les) Antilles, *s. f. pl.* The Antilles, the West Indies.
Antoine, *s. m.* Anthony.
Anvers, *s. m.* Antwerp.
Apennins, *s. m. pl.* Apennines.
Arabie, *s. f.* Arabia.
Argentine, *s. f.* Argentina, the Argentine.
Asie, *s. f.* Asia.
Assyrie, *s. f.* Assyria.
Athènes, *s. f.* Athens.
Atlantique, *s. m.* The Atlantic.
Auguste, *s.m.* Augustus.
Australie, *s. f.* Australia.
Austriche, *s. f.* Austria.
Azincourt, *s. m.* Agincourt.

Bâle, *s. f.* Basle.
Baltique, *s. f.* Baltic.

Barcelone, *s. f.* Barcelona.
Belgique, *s. f.* Belgium.
(les) Bermudes, *s. f. pl.* The Bermudas.
Bethléem, *s.m.* Bethlehem.
Beyrouth, *s.f.* Beirut, Beirout.
Birmanie, *s. f.* Burmah.
Bohême, *s. f.* Bohemia.
Bolivie, *s. f.* Bolivia.
Bosphore, *s. m.* The Bosphorus.
Bourgogne, *s.f.* Burgundy.
Brême, *s. f.* Bremen.
Brésil, *s. m.* Brazil.
Bretagne, *s. f.* Brittany.
Britanniques (Îles), *adj.* The British Isles.
Bruxelles, *s. f.* Brussels.
Bucarest, *s. m.* Bucharest.
Bulgarie, *s. f.* Bulgaria.

Cachemire, *s. m.* Kashmir.
(le) Caire, *s. m.* Cairo.
Calais, *s. m.* Calais.
Californie, *s. f.* California.
(le) Calvaire, *s. m.* (Mount) Calvary.
Cambodge, *s. m.* Cambodia.
(le) Cap, *s. m.* Capetown.
(les) Carpathes, *s. m. pl.* The Carpathian Mountains.
Carrache, *s. m.* Carracci.
Caspienne (la Mer), *s. f.* The Caspian Sea.
(le) Caucase, *s. m.* The

Caucasus.
César, *s. m.* Caesar.
Ceylan, *s. f.* Ceylon.
Chaldée, *s. f.* Chaldea.
Chili, *s. m.* Chile.
Chine, *s. f.* China.
Chypre, *s. f.* Cyprus.
Cléopâtre, *s. f.* Cleopatra.
Colombie, *s. f.* Columbia, Colombia.
Copenhague, *s. f.* Copenhagen.
Cordoue, *s. f.* Cordova, Cordoba.
Corée, *s. f.* Korea, Corea.
Cornouailles, *s.f. pl.* Cornwall.
Corse, *s. f.* Corsica.
Cracovie, *s. f.* Cracow.
Crimée, *s. f.* Crimea.
Croatie, *s. f.* Croatia.

Dalmatie, *s. f.* Dalmatia.
Danemark, *s. m.* Denmark.
Denis, *s. m.* Denis.
Dominique, *s. f.* Dominique.
Douvres, *s. m.* Dover.
Dresde, *s. f.* Dresden.
Dunkerque, *s. m.* Dunkirk.

Écosse, *s. f.* Scotland.
Édimbourg, *s. m.* Edinburgh.
Égypte, *s. f.* Egypt.
Élisabeth, *s. f.* Elizabeth.
Équateur, *s.m.* Ecuador.
Espagne, *s. f.* Spain.
Esthonie, *s. f.* Esthonia.
(les) États-Unis, *s. m. pl.* The United States.
Europe, *s. f.* Europe.

(les) Fidji, Viti, *s. f. pl.* The Fiji Islands.
Finlande, *s. f.* Finland.
Flandre, *s. f.* Flanders.
Florence, *s. f.* Florence.
Floride, *s. f.* Florida.
France, *s. f.* France.
Francfort, *s. m.* Frankfurt, Frankfort.
Fribourg, *s. m.* 1. *(Switzerland)* Fribourg; 2. *(Germany)* Freiburg.

Galilée, 1. *s. m.* Galileo; 2. *s. f.* Galilee.
Galles (Pays de), *s. m.* Wales.
Gambie, *s. f.* Gambia.
Gand, *f. m.* Ghent.
Gange, *f. m.* Ganges.
Gascogne, *s. f.* Gascony.
Gaule, *s. f.* Gaul.

Gédéon, *s. m.* Gideon.
Gênes, *s. f.* Genoa.
Genève, *s. f.* Geneva.
Georges, *s. m.* George.
Géorgie, *s. f.* Georgia.
Grande-Bretagne, *s. f.* Great Britain.
Grèce, *s. f.* Greece.
Groenland, *s. m.* Greenland.
Guinée, *s. f.* Guinea.

Hambourg, *s. m.* Hamburg.
Hanovre, *s. m.* Hanover.
(le) Havre, *s. m.* Havre.
Hawaï, *s. m.* Hawaii.
(la) Haye, *s. f.* the Hague.
Hongrie, *s. f.* Hungary.

Iéna, *s. f.* Jena.
Inde, *s. f.* India; *les* ~s *Occidentales* West In-

dies; *les ～s Orientales* East Indies.
Indonésie, *s. f.* Indonesia.
Irlande, *s. f.* Ireland.
Islande, *s. f.* Iceland.
Israël *s. m.* Israel.
Italie, *s. f.* Italy.

Jacques, *s. m.* James.
(la) Jamaïque, *s. f.* Jamaica.
Japon, *s. m.* Japan.
Jean, *s. m.* John.
Jeanne, *s. f.* Joan; Jean, Jane.
Jourdain *s. m.* Jordan.
Jupiter, *s.m.* Jupiter, Jove.

Laponie, *s. f.* Lapland.
Léon, *s. m.* Leo.
Lia, *s. f.* Leah.
Lisbonne, *s. f.* Lisbon.
Lithuanie, *s.f.* Lithuania.
Livourne, *s. f.* Leghorn.
Londres, *s. m.* London.
St. Luc, *s. m.* St Luke.
Luxembourg, *s. m.* Luxemburg.
Lyon, *s. m.* Lyons.

Mahomet, *s. m.* Mohammed, Mahomet.
(la) Manche, *s. f.* The English Channel.
Mantoue, *s. f.* Mantua.
St. Marc, *s. m.* Mark, St. Mark.
Marie, *s. f.* Mary.
Marseille, *s. m.* Marseilles.
Marthe, *s. f.* Martha.
(St) Matthieu, *s.m.* St. Matthew.
Maurice, (l'Île) *s. f.* Mauritius.
Moscou, *s. f.* Moscow.

Nicée, *s. f.* Nicaea.
Nil, *s. m.* The Nile.
Normandie, *s.f.* Normandy.
Norvège, *s. f.* Norway.
Nouvelle-Zélande, *s.f.* New Zealand.

Ostende, *s. f.* Ostend.
Oural, *s. m.* Ural.

Padoue, *s. f.* Padua.
Palerme, *s. f.* Palermo.
Parnasse, *s. m.* (Mount) Parnassus.
(les) Pays-Bas, *s. m. pl.* The Netherlands.
Pékin, *s. m.* Peking, Pekin.
Pensylvanie, *s.f.* Pennsylvania.
Pérou, *s. m.* Peru.
Perse, *s. f.* Persia.
Philadelphie, *s. f.* Philadelphia.
Philippes, *s. f.* Philippi.
Pierre, *s. m.* Peter.
Pise, *s. f.* Pisa.
Pologne, *s. f.* Poland.
(le) Pont-Euxin, *s. m.* The Black Sea.
Portugal, *s. m.* Portugal.
Pyrénées, *s.f. pl.* Pyrenees.

Raguse, *s. f.* Ragusa.
Reims, *s. m.* Rheims.
(le) Rhin, *s.m.* The Rhine.
Roumanie, *s.f.* Rumania.
Russie, *s. f.* Russia.
Salzbourg, *s. m.* Salzburg.
Sardaigne, *s. f.* Sardinia.
Scandinavie, *s. f.* Scandi-

navia.
Serbie, *s. f.* Serbia.
Sicile, *s. f.* Sicily.
Singapour, *s. m.* Singapore.
Sophie, *s. f.* Sophia.
Spitzberg, *s.m.* Spitzbergen.
Suède, *s. f.* Sweden.
Suisse, *s. f.* Switzerland.
Syrie, *s. f.* Syria.

Tchécoslovaquie, *s. f.* Czechoslovakia.
Thuringe, *s. f.* Thuringia.
Tunisie, *s. f.* Tunis.
Turquie. *s. f.* Turkey.

Upsal, *s. f.* Uppsala.

Vienne, *s. f.* Vienna.

Yougoslavie, *s. f.* Yugoslavia.

PHRASES

Bonjour. Bonsoir. Au revoir.
Je vous demande pardon. Pardon.
Comment allez-vous? Très bien — et vous?
Enchanté (de faire votre connaissance) monsieur (madame, mademoiselle).
Permettez-moi! Vous êtes très gentil.
Cela m'est égal.
A votre santé.
Permettez-moi de vous présenter à ...
Il fait beau (mauvais) temps.
Vous avez raison. Vous avez tort.
Ce n'est pas ma faute.
Faire son possible.
C'est très ennuyeux.
Vous vous moquez de moi.
Tant mieux (pis).
C'est un chic type.
Mettre les pieds dans le plat.
Rien ne va bien. Tout va mal.

Good morning. Good evening. Good-bye.
I beg your pardon. Excuse me.
How are you? Very well — and you?
How do you do (delighted to meet you).

Allow me! You are very kind.
It's all the same to me.
Your good health.
Allow me to introduce you to ...
It is fine (bad) weather.

You are right. You are wrong.
It is not my fault.
To do one's best.
It is very annoying.
You're pulling my leg.
So much the better (worse).
He's a jolly nice fellow.
To put one's foot in it.

Things are going badly.

Je suis anglais (anglaise).	I am an Englishmen (Englishwoman).
Je ne parle pas français.	I cannot speak French.
Je cherche . . .	I am looking for . . .
Je ne vous comprends pas.	I don't understand you.
Parlez lentement, s'il vous plaît!	Please speak slowly!
Y-a-t-il quelque'un qui parle anglais?	Is there anyone here who speaks English?
Où est le consulat britannique?	Where is the British Consulate?
C'est épatant, formidable !	It is wonderful, splendid !
Défense de . . . sous peine d'amende.	No . . . Trespassers will be prosecuted.
Entrée interdite.	No entry.
Les toilettes, les lavabos, les cabinets.	Lavatory.
Quelle heure est-il?	What time is it?
Il est une heure cinq.	It is five past one.
Nous sommes pressés.	We are in a hurry.
Combien de temps faut-il pour . . .?	How long does it take to . . . ?
Ce soir. Hier soir.	This evening, tonight. Last night.
Depuis quand êtes-vous ici?	How long have you been here?
Je suis ici depuis un mois.	I have been here a month.
Est-ce qu'on peut déjeuner (dîner) ici?	Can we lunch (dine) here?
Nous sommes quatre.	There are four of us.
Nous voudrions seulement un casse-croûte.	We only want a snack.
Voulez-vous nous donner le menu, s'il vous plaît.	Please give us the menu.
Apportez-nous la carte des vins, s'il vous plaît.	Bring us the wine list, please.
Nous voudrions du café noir (café au lait).	We would like black coffee (white coffee).
L'addition, s'il vous plaît.	The bill, please.
Je voudrais de l'essence (de l'huile, de l'eau).	I want some petrol (oil, water).
Je suis en panne.	I have had a breakdown.
Mon auto est sur la route à deux kilomètres d'ici.	My car is on the road two kilometres from here.
Connaissez-vous : route de . . .?	Do you know the road to . . .?

Is the post office (bank) near here?	Y a-t-il un bureau de poste (bureau de change) près d'ici?
Are there any letters for me?	Y a-t-il des lettres pour moi?
Do you sell ...?	Est-ce que vous vendez...?
You have given me the wrong change.	Vous vous êtes trompé en me rendant la monnaie.
Have you anything to declare?	Avez-vous quelque chose à déclarer?
I cannot find my ticket.	Je ne peux pas trouver mon billet.
J'ai laissé quelque chose dans le train.	I have left something in the train.
J'ai un train à prendre.	I have a train to catch.
A quelle heure est le premier (dernier) train pour ...?	What time is the first (last) train for ...?
Sur quel quai?	From which platform?
Où est-ce que je change pour ...?	Where do I change for ...?
Est-ce qu'il y a un hôtel où je peux passer la nuit?	Is there a hotel where I can stay the night?
Le dernier train est parti.	The last train has gone.
Je ne me sens pas bien.	I do not feel well.
Je veux descendre à ...	I want to get off at ...
Allez-vous près de ...?	Do you go near ...?
Puis-je avoir une chambre pour la nuit?	Can I have a room for the night?
Je reste deux ou trois jours seulement.	I am only staying for two or three days.
Je désire une chambre avec un grand lit.	I want a room with a double bed.
Pouvez-vous me donnez une chambre pour la nuit?	Can you put me up for the night?
Je serai de retour à trois heures.	I shall be back at three.
Avez-vous des journaux anglais?	Have you any English newspapers?
Combien met-on sur une lettre pour ...?	What does it cost to send a letter to ...?
Où puis-je acheter ...?	Where can I buy ...?
Voulez-vous me reserver cette place?	Will you reserve this place for me?

Acceptez-vous un cheque de voyage?	Will you take a traveller's cheque?
Voulez-vous faire suivre mon courrier à cette adresse?	Will you have letters sent on to this address?
J'ai besoin d'un guide qui parle anglais.	I need a guide who speaks English.
Est-ce bien la route pour . . .?	Is this the right road for . . .?
Combien de kilomètres d'ici à . . .?	How far is it from here to . . .?
Avez-vous des cartes postales?	Have you any post-cards?
Avez-vous une carte (un plan)?	Have you a map (plan)?
Savez-vous ce qu'on donne au cinéma (Théatre)?	Do you know what is on at the cinema (theatre)?
Ce chemin, ou mène-t-il?	Where does this road lead?
Pouvez-vous recommander un restaurant pas trop cher?	Can you recommend a cheap restaurant?
C'est trop cher. Avez-vous quelque chose de meilleur marché?	It is too dear. Have you anything cheaper?
Nous sommes perdus.	We are lost.
Avez-vous une pièce d'identite?	Have you any identification papers?
Avez-vous un sac en papier?	Have you a carrier bag?
Voici mon adresse.	Here is my address.
Je vous en prie.	That's all right.
Il n'y a pas de quoi.	Don't mention it.
Prenez ma place, madame.	Take my seat, madame.
Puis-je vous aider?	Can I help you?
Est-ce que je vous dérange?	Am I disturbing you?
Je suis navré (désolé).	I am terribly sorry.
Je vous remercie de votre hospitalité.	Thank you for your hospitality.
Nous nous sommes bien amusés.	We had a very good time.
C'est trop. C'est trop cher.	It's too much. It's too dear.

Attention!

Look out!

Vous avez raison. Vous avez tort.

You are right. You are wrong.

Ecoutez. Regardez.

Listen. Look.

Qu'est-ce qu-il y a?

What is the matter?

Parlez lentement, s'il vous plait.

Please speak slowly.

Attendez, je cherche la phrase dans ce livre.

Wait, I am looking for the phrase in this book.

Je vous ai déjà payé.

I have already paid you.

C'est tordant, c'est rigolo.

It's terribly funny.

Sans blague!

You don't say!

Vous plaisantez. Blague à part.

You are joking. Joking apart.

Entendu. D'accord.

Agreed. O.K.

Quel dommage!

What a pity!

Ne pas toucher.

Do not touch.

Prenez garde à la peinture.

Wet paint.

Vous avez tout le temps.

You have plenty of time.

Je n'ai pas le temps.

I have no time.

Avant-hier.

The day before yesterday.

Après-demain.

The day after tomorrow.

Garçon apportez-nous du pain, s'il vous plait.

Waiter, bring us some bread, please.

Encore un peu de . . .

A little more . . .

Que désirez-vous boire (comme boisson)?

What would you like to drink?

Le service (le couvert), est-il compris?

Is the service (the cover charge) included?

Vous pouvez garder la monnaie.

Keep the change.

Il y a une erreur dans l'addition.

There is a mistake in the bill.

Je vous en prie.

Please don't mention it.

Est-ce que le garage est ouvert la nuit?

Is the garage open all night?

Je veux partir demain de bonne heure.

I want to leave early tomorrow.

Combien de temps faut-il attendre?

How long shall I have to wait?

Pouvez-vous me prêter . . .?

Can you lend me . . . ?

Combien est-ce que je vous dois?

How much do I owe you?

J'ai deux places réservées en première (en seconde).	I have two first class (second class) seats reserved.
Pardon monsieur, cette place est à moi.	Excuse me, sir, that seat is mine.
Porteur, je veux mettre ces bagages à la consigne.	Porter I want to put this luggage in the cloakroom (left-luggage office).
Je vous suis.	I am coming with you.
Est-ce qu'il y a un porter de l'hôtel . . . ici?	Is there a porter from the . . . Hotel here?
Où est le bureau de renseignements?	Where is the enquiry office?
A quelle heure arrive-t-on à . . .?	When do we get to . . . ?
Combien de temps le train s'arrête-t-il ici?	How long does the train stop here?
L'avion pour . . . a déjà vingt minutes de retard.	The plane for . . . is twenty minutes late already.
L'avion de . . . est signalé.	The . . . plane is announced.
Où est le bureau de la compagnie aérienne?	Where is the Airline Office?
Je voudrais réserver une place dans l'avion qui part demain pour . .	I want to reserve a seat on the plane leaving tomorrow for . .
Est-ce qu'il y a un avion pour . . . audjourd'hui?	Is there a plane for . . . today?
Je ne me sens pas bien.	I do not feel well.
Apportez-moi du café (cognac, un verre d'eau), s'il vous plait.	Bring me some coffee (brandy, a glass of water), please.
Eteignez vos cigarettes et attachez vos ceintures, s'il vous plait.	Put out your cigarettes and fasten your seatbelts, please.
Appelez-moi un taxi.	Call me a taxi.
Dépêchez-vous, je suis très pressé.	Go quickly, I am in a great hurry.
Attendez-moi ici quelques minutes, s'il vous plait.	Please wait here for a few minutes.
Où est le bureau?	Where is the office?
Avez-vous une chambre avec salle de bains?	Have you a room with a private bathroom?
Quel est le prix d'une chambre par nuit?	What is the price of a room per night?

J'attends un monsieur (une dame, une demoiselle).	I am expecting a gentleman (a lady, a young lady).
Donnez-moi deux timbres de vingt-cinq centimes et deux de quinze.	Give me two 25 centime stamps and two at 15 centimes.
Je voudrais envoyer une dépêche.	I want to send a telegram.
Avez-vous l'horaire des trains pour . . . ?	Have you the time-table of trains for . . . ?
Peut-on avoir un petit déjeuner anglais?	Can we have an English breakfast?
Commandez un taxi pour neuf heures et demie, s'il vous plaît.	Order a taxi for 9.30, please.
Préparez la note, s'il vous plaît.	Please have my bill made out.
Nous voudrions être ensemble.	We want to be together.
Quelle distance d'ici à . . . ?	How far it to . . . ?
Quel est le nom de cette ville (ce village)?	What is the name of this town· (village)?
Où est le marché?	Where is the market place?
Si le temps le permet, nous comptons partir à l'aube.	Weather permitting, we hope to leave at dawn.
Voulez-vous me demander Molitor quarante-quatre, quatre-vingt-quatorze, s'il vous plaît.	Get me Molitor 44—94, please.
Combien vous dois-je pour la communication?	How much do I owe you for the call?
Puis-je prendre un rendezvous?	Can I make an appointment?
Puis-je avoir de la lecture?	Can I have something to read?
Pouvez-vous faire cette ordonnance, s'il vous plaît?	Can you make up this prescription, please?
Pouvez-vous me donner quelque chose pour les piqûres d'insectes (de fourmis, de moustiques)?	Can you give me something for insect (ant, mosquito) bites?

La peau me cuit; avez-vous quelque-chose de calmant?

My skin is smarting; have you anything to soothe it?

Pour l'usage externe.

For external use.

Je voudrais un film en couleur inversible (negatif).

I want a reversal (negative) colour film.

Est-ce que vous vendez ...?

Do you sell ...?

Avez-vous quelque chose de moins cher (de meilleure qualité)?

Have you anything cheaper (better)?

Je voudrais quelque chose comme ceci (cela).

I want something like this (that).

Pouvez-vous le (la) commander?

Can you order it for me?

Voulez-vous l'envoyer à cette adresse?

Will you send it to this address?

Voilà ce qu'il me faut.

That's exactly what I want.

Vous vous êtes trompé en me rendant la monnaie.

You have given me the wrong change.

Pouvez-vous le changer?

Can you change it?

Est-ce que vous vendez des cigarettes anglaises (du tabac anglais)?

Do you sell English cigarettes (tobacco)?

Il y a eu un accident.

There has been an accident.

Y a-t-il un médecin près d'ici?

Is there a doctor near here?

Je vous souhaite la bienvenue en Angleterre (France).

Welcome to England (France).

Avez-vous fait un bon voyage?

Did you have a good journey?

A quelle heure est le petit déjeuner (le déjeuner, le goûter, le diner)?

What time is breakfast (lunch, tea, dinner)?

Y a-t-il une banque (un bureau de change) près d'ici?

sithere a bank (money, exchange bureau) near here?

A

à, au, *prep.* to; at.
abaisser, *v. a.* lower, let down; s'∼ stoop.
abandonner, *v. a.* forsake, abandon.
abat-jour, *s. m.* lampshade.
abbaye, *s. m.* abbey.
abbé, *s. m.* abbot.
abdication, *s. f.* abdication.
abdiquer, *v. n.* abdicate; *v. a.* renounce.
abeille, *s. f.* bee.
abject, *adj.* abject, low.
abjurer, *v.a.* abjure; give up.
abolir, *v. a.* abolish.
abondance, *s. f.* plenty, abundance.
abondant, *adj.* abundant.
abonder, *v. n.* abound.
abonner: s'∼ subscribe to, take in.
abord, *adv.* d'∼ (at) first.
aboutir, *v. n.* end in, come to.
aboyer, *v. n.* bark.
abricot, *s. m.* apricot.
abrupt, *adj.* steep.
absence, *s. f.* absence; ∼ d'*esprit* absence of mind.
absent, *adj.* absent.
absenter: s'∼ leave, depart.
absolu, *adj.* absolute.
absorber, *v. a.* absorb;
absoudre*, *v. a.* absolve.
abstraction, *s. f.* abstraction.
abstrait, *adj.* abstract.
absurde, *adj.* absurd.
abus, *s. m.* abuse.

académie, *s. f.* academy.
accélérer, *v. a.* accelerate, hasten.
accent, *s.m.* accent, stress.
accentuer, *v.a.* accent.
accepter, *v. a.* accept; admit.
accès, *s. m.* access; fit.
accessible, *adj.* accessible.
accident, *s.m.* accident; *par* ∼ accidentally.
accidentel, -elle, *adj.* accidental.
acclamer, *v.a.* acclaim.
acclimater, *v.a.* acclimatize; 's'∼ become acclimatized.
accommoder, *v. a.* accommodate; fit up; s'∼ put up with, come to terms.
accompagner, *v. a.* accompany.
accomplir, *v. a.* accomplish, carry out.
accord, *s. m.* agreement, accord, harmony.
accorder, *v.a.* grant, confer; agree.
accoutumer, *v. a.* accustom; s'∼ get accustomed (to).
accréditer, *v. a.* accredit.
accrocher, *v. a.* hang up, hook; run against.
accroître, *v. a.* increase; s'∼ increase.
accueil, *s. m.* reception.
accueillir, *v. a.* receive, welcome.
accumuler, *v. a.* accumulate, heap up.
accusation, *s. f.* accusation, charge.

accuser, *v.a.* accuse.

achat, *s. m.* purchase; *faire des ~s* go shopping.

acheter, *v.a.* purchase, buy.

achèvement, *s. m.* completion.

achever, *v.a.* complete finish; achieve.

acide, *adj.* acid, sour; — *s. m.* acid.

acier, *s. m.* steel.

acoustique, *s. f.* acoustics.

acquérir*, *v.a.* acquire, purchase; get.

âcre, *adj.* acrid, sour.

acte, *s. m.* action, deed, act; transaction, document, certificate; *(theatre)* act.

acteur, *s. m.* actor.

actif, -ive, *adj.* active; — *s.m.* assets *(pl.);*

action, *s. f.* action; act, deed; effect; lawsuit; plot; story.

activité, *s. f.* activity.

actrice, *s. f.* actress.

actualité, *s. f.* topic of the hour; *~s* current events; news-reel.

actuel, -elle, present, of present interest; actual.

adapter, *v.a.* adapt; *s'~* adapt oneself.

addition, *s. f.* addition; bill.

additionner, *v. a.* add up.

adhérer, *v. a.* adhere, stick.

adieu, *s. m. (pl. -x)* goodbye; *faire ses ~x* take one's leave.

adjoint, *adj. & s. m.* assistant; deputy.

adjuger, *v. a.* adjuge.

administrateur, -trice,

s. m. f. manager, director.

administratif, -ive- *adj.* administrative.

administration, *s. f.* management, direction; administration.

administrer, *v.a.* administer; manage.

admirable, *adj.* admirable.

admiration, *s. f.* admiration.

admirer, *v. a.* admire, wonder at.

admission, *s. f.* admission, admittance.

adolescent, *s. m.* adolescent, youth.

adopter, *v.a.* adopt, pass.

adoption, *s. f.* adoption.

adorer, *v.a.* adore.

adresse, *s. f.* address; skill, dexterity.

adresser, *v. a.* address, direct; *s'~* apply (to).

adroit, *adj.* clever, skilful.

adulte, *adj. & s.* adult.

adversaire, *s. m.* adversary.

aérien, -enne, *adj.* aerial.

aérodrome, *s. m.* airport.

aéroport, *s. m.* airport.

affaiblir, *v. a.* weaken.

affaire, *s. f.* business, affair, matter; lawsuit.

affamé, *adj.* hungry.

affecter, *v. a.* affect, feign; move; assume.

affection, *s.f.* affection; disease.

affectueux, -euse, *adj.* affectionate.

affermir, *v. a.* strengthen; *s'~* become stronger.

affiche, *s. f.* poster, bill.

afficher, *v. a.* post up, stick up, placard.

affiler, *v.a.* sharpen.

affirmatif, -ive, *adj.* affirmative.

affirmer, *v. a.* affirm.

affliger, *v. a.* afflict.

affluer, *v. n.* flow into.

affranchir, *v. a.* (set) free; stamp.

affreux, -euse, *adj.* dreadful, terrible.

affronter, *v.a.* face.

afin, *conj.* ~ **de** in order to; ~ **que** in order that, so that.

africain (A.), *adj. & s. m. f.* African.

âge, *s. m.* age; period; *quel* ~ *avez-vous?* how old are you?

agence, *s. f.* agency.

agent, *s. m.* agent; policeman.

aggraver, *v.a.* aggravate.

agile, *adj.* agile, active.

agilité, *s. f.* agility.

agir, *v. n.* act; take effect; behave; s'~ be in question.

agitation, *s. f.* agitation.

agiter, *v. a.* agitate.

agneau, *s. m.* lamb.

agonie, *s. f.* agony.

agréable, *adj.* agreeable.

agréer, *v. a.* accept, receive favourably.

agrément, *s.m.* consent, approval; pleasure.

agressif, -ive, *adj.* aggressive.

agression, *s. f.* aggression, attack.

agriculture, *s.f.* agriculture.

aide, *s. f.* help.

aider, *v.a.* help.

aïeux, *s. m. pl.* ancestors.

aigle, *s. m.* eagle.

aigre, *adj.* sour, acid.

aigrir: s'~ turn sour.

aigu, *adj.* pointed, sharp; keen; *accent* ~ acute accent.

aiguille, *s.f.* needle; hand, index; point, switch; *grande* ~ minute hand.

aiguiser, *v. a.* sharpen.

ail, *s. m.* garlic.

aile, *s. f.* wing; flank; aisle; mudguard.

ailleurs, *adv.* somewhere else, elsewhere; d'~ in addition, besides.

aimable, *adj.* amiable, pleasant, kindly.

aimer, *v. a. & n.* like, love, be fond of, care to.

aîné, *adj. & s. m. f.* elder, eldest; senior.

ainsi, *adv. & conj.* so, thus; likewise; ~ *de suite* and so on; ~ *que* as well as.

air, *s. m.* air; look(s), appearance, manner; *(music)* air.

aisance, *s. f.* ease; comfort; facility; *être dans l'*~ be well off.

aise, *s. f.* ease, comfort.

aisé, *adj.* easy; well-off.

ajourner, *v.a.* adjourn.

alcool, *s. m.* alcohol.

alcoolique, *adj.* alcoholic.

algèbre, *s. f.* algebra.

aliment, *s. m.* aliment, food.

alimentation, *s.f.* alimentation; feeding.

alimenter, *v. a.* feed.

aliter, *v. a. être alité* be confined to bed, be laid up.

allaiter, *v. a.* give suck to; nurse.

allée, *s. f.* (garden) path, lane, walk, alley.

alléger, *v.a.* lighten; alleviate, soothe.

allégresse, *s. f.* gaiety, delight.

allemand (A.), *adj. & s. m. f.* German.

aller, *v. n.* go, proceed; get on; grow, get; ~ *à pied* walk; ~ *en auto* drive; ~ *en avion* fly; ~ *bien* be well; *comment allez-vous?* how are you?; *allons!* come on!; *allez!* indeed; *s'en* ~ go away, be off.

alliance, *s. f.* alliance, union; wedding-ring.

allié, -e, *s. m. f.* ally; — *adj.* allied.

allier, *v.a.* alloy; match; unite; *s'* ~ join with, unite.

allonger, *v.a.* lengthen, stretch out; prolong; ~ *le pas* step out; *s'* ~ get longer.

allumer, *v. a.* light (up), set on fire; excite.

allumette, *s. f.* match.

allure, *s. f.* gait, pace; manner, behaviour; direction.

allusion, *s. f.* allusion, hint; reference.

alors, *adv.* then.

alpinisme, *s. m.* mountaineering.

altérer, *v. a.* alter, change; *s'* ~ alter, degenerate.

alternance, *s. f.* alternation.

alternatif, -ive, *adj.* alternate, alternative.

alterner, *v. n. & a.* alternate.

altitude, *s. f.* altitude.

aluminium, *s. f.* aluminium.

amaigrir, *v.a.* make thin; *s'* ~ grow thin.

amant, -e, *s. m. f.* lover.

amas, *s.m.* heap, mass, pile.

amateur, *s. m.* amateur, lover, fancier.

ambassade, *s. f.* embassy.

ambassadeur, *s. m.* ambassador.

ambassadrice, *s. f.* ambassadress.

ambitieux, -euse, *adj.* ambitious.

ambition, *s. f.* ambition.

ambulance, *s. f.* ambulance; ~ *(automobile)* ambulance(-car).

âme, *s. f.* soul; mind.

améliorer, *v. a.* ameliorate, improve; *s'* ~ improve.

aménager, *v.a.* fit up, out.

amender, *v.a.* amend, improve.

amener, *v. a.* bring, draw; bring before, in, out; introduce; induce.

amer, -ère, *adj.* bitter.

américain, -e (A.), *adj. & s. m. f.* American.

ami, -e, *s. m. f.* friend; sweetheart; *bon* ~, *bonne* ~*e* sweetheart.

amical, *adj.* friendly, kind.

amiral, *s. m.* admiral.

amitié, *s. f.* friendship; affection; *meilleures* ~*s* kindest regards.

amortir, *v.a.* lessen, soften; pay (off), write off.

amortisseur, *s. m.* shock-absorber.

amour, *s. m.* love; *faire l'* ~ court, make love to; *mon* ~ my darling.

amoureux, -euse, *adj.* in

love *(de* with), enamoured *(de* of).

amplificateur, *s.m.* amplifier.

amplifier, *v. a.* amplify.

ampoule, *s. f.* blister; bulb.

amulette, *s. f.* amulet.

amusant, *adj.* amusing.

amusement, *s. m.* amusement, pastime, fun.

amuser, *v.a.* amuse, entertain; s'~ enjoy oneself.

an, *s. m.* year; *il y a un* ~ . a year ago.

analogie, *s. f.* analogy.

analogue, *adj.* analogous.

analyse, *s. f.* analysis.

analyser, *v. a.* analyse.

ananas, *s. m.* pineapple.

anatomie, *s. f.* anatomy.

ancêtre, *s. m. f.* ancestor.

ancien, -enne, *adj.* ancient, old, antique.

ancre, *s. f.* anchor; *lever l'*~ weigh anchor.

âne, *s. m.* ass.

anéantir, *v. a.* annihilate.

anecdote, *s.f.* anecdote.

ange, *s. m.* angel.

anglais, -e (A.), *adj.* English; — *s. m. f.* Englishman, Englishwoman.

angle, *s. m.* angle, corner; bend.

angoisse, *s.f.* anguish.

animal, *s.m.* animal; beast.

anneau, *s. m.* circle, ring.

année, *s. f.* year; ~ *scolaire* school-year; *bonne* ~ a happy New Year!

annexer, *v. a.* annex.

anniversaire, *s. m.* anniversary, b rthday.

annonce, *s. f.* announcement, advertisement.

annoncer, *v. a.* announce, give notice of; advertise.

annuaire, *s. m.* year-book, annual, directory.

annuel, -elle, *adj.* annual.

annuler, *v. a.* annul.

anonyme, *adj.* anonymous; *société* ~ joint-stock company.

anormal, *adj.* abnormal.

anse, *s. f.* handle; creek.

antécédent, -e, *adj. & s.m.* antecedent.

antenne, *s. f.* aerial.

antérieur, *adj.* anterior, previous.

antibiotique, *s. m.* antibiotic.

antichambre, *s. f.* entrance hall.

anticiper, *v. a. & n.* anticipate; encroach.

antipathie, *s.f.* antipathy.

antiquaire, *s. m.* antiquarian.

antique, *adj.* antique, ancient.

antiquité, *s. f.* antiquity.

antiseptique, *adj. & s. m.* antiseptic.

anxiété, *s.f.* anxiety.

anxieux, -euse, *adj.* anxious.

août, *s.m.* August.

apaiser, *v. a.* appease, pacify, quiet.

apercevoir, *v. a.* perceive, catch sight of; remark, notice.

aplanir, *v.a.* smooth, level, even off; s'~ become level.

aplatir, *v.a.* flatten.

apologie, *s. m.* apology, defence.

apoplexie, *s. f.* apoplexy.

apostolique, *adj.* apostolic(al).

apostrophe, *s. f.* apostrophe.

apôtre, *s. m.* apostle.

apparaître, *v. n.* appear.

appareil, *s. m.* apparatus, device, appliance, gear; camera; ~ de TV TV-set; ~ de direction steering-gear.

apparence, *s. f.* appearance, look(s); likelihood; en ~ apparently.

apparent, *adj.* apparent.

apparition, *s. f.* appearance; apparition.

appartement, *s.m.* flat; apartment.

appartenir, *v.n.* belong, appertain (à to).

appel, *s. m.* call; appeal; faire l'~ call the roll.

appeler, *v. a.* call in, out, up, down; ring up; name, term; en ~ appeal; faire ~ send for; s'~ be called, call oneself.

appendice, *s. m.* appendix.

appendicite, *s.f.* appedicitis.

appesantir, *v.a.* make heavy, weigh down.

appétit, *s. m.* appetite.

applaudir, *v. n.* applaud, clap.

application, *s. f.* application; diligence.

appliquer, *v. a.* apply; lay on.

apporter, *v.a.* bring.

appréciation, *s.f.* appreciation; estimation.

apprécier, *v. a.* value.

appréhension, *s. f.* apprehension, fear.

apprendre, *v. a.* learn, acquire; hear of; teach.

apprentissage, *s. m.* apprenticeship.

apprêter, *v. a.* prepare; season; dress; s'~ prepare oneself, get ready.

approbation, *s.f.* approbation, approval.

approche, *s. f.* approach, advance.

approcher, *v.a.* bring toward, forward.

approprié, *adj.* appropriate.

approprier: s'~ appropriate, take; accommodate, adapt oneself.

approuver, *v. a.* sanction; approve.

approximatif, -ive, *adj.* approximate.

approximation, *s.f.* approximation.

appui, *s. m.* support.

appuyer, *v. a.* support; lean; v. n. ~ sur lay stress (up)on; s'~ lean, rest, rely (upon).

après, *adv.* after; behind; next (to); ~ coup too late; ~ tout after all; d'~ after, according to; by.

après-demain, *adv. & s. m.* (the) day after tomorrow.

après-midi, *s. m.* afternoon.

à-propos, *adv.* in good time; — *s. m.* timely word; fitness.

apte, *adj.* apt, suitable.

aptitude, *s. f.* aptitude, ability, talent.

aquarelle, *s.f.* water-color.

arabe (A.), *adj. & s. m., f.* Arab, Arabian; Arabic.

araignée, *s. f.* spider.

arbitre, *s. f.* arbiter, judge;

umpire, referee.

arbre, *s. m.* tree; shaft; ~ *fruitier* fruit-tree; ~ *coudé* crank shaft.

arc, *s. m.* bow; arc(h).

arcade, *s. f.* arcade.

arche, *s. f.* arch, vault.

archet, *s. m.* bow.

archevêque, *s. m.* archbishop.

architecture, *s. f.* architecture.

archives *s. f. pl.* archives.

ardemment, *adv.* ardently.

ardent, *adj.* burning, fiery, ardent, eager.

ardeur, *s. f.* keenness; ardour, zeal.

arête, *s. f.* fish-bone; edge; ridge.

argent, *s. m.* silver; money; ~ *en caisse* cash in hand ~ *comptant* ready money; ~ *de la poche* pocket-money; *à-court d'~* pressed for money.

argenterie, *s. f.* plate.

argentin[1], *adj.* silvery.

argentin[2], -e (A.), *adj. & s. m. f.* Argentine.

argile, *s.f.* clay.

argot, *s. m.* slang.

argument, *s.m.* argument, proof, evidence.

aristocratie, *s.f.* aristocracy.

aristocratique, *adj.* aristocratic.

arme, *s.f.* arm, weapon; ~*s à feu* fire-arms; *faire des* ~*s* fence.

armée, *s. f.* army.

armer, *v.a.* arm; fortify; *s'*~ arm oneself.

armoire, *s.f.* cupboard; wardrobe.

armure, *s. f.* armour; armature.

arracher, *v.a.* pull (out), tear up; extract, draw; remove from.

arrangement, *s. m.* arrangement; agreement; settlement; ~*s* terms.

arranger, *v. a.* arrange, settle, fix (up); *s'*~ come to an agreement, make arrangements (for); make shift (to).

arrestation, *s. f.* arrest.

arrêt, *s. m.* stop (of bus, tram etc.); pause; standstill; sentence; arrest; ~ *facultatif* request stop; *sans* ~ non-stop.

arrêter, *v.a.* check, stop; arrest; engage, book; decide, decree; settle; *s'*~ stop; draw up; leave off.

arrière. *adv.* behind, backward; *en* ~ back(ward) ~ *s. m.* back part, rear.

arriéré, *adj.* overdue; backward; under-developed; — *s.m.* arrears (*pl.*).

arrivée, *s. f.* arrival; *à l'*~ on arrival.

arriver, *v. n.* arrive, come; turn up; happen; occur; ~ *à* attain, arrive at, reach; *le train arrive à* the train is due at.

arrogance, *s. f.* arrogance.

arroser, *v. a.* water, sprinkle; baste.

art, *s. m.* art; *les beaux* ~*s* the fine arts.

artère, *s.f.* artery; thoroughfare.

article, *s. m.* article; ~*s de grande consommation* consumer(s') goods.

articulation, *s. f.* joint.

articuler, *v.a.* articulate.

artificiel, -elle, *adj.* artificial.

artillerie, *s. f.* artillery.

artisan, *s. m.* craftsman.

artiste, *s. m. & f.* artist; player

ascenseur, *s. m.* lift.

asile, *s. m.* refuge, asylum.

aspect, *s.m.* aspect.

asperge, *s. f.* asparagus.

aspirateur, *s.m.* vacuum-cleaner.

aspiration, *s. f.* aspiration.

aspirer, *v.a.* inspire; *v. n.* aspire *(à* to).

assaillir*, *v. a.* assault.

assaisonner, *v.a.* season; dress.

assassin, *s. m.* assassin.

assassiner, *v. a.* assassinate, murder.

assaut, *s.m.* assault.

assemblage, *s. m.* assemblage, gathering, collection.

assemblée, *s.f.* assembly, meeting.

assembler, *v. a.* assemble; put together; gather; **s'~** assemble.

asseoir*, *v. a.* seat; place; **s'~** take a seat.

assez, *adv.* enough; pretty, fairly.

assiduité, *s.f.* assiduity.

assiéger, *v.a.* attack, besiege.

assiette, *s. f.* posture; seat; position; plate.

assimiler, *v. a.* assimilate *(* ` *1 * to).

assistance, *s.f.* presence, attendance; audience; assistance, help.

assister, *v. n.* attend, be present *(* `1` at); *v. a.* assist, help.

association, *s. f.* association; partnership, company.

associer, *v.a.* associate, link up; share interests with; **s'~** associate oneself *(avec* with).

assommant, *adj.* boring, dull.

assortir, *v.a.* match, assort; **s'~** be suitable, go well together.

assoupir, *v. a.* make drowsy, sleepy; **s'~** grow sleepy.

assujettir, *v.a.* subject, subjugate.

assumer, *v. a.* assume.

assurance, *s. f.* assurance; insurance; **~** *sur la vie* life-insurance.

assuré, *adj.* assured, confident, sure; insured.

assurer, *v. a.* assure, secure; insure; **s'~** make sure (of).

astre, *s. m.* star.

astronaute, *s. m.* astronaut, space man.

astronautique, *s. f.* astronautics, space travel.

astronef, *s. m.* spacecraft, space-ship.

atelier, *s.m.* workshop; studio.

athée, *s.m.f.* atheist.

athlète, *s.m.* athlete.

athlétique, *adj.* athletic.

atome, *s.m.* atom.

atomique, *adj.* atomic; *bombe* **~** atom(ic) bomb *énergie* **~** atomic energy.

attache, *s. f.* tie, fastener; bond, strap; *fig.* attachment.

attaché, *s. m.* attaché.

attacher, *v.a.* fasten, tie (up), attach; associate; engage; **s'~** attach (to),

become attached (to).

attaque, *s. f.* attack.

attaquer, *v.a.* attack.

attarder, *v.a.* delay; *être attardé* be delayed.

atteindre*, *v. a.* attain, reach; hit, stirke.

atteinte, *s. f.* blow, stroke; fit; injury; *hors d'~* out of reach.

attendre, *v. a. & n.* await, wait for, expect; s'~ hope for, expect.

attendrir, *v. a.* soften; *fig.* move, touch; s'~ be moved.

attendrissement, *s.m.* compassion; tenderness.

attente, *s. f.* waiting; hope

attentif, -ive, *adj.* attentive, considerate.

attention, *s.f.* attention, notice, heed, care; *(pl.)* attentions; *faire* ~ be careful, mind, take notice of, take heed (to); ~*!* look out!

atténuer, *v. a.* extenuate, attenuate.

atterrir, *v. n.* land.

atterrissage, *s. m.* landing; *piste d'~* landing-strip.

attester, *v.a.* attest.

attirail, *s. m.* implements *(pl.)*, utensils *(pl.)*, gear; tackle.

attirer, *v.a.* attract.

attitude, *s. f.* attitude.

attraction, *s.f.* attraction.

attrape, *s. f.* trap; catch.

attribuer, *v. a.* assign, allot; attribute, ascribe.

attribut, *s. m.* attribute.

au *(pl.* aux), to the, at the.

auberge, *s. f.* inn, tavern; ~ *de la jeunesse* youth hostel.

aucun, *adj. & pron.* no, none, no one, not any.

au-dessous, *adv.* below; ~ *de* under.

au-dessus, *adv.* (~ *de*) above, over.

audience, *s. f.* audience; public; sitting, session.

audiovisuel, -elle, *adj.* audio-visual.

auditeur, -trice, *s. m. f.* listener; auditor.

auditoire, *s. m.* audience; congregation.

auge, *s.m.* trough; bucket.

augmentation, *s.f.* augmentation, increase; rise.

augmenter, *v. a.* augment, increase; s'~ increase.

aujourd'hui, *adv.* today.

auparavant, *adv.* previously, earlier; before.

auprès, *adv.* near, by, close by; ~ *de* near.

auquel, *rel.pron.* to whom, to which.

aurore, *s.f.* dawn.

aussi, *adv.* also, too; ~ ... *que* as ... as; — *conj.* and so, therefore; ~ *bien que* as well as; ~ *bien* in fact.

austère, *adj.* austere, severe.

autant, *adv. & conj.* as much, as many, as far; ~ *que* as far as, as much as.

autel, *s. m.* altar.

auteur, *s. m.* author.

authentique, *adj.* authentic, genuine.

auto, *s. f.* car.

autobus, *s. m.* (motor-)bus.

autocar, *s. m.* (motor-)coach.

automatique, *adj.* automatic; — *s.m.* dial-telephone.

automne, *s. m. f.* autumn.

automobile, *s. m. f.* motor-car.

autonomie, *s.f.* autonomy.

autorisation, *s. f.* authorization, permission; licence.

autoriser, *v.a.* authorize.

autorité, *s. f.* authority; rule.

autoroute, *s. f.* motor-way.

auto-stop, *s. m.* hitch-hiking.

auto-stoppeur, -euse, *s. m. f.* hitch-hiker.

autour, *adv. & prep.* ~ de about, (a)round; *tout* ~ all round.

autre, *adj.* different, other, another, else; *un* ~ another; *d'*~ *part* on the other hand; ~ *part* elsewhere; *de temps* ~ now and then, at times; *i'*~ *jour* the other day; *l'un et l'*~ both; *l'un l'*~ each other.

autrefois, *adv.* formerly, long ago.

autrichien, -enne (A.), *adj. & s.m.f.* Austrian.

autrui, *pron.* others, other people.

avalanche, *s.f.* avalanche.

avaler, *v.a.* swallow; *fig.* endure, pocket.

avance, *s.f.* advance.

avancé, *adj.* advanced.

avancement, *s.m.* advance, progress; promotion.

avancer, *v.a.* advance, bring, put forward; pay in advance; — *v. n.*

advance, proceed, move on; s'~ come, move, go forward.

avant, *prep. & adv.* before, in front (of), in advance; ~ *tout* above all, before everything; *en* ~ forward, to the front; *mettre en* ~ bring forward; *en* ~ *de* in front of; — *s.m.* front (part); bow (of ship); forward.

avantage, *s. m.* advantage, benefit, profit; *(tennis)* vantage.

avantageux, -euse, *adj.* advantageous.

avant-hier, *adv.* day before yesterday.

avant-propos, *s. m.* foreword, preface.

avare, *s. m. f.* miser; — *adj.* avaricious, miserly.

avarice, *s.f.* avarice.

avec, *prep.* with.

avenir, *s. m.* future; *à l'*~ in the future.

aventure, *s. f.* adventure; chance, luck.

aventurer, *v.a.* risk; (s'~) venture.

aventurier, -ère, *s. m. f.* adventurer.

avenue, *s. f.* boulevard; avenue.

averse, *s.f.* shower (of rain).

aversion, *v. f.* aversion, dislike.

avertir, *v.a.* inform, let know; warn; *faire* ~ *de* give notice of.

avertissement, *s. m.* information, notification; advice; warning.

aveu, *s.m.* admission, confession; consent.

aveugle, *adj.* blind.

aveuglement, *s. m.* blindness.

avide, *adj.* greedy, eager.

avidité, *s.f.* avidity.

avilir, *v.a.* debase, disgrace, degrade.

avion, *v. a.* (aero)plane; ~ *de ligne* air-liner; ~ *à réaction* jet plane; *par* ~ by air-mail.

avis, *s. m.* opinion; advice, counsel; information, notice; hint; mind; *changer d'*~ change one's mind.

aviser, *v.a.* perceive; inform; let know; advise; *s'*~ *de* think, find.

avocat, *s. m.* barrister, advocate, counsel.

avoine, *s.f.* oat(s).

avoir*, *v. a.* have, possess; have on, wear; feel; ~ *raison* be right; ~ *faim* be hungry; ~ *de* take after; ~ *à* have to; *il y a* there is, there are; ago.

avorter, *v. n.* miscarry, have a miscarriage.

avorton, *s. m.* abortion.

avoué, *s. m.* attorney, solicitor; lawyer.

avouer, *v. a. & n.* admit, confess; acknowledge; approve.

avril, *s.m.* April.

axe, *s.m.* axis; axle.

azote, *s.m.* nitrogen.

B

baccalauréat, *s. m.* baccalaureate, bachelor's degree.

bachelier, *s. m.* bachelor

(of arts etc.).

bacille, *s.m.* bacillus.

bagage, *s. m.* luggage; *plier* ~ pack up one's kit.

bague, *s.f.* ring.

bai, *adj.* bay.

baie¹, *s. f.* bay.

baie², *s. f.* berry.

baigner: se ~ bathe.

baignoire, *s.m.* bath, bathtub; pit-box.

bâiller, *v. n.* yawn, gape.

bain, *s. m.* bath; *salle de* ~ bath-room.

baïonette, *s.f.* bayonet.

baiser, *v.a.* kiss.

baisse, *s.f.* fall; decline.

baisser, *v.a.* lower, let down; bring down; turn down; cast down; *v.n.* decline; fall; sink; se ~ stoop.

bal, *s. m.* ball; ~ *costumé* fancy-dress ball.

balai, *s.m.* broom, mop; (house-)brush; *donner un coup de* ~ sweep.

balance, *s. f.* balance, scales *(pl.)*.

balancer, *v.a.&n.* balance; weigh; swing, rock; give the sack; **se** ~ swing, wave; balance.

balayer, *v.a.* sweep (out), clear away.

balcon, *s. m.* balcony; dress-circle.

baleine, *s.f.* whale.

ballade, *s.f.* ballad.

balle, *s.f.* ball; bullet; bale.

ballon, *s.m.* balloon; (foot-)ball.

balnéaire, *adj.* pertaining to baths; *station* ~ watering place.

bambou, *s.m.* bamboo.

ban, *s. m.* ban; **~s** *de mariage* banns.

banal *adj.* banal, common, ordinary.

banane, *s. f.* banana.

banc, *s. m.* bench, form; bank; pew; stand.

bande, *s.f.* band, strip; bandage; troop, gang, set; **~** *de papier* slip of paper; **~** *transporteuse* conveyer belt.

bander, *v. a.* bind up.

bandit, *s. m.* bandit.

banlieue, *s. f.* outskirts, suburbs *(pl.).*

bannir, *v. a.* banish, exile.

banque, *s. f.* bank; *billet de* **~** banknote; *compte en* **~** bankaccount.

banquet, *s. m.* banquet, feast.

banquier, -ère, *s.m.f.* banker.

baptême, *s. m.* baptism.

baptiser, *v.a.* baptize.

barbare, *adj. & s.m.* barbarian.

barbarie, *s. f.* barbarousness, cruelty.

barbe, *s. f.* beard; *faire la* **~** *à* shave.

barbet, *s. m.* poodle.

barbier, *s. m.* barber.

baron, *s. m.* baron.

baronne, *s. f.* baroness.

barque, *s.f.* boat, barge.

barrage, *s.m.* barrier, barrage, dam.

barre, *s.f.* bar.

barreau, *s. m.* (small) bar; the Bar.

barrer, *v.a.* fasten, bar; cut off, shut out; steer.

barrière, *s.f.* barrier, town-gate, gate; bar;

obstacle.

barrique, *s.f.* barrel, cask.

bas¹, *adj.* low; *à* **~** *prix* cheap; *terre* **~se** lowland; *en* **~** (down) below, down(-wards), — *s. m.* bottom, lower part

bas², *s. m.* stocking; **~** *nylons* nylon stockings.

base, *s. f.* base; basis.

basique, *adj.* basic.

basse, *s.f.* bass; bass-viol.

bassesse, *s.f.* lowness, meanness.

basset, *s. m.* basset (dog).

bassin, *s. m.* basin, pool.

bataille, *s.f.* battle.

bataillon, *s. m.* battalion.

bateau, *s. m.* boat.

batelier, *s.m.* boatman.

bâtiment, *s. m.* building; building trade; ship.

bâtir, *v.a.* build, erect.

bâtisseur, -euse *s. m. f.* builder.

bâton, *s. m.* stick, staff.

batte, *s.f.* bat; beater.

battement, *s.m.* clap(ping); flapping.

batterie, *s.f.* battery; fight, row; percussive instruments *(pl.);* **~** *de cuisine* kitchen utensils *(pl.).*

battre*, *v. a. & n.* beat, strike, thrash; *se* **~** fight.

battu, *adj.* beaten.

bavard, -e *s.m.f.* gossip.

bavarder, *v.n.* chat(ter), gossip.

bazar, *s.m.* bazaar.

beau, bel; belle; beaux, belles, *adj.* beautiful, handsome, good-looking, fair; considerable; *il y a* ~ *temps que* it seems an age since; *un* ~ *jour* one fine day; — *s.m.* beauty.

beaucoup, *adv.* (~ *de)* a good deal, many, much; plenty (of); *a* ~ *près, de* ~ by far.

beau-frère, *s. m.* brother-in-law.

beau-père, *s. m.* father-in-law.

beauté, *s. f.* beauty.

beaux-arts, *s. m. pl.* (the) fine arts.

bébé, *s. m.* baby.

bec, *s. m.* beak, bill nib; mouth-piece; jet; ~ *de gaz* gas-burner, gas-jet.

bêche, *s. f.* spade.

bégayer, *v. n. &a.* stammer, stutter.

belge (B.), *adj.* & *s. m. f.* Belgian.

belle-fille, *s. f.* daughter-in-law; step-daughter.

belle-mère, *s. f.* mother-in-law; stepmother.

belle-sœur, *s. f.* sister-in-law.

bémol, *s. m.* & *adj.* flat (music).

bénédiction, *s. f.* benediction, blessing.

bénéfice, *s. m.* benefit, advantage, profit.

bénir, *v. a.* bless; praise.

berceau, *s. m.* cradle; *fig.* origin.

bercer, *v. a.* rock, lull (to sleep); *fig.* lull (with promises).

béret, *s.m.* beret.

berger, *s. m.* shepherd.

bergère, *s. f.* shepherdess; deep easy chair.

bésicles, *s. f. pl.* spectacles; goggles.

besogne, *s. f.* (piece of) work, job, task.

besoin, *s. m.* need, want; requirement; *avoir* ~ *de* want, need; *être dans le* ~ be poor.

bétail, *s. m.* cattle.

bête, *s. f.* beast; animal; — *adj.* foolish, silly, stupid, dull.

bêtise, *s. f.* foolishness, stupidity; nonsense; trifle.

beurre, *s. m.* butter.

biais, *s. m.* bias, slant, slope.

blaiser, *v. n.* slant, slope.

bibelot, *s. m.* trinket, gew-gaw.

biberon, *s. m.* feeding-bottle.

bible, *s. f.* Bible.

bibliothécaire, *s. m. f.* librarian.

bibliothèque, *s. f.* library; bookcase; bookstall.

bicyclette, *s. f.* bicycle, bike.

bicycliste, *s. m. f.* cyclist.

bien, *adv.* well, right, properly, fully; *assez* ~ fairly; *faire du* ~ benefit; *ou* ~ or else; *très* ~ very well, all right; ~ *avant* long before; very bad indeed; ~ *que* (al)though; – *s. m.* good, welfare, benefit; property, goods; *aller à* ~ prosper, be successful.

bien-être, *s. m.* welfare, well-being.

bienfaisance, *s. f.* beneficence.

bienfaisant, *adj.* charitable, kind; humane.

bienfait, *s. m.* kindness; benefaction.

bientôt, *adv.* soon, shortly; *à ~!* so long!

bienveillance, *s. f.* benevolence, kindness.

bienveillant, *adj.* kind(ly), benevolent, charitable.

bienvenu, *adj.* welcome; *soyez le ~* welcome!

bière, *s. f.* beer.

bifteck, *s. m.* beef-steak.

bijou, *s. m.* (*pl.* -x) jewel.

bijouterie, *s. f.* jewellery; jeweller's shop.

bijoutier, -ière *s. m. f.* jeweller.

bile, *s. f.* bile; *se faire de la ~* worry, fret.

bille, *s. f.* billiard-ball.

billet, *s. m.* note; ticket; certificate; *~ d'aller et retour* return ticket; *~ d'entrée* admission ticket; *~ de banque* banknote.

billot, *s. m.* block; yoke.

biographe, *s. m. f.* biographer.

biographie, *s. f.* biography.

biologie, *s. f.* biology.

biologiste, biologue, *s. m. f.* biologist.

bis, *int.* encore!

biscuit, *s. m.* biscuit.

bison, *s. m.* bison.

bistro, *s. m.* pub; wine-shop.

bizarre, *adj.* strange, odd.

blague, *s. f.* pouch.

blaireau, *s. m.* badger; shaving-brush.

blâme, *s. m.* blame, reprimand.

blâmer, *v. a.* blame; find fault with.

blanc, blanche, *adj.* white; hoary; blank.

blanchir, *v. a.* whiten, bleach; whitewash; *v. n.* turn white, whiten.

blasphème, *s. m.* blasphemy.

blasphémer, *v. a. & n.* blaspheme.

blé, *s. m.* wheat.

blême, *adj.* pale.

blesser, *v. a.* wound, injure, hurt; offend; *se ~* wound oneself; be offended.

blessure, *s. f.* wound, injury; offence.

bleu, *adj. & s. m.* blue; *~ marine* navy blue.

bloc, *s. m.* block; *en ~* in the lump.

blond, *adj.* fair, blond.

bloquer, *v. a.* blockade; block (up); tighten.

blouse, *s. f.* blouse, smock.

bobine, *s. f.* bobbin, spool.

bœuf, *s. m.* ox, beef.

bohème, *adj.* bohemian.

boire, *v. a. & n.* drink; swallow; *~ à la santé de X* drink X's health; — *s. m.* drink(ing).

bois, *s. m.* wood; timber; *de, en ~* wood(en).

boisson, *s. f.* drink, beverage.

boîte, *s. f.* box, case; can, tin; *~ aux lettres* letter-box; *~ de vitesse* gear-box; *en ~* tinned.

boiteux, -euse *adj.* lame.

bombardement, *s. m.* bombardment.

bombarder, *v. a.* bombard, shell.

bombe, *s. f.* bomb, shell; ~ *H* H-bomb.

bon, bonne, *adj.* good; kind, nice; right; valid; *c'est* ~! (all) right!; ~ *à rien* good for nothing; ~*ne année!* happy new year!; *de* ~*ne heure* early; — *s. m.* good(ness); bond, order.

bonbon, *s. m.* bonbon, sweet.

bond, *s. m.* bound, leap.

bondé, *adj.* crowded.

bonder, *v. a.* load, cram.

bondir, *v. n.* bound, leap, spring.

bonheur, *s. m.* happiness; good fortune; success.

bonhomme, *s. m.* good-natured man; simple man; fellow.

bonjour, *s. m.* good morning; salutation.

bonne, *s. f.* maid-servant; ~ *(d'enfants)* nursery-maid.

bonnet, *s. m.* cap, hood.

bonsoir, *s. m.* good evening.

bonté, *s. f.* goodness, kindness, benevolence.

bord, *s. m.* edge, border, brink, (b)rim, verge; side, board, bank; *à* ~ on board; *monter à* ~ go on board.

border, *v. a.* border, adjoin.

bordure, *s. f.* border, edging; verge; kerb.

borne, *s. f.* milestone; bound(ary), limit.

borner, *v. a.* bound, limit, restrict.

bosse, *s. f.* bump, protuberance; knob.

botanique, *adj.* botanical; — *s. f.* botany.

botte[1], *s. f.* (high) boot.

botte[2], *s. f.* bottle; truss.

bottine, *s. f.* boot.

bouche, *s. f.* mouth; orifice, muzzle.

boucher, *s. m.* butcher.

boucherie, *s. f.* butcher's (shop).

bouchon, *s. m.* plug, cork, stopper.

boue, *s. f.* mud, dirt.

bouger, *v. n.* stir, budge.

bougie, *s. f.* candle. (sparking-)plug.

bouillir*, *v. n. & a.* (also *faire* ~) boil.

bouillon, *s. m.* bubble; stock; ~ *de bœuf* beef-tea.

bouillotte, *s. f.* kettle.

boulanger, -ère, *s. m. f.* baker; baker's wife.

boulangerie, *s. f.* bakery, baker's (shop).

boule, *s. f.* ball, bowl.

boulevard, *s. m.* boulevard.

bouleverser, *v. a.* overthrow, upset; turn upside down; distract.

boulon, *s. m.* bolt, pin.

bouquet, *s. m.* cluster, bunch; bouquet.

bourdonnement, *s. m.* buzz(ing), humming.

bourdonner, *v. n.* buzz, hum, drone.

bourg, *s. m.* (small) town; village.

bourgeois, e, *s. m. f.* citizen; townsman.

bourgeoisie, *s. f.* citizens *(pl.)*; middle class.

bourse, *s. f.* purse; exchange; Stock Exchange; scholarship, bursary.

bousculade, *s. f.* hustling.

bousculer, *v. a.* upset, hustle, jostle; **se ~** hustle each other.

bout, *s. m.* end, extremity, tip, top, button; **un ~ de chemin** a short distance.

bouteille, *s. f.* bottle.

boutique, *s. f.* shop; booth, stall.

bouton, *s. m.* button; stud; bud; nipple; knob; **~s de manchette** cuff-links.

boutonnière, *s. f.* buttonhole.

boxer, *v. n.* box, fight.

boxeur, *s. m.* boxer.

bracelet, *s. m.* bracelet.

braconner, *v. n.* poach.

braconnier, *s. m.* poacher.

brancard, *s. m.* stretcher; shaft.

branche, *s. f.* branch.

branler, *v. a.* shake, totter, waver.

bras, *s. m.* arm; hand; branch.

braser, *v.a.* braze, solder.

brasserie, *s. f.* brewery; beershop.

brave, *adj.* brave; honest, worthy, good.

braver, *v. a.* face, brave.

bravoure, *s. f.* bravery, courage.

brebis, *s. f.* ewe, sheep.

brèche, *s. f.* breach, gap.

bref, brève, *adj.* brief, short.

bretelles, *s. f. pl.* braces.

brevet, *s. m.* patent; certificate.

bride, *s. f.* bridle, reins.

brièveté, *s. f.* brevity.

brigade, *s. f.* brigade.

brigadier, *s. m.* corporal, overseer.

brigand, *s. m.* brigand, armed robber.

brillant, *adj.* brilliant, shiny, glittering.

briller, *v.n.* shine, glitter, sparkle.

brin, *s. m.* shoot, sprig, blade (of grass).

brioche, *s. f.* brioche.

brique, *s. f.* brick; bar (of soap).

briquet, *s. m.* lighter.

briquette, *s.f.* briquette.

brise, *s. f.* breeze.

briser, *v. a.* break (to pieces), smash; *v. n.* break; **se ~** break to pieces.

britannique, *adj.* British.

broche, *s. f.* brooch; knitting-needle; spindle, spit.

brochure, *s. f.* pamphlet.

broder, *v. a.* embroider.

broderie, *s. f.* embroidery, braid.

bronchite, *s. f.* bronchitis.

bronze, *s. m.* bronze.

brosse, *s. f.* brush; **~ à barbe** shaving-brush; **~ à dents** tooth-brush; **~ à cheveux** hairbrush; **donner un coup de ~** a brush up.

brosser, *v.a.* brush; **se ~** brush oneself.

brouillard, *s. m.* mist, fog.

brouille, *s. f.* quarrel.

brouiller, *v.a.* mingle, mix; confuse, embroil;

shuffle (cards).

broyer, *v. a.* crush, pound.

bruire, *v.n.* rustle!

bruit, *s. m.* noise, din; fuss; rumour.

brûlant, *adj.* burning, hot, scorching; fiery.

brûler, *v. a.* & *n.* burn, scorch, roast; ~ *de long for.*

brume, *s. f.* mist, fog.

brumeux, -euse *adj.* foggy.

brun, *adj.* brown.

brusque, *adj.* sudden, curt, gruff.

brutal, *adj.* brutal, rude savage.

brute, *s. f.* brute.

bruyant, *adj.* noisy, loud.

budget, *s. m.* budget.

buffet, *s. m.* sideboard; buffet; refreshment room.

buisson, *s. m.* bush, shrub.

bulbe, *s. m.* bulb.

bulle, *s. f.* bubble; bull.

bulletin, *s.m.* bulletin.

bureau, *s. m.* (writing-)desk; bureau, office; department; board, committee; ~ *de location* box-office; ~ *de poste* post-office; ~ *de tabac* tobacconist's (shop); ~ *central* exchange.

burlesque, *adj.* burlesque, ridiculous; — *s.m.* burlesque.

but, *s. m.* butt, target; goal; aim, object, purpose; scope.

buter, *v.n.* stumble (*contre* against); se ~ grow obstinate.

butin, *s. m.* booty.

butte, *s. f.* hill, mound, knoll.

C

ça, *pron.* that; *comme* ~ in that way; — *adv.* here; — *int.* now then!

cabaret, *s. m.* tavern; wine-shop; night-club, music-hall.

cabine, *s. f.* cabin, berth; cage, car; ~ *téléphonique* call-box.

cabinet, *s. m.* small room; study; water-closet; office; business; cabinet (council); cabinet; ~ *de consultation* consulting room; surgery.

câble, *s. m.* rope, cable.

cabriolet, *s. m.* cabriolet.

cacao, *s. m.* cocoa.

cacher, *v.a.* hide, conceal; se ~ hide oneself.

cadeau, *s. m.* present, gift.

cadet, *adj.* & *s.m.* younger, junior; cadet.

café, *s. m.* coffee; café, coffee-house; ~ *au lait* white coffee; ~ *concert* music-hall.

cafetière, *s. f.* coffee-pot.

cage, *s.f.* cage; coop; case, crate.

cahier, *s. m.* exercise book.

caillou, *s.m.* pebble, stone.

caisse, *s.f.* box, case; cash(-box), till; cashier's office; drum; *en* ~ in hand.

caissier, -ère, *s.m.f.* cashier.

calcul, *s. m.* calculation, reckoning; arithmetic.

calculateur, *s. m.* calculator, computer.

calculer, *v.a. & n.* calculate, reckon, compute.

caleçon, *s. m.* pants *(pl.)*; ~ *de bain* bathing-drawers *(pl.)*.

calendrier, *s. m.* calendar.

calme, *adj.* quiet, calm; *fig.* cool; — *s. m.* calm.

calmer, *v. a.* quiet, calm.

calomnier, *v. a.* calumniate, slander.

calorie, *s. f.* calorie.

calorifère, *s. m.* heating apparatus.

calvaire, *s. m.* Calvary.

camarade, *s. m.* comrade, fellow; ~ *d'école* schoolfriend.

cambrioler, *v. a.* burgle, break into.

cambrioleur, *s. m.* burglar.

caméra, *s. f.* (cine-)camera.

camion, *s. m.* lorry.

camp, *s. m.* camp; side.

campagnard, *s. m.* countryman, peasant.

campagne, *s. f.* country-(side); fields *(pl.)*; campaign, expedition.

camper, *v. n.* camp.

camping, *s. m.* camping; *(terrain de)* ~ camping site; *matériel de* ~ camping equipment; *faire du* ~ camp.

canal, *s. m.* canal; channel.

canapé, *s. m.* sofa, couch.

canard, *s. m.* duck, drake.

candidature, *s. f.* candi-dature, candidacy.

canif, *s. m.* penknife.

canne, *s. f.* stick, cane; ~ *à péche* fishing-rod.

canon, *s. m.* gun, cannon.

canot, *s. m.* boat.

cantine, *s. f.* canteen.

canton, *s.m.* canton, district.

cantonade, *s.f.* wings *(pl.)*; *à la* ~ behind the scenes.

caoutchouc, *s.m.* rubber; waterproof, mackintosh.

capable, *adj.* capable, able; efficient; ~ *de* able to.

capacité, *s. f.* capacity, (cap)ability.

capitaine, *s. m.* captain, leader.

capital, *adj.* capital, chief; —*s.m.* main point; capital, fund.

capitale, *s.f.* capital; capital letter.

capitalisme, *s. m.* capital-ism.

capituler, *v. n.* capitulate.

caprice, *s. m.* caprice.

capricieux, *adj.* capricious, fickle.

capsule, *s. f.* capsule.

captif, -ive, *adj. & s. m. f.* captive.

captiver, *v. a.* captivate.

capturer, *v. a.* capture.

car, *conj.* for, because.

caractère, *s. m.* character, temper; nature; type, print, letter.

caractériser, *v.a.* characterize, distinguish.

caractéristique, *adj. & s.f.* characteristic.

cardinal, *s. m.* cardinal; — *adj.* chief, cardinal; *points card naux* cardinal points.

caresser, *v.a.* caress, fondle; foster.

caricature, *s. f.* caricature.

carnaval, *s. m.* carnival.

carnet, *s. m.* note-book, pocket-book; book of tickets; ∼ *de chèques* cheque-book.

carotte, *s. f.* carrot.

carreau, *s. m.* square; (paving-)tile; tile flooring; pane; diamond.

carrière, *s.f.* career; race-course; race; quarry.

carrosserie, *s.f.* body.

carte, *s.f.* card; map; ticket; bill (of fare); *partie de* ∼*s* game of cards; ∼ *postale* postcard; ∼ *routière* road-map; ∼ *de visite* visiting-card; ∼ *marine* chart; ∼ *d'entrée* admission ticket; ∼ *grise* driving licence; *à la* ∼ à la carte.

carton, *s. m.* pasteboard, cardboard; (paper) box.

cas, *s.m.* case; event; instance, fact; *dans le* ∼ *où, en* ∼ *de* in case; *en tout* ∼ in any case.

caserne, *s.f.* barracks *(pl.)*.

casquette, *s. f.* cap.

casser, *v. a. & n.* break; crack, snap; annul; dismiss; *se* ∼ break, get broken.

casserole, *s. v.* saucepan.

casuel, -elle, *adj.* casual, accidental.

catalogue, *s. m.* catalogue.

catastrophe, *s. f.* catastrophe, disaster.

catégorie, *s. f.* category, class.

cathédrale, *s. f.* cathedral.

catholicisme, *s. m.* catholicism.

catholique, *adj.* catholic.

cause, *s. f.* cause, reason, ground; case; *à* ∼ *de* on account of, owing to.

causer¹, *v. a.* cause.

causer², *v.n.* talk, converse, chat.

cavalerie, *s.f.* cavalry.

cavalier, *s. m.* horseman, cavalier.

cave, *s. f.* cave; cellar.

caverne, *s. f.* cave(rn).

ce¹, c', *pron.* this, it.

ce², cet; cette; *dem. adj. (pl.* **ces)** this *(pl.* these); that *(pl.* those).

ceci, *pron.* this.

céder, *v. a.* give up, yield, cede, make over; *v. n.* yield, give in, up.

ceinture, *s. f.* belt, girdle.

cela, *pron.* that, it; *c'est* ∼ that's right.

célébration, *s. f.* celebration.

célèbre, *adj.* celebrated.

célébrer, *v. a.* celebrate.

célibataire, *adj.* unmarried, single.

cellule, *s. f.* cell.

celtique, *adj.* Celtic.

celui, celle, *dem. pron. (pl.* **ceux, celles)** he, si e, they, those.

celui-ci, celui-là, celle-ci, celle-là, *dem. pron.*

(pl. ceux-ci, -là, celles-ci, -là) this one, this person, the latter, these ones.

cément, *s. m.* cement.

cendre, *s. f.* ash(es).

cendrier, *s. m.* ash-tray.

cent, *adj. & s. m.* hundred; pour ~ per cent.

centime, *s. m.* centime.

centimètre, *s. m.* centimetre.

central, *adj.* central.

centrale, *s. f.* ~ *électrique* power-plant, -station.

centre, *s. m.* centre.

cependant, *conj.* however, yet, still, nevertheless; in the meantime; ~ *que* while.

céramique, *s. f.* ceramics; — *adj.* ceramic.

cercle, *s. m.* circle, ring; party, club.

cercueil, *s. m.* coffin.

cérémonie, *s. f.* ceremony.

cerf, *s. m.* stag, hart,

cerise, *s. f.* cherry.

certain, *adj.* certain, sure.

certainement, *adv.* certainly, surely.

certificat, *s. m.* certificate, testimonial.

certifier, *v. a.* certify.

certitude, *s. f.* certainty.

cerveau, *s. m.* brain(s).

ces *see* ce²

cesse, *s. f.* ceasing, pause; sans ~ unceasingly.

cesser, *v. a. & n.* cease, stop; give up; *faire* ~ put an end to.

c'est-à-dire, *conj.* that

is to say, viz., i.e.

cet *see* ce².

ceux *see* celui.

chacun, *pron.* each, each one, every one; everybody.

chagrin, *s. m.* grief, sorrow, vexation; — *adj.* sad, sorrowful; sorry; gloomy.

chaine, *s. f.* chain; range (of mountains); ~ *de montage* assembly line.

chair, *s. f.* flesh; pulp (of fruit).

chaire, *s. f.* chair; pulpit; seat, see.

chaise, *s. f.* chair.

châle, *s. m.* shawl.

chaleur, *s. f.* heat; fire.

chambre, *s. f.* room; bedroom; chamber; apartment; hall; ~ *à coucher* bedroom; ~ *Haute* Upper House; ~ *de commerce* chamber of commerce.

chameau, *s. m.* camel.

champ, *s. m.* field, country; *fig.* space, opportunity, theme.

champagne, *s. m.* champagne.

champignon, *s. m.* mushroom.

champion, -onne, *s. m. f.* champion.

championnat, *s. m.* championship.

chance, *s. f.* chance, fortune, risk; luck.

chancelier, *s. m.* chancellor.

chancellerie, *s. f.* chancery.

chandail, *s. m.* sweater;

pullover.

chandelle, *s. f.* candle.

change, *s. m.* change, changing; succession; (foreign) exchange, barter; *agent de* ~ stockbroker; *bureau de* ~ exchange office; *lettre de* ~ bill of exchange.

changer, *v. a.* change, alter; exchange; *se* ~ betransformed; change one's clothes.

chanson, *s. f.* song.

chant, *s. m.* singing; song, tune; chant(ing).

chanter, *v. a. & n.* warble; chant; praise.

chanteur, -euse, *s. m. f.* singer

chantier, *s. m.* yard, timber-yard, work-yard.

chaoeau. *s. m.* hat; bonnet; cap.

chapelain, *s. m.* chaplain.

chapelle, *s. f.* chapel.

chapitre, *s. m.* chapter; subject, head.

chaque, *adj.* each, every.

charbon, *s. m.* coal; embers *(pl.)*; ~ *de bois* charcoal.

charcuterie, *s. f.* pork-butchery.

charcutier, -ière, *s. m. f.* pork-butcher.

charge, *s. f.* load, burden; post, function, charge, office; attack; accusation.

charger, *v. a. & n.* load; burden; charge; entrust.

charité, *s. f.* charity.

charmant, *adj.* charming.

charme, *s. m.* charm.

charpente, *s. f.* timber-work.

charpentier, *s. m.* carpenter.

charrette, *s. f.* cart, wagon.

charrue, *s. f.* plough.

charte, *s. f.* charter.

chasse, *s. f.* chase, hunt(ing), shooting.

chasser, *v. a. & n.* chase, pursue, hunt, shoot, go shooting; drive out.

chasseur, *s. m.* hunter; page-boy.

chaste, *adj.* chaste, pure.

chat, *s. m.* (he-)cat.

châtaigne, *s. f.* chestnut.

château, *s. m.* castle; palace.

chatte, *s. f.* (she-)cat.

chaud, *adj. & adv.* hot, warm: ardent.

chauffage, *s. m.* heating, warming; ~ *central* central heating.

chauffe-bain, *s. m.* geyser.

chauffer, *v. a. & n.* heat, warm; urge on; coach.

chauffeur, *s. m.* driver.

chausse, *s. f.* hose

chausser, *v. a. & n.* put on (shoes etc.), wear; *se* ~ put on one's stockings etc.

chaussette, *s. f.* sock.

chaussure, *s. f.* footwear, shoes *(pl.)*.

chauve, *adj.* bald.

chef, *s. f.* chief; ~ *de train* guard; ~ *d'orchestre* conductor.

chemin, *s. m.* road, way; lane; *se mettre en* ~ start; ~ *de fer* railway.

cheminée, *s. f.* chimney.

fireplace, funnel.

chemise, s. f. shirt.

chêne, s. m. oak(-tree).

chèque, s. m. cheque; ~ *en blanc* blank cheque; ~ *de voyage* traveller's cheque.

cher, chère, adj. dear.

chercher, v. a. seek, look for, search for.

chéri, -e, adj. dear; — s. m. f. darling.

cheval, s. m. horse; *à* ~ on horseback; *monter à* ~ ride.

chevalerie, s. f. chivalry.

chevalier, s. m. knight.

chevelure, s. f. hair.

cheveu, s. m. hair; *en* ~ bareheaded.

cheville, s.f. wooden pin, peg; ankle.

chèvre, s.f. (she-)goat.

chevreau, s.m. kid-(leather).

chez, prep. at, in, at the house of; ~ *X* at X's.

chic, adj. smart, spruce, fashionable; — s. m. chic; trick; elegance.

chien, -enne, s. m. f. dog.

chiffon, s. m. rag, scrap; chiffon.

chiffre, s. m. figure, digit; number.

chignon, s.m. knot (of hair), bun.

chimie, s.f. chemistry.

chimique, adj. chemical.

chimiste, s. m. f. chemist.

chinois, -e (Ch.), adj & s.m.f. Chinese.

chirurgie, s. f. surgery.

chirurgien, -enne, s.m.f. surgeon.

choc, s.m. shock, clash, collision.

chocolat, s. m. chocolate.

chœur, s. m. chorus; choir.

choisir, v.a. choose, pick out, select.

choix, s. m. choice.

chômage, s. m. stoppage, cessation of work; unemployment.

choquer, v. a. run into, strike against, collide with; shock, offend; *se* ~ come into collision; be shocked.

chose, s. f. thing, object, matter; goods; event; *quelque* ~ something, anything.

chou, s. m. cabbage, cole.

chou-fleur, s. m. cauliflower.

chrétien, -enne, adj. & s.m. f. Christian.

christianisme, s.m. Christianity.

chronique, adj. chronic; — s. f. chronicle.

chuchoter, v.n.&a. whisper.

chute, s. f. fall, downfall, descent; slope.

ci, adv. here.

ci-dessous, adv. below, underneath.

ci-dessus, adv. above; aforesaid.

cidre, s. m. cider.

ciel, s. m. (pl. **cieux**) heaven; sky; weather; climate.

cierge, s. m. wax candle.

cigare, s. m. cigar.

cigarette, s. f. cigarette.

cigogne, s. f. stork.

cil, s. m. eyelash.

cime, s, f. top, summit.

ciment, *s. m.* cement.

cimetière, *s. m.* cemetery; churchyard.

cinéma, *s. m.* cinema.

cinérama, *s. m.* cinerama.

cinq, *adj.* & *s. m.* five; fifth.

cinquante, *adj.* & *s. m.* fifty; fiftieth.

circonstance, *s.f.* circumstance; occurrence, occasion, event.

circuit, *s. m.* circuit.

circulation, *s. f.* circulation; currency; traffic.

circuler, *v. n.* circulate; *circulez!* move on!

cire, *s.f.* wax.

cirer, *v.a.* wax; polish.

ciseau, *s.m.* chisel.

ciseaux, *s. m. pl.* scissors.

citation, *s.f.* citation.

cité, *s. f.* city, town.

citer, *v.a.* cite; quote.

citoyen, **-enne**, *s.m.f.* citizen.

citron, *s. m.* lemon.

citronnade, *s.f.* lemon squash.

civil, *adj.* civil; — *s. m.* civilian.

civilisation, *s. f.* civilization, culture.

clair, *adj.* light, clear.

clapet, *s. m.* valve.

claquement, *s. m.* clap-(ping); snap.

claquer, *v. n. a.* crack, clap; chatter; bang.

clarté, *s. f.* light, brightness; clearness.

classe, *s. f.* class; order, rank; form, class-room.

classer, *v.a.* class, rank.

classifier, *v.a.* classify.

classique, *adj.* classic(al).

clause, *s. f.* clause.

clé, clef, *s. f.* key; spanner, wrench; *fig.* clue; ~ *de contact* ignition key.

clerc, *s. m.* clerk; scholar.

clergé, *s. m.* clergy.

clérical, *adj.* clerical.

client, *s. m.* client, customer, patron.

clientèle, *s.f.* clients (*pl.*).

cligner, *v. a.* & *n.* wink.

clignotant, *s. m.* indicator.

clignoter, *v.a.&n.* blink, wink.

climat, *s. m.* climate.

clinique, *adj.* & *s.f.* clinic, clinical.

cloche, *s.f.* bell.

cloître, *s. m.* cloister.

clore*, *v. a.* shut, close.

clos, *adj.* closed.

clôture, *s. f.* enclosure, fence; close.

clou, *s. m.* nail, stud; boil, furuncle.

clouer, *v. a.* nail (down).

club, *s. m.* club.

cocher, *s. m.* coachman, driver.

cochon, *s. m.* pig, swine.

code, *s. m.* code; law, rule.

cœur, *s. m.* heart; *fig.* mind, soul, courage; *par* ~ by heart.

coffre, *s. m.* chest.

coffre-fort, *s. m.* safe.

cognac, *s. m.* cognac.

cogner, *v. n.* & *a.* beat, knock, strike; *se* ~ knock against.

coiffer, *v. a.* put on (hat); dress, do s.o.'s hair.

coiffeur, **-euse**, *s.m.f.* hairdresser.

coiffure, s. f. head-dress, cap; hair-do; *salon de* ~ hairdresser.

coin, s. m. corner; angle.

coïncider, v.n. coincide.

coke, s.m. coke.

col, s.m. collar; neck.

colère, s.f. anger.

colis, s.m. parcel; item (of luggage).

collaborateur, -trice, s. m. f. fellow worker; collaborator.

collaborer, v.n. work jointly, collaborate.

collectif, -ive, adj. collective.

collection, s. f. collection.

collège, s.m. college; grammar school.

collègue, s.m.f. colleague, fellow worker.

coller, v.a. stick, paste.

collet, s.m. collar; neck.

collier, s.m. necklace; collar.

colline, s.f. hill.

collision, s.f. collision; *entrer en* ~ collide.

colombe, s. f. dove.

colonel, s.m. colonel.

colonie, s. f. colony; dominion.

colonne, s.f. column.

coloré, adj. coloured; colourful.

colossal, adj. colossal.

combat, s.m. fight, combat.

combattre, v.a.&n. fight (against), combat (with).

combien, adv. (~ *de*) how much, how many, how far; ~ *de temps?* how long?

combinaison, s.f. combination.

combiner, v.a. combine, unite; contrive, devise.

comédie, s.f. comedy.

comédien, s.m. comedian, actor.

comestible, adj. edible.

comique, adj. comic; — s. m. comic actor.

comité, s. m. committee.

commandant, s. m. commander.

commande, s.f. order.

commandement, s. m. command, order; commandment.

commander, v. a. command, order; control.

comme, adv. & conj. as, like; as . . . as; while; ~ *il faut* decent, proper; *tout* ~ just like; ~ *si* as if, as though.

commémorer, v.a. commemorate.

commençant, -e, s. m. f. beginner; — *cdj.* beginning.

commencement, s.m. beginning.

commencer, v. a. & n. begin, commence.

comment, adv. how, in what manner; why; ~ *allez-vous?* how are you?; ~ *(dites-vous)?* (I beg your) pardon?

commentaire, s. m. comment; commentary.

commenter, v. a. comment (on); criticize.

commerçant, -e, s. m. f. merchant, dealer.

commerce, s. m. commerce, trade; *voyageur*

de ~ commercial
traveller; ~ de gros
wholesale trade; faire
le ~ trade.

commercer, v. n. trade,
deal with, in.

commercial, adj. com-
mercial.

commettre, v. a. commit;
se ~ commit oneself.

commis, s.m. clerk,
employee.

commissaire, s.m. com-
misary; commissioner.

commissariat, s.m. police-
station.

commission, s. f. commission; charge; commit-
tee; errand.

commode, adj. conven-
ient, handy, comfort-
able; — s. f. chest of
drawers.

commun, adj. common;
joint; usual; vulgar;
peu ~ unusual; — s.m.
common people.

communauté, s. f. community.

commune, s. f. district.

communication, s. f.
communication, mes-
sage; call.

communier, v. n. com-
municate.

communion, s.f. com-
munion.

communiqué, s. m. communiqué.

communiquer, v. a. & n.
communicate.

compact, adj. compact.

compagnie, s.f. company.

compagnon, s. m. com-
panion, fellow.

comparaison, s. f. comparison.

comparer, v. a. compare.

compartiment, s. m.
compartment; ~ de
fumeurs smoking com-
partment; ~ pour non-
fumeurs non-smoker.

compas, s.m. compass-
(es).

compatriote, s. m. f.
compartiot, (fellow)
countryman.

compensation, s. f. compensation.

compenser, v.a.&n. com-
pensate.

compétent, adj. competent.

compétiteur, -trice, s. m.
f. competitor.

compétition, s.f. competition.

compilation, s. f. compilation.

compiler, v. a. compile.

complainte, s.f. com-
plaint.

complaisance, s. f. complaisance, kindness.

complaisant, adj. complaisant, obliging, kind.

complément, s. m. complement; object.

complémentaire, adj.
complementary.

complet, -ète, adj. complete, full.

compléter, v.a. complete.

complexe, adj. complex,
compound.

complication, s. f. complication.

compliment, s. m. compliment; congratula-
tion.

compliquer, v.a. complicate.

comploter, *v.a.* plot.

composant, -e, *adj. & s. f.* component.

composer, *v. a.* compose, se ~ de be composed of, consist of.

compositeur, -trice *,s. m. f.* composer.

composition, *s. f.* composition; paper.

comprendre, *v. a.* comprehend; understand.

comprimé, -e, *adj.* pressed; — *s. m.* tablet.

compromettre, *v. a.* compromise, commit; se ~ commit oneself.

compromis, *s. m.* compromise.

comptabilité, *s. f.* bookkeeping, accounts *(pl.)*

compte, *s.m.* account; amount, sum; ~ *courant* current account; *faire le* ~ *de* count; *régler un* ~ settle an account; ~ *rendu* report, account, statement; review; *tenir* ~ *de* take into account.

compter, *v. a. & n.* count, reckon, calculate.

comptoir, *s. m.* counter.

computer, *v. a.* compute.

comte, *s. m.* count.

comtesse, *s. f.* countess.

concéder, *v. a.* grant.

concentration, *s. f.* concentration; reduction.

concentrer, *v. a.* condense, concentrate.

concept, -tion, *s. m. f.* concept(ion), idea.

concernant, *prep.* concerning.

concerner, *v. a.* concern,

relate to.

concert, *s. m.* concert.

concevoir*, *v. a. & n.* conceive; think; imagine; apprehend.

concierge, *s. f. m.* porter.

concile, *s. m.* council.

concis, *adj.* concise.

conclure*, *v.a.&n.* conclude, end.

conclusion, *s.f.* conclusion, end.

concombre, *s. m.* cucumber.

concorder, *v.n.* agree.

concourir, *v. n.* contribute, concur; compte.

concours, *s. m.* concourse; help; assistance; competition.

concret, -ète, *adj.* concrete.

concurrence, *s. f.* competition; rivalry.

concurrent, *s. m.* competitor; rival.

condamnation, *s. f.* condemnation; sentence.

condamner, *v.a.* condemn, sentence.

condenser, *v. a.* condense.

condition, *s. f.* condition, state; service; stipulation, condition; *à* ~ *que* on condition that, provided that.

conditionnel, *adj.* conditional.

conditionnement, *s.m.* ~ *de l'air* air-conditioning.

conducteur, -trice, *s. m. f.* conductor; driver.

conduire*, *v. a. & n.* conduct, lead; drive; show (to), take (to); manage; *permis de* ~ driving licence.

conduit, *s. m.* pipe, tube.

conduite, *s. f.* conducting, leading; driving; behaviour, conduct.

cône, *s. m.* cone.

confection, *s. f.* ready-made clothes *(pl.)*.

confédération, *s. f.* confederation, confederacy.

conférence, *s. f.* comparison; conference; lecture; *maître de ∼s* lecturer; *faire une ∼* deliver a lecture.

conférencier, -ère, *s. m. f.* lecturer.

conférer, *v.a.* grant, confer, bestow; compare.

confesser, *v.a.* confess.

confession, *s. f.* confession.

confiance, *s.f.* confidence, trust, reliance; *avoir ∼* count on, trust.

confiant, *adj.* confident.

confidence, *s. f.* confidence.

confidentiel, -elle *adj.* confidential.

confier, *v.a.* trust; entrust, give in charge.

confinement, *s. m.* imprisonment.

confiner, *v. n. & a.* confine.

confirmation, *s.f.* confirmation.

confirmer, *v.a.* confirm.

confiserie, *s.f.* confectionery, sweet-shop.

confiture, *s.f.* jam, preserve.

conflit, *s. m.* conflict.

confondre, *v. a.* confound.

conformer, *v. a.* conform, adapt; *se ∼ à* conform oneself (to).

confort, *s.m.* comfort, ease.

confortable, *adj.* comfortable.

confrère, *s.m.* fellow-worker, colleague.

confronter, *v. a.* confront, compare.

confus, *adj.* confused.

confusion, *s. f.* confusion.

congé, *s. m.* leave, holiday; permission; discharge; warning; notice; *donner ∼* give notice (to); dismiss; *prendre ∼ de* take leave of; *être en ∼* be on holiday.

congédier, *v. a.* dismiss.

congratulation, *s. f.* congratulation.

congrès, *s.m.* congress, assembly.

conjecture, *s.f.* conjecture.

conjecturer, *v.a.&n.* conjecture, guess.

conjonction, *s.f.* conjunction, union.

connaissance, *s. f.* knowledge; acquaintance; *faire ∼ avec* get acquainted with.

connaître*, *v.a.* know, understand; be acquainted with.

connexion, *s.f.* connection.

conquérir*, *v. a. & n.* conquer; win (over).

conscience, *s.f.* consciousness; conscience; *avoir la ∼ de* be conscious of, be aware of.

conscient, *adj.* conscious.

conscrit, *s. m.* conscript.

conseil, *s. m.* counsel, advice; adviser; council, board, staff.

conseiller[1], **-ère**, *s. m. f.* counsellor, councillor.

conseiller[2], *v. a.&n.* advise, counsel.

consentir, *v. n.* consent, agree *(à* to).

conséquence, *s. f.* consequence, result.

conséquent, *adj.* consistent; *par* ~ consequently.

conservatoire, *s. m.* conservatory.

conserver, *v.a.* keep, preserve, tin.

considérable, *adj.* considerable.

considération, *s. f.* consideration; esteem.

considérer, *v. a.* consider; esteem.

consigne, *s. f.* cloak-room, left-luggage office.

consigner, *v.a.* deposit.

consister, *v.n.* consist (of), be made (of).

consoler, *v.a.* console.

consommateur, **-trice**, *s. m. f.* consumer, customer.

consommer, *v.a.* consummate; consume.

consomption, *s.f.* consumption.

consonne, *s.f.* consonant.

conspiration, *s.f.* conspiracy.

conspirer, *v. a. & n.* conspire, plot.

constant, *adj.* constant,

firm.

constipation, *s.f.* constipation.

constituer, *v. a.* constitute, compose.

constitution, *s. f.* constitution.

constitutionnel, **-elle**, *adj.* constitutional.

constructeur, *s. m.* builder.

construction, *s.f.* construction, building.

construire*, *v.a.* build, construct.

consul, *s. m.* consul.

consulat, *s. m.* consulate.

consulter, *v.a.* consult.

consumer, *v. a.* consume.

contact, *s.m.* contact, touch, switch.

contaminer, *v. a.* contaminate.

conte, *s.m.* story, tale.

contemplation, *s.f.* contemplation.

contempler, *v.a. & n.* contemplate.

contemporain, **-e**, *adj. & s. m. f.* contemporary.

contenance, *s. f.* capacity, contents *(pl.)*.

contenir, *v.a.* contain, hold; restrain; **se** ~ restrain oneself.

content, *adj.* content.

contentement, *s. m.* content, satisfaction.

contenter, *v.a.* content, satisfy; **se** ~ be contented, do with.

contenu, *s.m.* contents *(pl.)*.

conter, *v.a. & n.* tell, relate.

continent, *s. m.* continent.

continental, *adj.* conti-

nental:
check.

continuation, *s.f.* continuation, continuance.

continuel, -elle, *adj.* continual.

continuer, *v.a. & n.* go on (with), keep on; se ~ be continued.

contour, *s.m.* contour, outline.

contracter, *v. a.* contract, bargain for.

contradiction, *s. f.* contradiction.

contraindre*, *v. a.* compel, force; se ~ restrain oneself.

contrainte, *s.f.* constraint.

contraire, *adj. & s. m.* contrary; *au* ~ on the contrary.

contrairement, *adv.* ~ *à* contrary to.

contraste, *s. m.* contrast.

contraster, *v. n.* contrast *(avec* with).

contrat, *s.m.* contract.

contre, *prep.* against.

contrée, *s.f.* country.

contrefaçon, *s. f.* counterfeit(ing); forgery.

contrefaire, *v. a.* counterfeit; pirate, forge.

contre-partie, *s. f.* counterpart.

contresigner, *v.a.* countersign.

contribuant, *s. m.* contributor.

contribuer, *v. n.* contribute *(à* to).

contribution, *s.f.* contribution, tax.

contrôle, *s.m.* control, check; hall-mark.

contrôler, *v.a.* control,

contrôleur, *s. m.* ticket-collector.

contusion, *s. f.* bruise.

convaincre, *v.a.* convince.

convenable, *adj.* suitable, appropriate.

convenance, *s.f.* suitability, convenience.

convenir, *v.n.* suit, be convenient (to), fit.

conventionnel, -elle, *adj.* conventional.

conversation, *s.f.* conversation, talk.

converser, *v. n.* converse.

convertir, *v.a.* convert.

conviction, *s. f.* conviction.

convier, *v.a.* invite.

convive, *s.m.* guest.

convoi, *s.m.* convoy; funeral procession.

convoquer *v.a.* convoke.

coopération, *s. f.* co-operation.

coopérer, *v. n.* co-operate.

copie, *s. f.* (fair) copy.

copier, *v.a.* copy.

coq, *s. m.* cock.

coquille, *s. f.* shell.

coquin, *s.m.* rogue.

corail, *s.m.* coral.

corbeau, *s. m.* raven.

corbeille, *s. f.* basket.

corde, *s.f.* cord, rope.

cordial, *adj.* cordial.

cordonnier, *s.m.* shoemaker.

corne, *s. f.* horn; hooter.

corneille, *s. f.* crow, rook.

cornet, *s. m.* horn; cornet.

cornichon, *s. m.* gherkin.

corporation, *s. f.* corporation.

corps, s. m. body, corpse; corporation, corps.

correct, adj. correct.

correction, s. f. correction.

correspondance, s. f. correspondence; relation; communication; connection.

correspondant, adj. corresponding.

correspondre, v. n. correspond; communicate.

corriger, v.a. correct.

corrompre, v.a. corrupt, spoil; se ~ become corrupted.

corruption, s. f. corruption.

corset, s. m. stays (pl.).

cortège, s. m. escort.

cosmétique, adj. cosmetic; — s. m. ~s cosmetics.

cosmonaute, s. m. cosmonaut, spacemen.

costume, s. m. dress, costume; ~ de bain(s) bathing-costume.

côte, s. f. rib; slope; shore.

côté, s. m. side, part; à ~ by the side; de ~ on one side; d'un ~ on the one hand; de l'autre ~ on the other hand; passer à ~ pass by; à ~ de next (door) to; beside.

côtelette, s. f. chop.

coton, s. m. cotton.

cottage, s. m. cottage.

cou, s. m. neck.

couche, s. f. bed; napkin, diaper; coat; layer; (pl.) confinement.

coucher, v. a. put to bed; lay; v.n. lie down; sleep; être couché lie; se ~ go to bed, lie down; — s. m. bedtime; setting.

couchette, s.f. berth, bunk; napkin.

coude, s. m. elbow; angle, bend.

coudre*, v. a. & n. sew.

couler, v.n. flow, run, stream; leak; sink.

couleur, s.f. colour.

coulisse, s. f. groove; slip, wings (pl.); dans les ~s behind the scenes.

couloir, s.m. passage; corridor; lobby.

coup, s. m. blow, stroke, knock; smack; pull; kick; shot; draught; cast, move; d'un seul ~ at once; ~ de feu rush hours (pl.); de froid chill; ~ de main sudden attack; ~ d'œil glance, look; ~ de soleil sunstroke.

coupe, s.f. wine-cup.

couper, v.a. cut; cut down, off, up; divide; cross; mix; se ~ cut oneself, cut one's (finger etc.).

couple, s. f. pair, brace; m. couple.

cour, s. f. (court)yard; court; courting, courtship; faire la ~ à court, make love to.

courage, s. m. courage.

courageux, -euse, adj. courageous, brave.

courant, adj. current; running; — s.m. current; stream; course run; ~ d'air draught.

courbe, s. f. curve, bend.

courbé, adj. curved; bent.

courber, v. a. & n. bend, bow; se ~ bend, be bent; bow.

courir*, v. n. run; hurry; flow; be curent.

couronne, s.f. crown.

couronner, v.a. crown.

courrier, s. m. messenger, courier, post, mail.

cours, s. m. course; current, flow; currency.

course, s. f. race, run; course; drive.

court, adj. short, brief; — adv. short; suddenly; — s. m. tennis-court.

courtiser, v. a. pay court to, court.

courtois, adj. courteous, polite.

courtoisie, s. f. courtesy.

cousin, -e s. m. f. cousin.

coussin, s.m. cushion.

coût, s.m. cost, price.

couteau, s.m. knife.

coûter, v. n. & a. cost.

coûteux, -euse, adj. costly, expensive, dear; peu ~ inexpensive.

coutume, s.f. custom, habit; de ~ customary.

couture, s. f. sewing, seam; needlework; scar.

couturière, s.m. dressmaker.

couvent, s.m. convent.

couver, v.a. brood (on), sit; hatch; breed.

couvercle, s. m. cover, lid, cap.

couvert, adj. covered; covert, sheltered; cloudy; secret; —

s.m. set (of fork and spoon); cover; protection; mettre le ~ lay the table.

couverture, s. f. covering); blanket; ~s bedclothes.

couvrir*, v.a. cover; load; protect; be sufficent for.

crabe, s. m. crab.

cracher, v.n. & a. spit.

craie, s. f. chalk.

craindre, v.a. fear, be afraid of.

crainte, s. f. fear; de ~ de for fear of; de ~ que lest.

crampe, s.f. cramp.

crampon, s.m. cramp.

crâne, s. m. skull; — adj. bold.

craquer, v.n. crack.

cravate, s. f. (neck)tie.

crayon, s. m. pencil; crayon.

créance, s. f. credence, belief, trust.

créancier, -ère, s. m. f. creditor.

création, s. f. creation.

créature, s. f. creature.

crèche, s. f. crèche.

crédit, s. m. credit; à ~ on credit.

créditer, v.a. credit.

crediteur, s.m. creditor.

créer, v.a. create, make.

crème, s. f. cream, custard; ~ à raser shaving cream.

crémerie, s. f. dairy.

crêpe, s. m. crape, crêpe.

creuser, v. a. dig; deepen.

creux, -euse, adj. hollow, empty; — s. m. hollow.

crevaison, *s. f.* puncture.

crever, *v. a. & n.* burst; puncture; die.

cri, *s. m.* cry, scream; call, shout.

crible, *s.m.* sieve, screen.

cric, *s. m.* jack.

crier, *v.a. & n.* cry (out).

crime, *s. m.* crime, guilt.

criminel, **-elle**, *adj. & s. m. f.* criminal.

crise, *s. f.* crisis.

crisper, *v.a.* contract, shrivel.

cristal, *s. m.* crystal.

critique, *adj.* critical; — *s.f.* criticism, critique; *s.m.f.* critic, reviewer.

crochet, *s. m.* hook; crochet(-work); hanger.

croire*, *v. a. & n.* believe, credit, trust; think.

croiser, *v.a.* cross; *v.n.* cruise.

croître*, *v.n.* grow, increase; grow up; *v.a.* increase.

croix, *s. f.* cross.

croquis, *s.m.* sketch.

crouler, *v. n.* fall (to pieces), fall in.

croûte, *s. f.* crust; *casser la ~* have a snack.

croyance, *s.f.* belief, faith; creed.

croyant, **-e**, *s. m. f.* believer; — *adj.* faithful.

cru, *adj.* raw; crude.

cruauté, *s. f.* cruelty.

crue, *s. f.* rise, growth.

cruel, **-elle**, *adj.* cruel.

crypte, *s. f.* crypte.

cube, *s. m.* cube.

cueillir*, *v.a.* gather, pick, glean.

cuiller, **-ère**, *s. f.* spoon; *~ à pot* ladle; *~ à café* teaspoon.

cuir, *s. m.* skin; leather.

cuire*, *v. a. & n.* cook; boil; roast; burn; *faire trop ~* overdo.

cuisine, *s. f.* kitchen; cooking, cookery; *batterie de ~* kitchen utensils; *de ~* culinary; *livre de ~* cookery-book.

cuisinière, *s.f.* cook; kitchen range, cooker.

cuisse, *s. f.* thigh; leg.

cuit, *adj.* cooked, baked.

cuivre, *s. m.* copper.

cul, *s. m.* bottom.

culinaire, *adj.* culinary.

culotte, *s. f.* panties; breeches *(pl.).*

culte, *s. m.* cult, worship.

cultivateur, **-trice**, *s. m. f.* farmer.

cultiver, *v.a.* cultivate, till; *fig.* improve.

culture, *s.f.* culture.

culturel, **-elle**, *adj.* cultural.

cure, *s. f.* care; cure.

curé, *s. m.* priest; vicar.

cure-dent, *s.m.* toothpick.

curieux, **-euse**, *adj.* curious, strange, inquisitive.

curiosité, *s. f.* curiosity; *~s* sights.

cuve, *s. f.* tub, vat.

cuvette, *s. f.* ~ *(de lavabo)* wash-basin.

cycle, *s. m.* cycle.

cygne, *s. m.* swan.

cylindre, *s. m.* cylinder.

D

dactylo(graphe), *s. m. f.* typist.

dame, *s.f.* lady; queen.

danger, *s. m.* danger.

dangereux, -euse, *adj.* dangerous.

danois, -e (D.), *adj. & s. m. f.* Dane, Danish.

dans, *prep.* in, into; inside; during; ~ *le temps* formerly.

danse, *s. f.* dance.

danser, *v. n.* dance.

danseur, *s. m.* dancer.

danseuse: *s. f.* ballet-girl, dancer.

date, *s.f.* date; *prendre* ~ fix a day.

dater, *v. a. & n.* date.

datte, *s.f.* date.

davantage, *adv.* more, further; *bien* ~ much more; *pas* ~ no more; *en* ~ some more.

de, *prep.* of, from, out of, on account of.

dé, *s. m.* thimble.

déballer, *v. a.* unpack.

débarquer, *v. a. & n.* land, disembark, arrive.

débarrasser, *v. a.* clear (up), rid, free; *se* ~ get rid (of).

débat, *s. m.* debate.

débattre, *v. a. & n.* debate.

débit, *s. m.* sale; debit; output; utterance; ~ *de tabac* tobbaconist's shop.

déborder, *v. n. & a.* overflow, run over.

débouché, *s. m.* outlet, issue.

déboucher, *v. a.* uncork, open; *v. n.* run into.

débourser, *v. a.* disburse.

debout, *adv.* upright, standing; *être* ~ stand.

début, *s.m.* start, outset; first appearance.

débuter, *v. n.* begin, start; make one's first appearance.

décadence, *s.f.* decadence.

décagramme, *s.m.* decagramme.

décéder, *v.n.* die, decease.

décembre, *s. m.* December.

déception, *s. f.* deception, deceit; disappointment.

décharge, *s. f.* discharge; outlet.

décharger, *v.a.* unload, unburden; release; discharge; *se* ~ unburden oneself.

déchausser, *v.a.* take off (shoes).

déchéance, *s.f.* decadence, decay; decline.

déchiffrer, *v.a.* decipher; make out.

déchirer, *v.a.* tear, rend.

dechoir*, *v.n.* fall off, decay.

décider, *v. a. & n.* decide, settle; *se* ~ make up one's mind; be settled.

décilitre, *s. m.* decilitre.

décimal, -e, *adj. & s. f.* decimal.

décimètre, *s.m.* decimetre.

décisif, -ive, *adj.* decisive, final.

décision, *s.f.* decision.

déclaration, *s.f.* declaration, statement.

déclarer, *v.a.* declare, state; se ~ declare itself.

décliner, *v.n.* decline.

décolletage, *s.m.* low neck.

décolleter, *v.a.* cut low

turn; *tour à* ~ turning lathe.

décomposer, *v. a.* decompose; spoil; se ~ decompose.

décomposition, *s. f.* decomposition.

décompte, *s.m.* discount; particulars *(pl.)*.

décor, *s. m.* decoration; scene, environment; scenery.

décoratif, **-ive,** *adj.* decorative.

décorer, *v.a.* decorate; trim.

découper, *v.a.* cut out, carve.

décourager, *v.a.* discourage.

découverte, *s. f.* discovery.

découvrir*, *v. a.* discover, find out; uncover; se ~ uncover oneself, disclose oneself.

décret, *s. m.* decree, order.

décrier, *v.a.* cry down.

décrire, *v. a.* describe.

décrocher, *v.a.* unhook, take down.

décroissance, *s. m.* decrease.

décroître, *v. n.* decrease.

déçu, *adj.* disappointed.

dédain, *s.m.* disdain, scorn.

dedans, *adv.* within, inside; indoors, at home.

dédicace, *s. f.* dedication.

dédier, *v.a.* dedicate.

déduire*, *v.a.* deduct.

défaire, *v. a.* undo; break; unfasten; take off; defeat; se ~ come undone.

défaite, *s. f.* defeat.

défaut, *s. m.* defect, deficiency, want; fault; flaw; *à* ~ *de* for want of; *sans* ~ faultless.

défavorable, *adj.* unfavourable.

défendre, *v.a.* defend; forbid; se ~ defend oneself.

défense, *s.f.* defence, protection; prohibition; tusk; *se mettre en* ~ stand on one's guard.

défiance, *s.f.* distrust, mistrust.

défier, *v. a.* defy.

défigurer, *v. a.* disfigure, deface, spoil.

défiler, *v. n.* defile.

défini, *adj.* definite.

définir, *v. a.* define.

définitif, **-ive,** *adj.* definitive, final.

définition, *s.f.* definition.

défunt, **-e,** *adj. & s. m. f.* deceased, defunct.

dégager, *v.* a. redeem, release, disengage; emit.

dégorger, *v.a.* disgorge, discharge; *v.n.* discharge, overflow.

dégoût, *s. m.* disgust.

dégoûtant, *adj.* disgusting.

dégoûter, *v.a.* disgust; **se ~** get tired of.

dégradation, *s. f.* degradation.

dégrader, *v.a.* degrade; damage.

degré, *s. m.* degree.

déguisement, *s.m.* disguise.

déguiser, *v.a.* disguise, hide.

dehors, *adv.* out, outside, out of doors; *au ~* outside, abroad; *en ~ de* outside of, apart from.

déjà, *adv.* already; previously.

déjeuner, *s. m.* lunch(eon); *petit ~* breakfast; — *v.n.* have breakfast; take lunch.

delà, *prep.* beyond; *au ~ de* beyond.

délai, *s. m.* delay; *à bref ~* at short notice.

délégation, *s. f.* delegation.

déléguer, *v. a.* delegate.

délibération, *s. f.* deliberation, resolution; *en ~* under consideration.

délibérer, *v. n.* deliberate, ponder; *v.a.* bring under discussion.

délicat, *adj.* delicate; feeble; fastidious, dainty.

délicatesse, *s. f.* delicacy; delicateness; daintiness.

délice, *s. m.* delight.

délicieux, -euse, *adj.* delicious, delightful.

délier, *v. a.* untie; loosen.

délivrance, *s. f.* deliverance.

délivrer, *v.a.* deliver, (set) free.

déloyal, *adj.* disloyal, unfair.

demain, *adv.* tomorrow.

demande, *s. f.* request, application, inquiry, call, request, demand.

demander, *v.a.* ask, inquire (after); beg, demand; request, require; **se ~** wonder.

démanger, *v.n.* itch.

démarche, *s. f.* walk, gait; proceeding.

démasquer, *v. a.* unmask.

déménagement, *s. m.* removal, moving.

déménager, *v.n.&a.* move (house); remove.

démesuré, *adj.* immoderate, excessive.

demeure, *s.f.* delay; home, dwelling.

demeurer, *v.n.* live; stay.

demi, -e, *adj.* half; *à ~* by half; *une heure et ~e* half past one; an hour and a half; — *s. f.* half-hour.

demi-cercle, *s. m.* semicircle.

demi-heure, *s. f.* half an hour.

demi-jour, *s. m.* twilight.

démobiliser, *v.a.* demobilize.

démocratie, *s. f.* democracy.

démocratique, *adj.* democratic.

démodé, *adj.* old-fashioned.

demoiselle, *s.f.* young lady, miss.

démolir, *v. a.* demolish,

pull down.

démon, *s. m.* demon.

démonstratif, -ive, *adj.* demonstrative.

démonstration, *s. f.* demonstration.

démontrer, *v. a.* demonstrate.

dénaturé, *adj.* unnatural.

dénombrer, *v. a.* number.

dénomination, *s. f.* denomination.

dénoncer, *v. a.* denounce.

dénoter, *v. a.* denote; indicate.

dense, *adj.* dense, compact.

densité, *s. f.* density.

dent, *s. f.* tooth; *mal de ~s* toothache.

dental, *adj.* dental.

dentelle, *s. f.* lace.

dentier, *s. m.* set of (false) teeth, denture.

dentifrice, *s. m. pâte ~* tooth-paste.

dentiste, *s. m. f.* dentist.

dénué, *adj.* destitute.

dénuement, *s. m.* destitution.

départ, *s. m.* departure.

département, *s. m.* department; territory.

départir, *v. a.* grant, allot; *se ~* give up

dépasser, *v. a. & n.* pass, exceed, go beyond.

dépêche, *s. f.* despatch, wire, telegram.

dépêcher, *v. a.* dispatch; *v. n. & se ~* hurry.

dépendance, *s. f.* dependance.

dépendant, -e, *adj.* dependent; — *s. m. f.* dependant.

dépendre, *v. n.* depend.

dépense, *s. f.* expense; larder.

dépenser, *v. a. & n.* spend; waste.

dépit, *s. m.* spite; *en ~ de* in spite of.

déplacement, *s. m.* displacement; shift.

déplacer, *v.a.* displace, move, shift; *se ~* move.

déplaire, *v.n.* displease.

déplier, *v.a.* unfold, lay out.

déplorer, *v. a.* deplore.

déportation, *s. f.* transportation, deportation.

déposer, *v. a.* put down, set down; deposit; — *se ~* settle.

dépôt, *s.m.* deposit; store-room; warehouse; lock-up.

dépourvu, *adj.* needy.

dépraver, *v. a.* deprave.

déprécier, *v. a.* depreciate.

dépression, *s. f.* depression.

déprimer, *v. a.* depress.

depuis, *prep.* since, from; *~ longtemps* long since.

députation, *s. f.* deputation.

député, *s.m.* deputy; member of the French parliament.

dérangé, *adj.* deranged; upset.

déranger, *v. a.* upset, put out of order.

déraper, *v. n.* skid.

dérèglement, *s. m.* irregularity; disorder.

dérivation, *s. f.* derivation.

dériver, *v.n.* drift; be

derived.

dernier, -ère, *adj. & s. m. f.* latter, last, latest; *le* ~ the latter.

dernièrement, *adv.* lately.

dérober, *v. a.* rob, steal. **se** ~ steal away.

déroger, *v.n.* derogate (from).

dérouler, *v.a.* unroll, unfold.

déroute, *s.f.* defeat.

derrière, *adv. & prep.* behind, back; — *s. m.* back (part); bottom.

dès, *prep.* from, as early as, since; ~ *que* as soon as.

désagréable, *adj.* disagreeable, unpleasant.

désarmer, *v.a.* disarm.

désastre, *s.m.* disaster.

désavantage, *s. m.* disadvantage.

descendance, *s.f.* descent.

descendant, *adj.* descending; *en* ~ downward, downhill.

descendre, *v. n.* descend, come down, go down; alight; ~ *terre* land; — *v.a.* take down.

descente, *s.f.* descent; landing.

description, *s. f.* description.

désert¹, *s. m.* desert.

désert², *adj.* deserted, desolate.

déserter, *v. n. & a.* leave, desert.

désespérer, *v.n.* despair, give up.

désespoir, *s. m.* despair.

déshabiller, *v. a.* undress; take off clothes.

déshonneur, *s.m.* dishonour, disgrace.

déshonorer, *v. a.* dishonour, disgrace.

désigner, *v. a.* designate; denote; appoint.

desinfecter, *v. a.* disinfect.

désir, *s. m.* desire.

désirable: *adj.* desirable.

désirer, *v. a. & n.* desire, long for.

désireux, -euse, *adj.* desirous, anxious.

désobéir, *v.n.* disobey.

désobéissance, *s.f.* disobedience.

désobéissant, *adj.* disobedient.

désœuvré, *adj.* idle, unoccupied.

désolation, *s. f.* devastation; desolation.

désoler, *v.a.* desolate; afflict, distress; **se** ~ grieve, be sorry.

désordre, *s.m.* disorder.

dessert, *s. m.* dessert.

dessin, *s.m.* drawing, sketch; design; ~ *animé* cartoon.

dessiner, *v.a.* draw; sketch; design.

dessous, *adv. & prep.* under, underneath, below, beneath; — *s. m.* under-part; undies *pl.*

dessus, *adv. & prep.* on, upon, over, above, on top; — *s. m.* upper part, top.

destin, *s. m.* destiny, fate.

destinataire, *s. m. f.* receiver, addressee.

destination, *s. f.* destination.

destinée, *s.f.* destiny.

destiner, *v.a.* destine; mean (for); **se ~** be destined (*á* for).

détachement, *s. m.* disengagement; detachment.

détacher, *v.a.* loose(n), unfasten; detach; **se ~** get loose, come undone.

détail, *s.m.* detail, particular; retail; **en ~** in detail.

détention, *s. f.* detention.

détermination, *s.f.* determination.

déterminé, *adj.* definite, determinate; resolute; limited.

déterminer, *v.a.* determine, fix; limit; settle.

détestable, *adj.* hateful.

détester, *v.a.* detest.

détonation, *s.f.* detonation.

détour, *s.m.* turning, winding, turn; roundabout way; evasion.

détourner, *v.a.* turn aside; lead astray.

détroit, *s. m.* strait, pass.

détruire*, *v.a.* destroy, ruin; do away with.

dette, *s. f.* debt.

deuil, *s.m.* mourning.

deux, *adj. & s. m.* two; both.

deuxième, *adj.* second.

devancer, *v. a.* precede; anticipate.

devant, *prep. adv.* before; in front of; opposite to; **~ que** before; **au-~ de ~** in front ot; —

s. m. front; foreground.

dévaster, *v. a.* devastate, destroy.

développement, *s. m.* development, growth.

développer, *v.a.* (also **se ~**) develop.

devenir, *v.n.* become, get, turn, grow.

dévier, *v. a. & n.* deviate, turn away.

devise, *s. f.* device.

dévoiler, *v. a.* unveil, reveal.

devoir*, *v.a.* owe, be in debt for; have to, must, be bound to, ought to; — *s. m.* duty; task; work., prep.

dévorer, *v. a.* devour, eat up.

dévouement, *s. m.* devotion.

dévouer, *v. a.* devote, dedicate; **se ~** devote oneself.

diable, *s. m.* devil; trolley, truck.

diacre, *s. m.* deacon.

diadème, *s. m.* diadem.

diagnostic, *s. m.* diagnosis.

dialecte, *s. m.* dialect.

dialogue, *s. m.* dialogue.

diamant, *s. m.* diamond.

diapositive, *s. f.* transparency, slide.

diarrhée, *s. f.* diarrhoea.

dictée, *s. f.* dictation.

dicter, *v. a.* dictate.

dictionnaire, *s. m.* dictionary.

diesel, *s. m.* diesel engine.

dieu, *s. m.* (*pl. -x*) God.

différence, *s. f.* difference.

différent, *adj.* different.

différer, *v.a.* defer, put

off; *v.n.* differ, be different, vary.

difficile, *adj.* difficult, hard.

difficulté, *s. f.* difficulty, trouble.

diffusion, *s. f.* diffusion.

digne, *adj.* worthy; ~ *de* ... worthy of ...

dignité, *s.f.* dignity.

diligence, *s.f.* diligence.

diligent, *adj.* diligent.

dimanche, *s. m.* Sunday.

dimension, *s.f.* dimension.

diminuer, *v.a.* &. *n.* diminish, lessen, reduce.

dindon, *s.m.* turkey.

dîner, *s. m.* dinner; — *v. n.* dine.

diplomate, *s. m.* diplomat.

diplomatie, *s. f.* diplomacy.

diplomatique, *adj.* diplomatic.

diplôme, *s.m.* diploma.

dire*, *v.a.* say, tell; speak; ~ *à qn de faire qch.* tell s.o. to do sth.; *c'est à* ~ that is to say; *pour ainsi* ~ as it were; *vouloir* ~ mean; *dites donc!* look here!

direct, *adj.* direct.

directeur, *s.m.* director, manager; head master.

direction, *s.f.* direction; management; guidance; streering-gear.

directrice, *s. f.* directress; head mistress.

diriger, *v.a.* direct; lead, guide; manage; turn; steer.

disciple, *s.m.* disciple, follower.

discipline, *s. f.* discipline.

discorde, *s.f.* discord.

discours, *s.m.* discourse, speech.

discrédit, *s.m.* discredit.

discréditer, *v. a.* discredit.

discret, -ète *adj.* discreet; discrete.

discrètement, *adv.* discreetly.

discrétion, *s.f.* discretion.

discussion, *s. f.* discussion.

discuter, *v.a.* discuss, debate.

disparaître, *v.n.* disappear.

dispenser, *v. a.* dispense; se ~ *de* dispense with.

disposer, *v. a. & n.* dispose, lay out; se ~ prepare (to), be about (to); *bien disposé* willing.

disposition, *s. f.* disposition, arrangement; *la* ~ *de qn.* at s.o.'s disposal.

dispute, *s. f.* dispute.

disputer, *v. a. & n.* dispute, contest, argue; se ~ quarrel, dispute.

disqualifier, *v.a.* disqualify.

disque, *s. m.* disc, record; discus; ~ *microsillon* or *longue durée* long playing record.

dissimulation, *s. f.* dissimulation, dissembling.

dissimuler, *v.a. & n.* dissemble, conceal; se ~ conceal oneself.

dissolution, *s. f.* dissolution; undoing, breaking up.

dissoudre*, *v. a.* dissolve, disperse.

distance, *s. f.* distance; *a quelle* ~ *est-ce?* how far is it?

distant, *adj.* distant, far.

distiller, *v.a. & n.* distil.

distinct, *adj.* distinct, clear.

distinction, *s.f.* distinction.

distinguer, *v.a.* distinguish, discriminate; make out, tell.

distraction, *s. f.* abstraction; recreation; entertainment; distraction.

distraire, *v.a.* subtract; divert, distract; amuse, entertain.

distrait, *adj.* inattentive, absent-minded.

distribuer, *v. a.* distribute; deal out.

district, *s.m.* district.

divan, *s.m.* sofa, divan.

divergence, *s.f.* divergence; difference.

divers, *adj.* diverse, different, miscellaneous.

diversion, *s. f.* diversion.

divertir, *v.a.* divert, entertain; se ~ enjoy oneself.

divertissement, *s. m.* diversion; entertainment.

divin, *adj.* divine.

diviser, *v.a.* divide, separate.

division, *s.f.* division, department.

divorce, *s. m.* divorce.

divorcer *v n.* & *n.* divorce, be divorced.

dix, *adj. s. m.* ten.

dix-huit, *adj. & s.m.* eighteen.

dixième, *adj. & s.f.* tenth.

dix-neuf, *adj. & s.m.* nineteen.

dix-sept, *adj. & s.m.* seventeen.

dizaine, *s. f.* ten.

docteur, *s. m.* doctor.

document, *s.m.* document.

documentaire, *s. m.* documentary (film).

dogme, *s. m.* dogma.

doigt, *s.m.* finger; toe.

dollar, *s.m.* dollar.

domaine, *s.m.* domain; landed property.

dôme, *s. m.* dome.

domestique, *adj. & s. m. f.* domestic, servant.

domicile, *s. m.* domicile, dwelling.

domination, *s. f.* domination, rule.

dominer, *v. a. & n.* dominate, rule.

dommage, *s. m.* damage; pity.

dompter, *v. a.* subdue, master, tame.

don, *s. m.* present, gift.

donateur, *s.m.* giver.

donc, *conj.* therefore, then, so; of course.

donne, *s. f.* deal.

donner, *v. a.* give, grant, present with, afford, hand over; ~ *congé* give notice to; se ~ *pour* claim to be.

dont, *pron.* whose, of whom; of which.

dormir*, *v.n.* sleep.

dortoir, *s. m.* dormitory.

dos, *s. m.* back.

dose, *s. f.* dose.

dossier, *s. m.* back-piece; record, file.

dot, *s. f.* dowry.

doter, *v. a.* endow.

douane, *s.f.* customs; custom-house; duty; *déclaration de ~* customs declaration; *droits de ~* customs duties; *la visite de la ~* customs formalities.

douanier, *s.m.* custom-house officer.

double, *s.m.* double; *en ~* duplicate; *— adj.* double, dual.

doubler, *v. a.* double (up); line; dub.

doublure, *s.f.* lining; understudy.

douce see doux.

douceur, *s. f.* sweetness; gentleness.

douche, *s. f.* shower-bath.

douer, *v. a.* endow, gift.

douleur, *s. f.* pain, ache.

douloureux, -euse, *adj.* painful.

doute, *s. m.* doubt; *sans ~* no doubt, undoubtedly.

douter, *v. n.* doubt; *se ~* suspect.

douteux, -euse, *adj.* doubtful, dubious.

doux, douce, *adj.* sweet; mild, soft.

douzaine, *s.f.* dozen.

douze, *adj. & s. m.* twelve; twelfth.

douzième, *adj.* twelfth.

dramatique, *adj.* dramat-ic; *l'art ~* drama.

drame, *s.m.* drama.

drap, *s.m.* cloth, sheet.

drapeau, *s.m.* flag.

dresser, *v. a.* set up, erect; prepare; *se ~* stand up, get up.

drogue, *s. f.* drug.

droguerie, *s. f.* drugs *pl.*

droit, *s. m.* right; law; duty, due; *avoir ~ à* be entitled to; *~ de cité* citizenship; *~ d'auteur,* copyright; *exempt de ~s* duty-free; *~(s) de sortie,* export duty; *— adj.* right, direct, straight.

droite, *s. f.* right hand.

drôle, *adj.* droll, funny, strange; *— s. m.* rogue.

du, *art.* of the, some, any.

dû, *adj. & s. m.* due.

duc, *s. m.* duke.

duchesse, *s.f.* duchess.

duel, *s. m.* duel.

duplicata, *s. m.* duplicate, copy.

dur, *adj.* hard, tough.

durable, *adj.* lasting.

durant, *prep.* during, for.

durcir, *v. a. & n.* harden.

durée, *s.f.* duration, term.

durer, *v.n. & a.* last, endure, hold out.

dureté, *s. f.* hardness.

dynastie, *s.f.* dynasty.

E

eau, *s. f. (pl. -x)* water; *~ de mer* salt water; *~ de Seltz* soda-water.

ébaucher, *v.a.* sketch;

outline.

ébouriffer, *v.a.* ruffle.

ébullition, *s.f.* boiling.

écaille, *s.f.* scale.

écailler, *v.a.* scale.

écart, *s.m.* deviation; *à l'~* aside, apart.

écarter, *v.a.* set aside; dispel, take away; **s'~** turn aside.

ecclésiastique, *adj. & s.m.* ecclesiastic.

échafaud, *s. m.* scaffold-(ing).

échange, *s. m.* exchange.

échanger, *v. a.* exchange.

échapper, *v. n.* escape, get away.

échauder, *v.a.* scald.

échauffer, *v. a.* heat; **s'~** get hot.

échéance, *s. f.* expiration.

échéant, *adj.* due.

échec, *s. m.* check.

échecs, *s. m. pl.* chess.

échelle, *s.f.* ladder; scale.

échine, *s.f.* backbone.

écho, *s.m.* echo.

échoir*, *v.n.* expire, fall due; happen.

éclabousser, *v. a.* splash, spatter with mud.

éclair, *s.m.* lightning; flash.

éclairage, *s. m.* lighting; *~ au néon* strip-lighting.

éclaircir, *v. a.* make clear, clear up; clarify; throw light on; **s'~** become clear, clear up.

éclairer, *v. a.* light, illuminate; enlighten.

éclaireur, *s. m.* boy scout.

éclat, *s.m.* splinter; burst; brightness.

éclatant, *adj.* bright.

éclater, *v. n.* split; burst; break out; flash.

éclipser, *v. a.* eclipse; **s'~** be eclipsed; take French leave.

école, *s.f.* school; *maître d'~* schoolmaster; *~ normale* teachers' training college; *~ secondaire* grammar-school.

écolier, *s. m.* schoolboy.

écolière, *s. f.* schoolgirl.

économe, *adj.* economical; — *s. m.* bursar.

économie, *s. f.* economy; thrift; *~ politique* political economy; *~s* savings; *faire des ~s* save up.

économique, *adj.* economic; economical.

économiser, *v. a. & n.* economize, save, spare.

écorce, *s. f.* bark; rind.

écossais, *adj.* Scottish, Scotch.

Écossais, *s. m.* Scotsman.

écouler, *v.a.* sell.

écouter, *v.a.* listen to; hear.

écouteur, *s.m.* head-phone; receiver.

écran, *s.m.* screen; *le petit ~* television.

écrier: **s'~** cry out.

écrire*, *v. a.* write (down); *machine à ~* type-writer.

écrit, *adj.* written; — *s. m.* writing; *par ~* in writing.

écriture, *s.f.* writing; handwriting; style.

écrivain, *s.m.* writer,

author.

écuelle, s. f. bowl, basin, dish.

écume, s.f. foam.

écureuil, s.m. squirrel.

écurie, s. f. stable.

édifice, s.m. building.

édifier, v.a. build, erect; edify.

édit, s.m. edict, decree.

éditer, v. a. publish; edit.

éditeur, s. m. publisher.

édition, s. f. publication; edition.

éducation, s. f. education; training.

effacer, v. a. efface, rub out; wipe out.

effectif, -ive adj. actual, real.

effectuer, v.a. effect, carry out.

effet, s. m. effect, result; impression; bill (of exchange); (pl.) clothes, belongings.

efficacité, s. f. efficacy.

effondrer: s'~ fall in, collapse.

effort, s. m. effort, exertion, endeavour.

effrayant, adj. frightful.

effrayé, adj. afraid.

effrayer, v.a. frighten; s'~ be frightened.

effroi, s.m. fright.

effroyable, adj. frightful.

effusion, s.f. effusion, gush.

égal, adj. equal, like, alike; (all the) same; even.

également, adv. equally.

égaler, v.a. equal.

égalité, s.f. equality.

égard, s. m. regard; à cet ~ on that account; à l'~ de with regard to; en ~ à considering.

égarer, v. a. mislead, misguide; s'~ lose one's way.

égayer, v. a. cheer (up); s'~ cheer up.

église (É), s. f. church.

égoïste, adj. egoistic, selfish.

egyptien, -enne (É), adj. & s.m.f. Egyptian.

eh, int. ah!; ~ bien! well!

élaborer, v. a. work out, think out, elaborate.

élan, s.m. dash; run; élan, zest.

élancé adj. slim.

élancer, v. n. shoot; s'~ bound, dash, rush; soar.

élargir, v. a. make wider, enlarge; set at liberty.

élastique, adj. & s. m. elastic.

électeur, -trice, s. m. f. voter.

élection, s.f. election.

électricien, -enne, s. m. f. electrician.

électricité, s.f. electricity; usine d'~ power-plant, -station.

électrique, adj. electric(al).

électron, s.m. electron.

électronique, adj. electronic.

élégance, s.f. elegance.

élégant, adj. elegant.

élément, s. m. element.

élémentaire, adj. elementary.

éléphant, s. m. elephant.

élévation, s.f. elevation.

élève, *s.m.f.* pupil.

élevé, *adj.* educated.

élever, *v. a.* raise, lift up; increase; bring up, educate; rear; s'~ rise; exalt oneself.

éliminer, *v. a.* eliminate.

élire, *v. a.* choose; elect.

elle, *pron. (pl.* elles) she, it, her; they.

elle-même, *pron.* herself.

éloigné, *adj.* far, distant.

éloigner, *v.a.* remove; take away; set aside.

émail, *s. m.* enamel.

émaner, *v.n.* emanate.

emballer, *v.a.* pack up; pack off.

embarquement, *s. m.* embarking; shipment.

embarquer, *v.a.* ship, embark; *v.n.* go on board.

embarrasser, *v. a.* embarrass.

embellir, *v. a.* embellish.

embêter, *v.a.* bore; annoy.

emblème, *s. m.* emblem.

embouchure, *s. f.* mouthpiece; mouth (of river).

embranchement, *s.m.* branchline; junction.

embrasser, *v. a.* embrace; kiss; s'~ kiss.

embrayage, *s. m.* clutch, coupling.

embrouillement, *s.m.* tangle; muddle.

embrouiller, *v. a.* embroil, entangle; muddle; s'~ become confused.

émetteur, *s. m.* transmitter.

émettre *v. a.* emit; trans-

mit, broadcast.

émigration, *s. f.* emigration.

émigré, -e, *s.m.f.* emigrant.

émigrer, *v.n.* emigrate.

éminent, *adj.* eminent.

emmener, *v.a.* take away.

émotion, *s.f.* emotion; feeling.

émouvoir, *v.a.* move, touch; s'~ be moved.

emparer: s'~ *de* get hold of, seize.

empêchement, *s. m.* hindrance.

empêcher, *v.a.* keep from; prevent; hinder.

empire, *s.m.* empire.

emplette, *s. f.* purchase.

emplir, *v.a.* fill (up).

emploi, *s.m.* employment, job; use.

employé, -e, *s.m.f.* employee; clerk; attendant.

employer, *v.a.* employ; use.

empoigner, *v.a.* grasp, grip; lay hands on.

empoisonner, *v. a.* poison.

emporter, *v.a.* carry, take away, carry off, remove; s'~ get angry, lose one's temper.

empreinte, *s. f.* stamp, print, impression.

empresser: s'~ hurry, hasten.

emprisonnement, *s.m.* imprisonment.

emprisonner, *v.a.* imprison.

emprunter, *v. a.* borrow.

en, *prep.* in; to; into; at; like, as; by; through;

— *pron.* of him, of her, of it, of them, their; any, some.

encan, *s.m.* auction.

enceinte, *adj.* pregnant.

enchaîner, *v.a.* chain; link up; detain.

enchantement, *s. m.* spell; delight.

enchanter, *v.a.* charm, delight.

enclore, *v.a.* enclose.

enclose, *s. m.* enclosure; close.

enclume, *s.f.* anvil.

encombrement, *s. m.* stoppage; (traffic) jam.

encombrer, *v. a.* block up, jam.

encore, *adv.* yet, still; again; *pas* ~ not yet; ~ *une fois* once again; ~ *que* although; ~ *du* some more; ~ *quelque chose, Madame?* anything else, madam?

encouragement, *s. m.* encouragement.

encourager, *v. a.* encourage; cheer.

encre, *s.f.* ink.

encyclopédie, *s. f.* encyclopaedia.

endommager, *v.a.* damage; injure.

endormir, *v.a.* put to sleep; s'~ go to sleep, fall asleep.

endosser, *v.a.* endorse.

énergie, *s. f.* energy; ~ *atomique* atomic energy.

énergique, *adj.* energetic.

enfance, *s.f.* infancy, childhood.

enfant, *s. m. f.* infant, child; *chambre d'*~*s* nursery; *d'*~*s* juvenile.

enfermer, *v.a.* shut in, up, lock up.

enfin, *adv.* at last; finally; in short.

enflammer, *v. a.* set on fire; s'~ take fire.

enfler, *v. a.* swell (up); s'~ swell.

enflure, *s. f.* swelling.

engagement, *s. m.* obligation; commitment; engagement.

engager, *v. a. & n.* pledge; pawn; engage, sign on.

engloutir, *v. a.* swallow up, devour.

engraisser, *v.a.* fatten; *v.n.* grow fat.

enlèvement, *s.m.* removal.

enlever, *v.a.* remove, clear away, take away.

ennemi, *s.m.* enemy.

ennui, *s. m.* bore(dom); vexation; nuisance.

ennuyer, *v. a.* bore, weary; s'~ be bored.

ennuyeux, **-euse**, *adj.* boring, tedious.

énoncer, *v.a.* state.

énorme, *adj.* enormous.

enquérir: s'~ *de* inquire about.

enrager, *v. n.* be enraged.

enregistrer, *v. a.* register, enter, record.

enrhumer, *v.a. être enrhumé* have a cold; s'~ catch a cold.

enrôler, *v. a.* enrol, draft.

enroué, *adj.* hoarse.

enrouler, *v. a.* roll (up).

enseignement, *s. m.* instruction, tuition.

enseigner, *v.a. & n.*

teach, instruct (in).

ensemble, *adv.* together; — *s. m.* whole, mass; unity; two-piece suit; set of furniture, suite.

ensuite, *adv.* then; next.

ensuivre: s'~ follow, ensue.

entasser, *v.a.* heap up.

entendement, *s. m.* understanding.

entendre, *v. a. & n.* hear; understand; ~ *parler de* hear of; *ne pas* ~ miss; *qu'entendez-vous par là?* what do you mean by that?; *bien entendu* of course; *c'est entendu!* that's settled!; agreed!

entente, *s.f.* meaning; understanding; agreement.

enterrement, *s. m.* burial.

enterrer, *v.a.* bury.

enthousiasme, *s. m.* enthusiasm.

enthousiaste, *adj.* enthusiastic; keen.

entier, -ère, *adj.* entire.

entièrement, *adv.* entirely, wholly.

entorse, *s.f.* sprain; *donner une* ~ *à* sprain one's (foot, ankle).

entourage, *s. m.* circle of friends; surroundings *(pl.)*; attendants *(pl.)*.

entourer, *v.a.* surround; encircle.

entracte, *s. m.* interval.

entrailles, *s.f. pl.* entrails.

entraîner, *v.a.* draw along; carry away; involve, entail; coach.

entraîneur, *s. m.* trainer, coach.

entre, *prep.* between, among; into, in.

entrée, *s. f.* entry, entrance, beginning; free access; duty.

entremets, *s. m.* second course.

entreprendre, *v.a.* attempt, undertake, contract for; worry.

entrepreneur, *s.m.* contractor.

entreprise, *s. f.* undertaking, enterprise.

entrer, *v. n.* enter; come in, go in; get in; get into; *faire* ~ show in.

enveloppe, *s. f.* envelope; wrapper, cover.

envelopper, *v. a.* wrap up, do up; envelop.

envers, *prep.* towards, to.

enviable, *adj.* enviable.

envie, *s. f.* envy; desire.

envier, *v. a.* envy; desire.

environ, *adv. & prep.* about.

environner, *v.a.* surround.

environs, *s. m. pl.* surroundings.

envoi, *s. m.* sending; consignment, shipment.

envoler: s'~ fly away, take wing.

envoyer*, *v.a.* send, dispatch, forward.

envoyeur, *s.m.* sender.

épais, -aisse, *adj.* thick.

épaisseur, *s. f.* thickness.

épargne, *v.s.f.* savings *(pl.)*.

épargner, *v. a.* save (up).

épaule, *s.f.* shoulder.

épée, *s.f.* sword.

éperon, *s.m.* spur.

épice, *s. f.* spice.

épicerie, *s.f.* grocery, grocer's (shop).

épicier, -ère, *s. m. f.* grocer.

épidémie, *s. f.* epidemic.

épinard, *s.m.* spinach.

épine, *s. f.* thorn; spine, backbone; obstacle.

épingle, *s. f.* pin; ~ *de sûreté* safety-pin.

épisode, *s.m.* episode.

éplucher, *v. a.* peel; pick; sift, preen, thin out.

éponge, *s.f.* sponge.

éponger, *v. a.* sponge; mop (up).

époque, *s. f.* period, age, epoch, time.

épouse, *s.f.* wife.

épouser, *v.a.* marry.

épouvante, *s.f.* fright.

époux, *s. m.* husband.

épreuve, *s. f.* test, trial; proof; print.

éprouver, *v. a.* test, prove; feel; experience.

épuisé, *adj.* exhausted; out of print.

épuiser, *v. a.* exhaust; use up; wear out.

équation, *s.f.* equation.

équilibre, *s.m.* balance, equilibrium.

équipage, *s. m.* suite, retinue; carriage; crew.

équipe, *s. f.* gang, shift; crew, team, side; train.

équipement, *s. m.* equipment.

équiper, *v.a.* equip.

équivalent, *adj.* equivalent.

ère, *s.f.* era.

errant, *adj.* wandering.

errer, *v. n.* stray; err.

erreur, *s.f.* error, mistake.

érudit, *adj.* learned.

érudition, *s.f.* learning.

escalateur, *s. m.* escalator.

escale, *s.f.* port; landing; *sans* ~ non-stop.

escalier, *s. m.* stairs *(pl.)*, staircase; ~ *de sauvetage* fire-escape; ~ *de service* backstairs *(pl.)*; ~ *roulant* escalator.

escargot, *s.m.* snail.

escarpins, *s. m. pl.* pumps.

esclavage, *s.m.* slavery.

esclave, *s. m. f.* slave; — *adj.* slavish.

escrime, *s.f.* fencing; *faire de l'*~ fence.

escrimer, *v.n.* fence.

espace, *s. m.* space; room.

espagnol, -e (E.), *adj.* Spanish; — *s. m. f.* Spaniard; Spanish.

espèce, *s. f.* species, kind.

espérance, *s. f.* hope, expectation.

espérer, *v. a.* hope (for).

espion, -onne, *s.m.f.* spy.

espionnage, *s. m.* espionage, spying.

espoir, *s.m.* hope.

esprit, *s. m.* spirit; mind; character; wit; sense.

esquille, *s.f.* splinter.

esquiver, *v.a.* evade.

essai, *s.m.* trial, test; essay; attempt.

essayer, *v. a.* try, attempt; essay; assay.

essence, *s.f.* essence; petrol.

essentiel, -elle, *adj.* essential.

essieu, *s.m.* axle.

essor, *s.m.* flight.

essoreuse, *s. f.* spin-drier.

essuie-glace, *s. m.* windscreen wiper.

essuie-main(s), *s. m. (pl.)* towel; ~ *à rouleau* roller-towel.

essuyer, *v.a.* dust; wipe; dry; mop up.

est, *s. m.* cast.

esthétique, *adj.* aesthetic.

estime, *s.f.* esteem.

estimer, *v.a. & n.* estimate, value; esteem, regard; consider.

estomac, *s.m.* stomach.

estrade, *s.f.* platform.

estuaire, *s.m.* estuary.

et, *conj.* and; ~ ...~ both ... and.

étable, *s.f.* cow-shed; ~ *à porcs* pigsty.

établi, *s.m.* (joiner's) bench.

établir, *v.a.* establish, found, settle, set up; build; prove; s'~ settle (down).

établissement, *s. m.* establishment.

étage, *s. m.* floor, stor(e)y.

étagère, *s. f.* shelf.

étaler, *v.a.* display; spread (out); show off; s'~ stretch oneself out.

étang, *s.m.* pond.

étape, *s.f.* stage.

état, *s.m.* state; condition; profession, station office; statement; *homme d'*~ statesman; *coup d'*~ revolt.

été, *s.m.* summer.

éteindre*, *v.a.* put out, extinguish; turn off; s'~ be extinguished.

étendre, *v. a.* spread out; stretch out; extend; s'~ lie down; stretch

one-self out.

étendu, *adj.* wide, vast, extensive.

étendue, *s.f.* expanse, reach, range; extent.

éternel, -elle, *adj.* eternal.

éternuement, *s. m.* sneeze.

éternuer, *v.n.* sneeze.

étincelle, *s.f.* spark.

étiquette, *s.f.* ticket, label; etiquette.

étoffe, *s.f.* cloth, material.

étoile, *s.f.* star.

étonnant, *adj.* astonishing, amazing.

étonnement, *s. m.* astonishment, wonder.

étonner, *v.a.* astonish, amaze; s'~ be astonished.

étouffer, *v.a.* choke.

étrange, *adj.* strange.

étranger, -ère, *adj.* foreign, strange; —-*s.m.f.* foreigner; *à l'*~ abroad.

être*, *v.n.* be, exist; *il est... it is...;* ~ *bien* be good-looking; be well; *c'est que* the fact is; ~ *à* belong to; — *s.m.* being.

étreindre*, *v.a.* clasp; press; embrace.

étreinte, *s.f.* embrace.

étrier, *s. m.* stirrup.

étroit, *adj.* narrow, strait; close.

étude, *s. f.* study; chambers *(pl.)*.

étudiant, -e, *s.m.f.* student, undergraduate.

étudier, *v. a.* study, read; practise.

étui, *s.m.* case, box.

étuver, *v.a.* stew, steam.
eucharistie, *s.f.* eucharist.
européen, -enne, *adj.* European.
eux, *pron. m.* they, them.
évader: s'~ escape; get away.
évaluer, *v. a.* value, estimate.
évangélique, *adj.* evangelical.
évangile, *s.m.* gospel.
évaporer, *v. a.* evaporate; **s'~** evaporate.
éveil, *s. m.* **en ~** on the lookout.
éveiller, *v. a.* awaken; **s'~** wake up.
événement, *s.m.* event.
éventail, *s.m.* fan.
éventuel, -elle, *adj.* eventual.
évêque, *s.m.* bishop.
évidemment, *adv.* evidently, obviously.
évidence, *s.f.* evidence.
évident, *adj.* evident, obvious.
éviter, *v. a.* avoid, evade.
évoluer, *v.n.* evolve.
évolution, *s. f.* evolution.
exact, *adj.* exact, accurate.
exactement, *adv.* exactly.
exactitude, *s.f.* exactitude, precision.
exagérer, *v. a.* exaggerate.
examen, *s. m.* exam(ination); test.
examiner, *v. a.* examine; investigate, look into.
excédent, *s.m.* surplus; **~s de bagages** excess luggage.
excéder, *v. a.* exceed, surpass; tire out.
excellence, *s.f.* excellence; excellency.
excellent, *adj.* excellent.
excepté, *adj.* excepted; — *prep.* except(ing), but.
excepter, *v.a.* except.
exception, *s. f.* exception.
exceptionnel, -elle, *adj.* exceptional.
excès, *s. m.* excess.
excessif, -ive, *adj.* excessive.
excitation, *s.f.* excitement.
exciter, *v.a.* excite, stir up; urge on.
exclamation, *s.f.* exclamation.
exclure*, *v.a.* exclude.
exclusif, -ive, *adj.* exclusive.
excursion, *s. f.* excursion.
excursionniste, *s.m.f.* holiday-maker, tourist.
excuse, *s.f.* excuse; apology; *faire des ~s* apologize.
excuser, *v.a.* excuse; pardon; apologize for; **s'~** apologize; ask to be excused; *excusez-moi* I beg your pardon; excuse me.
exécuter, *v.a.* execute, carry out, perform.
exécutif, -ive, *adj.* executive.
exécution, *s. f.* execution.
exemplaire, *s.m.* copy.
exemple, *s. m.* example; *par ~* for example; *sans ~* unprecedented.
exempt, *adj.* exempt, free (*de* from).
exemption, *s.f.* exemp-

tion.

exercer, *v.a.* exercise; practise; carry on; s'~ practise.

exercice, *s.m.* exercise.

exhibition, *s.f.* exhibition; display.

exigence, *s.f.* demand; exigency.

exil, *s.m.* exile.

existence, *s. f.* existence.

exister, *v. n.* exist.

expansif, **-ive**, *adj.* expansive.

expansion, *s.f.* expansion.

expédient, *s.m.* expedient, device.

expédier, *v.a.* forward, send off.

expéditeur, **-trice**, *s. m. f.* sender, shipping-agent.

expédition, *s. f.* consignment; expedition, forwarding, dispatch.

expérience, *s.f.* experience; experiment; *faire des* ~*s* to experiment.

expérimental, *adj.* experimental.

expert, *adj.* expert.

expirer, *v.n.* expire; die.

explication, *s.f.* explanation.

expliquer, *v.n.* explain, account for, show.

exploration, *s. f.* exploration.

explorer, *v. a.* explore.

explosion, *s.f.* explosion.

exportateur, *s.m.* exporter.

exportation, *s. f.* export, exportation.

exporter, *v. a.* export.

exposé, *s.m.* statement.

exposer, *v.a.* expose, show; state; set forth.

exposition, *s. f.* exhibition, display; statement, exposure; exposition.

exprès, *adv.* on purpose.

express, *adj.* express; — *s.m.* express (train).

expression, *s.f.* expression.

exprimer, *v.a.* express.

expulser, *v.a.* expel.

expulsion, *s.f.* expulsion.

extension, *s. f.* extension; extent.

exténuer, *v.a.* tire out, exhaust.

extérieur, *s. m.* exterior; outside; à l'~ outwards — *adj.* outward.

extinction, *s.f.* extinction; quenching.

extraire, *v. a.* extract; draw, pull out.

extraordinaire, *adj.* extraordinary, unusual.

extravagant, *adj.* extravagant.

extrême, *adj.* extreme.

extrêmement, *adv.* extremely, very.

extrémité *s. f.* extremity; last moment.

F

fabricant, *s.m.* manufacturer, maker.

fabrication, *s.f.* manufacture; fabrication.

fabrique, *s.f.* factory, works.

fabriquer, *v.a.* manufacture, make.

façade, *s.f.* front.

face, *s.f.* face; look;

en ~ de opposite, in front of.

facétieux, -euse, *adj.* facetious; humorous.

fâché, *adj.* offended.

fâcher, *v. a.* offend; make angry; **se ~** get angry.

facile, *adj.* easy; fluent.

facilité, *s. f.* ease; facility; convenience.

faciliter, *v.a.* facilitate; make easy.

façon, *s. f.* making; fashion, shape; way, manner; **de ~** *a* so as to; **de ~ que** so that; **en aucune ~** by no means; **d'une ~ quelconque** somehow.

facteur, *s.m.* factor; postman; porter, carrier; *fig.* circumstance.

faction, *s.f.* faction; sentry, watch.

facture, *s.f.* bill, invoice.

facultatif, -ive, *adj.* optional.

faculté, *s.f.* faculty.

fade, *adj.* flat, insipid.

faible, *adj.* weak; feeble.

faiblesse, *s. f.* weakness.

faiblir, *v. n.* become weak.

faillir, *v. n.* fail, fall short; err; **~ + inf.** nearly; **j'ai failli manquer le train** I nearly missed the train.

faim, *s. f.* hunger; *avoir* **~** be hungry.

faire*, *v.a.* make; do; build; cause; **~ allusion** refer to; **~ attention** (*a*) pay attention (to); **~ une chambre** do a room; **~ le commerce** trade; **~ la cuisine** do the cooking; **~ ses études** study; be at school; **~ la guerre** make war; **~ un lit** make a bed; **~ mal à** hurt; **~ part à** let know; **~ des progrès** make progress; **~ une promenade** take a walk; **~ queue** queue; **~ savoir** let know, inform (of); **~ usage (de)** make use (of); **~ voir** show; **que ~?** what's to be done?; **qu'est-ce que cela fait?** what does it matter?; **n'avoir rien à ~** have nothing to do; **deux et deux font quatre** two and two make four; **~ 70 km. à l'heure** do 70 km. an hour; **il fait du vent** it is windy; **il fait chaud** it is warm; **il fait jour** it is daylight; **— se ~** be made, be done; get used (to).

faisan, *s. m.* pheasant.

fait, *s. m.* fact; **en ~** in fact, after all, as a matter of fact.

falloir*, *v. impers.* be necessary, be required; must, have to, should, ought to; *comme il faut* proper, decent; **s'en ~** be wanting.

fameux, -euse, *adj.* famous.

familier, -ière, *adj.* familiar.

famille, *s. f.* family.

faner, *v.n.* fade.

fantaisie, *s.f.* fancy.

fantastique, *adj.* fantastic.

fardeau, *s.m.* burden.

farine, *s.f.* flour, meal.

fatal, *adj.* mortal, fatal.

fatigant, *adj.* fatiguing.

fatigue, *s.f.* fatigue.

fatigué, *adj.* tired, weary.

fatiguer, *v. a.* tire, weary, fatigue.

faubourg, *s.m.* suburb.

faucher, *v.a.* mow, cut.

faucheuse, *s.f.* ~ (*à moteur*) (lawn-)mower.

faucille, *s. f.* sickle.

faucon, *s.m.* falcon.

faute, *s. f.* mistake, error, fault; lapse; want; *faire* ~ fail.

fauteuil, *s. m.* arm-chair, easy chair; stall, dress-circle seat.

fauve, *s.m.* wild beast.

faux¹, fausse, *adj.* false.

faux², *s. f.* scythe.

faveur, *s. f.* favour; *en* ~ *de* in favour of, on behalf of.

favorable, *adj.* favourable.

favori, -ite, *adj.* favorite.

fécond, *adj.* fertile.

féconder, *v.a.* fertilize.

fédéral, *adj.* federal.

fédération, *s.f.* federation.

fédéré, -e, *adj. & s. m. f.* federate.

feindre*, *v. a. & n.* feign.

félicitation, *s.f.* congratulation.

félicité, *s.f.* happiness.

féliciter, *v.a.* congratulate.

féminin, *adj.* feminine.

femme, *s.f.* woman; wife.

fendre, *v. a.* split; rend.

fenêtre, *s. f.* window.

fente, *s. f.* crack, split.

fer, *s. m.* iron; ~ *à cheval* horseshoe.

férié, *adj. jour* ~ holiday.

ferme¹, *adj.* firm; — *adv.* fast; firmly.

ferme², *s. f.* farm.

fermé, *adj.* closed.

fermer, *v. a.* close, shut; *se* ~ close, be shut.

fermeté, *s. f.* firmness.

fermeture, *s. f.* shutting; shutter; ~ *éclair* zip fastener, zipper.

fermier, *s. m.* farmer.

féroce, *adj.* wild, cruel.

férocité, *s. f.* ferocity.

ferronnerie, *s.f.* iron-works.

fertile, *adj.* fertile.

fervent, *adj.* fervent.

ferveur, *s. f.* fervour.

fesse, *s.f.* buttock.

festin, *s.m.* feast.

fête, *s. f.* feast, holiday; birthday.

fêter, *v. a.* observe; celebrate.

fêteur, -euse, *s. m. f.* holiday-maker.

feu, *s.m.* fire, flame; light; *mettre le* ~ *à* set on fire; *prendre* ~ take fire; ~ *d'artifice* fireworks *(pl.);* ~*x de circulation* traffic lights; ~*x d'arrière* tail lights.

feuillage, *s.m.* foliage.

feuille, *s.f.* leaf; sheet.

février, *s.m.* February.

fiancé, -e, *s. m. f.* fiancé, -e.

fiancer, *v.a.* engage; se

~ be engaged.

fibre, *s. f.* fibre.

ficelle, *s. f.* string.

fiche, *s. f.* pin, peg; slip (of paper).

ficher, *v. a.* drive in, fix; do, work; deal (a blow).

fidèle, *adj.* faithful.

fidélité, *s. f.* fidelity.

fier: se ~ trust, count on.

fierté, *s. f.* pride.

fièvre, *s. f.* fever.

figue, *s. f.* fig.

figure, *s. f.* form, shape; face; figure.

figurer, *v.a.* figure, represent; se ~ imagine.

fil, *s.m.* thread, yarn; edge; clue; ~ *(de fer)* wire.

file, *s. f.* row, file, line.

filer, *v.a.* & *n.* spin.

filet, *s.m.* net; fillet; rack.

fille, *s. f.* daughter; girl; maid; *jeune* ~ young lady.

fillette, *s.f.* little girl.

filleul, -e, *s. m. f.* godson, god-daughter.

film, *s. m.* film; *le grand* ~ feature film; ~ *avec* film featuring ...; ~ *annonce* trailer.

fils, *s. m.* son.

fin¹, *s.f.* end; close; *à la* ~ in the end, finally; *mettre* ~ *à* put an end to; *tirer à sa* ~ come to an end; ~ *de semaine* week-end.

fin², *adj.* fine; nice.

final, *adj.* final.

finance, *s. f.* finance.

financier, *adj.* financial.

fini, *adj.* finished; ended; over.

finir, *v. a.* & *n.* end, finish, put an end to; eat up.

finlandais, -e (F.), *adj.* Finnish; — *s. m. f.* Finn; Finnish.

fixe, *adj.* fixed, firm.

fixer, *v.a.* fix, fasten; stare at; settle.

flacon, *s. m.* flagon, bottle.

flagrant, *adj.* flagrant.

flairer, *v. a.* smell, scent.

flambeau, *s. m.* torch.

flamboyer, *v.n.* flame, flare.

flamme, *s.f.* flame.

flanelle, *s. f.* flannel.

flanquer, *v.a.* fling.

flatter, *v. a.* caress; flatter.

flatterie, *s.f.* flattery.

flèche, *s. f.* arrow.

fléchir, *v. a.* bend, bow; *fig.* move.

fleur, *s. f.* flower, blossom.

fleurir, *v.n.* flower, blossom.

fleuve, *s. m.* river.

flirter, *v. n.* flirt.

flocon, *s. m.* flake *(snow etc.).*

flot, *s. m.* wave; flood; *être à* ~ be floating.

flottant, *adj.* floating.

flotte, *s.f.* fleet; navy.

flotter, *v.n.* & *a.* float.

fluide, *s. m.* & *adj.* fluid.

flute, *s. f.* flute.

foi, *s.f.* faith, belief; credit.

foie, *s. m.* liver.

foin, *s.m.* hay; grass.

foire, *s.f.* fair, market.

fois, *s.f.* time; *une* ~ once; *encore une* ~ again; *deux* ~ twice; *à la* ~ at same time;

chaque ~ every time.

folie, *s. f.* folly, madness.

folle *see* **fou.**

foncer, *v. a.* sink; darken, deepen.

fonction, *s.f.* function, duty.

fonctionnaire, *s.m.f.* functionary, official.

fonctionner, *v.n.* function, operate, work.

fond, *s. m.* bottom, ground, foundation; *à* ~ thoroughly.

fondamental, *adj.* fundamental, basic.

forcer, *v. a.* force; break open; compel, impel.

forêt, *s. f.* forest.

forger, *v. a.* forge.

formalité, *s. f.* formality.

forme, *s. f.* form, shape.

formel, -elle, *adj.* formal, express; flat.

former, *v. a.* form, shape.

formidable, *adj.* formidable, terrible.

formule, *s.f.* formula.

formuler, *v. a.* formulate, draw up.

fort, *adj.* strong, robust; fat; stout, stiff; skilful; heavy; *être* ~ *en* be well up in; — *adv.* very (much), highly, hard; ~ *bien* very well; — *s. m.* strong man; stronghold.

forteresse, *s.f.* fortress.

fortification, *s. f.* fortification.

fortifier, *v. a.* strengthen, fortify.

fortune, *s.f.* fortune, chance; luck; wealth, property.

fou, fol, folle, *adj.* mad, foolish; crazy.

foudre, *s.f.* lightning, thunderbolt.

fouille, *s. f.* excavation.

fouiller, *v. a. & n.* dig, excavate.

fouillis, *s.m.* muddle, mess.

foule, *s. f.* crowd, mass.

four, *s. m.* oven, furnace.

fourchette, *s.f.* fork (*table*).

fourgon, *s. m.* (delivery) van; wagon; ~ *(aux bagages)* luggage-van.

fourmi, *s.f.* ant.

fourneau, *s.m.* stove, range; ~ *à gaz* gas-ring, -stove; ~ *électrique* electric cooker.

fourniment, *s.m.* outfit, kit.

fournir, *v.a.* furnish (with); supply; provide (with).

fourreau, *s.m.* sheath, case, scabbard.

fourreur, *s.m.* furrier.

fourrure, *s.f.* fur.

foyer, *s.m.* fireside, home; foyer, lounge.

fracas, *s.m.* crash; uproar; fuss; noise.

fracasser, *v.a.* shatter, smash.

fraction, *s.f.* fraction; portion; instalment.

fracture, *s.f.* fracture.

fragile, *adj.* fragile.

frais[1], fraîche, *adj.* fresh, cool; chilly.

frais[2], *s. m. pl.* expenses, charges, fees.

fraise, *s.f.* strawberry.

framboise, *s. f.* raspberry.

franc, franche, *adj.* frank,

free, open.

français (F.), *adj.* French; — *s. m.* Frenchman; French (language).

Française, *s.f.* French-woman.

franchir, *v.a.* clear, jump over, cross.

franchise, *s. f.* exemption; frankness.

frapper, *v.a.* strike, hit, knock; impress; surprise.

frein, *s. m.* bit (of bridle); brake; *fig.* check.

frêle, *adj.* weak, frail.

fréquent, *adj.* frequent.

frère, *s.m.* brother.

fricassée, *v.a.* fricassee.

friction, *s.f.* friction.

frigidaire, *s.m.* refrigerator.

frigo, *s.m.* fridge.

frileux, -euse, *adj.* chilly.

frire*, *v.n.* & *a.* fry.

friser, *v.a.* & *n.* curl.

frissonner, *v. n.* shiver, tremble.

frivole, *adj.* frivolous, flimsy.

froid, *s. m.* cold; *avoir* ~ feel cold; — *adj.* cold, cool; *il fait froid* it is cold.

froisser, *v.a.* rumple, crumple; bruise; *fig.* offend, hurt; *se* ~ take offence.

frôler, *v.a.* graze.

fromage, *s.m.* cheese.

front, *s.m.* forehead; face; front (part).

frontière, *s.f.* frontier, border.

frotter, *v. a.* rub.

fruit, *s.m.* fruit; pro-duce.

fruitier, *s.m.* fruiterer, greengrocer.

fuir*, *v. n.* & *a.* run away, flee.

fuite, *s. f.* flight; leakage, leak.

fumée, *s.f.* smoke.

fumer, *v. a.* & *n.* smoke.

fumeur, -euse *s.m.f.* smoker.

fumier, *s.m.* dung.

funèbre, *adj.* funereal.

funérailles, *s.f.pl.* funeral.

funiculaire, *s.m.* rope railway.

fureur, *s. f.* fury, rage.

furie, *s. f.* fury.

furieux, -euse, *adj.* furious.

furoncle, *s.m.* boil, furuncle.

fusée, *s.f.* fuse; rocket.

fusil, *s.m.* gun.

fusillade, *s.f.* firing, shooting.

futur, *adj.* & *s. m.* future.

fuyant, *adj.* flying, fleeing; passing.

G

gâchis, *s.m.* mortar; mire; *fig.* muddle, mess.

gaffe, *s. f.* blunder.

gage, *s. m.* pledge; security; ~s wages.

gagner, *v. a.* gain; win.

gai, *adj.* gay, cheerful.

gaieté, *s.f.* gaiety.

gain, *s.m.* gain, profit.

galant, *adj.* courteous.

galerie, *s. f.* gallery.

galop, *s. m.* gallop.

gamin, *s.m.* urchin.

gamme, *s. f.* scale; range.

gant, *s. m.* glove.

garage, *s.m.* garage; siding.

garantie, *s. f.* guarantee.

garantir, *v. a.* guarantee.

garçon, *s. m.* boy; young man; fellow; bachelor; waiter.

garde¹, *s.f.* guard; watch; police; nurse.

garde², *s.m.* warden, guardian; watch.

garde-bébé, *s. m.* baby-sitter, sitter-in.

garde-boue, *s.f.* mud-guard.

garde-chasse, *s. m.* game-keeper.

garder, *v.a.* keep, take care of; attend (to).

garde-robe, *s.f.* wardrobe.

gardien, -enne, *s.m.f.* guardian, keeper; warden; watch(man); ~ de la paix constable; ~ (de but) goalkeeper.

gare, *s. f.* station; depot; ~ des marchandises goods station; aller recevoir qn à la ~ meet sy at the station.

garni, *s.m.* furnished lodgings (pl.), digs.

garnir, *v. a.* furnish; fit up, trim.

garnison, *s. f.* garrison.

garniture, *s.f.* fittings (pl.); set; garnishing.

gâteau, *s. m.* cake.

gâter, *v. a.* waste, impair; spoil.

gauche, *adj.* left.

gaz, *s. m.* gas; usine à ~ gas-works.

gazon, *s. m.* grass; lawn.

géant, *s. m.* giant.

gelée, *s. f.* jelly.

gémir, *v. n.* groan.

gênant, *adj.* inconvenient, annoying.

gendre, *s. m.* son-in-law.

gêne, *s. f.* inconvenience; trouble; être dans la ~ be hard-up.

gêné, *adj.* uneasy; stiff; embarrassed.

gêner, *v.n.* inconvenience; be in the way of; interfere with.

général, *adj. & s. m.* general; en ~ in general, generally.

généraliser, *v.a. & n.* generalize.

générateur, *s.m.* generator.

génération, *s.f.* generation.

généreux, -euse, *adj.* generous.

générosité, *s.f.* generosity.

génie, *s. m.* genius; corps of engineers.

genou, *s.m.* (pl. -x) knee; (pl.) lap; se mettre à ~s kneel down.

genre, *s. m.* genus, kind.

gens, *s.m. f.* people; attendants.

gentil, -ille, *adj.* gentle.

géographie, *s.f.* geography.

géographique, *adj.* geographic(al).

géologie, *s. f.* geology.

géométrie, *s. f.* geometry.

géométrique, *adj.* geometric(al).

gérant, -e, *s. m. f.* manager; manageress.

gérer, *v. a.* manage.

germanique, *adj.* Germanic.

germe, *s.m.* germ.

gésir*, *v.n.* lie.

geste, *s.m.* gesture.

gesticuler, *v. n.* gesticulate.

gibier, *s. m.* game.

gifle, *s. f.* slap, box on the ear.

gifler, *v. a.* give s.o. a slap (in the face).

gilet, *s.m.* waistcoat, vest.

girafe, *s. f.* giraffe.

glace, *s. f.* ice; ice-cream; mirror; *mer de* ~ glacier.

glacer, *v. a.* freeze, chill.

glacial, *adj.* icy, glacial.

glacier, *s. m.* glacier.

glissade, *s. f.* slide; slip.

glissant, *adj.* slippery.

glisser, *v.n.* slide; slip; glide over; **se** ~ slip, creep (into).

globe, *s. m.* globe; earth.

gloire, *s. f.* glory, fame.

glorieux, -euse, *adj.* glorious; proud.

gober, *v.a.* swallow.

golfe, *s. m.* gulf.

gomme, *s. f.* gum; india-rubber.

gommer, *v. a.* gum.

gonfler, *v.a.* inflate.

gorge, *s.f.* throat, gullet.

gorgée, *s. f.* gulp.

gosse, *s.m.* kid, brat.

gothique, *adj.* Gothic.

goudron, *s. m.* tar.

gourmand, *adj.* greedy.

goût, *s. m.* taste; savour.

goûter, *v. a.* taste; relish, enjoy; — *s.m.* tea *(meal)*.

goutte, *s. f.* drop.

gouvernail, *s. m.* rudder, helm.

gouvernante *s. f.* governess.

gouvernement, *s.m.* government.

gouverner, *v. a.* govern, control, rule; manage; steer.

gouverneur, *s. m.* governor; tutor, preceptor.

grâce, *s. f.* grace; pardon; thanks *(pl.)*; favour.

gracieux, -euse, *adj.* graceful; gracious.

grade, *s. m.* rank, grade.

grain, *s. m.* grain, berry, corn; a touch (of).

graine, *s. f.* seed, berry.

graissage, *s. m.* lubrication.

graisse, *s. f.* fat, grease, lard.

graisser, *v.a.* grease, lubricate.

grammaire, *s.f.* grammar.

grammatical, *adj.* grammatical.

gramme, *s. m.* gramme.

gramophone, *s. m.* gramophone.

grand, *adj.* great; large; big; tall; grand.

grandeur, *s.f.* size; length; breadth; greatness.

grandir, *v.n.* grow (up); grow big, tall.

grand'mère, *s. f.* grandmother.

grand-père, *s. m.* grandfather.

granit, *s. m.* granite.

grappe, *s. f.* bunch; ~ *de raisin* bunch of grapes.

gras, grasse, *adj.* fat; thick.

gratitude, *s.f.* gratitude.

gratter, *v. a. & n.* scratch, overtake; brush.

gratuit, *adj.* free (of charge).

grave, *adj.* grave; heavy.

graver, *v.a.* engrave.

gravure, *s.f.* engraving.

grec, grecque (G.), *adj. & s. m. f.* Greek.

grêle, *adj.* slender, delicate, slim.

grelotter, *v.n.* shiver.

grenier, *s. m.* loft; granary.

grenouille, *s. f.* frog.

grève, *s. f.* strike; beach.

grief, *s. m.* grievance.

griffe, *s. f.* claw; clutch.

grill, *s. m.* grill, gridiron.

grille, *s. f.* iron railing, grating.

griller, *v.a.* grill, toast.

grimace, *s.f.* grimace.

grimacer, *v.a.* grimace.

grimper, *v. n. & n.* climb.

grincer, *v. n. & a.* grind, grate; creak.

grippe, *s.f.* influenza.

gris, *adj.* gray.

grogner, *v.n.* groan; grunt, grumble.

gronder, *v. n.* roar; rumble; *v.a.* scold.

gros, grosse, *adj.* large, big; stout; great; thick; — *s. m.* bulk; wholesale; *en* ~ roughly; wholesale.

grossier, *adj.* coarse, gross.

grossir, *v. a.* make bigger; increase; *v. n.* grow bigger.

grotesque, *adj.* grotesque.

groupe, *s.m.* group.

grouper, *v.a.* group.

grue, *s.f.* crane.

gué, *s. m.* ford (*across river*).

guêpe, *s. f.* wasp.

guérir, *v.a.* cure, heal; *v. n. & se* ~ be cured, get well again.

guerre, *s. f.* war.

gueule, *s. f.* mouth, jaws *(pl.);* opening.

guichet, *s.m.* ticket window; counter; booking-office.

guide, *s. m.* guide; conductor; guide-book.

guider, *v. a.* guide, lead.

guillemets, *s. m. pl.* inverted commas.

guise, *s. f.* way, manner; *à votre* ~ as you like.

guitare, *s. f.* guitar.

gymnastique, *s. f.* gymnastics.

H

habile, *adj.* able, clever.

habileté, *s. f.* skill, cleverness; ability.

habiller, *v. a.* clothe; dress (up); *s'*~ dress, put on one's clothes.

habit, *s. m.* (dress-)suit; coat; ~*s* clothes.

habitant, -e, *s.m.f.* inhabitant.

habitation, *s. f.* habitation, dwelling.

habiter, *v. a. & n.* inhabit, live in, dwell in.

habitude, *s. f.* habit, use.

habituel, -elle, *adj.* habitual, usual.

habituer, *v. a.* accustom; **s'~** *à* get accustomed to, get used to.

hache, *s. f.* axe.

hacher, *v.a.* chop, cut up, hack, mince.

hachis, *s. m.* hash.

haine, *s. f.* hate, hatred.

haïr*, *v.a.* hate.

haleine, *s. f.* breath.

hall, *s. m.* lounge; **~** *de montage* erecting shop.

halle, *s.f.* market-hall.

hanche, *s.f.* haunch, hip.

hangar, *s. m.* shed, hangar.

happer, *v.a.* snap up.

harasser, *v.a.* harass.

hardi, *adj.* bold, daring.

hareng, *s.m.* herring.

haricot, *s.m.* bean; **~s** *verts* French-beans.

harmonie, *s. f.* harmony.

harmonieux, -euse, *adj.* harmonious.

harnais, *s.m.* harness.

harpe, *s.f.* harp.

hasard, *s. m.* hazard, risk; *par* **~** by chance.

hasarder, *v.a.* hazard, risk, stake.

hasardeux, -euse, *adj.* risky; unsafe.

hâte, *s. f.* haste, hurry, rush; *à la* **~** in a hurry.

hâter, *v. a.* hasten, urge on; **se ~** hurry (up).

hausse, *s. f.* rise.

hausser, *v. a. & n.* raise, lift; **se ~** rise.

haut, *adj.* high; elevated; upright; loud; upper; *terre* **~e** highland; *à voix* **~e** aloud; — *adv.* high, highly, up; aloud; *en* **~** at the top; upstairs; — *s. m.* top, height, summit.

hauteur, *s.f.* height, altitude.

haut-parleur, *s. m.* loudspeaker.

havresac, *s.m.* haversack, knapsack.

hebdomadaire, *adj. & s.m.* weekly.

hébreu (H.), *adj. & s. m.* Hebrew.

hectare, *s.m.* hectare.

hélice, *s.f.* air-screw, propeller.

hélicoptère, *s.m.* helicopter.

herbe, *s.f.* herb, grass; pot-herb.

herbeux, -euse, *adj.* grassy.

hérédité, *s.f.* heredity.

hérisser, *v.a.* bristle; ruffle; **se ~** bristle up, stand on end.

hérisson, *s. m.* hedgehog.

héritage, *s. m.* inheritance, heritage.

hériter, *v.a. & n.* inherit.

héritier, *s.m.* heir.

héritière, *s.f.* heiress.

héroïne, *s.f.* heroine.

héros, *s. m.* hero.

hésitation, *s.f.* hesitation.

hésiter, *v.n.* hesitate.

heure, *s. f.* hour, time; *quelle* **~** *est-il?* what time is it?; *il est dix* **~s**

moins le quart it's a quarter to ten; *dix ~s* ten o'clock; *dix ~s et quart* a quarter past ten; *dix ~s et demie* half past ten; *de bonne ~* early; *~s de pointe* rush hours; *~s d'ouverture* business hours; *~s supplémentaires* overtime.

heureux, -euse, *adj.* happy, fortunate, successful.

heurter, *v. a. & n.* knock against, hit, run into, against; *se ~* run, hit, dash against, collide.

hibou, *s. m. (pl. -x)* owl.

hideux, -euse, *adj.* hideous, terrible.

hier, *adv.* yesterday; *~ soir* last night.

hirondelle, *s. f.* swallow.

histoire, *s. f.* (hi)story, tale.

historique, *adj.* historic.

hiver, *s.m.* winter.

hollandais, -e (H.), *adj. & s. m. f.* Dutch(man), Dutch-woman.

homard, *s.m.* lobster.

homme, *s.m.* man; *~ d'affaires* business man; *~ d'état* statesman.

hongrois, -e, (H.), *adj. & s.m.f.* Hungarian.

honnête, *adj.* honest.

honnêteté, *s. f.* honesty.

honneur, *s.m.* honour; credit.

honorable, *adj.* honourable.

honoraires, *s. m. pl.* fee(s).

honorer, *v.a.* honour.

honte, *s.f.* shame; *avoir ~ de* be ashamed of.

honteux, -euse, *adj.* shameful, disgraceful.

hôpital, *s. m. (pl. -aux)* hospital.

hoquet, *s.m.* hiccup.

horaire, *s.m.* time-table.

horizon, *s.m.* horizon.

horizontal, *adj.* horizontal.

horloge, *s.f.* clock.

horloger, *s.m.* watch-maker.

horreur, *s. f.* horror.

horrible, *adj.* horrible.

hors, *adv.* out, outside; *— prep.* out of, outside.

hospitalité, *s. f.* hospitality.

hostie, *s.f.* wafer *(Church).*

hostile, *adj.* hostile.

hostilité, *s.f.* hostility.

hôte, *s.m.* host; guest.

hôtel, *s.m.* hotel; large house; *~ de ville* town-hall.

hôtesse, *s. f.* hostess; *~ de l'air* air-hostess.

houe, *s. f.* hoe.

houillère, *s.f.* colliery.

hublot, *s.m.* window.

huile, *s. f.* oil.

huissier, *s. m.* usher.

huit, *adj. & s. m.* eight.

huitième, *adj.* eighth.

huître, *s. f.* oyster.

humain, *adj.* human.

humanité, *s. f.* humanity.

humble, *adj.* humble.

humecter, *v.a.* wet.

humer, *v. a.* inhale, suck in.

humide, *adj.* humid, wet.

humidité, *s. f.* humidity.

humiliation, *s. f.* humiliation.

humilier, *v. a.* humiliate.

humilité, *s. f.* humility.

humoristique, *adj.* humorous.

humour, *s. m.* humour.

hurlement, *s. m.* howl-(ing), roar(ing).

hurler, *v.n.* howl, roar.

hutte, *s.f.* hut, cabin.

hydrogène, *s. m.* hydrogen.

hygiène, *s. f.* hygiene.

hymne, *s. m.* hymn.

hypocrite, *s. m. f.* hypocrite; — *adj.* hypocritical.

hypothèse, *s. f.* supposition; hypothesis.

hystérique, *adj.* hysterical.

I

ici, *adv.* here; *d'~* from here; *par ~* this way.

idéal, -e, *adj.* ideal.

idéalisme, *s. m.* idealism.

idéaliste, *s. m. f.* idealist.

idée, *s. f.* idea, notion; *il m'est venu à l'~* it occurred to me.

identique, *adj.* identical.

identité, *s.f.* identity.

idiome, *s. m.* language, dialect.

idiot, *adj.* idiotic; — *s. m.* idiot.

idiotisme, *s. m.* idiom.

ignition, *s. f.* ignition.

ignorance, *s. f.* ignorance.

ignorant, *adj.* ignorant.

ignorer, *v.a.* not know, be ignorant of, be unaware of.

il, elle, *pron.* *(pl.* **ils**, **elles**) he, she, it; they; there.

île, *s. f.* island.

illégal, *adj.* illegal.

illicite, *adj.* illicit, unlawful.

illumination, *s. f.* illumination; *~ par projecteurs* flood-lighting.

illuminer, *v. a.* illuminate, light up; *~ par projecteurs* flood-light.

illusion, *s.f.* illusion, delusion.

illustration, *s. f.* illustration.

illustrer, *v.a.* illustrate, explain.

image, *s. f.* image, picture, likeness.

imagé, *adj.* vivid.

imaginaire, *adj.* imaginary, fantastic.

imaginatif, -ive, *adj.* imaginative.

imagination, *s. f.* imagination, fancy.

imaginer, *v.a.* s'~ imagine.

imbécile, *s.m. f.* fool, idiot; — *adj.* foolish.

imitation, *s.f.* imitation, copy.

imiter, *v. a.* imitate, copy.

immédiat, *adj.* immediate.

immense, *adj.* immense.

immeuble, *s. m.* real estate, landed property.

immigrant, -e, *adj.* & *s. m. f.* immigrant.

immigration, *s.f.* immigration.

immigrer, *v. a.* immigrate.

immobile, *adj.* immobile.

immoral, *adj.* immoral.

immortel, -elle, *adj.* immortal.

imparfait, *adj.* & *s. m.* imperfect.

impartial, *adj.* impartial.

impatience, s. f. impatience.

impatient, adj. impatient.

impayé, adj. unpaid.

impératif, -ive, adj. & s. m. imperative.

impératrice, s. f. empress.

imperfection, s.f. imperfection.

impérial, adj. imperial.

impérialisme, s.m. imperialism.

imperméable, adj. impermeable; waterproof.

impertinent, adj. impertinent.

impétueux, -euse, adj. impetuous, headlong.

impliquer, v. a. implicate, involve, imply.

implorer, v.a. implore, beg.

impoli, adj. impolite.

impopulaire, adj. unpopular.

importance, s.f. importance.

important, adj. important.

importateur, -trice, s. m. f. importer.

importation, s.f. importation; ~s imports.

importer, v.n. matter, be of moment; n'im-porte it does not matter.

importun, adj. troublesome, importunate.

importuner, v.a. annoy, molest, worry.

imposer, v.a. impose, inflict, lay (on); levy.

impossible, adj. impossible.

impôt, s. m. tax, duty.

impression, s. f. impression; print, edition; faute d'~ misprint.

impressionner, v. a. impress, affect.

imprimé, s.m. printed matter.

imprimer, v. a. (im)print, impress; publish.

imprimerie, s. f. printing; printing office.

impropre, adj. unfit, improper.

imprudent, adj. imprudent.

impuissant, adj. powerless, ineffectual, helpless.

impulsion, s. f. spur, impulse.

inaccoutumé, adj. unaccustomed.

inachevé, adj. unfinished.

inanimé, adj. inanimate.

inapplicable, adj. inapplicable, irrelevant.

inattendu, adj. unexpected.

inattentif, -ive, adj. inattentive, heedless.

incapable, adj. incapable, unable, inefficient.

incendie, s. m. fire.

incendier, v. a. set fire to.

incertain, adj. uncertain.

incessant, adj. incessant.

incident, s. m. incident; — adj. incidental.

inciter, v.a. incite, urge.

inclinaison, s. f. inclination, gradient.

inclination, s. f. inclination; bent; love.

incliner, v. a. & n. incline, bend; slope; slant; s'~ bow down, bend.

inclusif, -ive adj. inclusive.

incommode, adj. inconvenient, uncomfortable.

incommoder, v.a. inconvenience, annoy.

incomparable, adj. incomparable.

incompatible, adj. incompatible.

incompétent, adj. incompetent.

incomplet, adj. incomplete, imperfect.

inconscient, adj. unconscious.

inconséquent, adj. inconsistent.

inconvenant, adj. improper, unsuitable.

inconvénient, s.m. inconvenience.

incorrect, adj. incorrect.

incroyable, adj. incredible.

incurable, adj. incurable.

indécis, adj. uncertain.

indécision, s. f. indecision.

indéfini, adj. indefinite, undefined.

indépendance, s.f. independence.

index, s.m. forefinger, index.

indicateur, s. m. indicator, gauge; time-table.

indication, s. f. indication; direction; sign.

indice, s. m. sign, token, mark; index.

indien, -enne (I.), adj. & s.m.f. Indian.

indifférent, adj. indifferent.

indigestion, s. f. indigestion.

indignation, s. f. indignation.

indiquer, v.a. indicate, point out, show.

indirect, adj. indirect.

indiscret, -ète, adj. indiscreet.

indiscrétion, s. f. indiscretion.

indispensable, adj. indispensable, essential.

indisposé, adj. unwell; upset.

individu, s. m. individual, person.

individuel, -elle, adj. individual.

indulgence, s. f. indulgence.

indulgent, adj. indulgent.

industrie, s. f. industry.

industriel, -elle, adj. industrial; — s. m. manufacturer.

inefficace, adj. inefficient.

inégal, adj. unequal.

inégalité, s. f. inequality.

inerte, adj. inert; dull.

inévitable, adj. inevitable.

inexpérimenté, adj. inexperienced.

inexplicable, adj. inexplicable.

infâme, adj. infamous.

infanterie, s. f. infantry.

infection, s. f. infection.

inférieur, adj. inferior.

infinitif, s. m. infinitive.

infirmerie, s. f. infirmary.

infirmier, -ère, s. m. f. nurse.

influence, s. f. influence.

influencer, v. a. influence.

information, s. f. information.

informer, *v. a.* inform, let know; s'~ *de* inquire about.

infructueux, -euse, *adj.* unsuccessful.

ingénieur, *s. m.* engineer.

ingénieux, -euse, *adj.* ingenious.

ingéniosité, *s. f.* ingenuity.

ingrat, *adj.* ungrateful.

ingrédient, *s. m.* ingredient.

inhabité, *adj.* uninhabited.

inintéressant, *adj.* uninteresting.

initial, -e, *adj. & s. f.* initial.

initiative, *s. f.* initiative; syndicat d'~ tourist office.

injection, *s. f.* injection.

injure, *s.f.* injury.

injurier, *v.a.* insult.

injurieux, -euse, *adj.* injurious.

injuste, *adj.* unjust.

injustice, *s. f.* injustice.

innocence, *s. f.* innocence.

innocent, *adj.* innocent.

innombrable, *adj.* innumerable, countless.

inoccupé, *adj.* unoccupied.

inoculer, *v.a.* inoculate.

inondation, *s. f.* flood.

inonder, *v. a.* flood.

inquiet, -ète *adj.* anxious, restless, uneasy.

inquiéter, *v.a.* worry.

insecte, *s.m.* insect.

insensé, *adj.* insane, mad.

insensible, *adj.* insensible.

inséparable, *ad.j* inseparable.

insigne, *s. m.* badge.

insignifiant, *adj.* insignificant.

insipide, *adj.* dull, flat.

insister, *v. a.* insist, lay stress on.

insolence, *s. f.* insolence.

insolent, *adj.* insolent.

insouciant, *adj.* careless.

inspecter, *v.a.* inspect, survey.

inspiration, *s. f.* inspiration.

inspirer, *v.a.* inspire, suggest; inhale.

installation, *s. f.* installation; fitting up.

installer, *v.a.* install; fit up; *v.n.* s'~ to settle down.

instant, *adj.* instant, pressing; — *s.m.* instant, moment; à l'~ instantly, at once.

instantané, *s.m.* snap(shot).

instinct, *s. m.* instinct.

instituer, *v.a.* institute.

institut, *s.m.* institute.

institution, *s. f.* institution; boarding-school.

instruction, *s. f.* instruction, tuition; knowledge, learning; direction; inquiry.

instruire*, *v.a.* instruct, teach.

instrument, *s. m.* instrument, implement, tool.

instrumental, *adj.* instrumental.

insuffisance, *s. f.* insufficiency.

insuffisant, *adj.* insufficient, deficient.

insulte, *s. f.* insult.

insulter, *v. a. & n.* insult.

insupportable, *adj.* intolerable, unbearable.

intact, *adj.* intact, entire.

intégral, *adj.* integral.

intégrité, *s.f.* integrity.

intellectuel, -elle, *adj.* & *s.m.* intellectual.

intelligence, *s. f.* intelligence, understanding.

intelligent, *adj.* intelligent, clever.

intendant, *s. m.* manager.

intense, *adj.* intense.

intensité, *s. f.* intensity.

intention, *s. f.* intention, purpose; *avoir l'~* intend, mean.

interdire, *v. a.* forbid.

intéressant, *adj.* interesting; *peu ~* uninteresting.

intéressé, *adj.* interested, concerned.

intéresser, *v. a.* & *n.* interest; concern; *s'~* take an interest (*à* in); be concerned.

intérêt, *s.m.* interest; concern; share; *avoir ~ à* have an interest in.

intérieur, *s.m.* inside, interior; *à l'~* inside, indoors; *Ministre de l'Intérieur* Home Secretary.

intermédiaire, *adj.* intermediate; — *s. m. f.* intermediary.

international, *adj.* international.

interne, *adj.* internal, inward.

interpellation, *s. f.* interpellation.

interpeller, *v. a.* interpellate, question.

interposer, *v. a.* interpose.

interprétation, *s. f.* interpretation.

interprète, *s. m. f.* interpreter.

interpréter, *v.a.* interpret; render.

interrogation, *s. f.* interrogation; inquiry.

interrogatoire, *s.m.* (cross-)examination.

interroger, *v.a.* interrogate, cross-examine, question.

interrompre, *v.a.* interrupt.

interrupteur, *s. m.* interrupter; switch.

interruption, *s. f.* interruption.

intervalle, *s.m.* interval; *dans l'~* in the meantime.

intervenir, *v.n.* intervene, interfere, go between.

intervention, *s. f.* intervention.

interview, *s. f. m.* interview.

intime, *adj.* intimate.

intimité, *s.f.* intimacy.

intolérable, *adj.* intolerable.

intrigue, *s.f.* intrigue.

intriguer, *v.n.* & *n.* intrigue.

introduction, *s. f.* introduction.

introduire, *v.a.* introduce; show in.

inutile, *adj.* useless.

invalide, *adj.* invalid, dis-

abled.
invasion, s. f. invasion.
inventer, v.a. make up.
inventeur, s. m. inventor.
invention, s. f. invention.
investigation, s. f. investigation, inquiry.
invisible, adj. invisible.
invitation, s.f. invitation.
invité, -e, s. m. f. guest.
inviter, v. a. invite.
iris, s. m. iris.
irlandais (I.), adj. Irish; — s. m. Irishman.
ironie, s. f. irony.
ironique, adj. ironical.
irradier, v. a. (ir)radiate.
irréel, adj. unreal.
irrésistible, adj. irresistible.
irritation, s. f. irritation.
irriter, v.a. irritate.
isolement, s. m. isolation.
isoler, v.a. isolate.
isotope, s.m. isotope.
issue, s. f. issue, outlet, way out.
italien, -enne (I.), adj. & s. m. f. Italian.
itinéraire, adj. itinerary; — s.m. guide-book.
ivre, adj. drunk.

J

j' see je.
jadis, adv. once, long ago, formerly.
jalousie, s.f. jealousy; blind.

jaloux, -se, adj. jealous.
jamais, adv. never, ever.
jambe, s. f. leg, shank.
jambon, s. m. ham.
janvier, s. m. January.
japonais, -e (J.), adj. & s. m. f. Japanese.
jardin, s. m. garden.
jardinier, -ère, s. m. f. gardener.
jarre, s. f. jar.
jarretière, s. f. garter.
jauge, s. f. gauge.
jauger, v. a. gauge.
jaune, adj. yellow; — s. m. yolk.
je, j', pron. I.
jersey, s. m. jersey.
jet, s.m. throw(ing).
jeter, v.a. throw, throw away, down; cast, fling; shoot; discharge; se ~ rush.
jeton, s. m. counter.
jeu, s.m. game, play, set.
jeudi, s. m. Thursday.
jeune, adj. young.
jeûne, s.m. fast(ing).
jeûner, v.n. fast.
jeunesse, s. f. youth.
joie, s. f. joy, delight.
joindre*, v. a. & n. join, unite; se ~ join.
joint, s. m. joint, articulation.
jointure, s. f. joint.
joli, adj. pretty, nice.
jonction, s. f. junction.
jongleur, s. m. juggler.
joue, s. f. cheek (face).
jouer, v. a. & n. play; gambol; gamble.
jouet, s. m. toy.
joueur, -euse, s. m. f. player; gambler.
joug, s. m. yoke.

jouir, *v.n.* (**~** *de*) enjoy.

jouissance, *s.f.* enjoyment, pleasure, joy.

jour, *s. m.* day; daylight, light; life; **~** *de fête* holiday; **~** *de semaine* week-day; *un* **~** some day; *tous les* **~s** every day; *à* **~** up to date.

journal, *s. m.* (news)paper; journal, diary.

journalier, -ère, *adj.* daily; — *s.m.* day-labourer.

journaliste, *s. m. f.* journalist.

journée, *s. f.* day; day's wages *(pl.)*; day's work.

joyau, *s. m.* jewel.

joyeux, -euse, *adj.* joyful. merry.

judiciaire, *adj.* judicial, legal.

judicieux, -euse, *adj.* judicious, sensible, reasonable.

juge, *s. m.* judge.

jugement, *s. m.* judg(e)ment; sentence.

juger, *v. a. & n.* judge.

juif, -ive (J.), *adj.* Jewish; — *s. m. f.* Jew.

juillet, *s. m.* July.

juin, *s. m.* June.

jumeau, -elle *adj. s. m. f.* twin; *f. pl.* binoculars.

jungle, *s. f.* jungle.

jupe, *s. f.* skirt.

juré, *s. m.* juryman.

jurer, *v. a. & n.* swear.

jurisprudence, *s..f* jurisprudence.

juron, *s. m.* oath.

jury, *s. m.* jury.

jus, *s.m.* juice.

jusque, jusqu'à, *prep.* till; as far as.

juste, *adj.* just, right; fair.

justice, *s.f.* justice.

justification, *s.f.* justification.

justifier, *v.a.* justify.

juvénile, *adj.* juvenile.

K

kangourou, *s. m.* kangaroo.

kayak, *s. m.* kayak.

képi, *s. m.* cap.

kilogramme, *s.m.* kilogram(me).

kilomètre, *s.m.* kilometre.

kiosque, *s. n.* kiosk.

L

l' = **le** or **la**.

la, *art.* the; —*pron.* her, it.

là, *adv.* there; here.

labeur, *s.m.* labour, work.

laboratoire, *s.m.* laboratory.

laborieux, -euse, *adj.* laborious, hard-working.

labourer, *v.a.* plough.

lac, *s. m.* lake.

lacer, *v. a.* lace.

lacet, *s. m.* lace; braid; bowstring; shoe-lace.

lâche, *adj.* loose; cowardly; — *s. m.* coward.

lâcher, *v.a.* loosen, slacken; let go.

lactation, *s. f.* lactation.

laid, *adj.* ugly; plain.

laideur, *s. f.* ugliness.

lainage, *s.m.* woollen goods *(pl.);* wool.

laine, *s. f.* wool; *pure* ~ all wool.

laïque, *adj.* lay.

laisser, *v.a.* leave, quit; give up; let alone; leave behind, off; ~ *aller* let go, neglect.

lait, *s. m.* milk.

laiterie, *s. f.* dairy.

laitier, *s. m.* milkman, dairyman.

laitière, *s. f.* dairymaid.

laitue, *s. f.* lettuce.

lambeau, *s. m.* rag, strip.

lame, *s. f.* blade; plate, sheet; ~ *de rasoir* razor-blade.

lamentation, *s. f.* lamentation.

lampe, *s. f.* lamp.

lancement, *s.m.* throwing; launching.

lancer, *v. a.* throw, fling; se ~ dart, rush.

langage, *s. m.* language; tongue; speech, way of speaking.

lange *s. m.* baby's nappy.

langue, *s. f.* tongue; language; ~ *maternelle* mother-tongue.

laper, *v. a.* lap (up).

lapin, *s. m.* rabbit.

laps, *s. m.* lapse, space (of time).

lapsus, *s. m.* lapse, slip.

laque, *s. f.* lacquer.

lard, *s. m.* bacon.

large, *adj.* broad, wise; generous; liberal; — *s.m.* room, breadth.

largeur, *s. f.* width.

larme, *s. f.* tear.

las, lasse, *adj.* weary.

lasser, *v.a.* tire, wear out; se ~ *de* get tired of.

latéral, *adj.* lateral, side.

latin, -e, *adj. & s. m. f.* Latin.

latitude, *s.f.* latitude; scope, freedom.

lavable, *adj.* washable.

lavabo, *s. m.* wash-basin; lavatory.

lavage, *s.m.* washing; ~ *de vaisselle* washing-up.

lavande, *s. f.* lavender.

laver, *v. a.* wash; se ~ wash (oneself); *machine à* ~ washing-machine.

layette, *s. f.* baby-linen.

le, la, l', *art.* the; — *pron.* *(pl.* les) him, her, it; them.

lécher, *v. a.* lick, lap.

leçon, *s. f.* lesson; lecture.

lecteur, -trice, *s. m. f.* reader; lector.

lecture, *s. f.* reading.
légal, *adj.* legal, lawful.
légende, *s. f.* legend.
léger, -ère *adj.* light, slight; loose.
légèreté, *s. f.* lightness; ease.
légion, *s. f.* legion.
législation, *s.f.* legislation.
législature, *s. f.* legislature.
légitime, *adj.* legitimate, lawful.
légume, *s.m.* vegetable.
lendemain, *s.m.* next day, day after.
lent, *adj.* slow; tardy.
lenteur, *s.f.* slowness.
lentille, *s.f.* lentil; lens.
léopard, *s.m.* leopard
lequel, laquelle, *rel. pron. (pl.* **lesquels, lesquelles)** who, whom; which, that.
lettre, *s.f.* letter; type character; ~s literature; arts; *à la* ~ literally, word for word; ~ *de change* bill of exchange; ~ *de crédit* letter of credit; ~ *recommandée* registered letter; *boîte aux* ~s letter-box.
lettré, *adj.* learned; literary.
leur, *poss. adj. (pl.* **-s)** their; — *pron.* to them, them; *le* or *la* ~, *les* ~s theirs, their own.
levée, *s.f.* raising; removal; levy.
lever, *v. a.* lift (up), raise; hoist; *v. n.* rise; *se* ~ rise get up.

levier, *s. m.* lever; ~ *des vitesses* gear-lever.
lèvre, *s. f.* lip.
lexique, *s.m.* lexicon.
liaison, *s.f.* joining, junction; union; connection; tie; liaison.
libéral, *adj.* liberal.
libérer, *v.a.* liberate.
liberté, *s.f.* liberty.
libraire, *s.m. f.* bookseller.
librairie, *s. f.* bookshop.
libre, *adj.* free; unoccupied.
licence, *s.f.* licence, degree.
licencié, -e, *s. m. f.* licenciate; licensee.
licencieux, -euse, *adj.* licentious.
lie, *s. f.* dregs, grounds *(pl.).*
liège, *s.m.* cork.
lien, *s.m.* tie; bond; band, strap, cord; link.
lier, *v. a.* bind, tie (up); fasten; link up.
lieu, *s. m.* place; *au* ~ *de* instead of; *avoir* ~ take place.
lieutenant, *s. m.* lieutenant.
lièvre, *s. m.* hare.
ligne, *s. f.* line; ~ *aérienne* air-line.
lilas, *s. m.* lilac.
limace, *s.f.* slug.
limaçon, *s. m.* snail.
lime, *s. f.* file.
limer, *v. a.* file.
limite, *s.f.* bound(s), border, limit.
limiter, *v.a.* limit, restrict.
limon, *s.m.* mud, silt.

limonade, *s. f.* lemonade.
lin, *s. m.* flax.
linge, *s. m.* linen.
linger, **-ère**, *s.m.f.* linendraper.
lingerie, *s. f.* ladies' underclothing, lingerie.
lion, *s. m.* lion.
liqueur, *s. f.* liqueur.
liquide, *adj.* liquid.
liquider, *v.a.* liquidate.
lire*, *v.a.* read.
liste, *s. f.* list, roll; panel.
lit, *s. m.* bed.
litre, *s. m.* litre.
littéraire, *adj.* literary.
littérature, *s.f.* literature.
livraison, *s.f.* delivery; part (of book).
livre[1], *s. m.* book; work; *teneur de ~s* bookkeeper.
livre[2], *s. f.* pound.
livrer, *v.a.* deliver; give up.
local, *s.m.* spot, premises; — *adj.* local.
localité, *s. f.* place, spot.
locataire, *s. m. f.* tenant, lodger.
location, *s. f.* letting out; hiring, renting; *prendre en ~* hire; *bureau de ~* box-office; *~ des places* seat reservation.
locomotive, *s.f.* (railway) engine.
loge, *s.f.* hut. cabin; box.
logement, *s. m.* lodging.
loger, *v.a.* accommodate, lodge; house; *v.n.* reside, live (in).
logeur, *s. m.* landlord.
logeuse, *s. f.* landlady.
logique, *s. f.* logic; — *adj.* logical.
loi, *s.f.* law, statute; *projet de ~* bill, draft.
loin, *adv.* far, far off, away; *au ~* far off.
lointain, *adj.* far, remote.
loisif, *s. m.* spare time, leisure.
long, **longue**, *adj. & s. m. f.* long; *être ~ à* be long in.
longitude, *s. f.* longitude.
longtemps, *adv.* long, a long time; *depuis ~* for a long time, long since.
longueur, *s. f.* length.
loquet, *s. m.* latch.
lors, *adv.* then; *dès ~* from that time.
lorsque, *conj.* when.
lot, *s. m.* lot, fate; prize.
loterie, *s. f.* lottery.
lotion, *s. f.* lotion.
louage, *s.m.* hiring; hire.
louche, *s.f.* ladle.
louer[1], *v.a.* hire (out); let; *à ~* for hire; to let.
louer[2], *v. a.* praise.
loup, *s. m.* wolf.
lourd, *adj.* heavy; clumsy.
louve, *s. f.* she-wolf.
loyal, *adj.* loyal, true.
loyauté, *s. f.* honesty.
loyer, *s. m.* rent; hire.
lubrifier, *v.a.* lubricate.
lucratif, **-ive**, *adj.* lucrative.
luge, *s. f.* sledge.
lugubre, *adj.* dismal.
lui, *pron.* (to) him, (to) her, (to) it.
lui-même, *pron.* himself.

luire*, *v. n.* shine, gleam.
lumière, *s. f.* light, daylight.
lumineux, -euse, *adj.* luminous, bright.
lundi, *s. m.* Monday.
lune, *s. f.* moon; ~ *de miel* honeymoon.
lunette, *s. f.* telescope; *(pl.)* spectacles, specs; ~s *de soleil* sun-glasses.
luthérien, -enne, *adj.* & *s. m. f.* Lutheran.
lutte, *s. f.* wrestling; fight, struggle.
lutter, *v.n.* wrestle, fight.
lutteur, *s. m.* wrestler.
luxe, *s. m.* luxury.
luxeux, -euse, *adj.* luxurious.
lycée, *s.m.* secondary school, grammar-school.

M

m' *see* **me**.
ma *see* **mon**.
mâcher, *v. a.* chew.
machine, *s. s.* machine, engine, apparatus; ~ *à coudre*, sewing-machine.
mâchoire, *s. f.* jaw.
maçon, *s m.* mason.
madame, *s. f. (pl.* mesdames) madam.
mademoiselle, *s. f. (pl.* mesdemoiselles) miss.
magasin, *s.m.* shop; store; warehouse; *grand* ~ department store.
magique, *adj.* magic.
magnétique, *adj.* magnetic.
magnétophone, *s.m.* tape-recorder.

magnifique, *adj.* magnificent.
mai, *s. m.* May.
maigre, *adj.* lean, thin.
maigrir, *v.n.* grow lean, get thin.
maille, *s. f.* stitch; knot.
maillot, *s.m.* tights *(pl.)*; ~ *(de bain)* bathing-costume.
main, *s. f.* hand; lead; *en* ~ in hand; *se donner la* ~ shake hands; *tenir la* ~ *à* see to, see that; *de seconde* ~ second-hand.
maintenant, *adv.* now, at present
maintenir, *v. a.* (up)hold, support, keep (up), maintain.
maintien, *s. m.* maintenance.
maire, *s. m.* mayor.
mais, *conj.* but.
maïs, *s. m.* maize.
maison, *s. f.* house, residence; home; firm; *à la* ~ at home, indoors; *tenir* ~ keep house.
maître, *s.m.* master; proprietor; teacher; ~ *d'école* schoolmaster; ~ *de maison* host.
maîtresse, *s. f.* mistress; (land)lady; sweetheart; ~ *d'école* schoolmistress.
maîtrise, *s.f.* mastery, control.
maîtriser, *v.a.* master.
majesté, *s. f.* majesty.
majeur, *adj.* major; main; chief; — *s. m.* major.
majorité, *s. f.* majority.

majuscule, *s. f.* capital letter.

mal, *s. m.* ill, evil, wrong; pain, harm; trouble, hardship; *avoir ~ à* have a pain in; — *adv.* wrong, badly, ill.

malade, *adj.* sick; ill; *tomber ~* fall ill, be taken ill; — *s. m. f.* invalid, patient.

maladie, *s.f.* illness; sickness; disease.

maladroit, *adj.* awkward, clumsy.

malaise, *s. m.* uneasiness.

malchance, *s.f.* bad luck.

mâle, *s. m.* male.

malentendu, *s. m.* misunderstandig.

malgré, *prep.* in spite of; *~ tout* for all that.

malheur, *s. m.* misfortune, ill luck; mischance; accident.

malheureux, -euse, *adj.* unfortunate, unlucky.

malice, *s. f.* malice.

malin, maligne, *adj.* malicious, malignant; evil.

malle, *s. f.* trunk; mail; *faire la ~* pack.

mallette, *s.f.* suitcase.

malpropre, *adj.* dirty, filthy; untidy.

malsain, *adj.* unhealthy.

malveillant, *adj.* malevolent, evil-minded.

maman, *s.f.* mamma.

manche[1], *s.m,* handle. holder.

manche[2], *s. f.* sleeve.

Manche, *s.f.* English Channel.

manchette, *s. f.* cuff.

mandat, *s. m.* mandate; money-order.

manger, *v.a.* eat; *donner à ~* feed; *salle à ~* dining-room; — *s. m.* eating; food.

manicure, *s. m. f.* manicure.

manier, *v.a.* handle.

manière, *s. f.* manner, way, fashion; *(pl.)* manners.

manifestation, *s. f.* manifestation.

manifester, *v.a.* manifest, show; *se ~* manifest oneself.

manipuler, *v. a.* manipulate, operate.

manœuvre, *s.f.* action; proceeding; manœuvre; *s. m.* labourer.

manœuvrer, *v. a. & n.* handle, manœuvre, work.

manoir, *s. m.* manor.

manque, *s.m.* want; deficiency.

manquer, *v. a.* miss; *v. n.* fail; be missing, be wanting.

mansarde, *s.f.* garret.

manteau, *s. m.* coat.

manuel, -elle, *adj.* manual; — *s. m.* manual, handbook.

manufacture, *s. f.* manufacture; factory.

manufacturer, *v. a.* manufacture.

manuscrit, *s. m.* manuscript.

maquillage, *s.m.* make-up.

marbre, *s. m.* marble.

marchand, -e, *s. m. f.* merchant, tradesman; shopkeeper.

marchandise, *s. f.* merchandise, goods *(pl.)*.

marche, *s. f.* walk; march; progress; move.

marché, *s. m.* market; bargain; agreement: *bon* ~ cheap.

marcher, *v.n.* walk; travel; march; work; run; proceed.

mardi, *s. m.* Tuesday; ~ *gras* Shrove Tuesday.

mare, *s. f.* pool, pond.

maréchal, *s. m.* marshal.

marée, *s. f.* tide, flood.

margarine, *s. f.* margarine.

marge, *s. f.* margin.

mari, *s. m.* husband.

mariage, *s. m.* marriage.

marié, -e, *adj.* married; — *s. m. f.* bridegroom, married man; bride, married woman.

marier, *v. a.* marry; match; — *se* ~ marry, get married.

marin, *adj.* marine; — *s.m.* seaman, sailor, mariner.

marmelade, *s. f.* marmalade.

marque, *s. f.* mark, imprint; trade-mark.

marquer, *v.a.* mark; stamp; brand.

marron, *s. m.* chestnut.

mars, *s. m.* March.

marteau, *s. m.* hammer.

martyr, -e, *s.m.f.* martyr.

masque, *s. m.* mask.

masquer, *v.a.* mask.

massacre, *s. m.* massacre.

massage, *s. m.* massage.

masse, *s. f.* mass; heap.

massif, -ive, *adj.* massive, bulky, clumsy.

mât, *s. m.* mast.

match, *s. m.* match.

matelas, *s. m.* mattress.

matelot, *s.m.* sailor, seaman.

matérialisme, *s. m.* materialism.

matériaux, *s.m.pl.* material(s).

matériel, -elle, *adj.* material; — *s. m.* matter; material; implements *(pl.)*.

maternel, -elle, *adj.* maternal; motherly; *école* ~*le* infant-school.

mathématicien, -enne, *s. m. f.* mathematician.

mathématique, -elle, *adj.* mathematical; — *s. f.* mathematics.

matière, *s.f.* matter; material; substance; ~ *première* raw material.

matin, *s.m.* morning; *le* ~ in the morning; *du* ~ a.m.

matinal, *adj.* morning.

matinée, *s.f.* morning; matinée.

matrice, *s. f.* womb.

maturité, *s. f.* maturity.

maudire*, *v.a.* curse.

mauvais, *adj.* bad, ill, evil; — *s. m.* bad.

me, m' *pron.* (to) me; (to) myself.

mécanicien, *s. m.* mechanic; engine-driver.

mécanique, *adj.* mechanic(al); — *s.m.* mechanics; machine; mechanism.

mécaniser, *v. a.* mechanize.

mécanisme, *s. m.* mechanism; machinery.

méchant, *adj.* evil, bad.

mécontent, *adj.* displeased, dissatisfied, unhappy.

mécontenter, *v. a.* dissatisfy.

médaille, *s. f.* medal.

médecin, *s.m.* doctor, physician.

médecine, *s. f.* medicine.

médical, *adj.* medical.

médicament, *s. m.* medicament; medicine.

médiéval, *adj.* medieval.

méditation, *s. m.* meditation.

méditer, *v. a. & n.* meditate.

méfiance, *s.f.* mistrust.

méfier: se ~ be suspicious (*de* of); mistrust.

meilleur, -e, *adj.* better; — *s. m. f.* the best.

mélancolie, *s. f.* melancholy, gloom.

mélancolique, *adj.* melancholy, sad.

mélange, *s.m.* mixture, blend.

mélanger, *v.a.* mix, blend.

mêler, *v.a.* mix (up), mingle; **se ~** mingle, be mixed; interfere with.

mélodie, *s. f.* melody.

melon, *s.m.* melon.

membre, *s.m.* member, limb.

même, *adj.* same; self; — *adv.* even, also, likewise; *de ~* in the same way; *de ~ que* as well as; *quand ~* even if.

mémoire, *s.f.* memory; *s.m.* memorandum; bill; (*pl.*) memoirs.

menace, *s.f.* menace.

menacer, *v.a.* threaten.

ménage, *s. m.* housekeeping; household.

ménager, *v. a.* be sparing of; take care of; manage.

ménagère, *s.f.* housewife, housekeeper.

mendiant, -e, *s.m.f.* beggar.

mendier, *v. a. & n.* beg.

mener, *v.a.* guide, conduct, lead.

mensonge, *s.m.* lie.

mensuel, *adj.* monthly.

mental, *adj.* mental.

mention, *s.f.* mention.

mentionner, *v. a.* mention.

mentir*, *v.n.* lie, tell a lie.

menton, *s.m.* chin.

menu, *adj.* slim; small; minute; — *s. m.* bill of fare, menu.

menuisier, *s. m.* joiner, carpenter.

méprendre: se ~ make a mistake, be mistaken.

mépris, *s.m.* contempt.

mer, *s.f.* sea; *par ~* by sea; *bord de la ~* seaside.

mercerie, *s. f.* haberdashery.

merci, *s. f.* mercy; — *int.* thanks!, (no) thank you!

mercredi, *s. m.* Wednesday.

mercure, *s.m.* mercury.

mère, *s.f.* mother.

mérite, *s. m.* merit, worth.

mériter, *v.a.* merit, deserve.

merveille, *s.f.* wonder.

merveilleux, -euse, *adj.* wonderful.

message, *s.m.* message.

messe, *s.f.* mass.

mesure, *s.f.* measure, gauge, measurement; size; metre.

mesurer, *v.a.* measure.

métal, *s.m.* metal.

métallique, *adj.* metallic.

météorologie, *s. f.* meteorology.

méthode, *s.f.* method.

méthodique, *adj.* methodical, systematic.

métier, *s. m.* trade; business; employment, occupation.

mètre, *s. m.* metre.

métro, *s. m.* tube, underground.

métropolitain, *adj.* metropolitan; underground.

mets, *s.m.* dish, food.

mettre*, *v.a.* put, set, place; put in, on; bring; ~ de c té set aside, save; ~ en ordre set in order, tidy up; se ~ sit down; se ~ à set about, take to.

meuble, *s. m.* (piece of) furniture; — *adj.* movable; biens ~s personal property.

meubler, *v.a.* furnish, fit up.

meunier, *s.m.* miller.

meurtre, *s.m.* murder.

meurtrier, *s. m.* murderer.

meurtrir, *v.a.* bruise, injure.

mi-, half, mid.

microbe, *s. m.* microbe.

microphone, *s. m.* microphone.

microscope, *s. m.* microscope.

midi, *s. m.* noon, midday; south.

miel, *s. m.* honey.

mien, *pron.* mine, my own.

miette, *s. f.* crumb.

mieux, *adv.* better.

mignon, -onne, *adj.* tiny; — *s.m.f.* darling.

migraine, *s. f.* headache.

milieu, *s.m.* middle, centre; environment.

militaire, *adj.* military; — *s. m.* soldier.

mille[1], *adj.* & *s.m.* thousand.

mille[2], *s. m.* mile (= 1609 metres).

millier, *s.m.* thousand.

million, *s.m.* million.

millionaire, *s. m. f.* millionaire.

mince, *adj.* thin, slim.

mine[1], *s.f.* mine.

mine[2], *s.f.* look(s); de bonne ~ good-looking.

miner, *v. a.* (under)mine.

mineral, *s.m.* ore.

minéral, *adj.* mineral.

mineur[1], *s.m.* miner.

mineur[2], -e, *adj.* & *s. m. f.* minor.

ministère, *s. m.* ministry.

ministre, *s. m.* minister; premier ~ prime minister, premier.

minorité, *s. f.* minority.
minuit, *s.m.* midnight.
minuscule, *s.f.* small letter.
minute, *s.f.* minute; instant.
miracle, *s.m.* miracle.
miraculeux, -euse, *adj.* miraculous, wonderful.
miroir, *s.m.* mirror.
misérable, *adj.* miserable.
misère, *s. f.* misery.
miséricorde, *s. f.* mercy.
mission, *s.f.* mission.
missionnaire, *adj. & s. m. f.* missionary.
mite, *s. f.* moth.
mobile, *adj.* movable, mobile.
mobilier, *s. m.* furniture, suite.
mobilisation, *s. f.* mobilization.
mobiliser, *v.a.&n.* mobilize.
mode¹, *s.f.* fashion, vogue; *à la ~* in vogue, in fashion.
mode², *s. m.* mode, way; mood.
modèle, *s.m.* model.
modération, *s. f.* moderation.
modérer, *v.a.* moderate.
moderne, *adj.* modern.
modeste, *adj.* modest.
modestie, *s.f.* modesty.
modification, *s. f.* modification, change.
modifier, *v.a.* modify.
modiste, *s.f.* milliner.
moelleux, -euse, *adj.* soft, mellow.
mœurs, *s. f. pl.* manners, customs, ways.
moi, *pron.* me, to me.

moi-même, *pron.* myself.
moindre, *adj.* less, lesser, smaller; *le ~* the least.
moineau, *s. m.* sparrow.
moins, *adv. & s. m.* less *(que, de* than); fewer *(de* than); minus; *le ~* the least; *à ~ que* unless; *au ~* at least.
mois, *s. m.* month; *par ~* monthly; a month.
moisson, *s.f.* harvest, crop.
moissonner, *v. a.* harvest, reap.
moitié, *s.f.* half.
molécule, *s. f.* molecule.
mollet, *s.m.* calf *(of leg).*
moment, *s. m.* moment, instant.
mon, ma, *pron.* (pl. **mes**) my.
monarchie, *s. f.* monarchy
monastère, *s. m.* monastery, convent.
mondain, *adj.* worldly.
monde, *s.m.* world; people, company; *mettre au ~* give birth to; *tout le ~* everybody.
monnaie, *s.f.* money, coin, change; currency; *~ légale* legal tender; *~ étrangère* foreign currency.
monopole, *s.m.* monopoly.
monotone, *adj.* monotonous.
monseigneur, *s.m.* my lord, your lordship.
monsieur, *s. m.* gentleman; *M.* Mr.
monstrueux, -euse, *adj.* monstrous.
mont, *s. m.* mountain.
montage, *s. m.* carrying

up; mounting, setting; wiring.

montagne, *s. f.* mountain.

montagneux, -euse, *adj.* mountainous.

montant, *adj.* ascending, uphill; **en ~** upwards.

monte-charge, *s. m.* goods lift.

montée, *s. f.* rise, slope.

monter, *v.n.* go up, come up, ascend, climb; mount; ride; amount *(à* to); equip, fit up; **~** *à cheval* ride; *faire* **~** *qn. (dans sa voiture)* give s.o. a lift.

montre¹, *s.f.* watch.

montre², *s.f.* display, show; show-window.

montrer, *v.a.* show, display, point out; **se ~** show oneself.

montueux, -euse, *adj.* hilly, steep.

monument, *s. m.* monument.

monumental, *adj.* monumental.

moquerie, *s. f.* mockery.

moral, *adj.* moral.

morale, *s.f.* ethics; morality.

moralité, *s. f.* morality, morals *(pl.).*

morceau, *s. m.* piece, morsel, bit; snack.

mordre, *v. a.* bite; gnaw.

mors, *s. m.* bit; *fig.* check.

mort, *s. f.* death; — *adj.* dead, lifeless.

mortel, -elle, *adj.* mortal; boring, tedious.

mot, *s. m.* word; short note; **~s** *croisés* crossword (puzzle).

motel, *s. m.* motel.

moteur, *s. m.* motor, engine.

motif, *s. m.* motive; cause.

motion, *s.f.* motion, movement.

motocyclette, *s. f.* motor-(bi)cycle, motor-bike.

mou, mol, molle, *adj.* soft; loose.

mouche, *s. f.* fly.

moucher: se ~ blow one's nose.

mouchoir, *s. m.* handkerchief.

moudre*, *v.a.* grind.

mouette, *s.f.* gull.

mouiller, *v.a.* & *n.* soak, wet.

moule, *s. m.* mould, cast.

moulin, *s. m.* mill; **~** *à vent* windmill; **~** *à café* coffee-mill.

mourant, *adj.* dying, expiring.

mourir*, *v. n.* die, expire.

mousse, *s. f.* foam, froth, lather; moss.

moustache, *s. f.* moustache.

moustique, *s.m.* mosquito.

moutarde, *sf.* mustard.

mouton, *s.m.* sheep; mutton.

mouvement, *s. m.* movement, motion, move.

mouvoir*, *v.a.* move; start; **se ~** move, stir.

moyen, -enne, *adj.* mean, middle, average; *le* **~** *âge* the Middle Ages; — *s. m.* means, way, manner; *au* **~** *de* by means of; *avoir les* **~s** *de* can afford.

moyenne, *s. f.* average, mean; *en ~* on the average.

muet, -ette, *adj.* dumb, mute; speechless.

multiplication, *s. f.* multiplication.

multiplier, *v.a.&n.* multiply.

multitude, *s. f.* multitude, crowd.

municipal, *adj.* municipal, city.

munir, *v.a.* provide *(de* with).

munition, *s. f.* (am)munition.

mur, *s. m.* wall.

mûr, *adj.* ripe; mature.

mûrir, *v. a. & n.* ripen.

murmure, *s.m.* murmur.

murmurer, *v.n.* murmur.

muscle, *s.m.* muscle.

muse, *s. f.* muse.

museau, *s. m.* muzzle.

musician; — *adj.* musical.

musical, *adj.* musical.

musicien, -enne, *s. m. f.*

musique, *s.f.* music; *instrument de ~* musical instrument.

mutuel, -elle, *adj.* mutual.

myope, *adj.* short-sighted.

mystère, *s.m.* mystery.

mystérieux, -euse, *adj.* mysterious.

mystification, *s. f.* mystification.

mystique, *adj.* mystic.

N

nacre, *s.f.* mother-of-pearl.

nage, *s.f.* swimming; rowing, paddling.

nager, *v.n.* swim; float; row.

nageur, -euse, *s. m. f.* swimmer.

naïf, -ïve, *adj.* naïve.

nain, -e, *s. m. f.* dwarf.

naissance, *s. f.* birth; *lieu de ~* birth-place.

naître*, *v. n.* be born; arise (from).

nappe, *s.f.* table-cloth.

narine, *s.f.* nostril.

nasal, *adj.* nasal.

natal, *adj.* natal, native, birth.

natif, -ive, *adj. & s. m. f.* native.

nation, *s.f.* nation.

national, *adj.* national.

nationalité, *s.f.* nationality.

naturaliser, *v.a.* naturalize.

nature, *s.f.* nature.

naturel, -elle, *adj.* natural, native.

naturellement, *adv.* naturally, of course.

naufrage, *s. m.* shipwreck; *faire ~* be shipwrecked.

nausée, *s.f.* nausea.

nautique, *adj.* nautical.

naval, *adj.* naval.

navigateur, *s.m.* navigator.

navigation, *s.f.* navigation; sailing; *compagnie de ~* shipping company; ~ *spatiale* space-flight.

naviguer, *v. a. & n.* navigate.

navire, *s.m.* ship; ~s shipping.

ne, n', *adv.* not; ~... *pas* not; ~ ... *que* only.

né, -e, *adj.* born; née.

nécessaire, *adj.* necessary.

nécessité, *s. f.* necessity.

nécessiter, *v.a.* necessitate, make necessary.

nef, *s. f.* ship, vessel; nave; ~ *latérale* aisle.

négatif, -ive, *adj. & s. m.* negative.

négative, *s. f.* negative.

négligence, *s. f.* neglect, negligence.

négligent, *adj.* negligent.

négliger, *v.a.* neglect.

négociant, -e, *s. m. f.* merchant, trader.

négociation, *s. f.* negotiation, transaction.

nègre, *s.m.* negro.

neige, *s.f.* snow.

neiger, *v.n.* snow.

neigeux, -euse, *adj.* snowy.

néon, *s. m.* neon.

nerf, *s. m.* nerve; sinew.

nerveux, -euse, *adj.* nervous.

net, nette, *adj.* clean, neat, clear, tidy; net; — *adv.* flatly, point-blank.

nettoyage, *s. m.* cleaning, cleansing.

nettoyer, *v.a.* clean, cleanse, clear.

neuf¹, *adj. & s. m.* nine.

neuf², *neuve, adj.* new.

neutre, *adj.* neutral.

neuvième, *adj.* ninth.

neveu, *s.m.* nephew.

nez, *s.m.* nose.

ni, *conj.* ~ ... ~ (n)either ... (n)or; ~ *l'un* ~ *l'autre* neither (one).

nid, *s.m.* nest; berth.

nièce, *s.f.* niece.

nier, *v.a.* deny.

niveau, *s. m.* level.

noble, *adj.* noble.

noblesse, *s.f.* nobility.

noce, *s. f. (often pl.)* wedding; *(sing.)* revelry.

Noël, *s. m.* Christmas; *veillée de* ~ Christmas eve.

nœud, *s. m.* knot, bow, tie.

noir, *adj.* black.

noix, *s. f.* (wal)nut; ~ *de coco* coconut.

nom, *s. m.* name, surname; fame; noun; ~ *de famille* surname.

nombre, *s.m.* number.

nombreux, -euse, *adj.* numerous.

nomination, *s. f.* nomination, appointment.

nommer, *v. a.* name, give name to; appoint, nominate.

non, *adv.* no, not.

nonne, *s. f.* nun.

nord, *s. m.* north; *du* ~, *au* ~ northern.

nord-est, *s. m.* northeast.

nord-ouest, *s. m.* northwest.

normal, *adj.* normal.

norvégien, -enne (N.), *adj. & s. m. f.* Norwegian.

nos, *poss. adj.* our.

notable, *adj.* notable, remarkable.

notaire, *s. m.* notary (-public).

note, *s. f.* note, mark; bill, account; note *(music)*; ~ *(au bas de la page)* foot-note.

noter, *v.a.* note, jot down; notice.

notice, *s. f.* notice.

notion, *s. f.* notion, idea.

notre, *poss. adj.* our.

nôtre, *pron. poss.* ours, our own.

nourrir, *v.a.* nourish, feed.

nourriture, *s. f.* nourishment food.

nous, *pron.* we; us.

nous-mêmes, *pron.* ourselves.

nouveau, -el, -elle, *adj.* new; further; de ~ again.

nouvelle, *s. f.* news; short story.

novembre, *s. m.* November.

noyau *s.m.* stone, kernel; nucleus, core.

noyer[1], *v. a.* drown; se ~ be drowning; drown oneself.

noyer[2], *s. m.* walnut-tree.

nu, *adj.* naked, bare.

nuage, *s. m.* cloud.

nuageux, -euse, *adj.* cloudy, clouded.

nuance, *s. f.* shade, tint, nuance.

nucléaire. *adj.* nuclear.

nuire*, *v. n.* hurt, harm, be harmful.

nuit, *s. f.* night; il (se) fait ~ it is night, it is getting dark; de ~ by night; la ~ at night, bonne ~! good night!

nul, nulle, *adj.* not one, not any; null, nil; — *pron.* no one, nobody.

numéro, *s. m.* number, size; ticket; copy, issue.

nu-pied, *adv.* barefoot.

nylon, *s. m.* nylon.

O

obéir, *v.n.* obey.

obéissance, *s. f.* obedience.

objectif, -ive, *adj.* objective; — *s. m.* object, purpose; lens.

objection, *s. f.* objection.

objet, *s. m.* object, thing, article; purpose; ~ d'art work of art.

obligation, *s. f.* obligation.

obligatoire, *adj.* compulsory, obligatory.

obliger, *v.a.* oblige, compel.

obscur, *adj.* dark, dim.

obscurité, *s. f.* darkness, dimness; dans l'~ in the dark.

observation, *s.f.* observation; remark.

observer, *v. a. & n.* observe, watch; keep.

obstacle, *s. m.* obstacle; hindrance; bar.

obstine, *adj.* obstinate.

obtenir, *v. a.* obtain, get.

occasion, *s. f.* occasion, chance, event; a l'~ if need be, eventually; d'~ second-hand.

occidental, *adj.* western, occidental.

occupant, -e, *s. m. f.* occupier, occupant.

occupation, *s. f.* occupation; pursuit.

occupé, *adj.* occupied, busy, engaged; *non ~* unoccupied.

occuper, *v.a.* occupy, employ; *s'~* occupy oneself *(de* with), be engaged; think *(de* of).

occurrence, *s.f.* occurrence; *en l'~* in this case.

océan, *s.m.* ocean.

octobre, *s.m.* October.

odieux, -euse, *adj.* odious.

œil, *s. m. (pl.* yeux) eye, sight; *coup d'~* glance; *au premier coup d'~* at first sight, at a glance; *ouvrez l'~!* look out!

œillet, *s.m.* carnation; eyelet.

œuf, *s.m.* egg; *~ à la coque* boiled egg; *~s brouillés* scrambled eggs; *~s durs* hard-boiled eggs; *blanc d'~* white of egg; *jaune d'~* egg-yolk.

œuvre, *s. f.* work; composition; *~ d'art* work of art.

offense, *s. f.* offence, insult; trespass.

offenser, *v.a.* offend, shock, injure; *s'~* take offence, be offended *(de* with), be angry.

office, *s.m.* office; service; post; agency; *exercer un ~* hold an office.

officiel, -elle, *adj.* official.

officier, *s.m.* officer.

offre, *s. f.* offer, tender.

offrir*, *v. a.* offer, present, hold out; *s'~* offer, propose oneself.

oh!, *int.* oh!, O!, indeed!

oie, *s.f.* goose.

oignon, *s. m.* onion; bulb.

oiseau, *s. m.* bird.

olympique, *adj.* Olympic; *les jeux ~* the Olympic games.

ombre, *s.m.* shade; ghost; obscurity, darkness.

ombreux, -euse, *adj.* shady, shaded.

omelette, *s.f.* omelet.

omettre, *v. a.* omit.

omission, *s. f.* omission, oversight.

omnibus, *s. m.* bus; — *adj.* slow; *train ~* slow train.

on, *pron.* one, we, people *(pl.)*; you; they; somebody; some one; *~ dit* they say, it is said, people say; *ferme!* closing time!

oncle, *s.m.* uncle.

onde, *s. f.* wave; undulation;

ondulation, *s. f.* undulation; waving.

onduler, *v. a. & n.* undulate, wave; ripple.

ongle, *s.m.* nail *(finger).*

onze, *adj. & s. m.* eleven; eleventh.

opéra, *s. m.* opera; opera-house; *~ comique* comic opera.

opérateur, *s. m.* operator; cameraman.

opération, *s. f.* operation; *salle d'~* operating-theatre.

opérer, *v. a. & n.* operate (on); *se faire ~* undergo an operation.

opérette, *s.f.* operetta.

opinion, *s.f.* opinion.

opportun, *adj.* opportune, timely.

opposer, *v.a.* oppose.

opposition, *s. f.* opposition.

oppression, *s. f.* oppression.

opprimer, *v. a.* oppress.

optimiste, *adj.* optimistic; — *s. m. f.* optimist.

optique, *adj.* optic(al); — *s. f.* optics.

or, *s. m.* gold; *d'~, en ~* golden.

orage, *s.m.* storm.

orange, *s.f.* orange.

orateur, *s.m.* speaker.

orbite, *s. f.* orbit.

orchestre, *s. m.* orchestra.

ordinaire, *adj.* ordinary, usual, common.

ordinairement, *adv.* usually, generally.

ordonnance, *s. f.* order; statute; prescription.

ordonner, *v.a.* order, command.

ordre, *s. m.* order, command; *mettre en ~* arrange, clear up.

ordure, *s. f.* refuse, rubbish.

oreille, *s. f.* ear; hearing; *prêter l'~ à* listen to, lend an ear to.

oreiller, *s.m.* pillow.

organe, *s.m.* organ.

organique, *adj.* organic.

organisation, *s. f.* organization, arrangement.

organiser, *v. a.* organize.

organisme, *s. m.* organism, system.

orgue, *s.m.* organ.

orgueil, *s.m.* pride.

orient, *s. m.* the East; *de l'~* eastern.

oriental, *adj.* oriental, eastern.

original, *adj.* original.

origine, *s. f.* origin, source; *avoir ~* come from.

ornement, *s. m.* ornament, adornment.

orner, *v. a.* adorn, ornament, trim, decorate.

orphelin, -e, *s. m. f.* orphan.

orthographie, *s. f.* spelling.

os, *s. m.* bone.

osciller, *v.n.* oscillate.

oser, *v. a. & n.* dare, venture.

ôter, *v.a.* take away, take off, remove, pull off; *s'~* remove oneself.

ou, *conj.* or, either, else.

où, *adv.* where; whence; at which, in which; *n'importe ~* anywhere.

ouate, *s.f.* cotton-wool.

oublier, *v. a. & n.* forget; overlook.

ouest, *s. m.* west; *à l'~* to, in the west, westward; *de l'~* western.

oui, *adv.* yes.

ouragan, *s. m.* hurricane.

ours, *s.m.* bear.

ourse, *s.f.* she-bear.

outil, *s.m.* tool.

outré, *adj.* exaggerated.

ouvert, *adj.* open; free; open-hearted; *à bras* ~s with open arms.

ouverture, *s. f.* opening; overtures *(pl.)*, proposal; overture.

ouvrage, *s. m.* (piece of) work.

ouvre-boîte, *s. m.* tin-opener.

ouvreuse, *s. f.* box-opener, attendant.

ouvrier, -ère, *s. m. f.* workman, worker; workwoman, hand; *premier* ~ foreman.

ouvrir*, *v. a. & n.* open (up); break open; s'~ be opened, open.

oxygène, *s. m.* oxygen.

P

pacifique, *adj.* pacific, peaceful; *l'Océan* ~ the Pacific Ocean.

pacte, *s. m.* pact.

page¹, *s. f.* page; *être à la* ~ be up to date.

page², *s. m.* page *(boy).*

paiement *see* **payement.**

paille, *s. f.* straw, chaff.

pain, *s. m.* bread, loaf; cake, tablet.

pair¹, *adj.* equal, even; *au* ~ at par; "au pair".

pair², *s. m.* peer.

paire, *s. f.* pair; couple.

paisible, *adj.* peaceful.

paître*, *v. a. & n.* graze, feed.

paix, *s. f.* peace; calm.

palais¹, *s. m.* palace.

palais², *s. m.* palate.

pâle, *adj.* pale.

paletot, *s. m.* overcoat.

pâleur, *s. f.* pallor.

pâlir, *v. n. & a.* (grow) pale.

palmier, *s.m.* palm-tree.

palpiter, *v.n.* palpitate.

pamphlet, *s.m.* pamphlet.

pamplemousse, *s. m.* grapefruit.

pan, *s. m.* flap; coat-tail.

panache, *s.m.* plume.

panier, *s. m.* basket.

panique, *s. f.* panic.

panne, *s.f.* break-down; power-cut.

panneau, *s. m.* panel.

panorama, *s. m.* panorama.

pansement, *s. m.* dressing, bandage.

pantalon, *s. m.* trousers *(pl.).*

pantoufle(s), *s. f. (pl.)* slipper(s).

papa, *s. m.* dad, daddy.

papauté, *s. f.* papacy.

pape, *s. m.* pope.

papeterie, *s. f.* paper-mill; stationery.

papetier, *s. m.* stationer.

papier, *s. m.* paper; ~ *hygiénique* toilet-paper; ~ *peint* wallpaper.

papillon, *s. m.* butterfly.

pâques, *s. m. pl.* Easter.

paquet, *s.m.* packet, parcel.

par, *prep.* by, by way of, by means of; across; through; per; for.

parade, *s. f.* parade, show.

paragraphe, *s. m.* paragraph.

paraître*, *v.n.* appear,

come in sight; come out; *faire* ~ publish.

parallèle, *adj.* & *s. f.* parallel.

paralysie, *s. f.* paralysis.

paralytique, *s. m. f.* paralytic.

parapluie, *s. m.* umbrella.

paratonnerre, *s. m.* lightning-conductor.

parbleu, *int.* indeed!

parc, *s. m.* park; fold.

parce que, *conj.* because, on account of.

parcourir, *v.n.* travel through, go over; cover; run over, look over.

parcours, *s.m.* course, run; distance; mileage.

pardessus, *s. m.* overcoat.

par-dessus, *prep.* above.

pardon, *s. m.* pardon; *je vous demande* ~! I beg your pardon!; pardon me!; excuse me!; ~? (I beg your) pardon?

pardonner, *v.a.* pardon.

pare-boue, *s.m.* mudguard.

pare-brise, *s.m.* windscreen.

pare-choc, *s. m.* bumper.

pareil, -eille, *adj.* like, similar; such; same.

parent, *s. m. f.* relative, relation; ~s parents; relatives.

parer, *v. a.* adorn, trim; parry, ward off.

paresseux, -euse, *adj.* lazy, idle.

parfait, *adj.* & *s. m.* perfect.

parfaitement, *adv.* perfectly; ~! quite so!

parfois, *adv.* sometimes.

parfum, *s. m.* perfume.

parfumer, *v. a.* perfume.

parfumerie, *s. f.* perfumery.

parier, *v. a.* bet, stake.

parisien, -enne, *adj.* & *s. m. f.* Parisian.

parlement, *s. m.* parliament.

parlementaire, *adj.* parliamentary.

parler, *v. n.* & *a.* speak, talk; — *s. m.* speech, utterance; parlance.

parmi, *prep.* among.

paroi, *s. f.* wall, partition.

paroisse, *s. f.* parish.

parole, *s. f.* speech, utterance; language; word.

parquet, *s. m.* parquet.

part, *s. f.* part, share; side; *prendre* ~ *à* take part in, participate; *faire* ~ *a* inform (of), let know; *à* ~ apart; *d'une* ~ ... *d'autre* ~ on the one hand ... on the other (hand).

partager, *v.a.* divide, share out; share.

partenaire, *s. m. f.* partner.

parterre, *s. m.* flower-bed; pit.

parti, *s. m.* party; side.

participant, -e, *s. m. f.* & *adj.* participant.

participation, *s. f.* participation, share.

participe, *s. m.* participle; ~ *passé* past participle.

participer, *v.n.* participate, take part (*à* in).

particulier, -ère, *adj.* particular, special, specific; peculiar; private;

— s. m. f. private person; en ~ in particular.

partie, s. f. part; match, game; party; en ~ partly, in part.

partir*, v. n. start, leave, go (away), set out.

partisan, s. m. partisan, follower.

partition, s. f. score.

partout, adv. everywhere.

parure, s. f. ornament; set.

parvenir, v. n. attain (à to), reach.

pas¹, s. m. step, pace.

pas², adv. no, not, not any; ~ du tout not at all; ~ nécessaire unnecessary.

passage, s. m. passing; passage; corridor; crossing; thoroughfare ~ clouté pedestrian crossing; ~ à niveau level-crossing; ~ interdit no thoroughfare.

passager, -ère, adj. passing, transient, fugitive; — s. m. f. passenger.

passant, -e, adj. en ~ by the way, cursorily; — s. m. f. passer-by.

passe, s. f. pass, passage; channel; permit.

passé, adj. past; — prep. after, beyond.

passeport, s. m. passport.

passer, v. n. & a. pass; pass along, by; cross; go on, pass on; hand; pass away; omit; forgive; strain; en ~ par là submit to it; ~ un examen take an examination; ~ la nuit

spend the night; se ~ happen; disappear; do without.

passif, -ive, adj. passive — s.m. liabilities (pl.).

passion, s. f. passion.

passionné adj. passionate.

pastel, s. m. pastel.

pastille, s.f. pastille.

pâte, s. f. paste; dough.

pâté, s. m. pie, pasty; block (of buildings); blot.

patente, s.f. patent, licence.

patience, s. f. patience.

patient, -e, adj. & s. m. f. patient.

patin, s. m. skate.

patinage, s. m. skating.

patiner, v.n. skate.

patinoire, s.f. skating-rink.

pâtisserie, s.f. pastry; pastry-shop, cake-shop.

pâtissier, -ère, s. m. f. pastry-cook.

pâtre, s. m. shepherd.

patrie, s. f. country.

patriote, adj. patriotic; — s. m. f. patriot.

patron¹, -onne, s. m. f. patron; employer, boss.

patron², s. m. model, pattern.

patronage, s. m. patronage, support.

patronner, v. a. patronize, protect.

patrouille, s.f. patrol.

patte, s. f. paw, foot.

pâture, s. f. fodder, pasture.

paume, s. f. palm.

paupière, s. f. eyelid.

pause, s. f. pause, stop,

break; rest.

pauvre, *adj.* poor.

pauvreté, *s. f.* poverty.

pavé, *s. m.* paving-stone; pavement; street.

paver, *v. a.* pave.

pavillon, *s. m.* pavilion, summer-house; flag.

payable, *adj.* payable, due.

paye, *s.f.* pay, wages *pl.*

payement, paiement, *s. m.* payment.

payer, *v.a.* pay; pay down, for, off; repay.

pays, *s. m.* country, land; home; nation; district, region.

paysage, *s. m.* landscape; scenery.

paysan, -anne, *s. m. f.* peasant, countryman; countrywoman.

peau, *s. f.* skin; hide; leather.

pêche¹, *s. f.* peach.

pêche², *s. f.* fishing; angling; ∼ *à la ligne* angling.

péché, *s. m.* sin, trespass.

pécher, *v. n.* sin, trespass.

pêcher, *v. a. & n.* fish, angle.

pécheur, -eresse, *s. m. f.* sinner.

pêcheur, *s.m.* angler, fisher.

pécuniaire, *adj.* pecuniary.

pédagogie, *s. f.* pedagogy.

pédale, *s. f.* pedal.

pédant, *adj.* pedant.

pédicure, *s. m.* pedicure.

peigne, *s. m.* comb.

peigner, *v. a.* comb.

peignoir, *s.m.* wrapper, dressing-gown.

peindre*, *v.a.* paint.

peine, *s. f.* punishment; pain, grief; trouble.

peintre, *s. m.* painter.

peinture, *s. f.* painting.

pêle-mêle, *adv.* pell-mell, in a muddle.

pelle, *s. f.* shovel, spade.

pellicule, *s. f.* film.

pelote, *s. f.* ball.

pelouse, *s. f.* lawn.

pelure, *s. f.* rind, peel.

pénalité, *s. f.* penalty.

penchant, *s. m.* slope, slant; bent, liking.

pencher, *v. a. & n.* incline, bend; stoop; lean (towards).

pendant¹, *adj.* hanging, pendent; — *s. m.* pendant; match.

pendant², *prep.* during; ∼ *que* while.

pendre, *v. a. & n.* hang (up); suspend; hang down; be hanging.

pendule, *s. f.* clock.

pénétrer, *v. a. & n.* penetrate, go through; search; see through.

pénitence, *s. f.* penitence.

pensée, *s.f.* thought, thinking; mind, pansy.

penser, *v. n. & a.* think.

pension, *s.f.* pension; board (and lodging); boarding-house; boarding-school; life annuity; ∼ *et chambre(s)* board and lodging; ∼ *pour étudiants* hostel.

pensionnaire, *s.m.f.* boarder; paying guest.

pensionnat, *s. m.* boarding-school.

pente, *s. f.* slope, descent; en ~ downhill.

Pentecôte, *s. f.* Whitsuntide; *dimanche de la* ~ Whit Sunday.

pépier, *v.n.* chirp.

pépin, *s. m.* pip, stone.

perçant, *adj.* piercing.

perception, *s.f.* perception.

percer, *v. a. & n.* pierce, bore; punch; tap.

percevoir, *v. a.* perceive, understand.

perdre, *v. a. & n.* lose; waste; be the ruin of; se ~ get lost, disappear; be ruined.

perdrix, *s. f.* partridge.

père, *s. m.* father.

perfection, *s.f.* perfection.

perforation, *s. f.* perforation.

perforer, *v.a.* perforate.

peril, *s.m.* peril, danger.

période, *s. f.* period, term.

périodique, *adj.* periodic, periodical.

périr, *v. n.* perish.

perle, *s. f.* pearl, bead.

permanent, *adj.* permanent.

permanente, *s. f.* perm.

permettre, *v.a.* allow, permit, let; *permettez-moi de* allow me to; *vous permettez?* may I?

permis, *s.m.* permit, licence.

permission *s. f.* permission, leave (of absence).

perron, *s. m.* stair, steps *(pl.).*

perroquet, *s. m.* parrot.

persan, *-e* (P.), *adj. & s. m. f.* Persian.

persécuter, *v. a.* persecute.

persécution, *s. f.* persecution.

persil, *s. m.* parsley.

persister, *v.n.* persist.

personnage, *s. m.* personage, person.

personnalité, *s. f.* personality.

personne, *s.f.* person; *grande* ~ grown-up; — *pron.* any one; anybody; no one.

personnel, -elle, *adj.* personal; — *s. m.* personnel, staff.

perspective, *s. f.* perspective, prospect, outlook.

persuader, *v.a.* persuade, convince.

persuasion, *s. f.* persuasion, conviction.

perte, *s.f.* loss; ruin.

pertinent, *adj.* pertinent.

peser, *v. a.* weigh; ponder.

pessimiste, *s. m. f.* pessimist; — *adj.* pessimistic.

petit, *adj.* small, little.

petite-fille, *s.f.* granddaughter.

petit-fils, *s. m.* grandson.

pétition, *s.f.* petition, request.

petits-enfants, *pl.* grandchildren.

pétrole, *s.m.* petroleum.

peu, *adv. & s. m.* little, bit, few; ~ a ~ little by little, bit by bit; *un (petit)* ~ a (little) bit; *quelque* ~ somewhat; ~ *abondant* scanty; ~ *commun* unusual; ~ *confortable* uncomfortable; ~ *nécessaire* unnecessary.

peuple, *s. m.* people.

peur, *s. f.* fear; fright; *avoir* ~ *(de)* be afraid (of); *de* ~ *que* for fear that.

peut-être, *adv.* perhaps.

phare, *s. m.* lighthouse; headlight.

pharmacie, *s.f.* pharmacy, chemist's (shop).

pharmacien, -enne, *s. m. f.* chemist.

phase, *s.f.* phase.

phénomène, *s. m.* phenomenon.

philologie, *s. f.* philology.

philosophe, *s.m.* philosopher.

philosophie, *s. f.* philosophy.

philosophique, *adj.* philosophical.

phono(graphe), *s.m.* gramophone.

photo, *s. f.* photo, snap.

photographe, *s.m.* photographer.

photographie, *s. f.* photograph; photography.

photographier, *v. a.* photograph.

photographique, *adj.* photographic; *appareil* ~ camera.

phrase, *s. f.* phrase; sentence.

phtisie, *s. f.* consumption.

physicien, -enne, *s. m. f.* physicist.

physique, *adj.* physical; — *s. f.* physics; ~ *nucléaire* nuclear physics; — *s. m.* physique, constitution.

pianiste, *s. m. f.* pianist.

piano(forte), *s. m.* piano.

pièce, *s. f.* piece, part, bit, coin; play; room; joint.

pied, *s. m.* foot, leg; *à* ~ on foot; *aller à* ~ walk.

pierre, *s. f.* stone; rock.

piéton, *s. m.* pedestrian.

pieu, *s. m.* stake, post.

pieux, -euse, *adj.* pious.

pigeon, -onne, *s. m. f.* dove, pigeon.

pile, *s. f.* pile, heap; battery.

pilier, *s. m.* pillar, post, column.

piller, *v. a. & n.* pillage.

pilot, *s. m.* pile.

pilote, *s. m.* pilot.

piloter, *v.a.* pilot, guide.

pilule, *s. f.* pill.

pin, *s. m.* pine(-tree).

pince, *s. f.* pinch; pincers, pliers, tongs *(pl.)*.

pincer, *v. a.* pinch.

pipe, *s. f.* pipe.

piquant, *adj.* pungent, sharp; piquant.

pique, *s. f.* pike; *s. m. (cards)* spade.

pique-nique, *s. m.* picnic.

piquer, *v. a. & n.* prick, sting; lard; goad, spur.

piqûre, *s. f.* prick, sting; puncture; injection.

pirate, *s. m.* pirate.

pire, *adj.* worse.

pis, *adv.* worse.

piscine, *s. f.* swimming-pool.

piste, *s. f.* track; trace; runway.

pistolet, *s. m.* pistol.

pitié, *s.f.* pity.

placard, *s. m.* placard, poster; cupboard.

place, s. f. place; room; seat; square.

placement, s. m. placing; investment; *bureau de* ~ labour-exchange.

placer, v. a. place, put, set; invest; sell.

plafond, s. m. ceiling.

plage, s. f. beach.

plaider, v. a. & n. plead.

plaindre, v. a. pity, feel compassion for; se ~ complain.

plaine, s. f. plain.

plainte, s. f. complaint.

plaire*, v. n. please; *vous plaît-il de?* would you like to?; *s'il vous plaît* (if you) please; se ~ take pleasure, enjoy.

plaisant, adj. pleasant, pleasing.

plaisanterie, s. f. joke, jest; *par* ~ as a joke.

plaisir, s. m. pleasure.

plan, s. m. plan; design; plane.

planche, s. f. board, plank.

plancher, s. m. floor.

planer, v. a. plane.

plante, s. f. plant; sole.

planter, v. a. plant; set.

planteur, s. m. planter.

plaque, s. f. plate; slab; plaque; ~ de police number-plate.

plaquer, v. a. plate; lay on.

plastique, adj. plastic; — s. f. plastic art; figuré; — s. m. plastics *pl.*

plastron, s. m. (shirt-) front; plastron; stiff shirt.

plat, adj. flat; plain; dull; — s. m. flat (part);

blade.

plateau, s.m. tray; scale (of balance); plateau.

plate-bande, s. f. flower-bed.

plate-forme, s.f. platform.

plâtre, s. m. plaster.

plein, adj. full; filled; *en* ~ fully, entirely.

pleurer, v. n. cry, weep.

pleuvoir: *il pleut* it rains.

pli, s. m. fold, crease.

pliant, adj. flexible, pliant; folding.

plier, v. a. & n. fold (up), bend; se ~ submit (à to).

plisser, v. a. & n. plait, fold, tuck; wrinkle.

plomb, s.m. lead.

plombage, s. m. filling.

plombier, s. m. plumber.

plonger, v. a. & n. plunge, immerse, dip, dive.

pluie, s. f. rain.

plume, s. f. feather, plume, pen.

plupart, s. f. most, the greatest part, majority.

pluriel, s. m. plural.

plus, adv. more, most; further, longer; any more; *de* ~ *en* ~ more and more; *en* ~ *de* in addition to; *ne . . .* ~ no more, no longer.

plusieurs, adj. several, many, some, a few; — pron. several people.

plutôt, adv. rather, preferably.

pluvieux, -euse, adj. rainy, wet.

pneu(matique), s. m. tyre.

pneumonie, s. f. pneumonia.

poche, *s. f.* pocket; pouch.

poêle¹, *s. m.* stove.

poêle², *s. f.* frying pan.

poème, *s. m.* poem.

poésie, *s. f.* poetry; poesy.

poète, *s. m.* poet.

poétique, *adj.* poetic(al).

poids, *s. m.* weight.

poignant, *adj.* poignant.

poigne, *s. f.* grip, grasp.

poignée, *s. f.* handle; hilt; handful.

poignet, *s. m.* wrist; cuff.

poil, *s. m.* hair; bristle; coat.

poinçon, *s.m.* punch, bodkin.

poinçonner, *v. a.* punch, clip; stamp.

poing, *s.m.* fist.

point, *s. m.* point, dot; full stop; *deux ~s* colon; *~ et virgule* semicolon; *à ~* just in time; *être sur le ~ de* be about to; *~ de vue* point of view.

pointe, *s. f.* point, head, tip.

pointer, *v. a. & n.* point.

pointu, *adj.* sharp, pointed.

poire, *s. f.* pear.

pois, *s. m.* pea.

poison, *s. m.* poison.

poisson, *s. m.* fish.

poissonnier, -ère, *s. m. f.* fishmonger.

poitrine, *s.f.* chest, breast.

poivre, *s. m.* pepper.

pôle, *s. m.* pole.

poli, *adj.* polished; polite.

police, *s. f.* police; policy; *agent de ~* policeman.

policier, *s. m.* policeman.

policlinique, *s.f.* outpatients' department.

polir, *v. a.* polish, refine.

politesse, *s. f.* politeness.

politicien, -enne, *s. m. f.* politician.

politique, *s. f.* politics.

polonais, -e (P.), *adj.* Polish; *— s. m.* Pole; *s. f.* Polish woman; polonaise.

pomme, *s. f.* apple; *~ de terre* potato.

pommier, *s. m.* apple tree.

pompe¹, *s. f.* pomp, ceremony.

pompe², *s. f.* pump; *~ à incendie* fire-engine; *~ à essence* petrol pump.

pompier, *s. m.* fireman; *les ~s* fire-brigade.

ponctuel, -elle, *adj.* punctual.

pont, *s. m.* bridge; deck; *~ suspendu* suspension-bridge; *~ inférieur* lower deck.

populaire, *adj.* popular; vulgar, common.

popularité, *s. f.* popularity.

population, *s. f.* population.

populeux, -euse, *adj.* populous.

porc, *s. m.* pig, hog; pork.

porcelaine, *s. f.* porcelain, china(ware).

pore, *s. m.* pore.

poreux, -euse *adj.* porous.

port¹, *s.m.* harbour (sea)port; *arriver à bon ~* arrive safely.

port², *s. m.* bearing; gait; carriage; postage; *~ payé* postage paid.

portable, *adj.* portable.

porte, *s. f.* door(way), entrance; ~ *d'entrée* front-door.

porte-cigarettes, *s. m. pl.* cigarette-case.

portée, *s. f.* litter; range, scope; ~ within reach.

portemanteau, *s.m.* coat-stand; suit-case.

porter, *v. a. & n.* bear; carry; convey; wear, have on; hold; ~ *intérêt* yield interest; show interest; ~ *la santé de B* drink B's health; se ~ be worn, be carried; *comment vous portez-vous?* how are you?

porteur, *s. m.* porter, carrier; bearer.

portier, -ère, *s. m. f.* porter, door-keeper.

portière, *s. f.* door (on vehicle); (door-)curtain.

portion, *s. f.* portion, part, share; helping.

portrait, *s. m.* portrait.

portugais, -e (P.), *adj. & s. m. f.* Portuguese.

posemètre, *s. m.* light-meter.

poser, *v. a. & n.* place, lay down, put; state.

positif, -ive, *adj. & s. m. f.* positive.

position, *s.f.* position, situation; attitude.

posséder, *v.a.* possess.

possession, *s.f.* possession; property.

possibilité, *s.f.* possibility.

possible, *adj.* possible; *faire tout son* ~ do one's best.

postal, *adj.* postal; post; *carte* ~*e* post-card.

poste¹, *s. f.* post(-office), mail; *mettre à la* ~ post (a letter); *bureau de* ~ post-office; *timbre* ~ stamp; ~ *aérienne* air-mail.

poste², *s. m.* post, station, office; police-station; receiver; set; ~ *de T. S. F.* wireless-set.

postulant, -e, *s. m. f.* applicant; candidate.

pot, *s. m.* pot, can, jug, vessel; pitcher.

potager, *s.m.* kitchen garden.

poteau, *s. m.* post.

poterie, *s. f.* pottery.

potin, *s. m.* noise; (piece of) gossip.

poubelle, *s. f.* dustbin.

pouce, *s.m.* thumb.

pouding, *s. m.* pudding.

poudre, *s. f.* powder, dust.

poudrier, *s. m.* compact.

poule, *s.f.* hen; fowl.

poulet, *s.m.* chicken, fowl.

pouls, *s. m.* pulse.

poumon, *s. m.* lung(s).

poupée, *s. f.* doll.

pour, *prep.* for; ~ *cent* per cent; ~ *que* in order that.

pourboire, *s. m.* tip.

pourquoi, *conj. & adv.* why; what for; for what reason.

poursuite, *s. f.* pursuit, chase; ~*s* suit, action.

poursuivre, *v. a.* pursue, chase, prosecute.

pourtant, *adv.* however, still.

pourvoir, *v. n. & a.* provide (*à* for), supply, cater (*à* for).

pousser, *v. a. & n.* push; shove; urge; impel; grow; utter.

poussière, *s. f.* dust

poussièreux, -euse *adj.* dusty.

pouvoir*, *v. a. & n.* be able, may; **se** ~ be possible; *cela se peut* that may be; — *s. m.* power.

pratique, *s. f.* practice, execution; experience; customers (*pl.*); — *adj.* practical, convenient.

pratiquer, *v. a.* practise, carry out; exercise.

préalable, *adj.* previous, *au* ~ first of all.

précédent, *adj.* precedent, previous; — *s. m.* precedent.

précéder, *v. a. & n.* precede; come before.

prêcher, *v. a. & n.* preach.

prêcheur, *s. m.* preacher.

précieux, -euse, *adj.* precious, valuable, costly.

précipice, *s. m.* precipice.

précipitation, *s. f.* precipitation, haste, hurry.

précipité, *adj.* hasty.

précipiter, *v.a.* precipitate; hasten, hurry.

précis, *adj.* exact, precise; — *s. m.* summary.

préciser, *v.a.* specify.

prédécesseur, *s. m.* predecessor.

prédire, *v.a.* foretell.

préfabriqué, *adj.* prefabricated.

préface, *s.f.* preface.

préférable, *adj.* preferable, better.

préférer, *v.a.* prefer; like better.

préfet, *s.m.* prefect.

préjugé, *s. m.* prejudice, presumtion.

prélat, *s.m.* prelate.

préliminaire, *adj.* preliminary.

premier, -ère, *adj.* first, former; ~ *plan* foreground; close-up; *de* ~ *ordre* first-rate; ~ — *s. m.* first floor.

première, *s. f.* first night; first class (in a carriage).

prendre*, *v. a.* take, take up, seize; receive, accept; put on; wear; charge; catch; ~ *place* take a seat; *à tout* ~ on the whole; ~ *pour* mistake for; ~ *du corps* put on weight; ~ *l'air* take a walk; *se* ~ be taken, be caught.

prénom, *s. m.* Christian name.

préoccuper, *v. a.* preoccupy, engross; worry; *se* ~ trouble oneself.

préparatifs, *s.m.pl.* preparations.

préparation, *s. f.* preparation.

préparer, *v. a.* prepare, make ready; read for; *se* ~ prepare oneself, get ready.

préposition, *s. f.* preposition.

prérogative, *s. f.* prerogative, privilege.

près, *adv. & prep.* near, close by, close to; nearly; *à peu ~* nearly (so); *de ~* closely.

prescription, *s. f.* prescription.

prescrire*, *v. i.* prescribe.

présence, *s. f.* presence, attendance; *en ~ de* in the presence of.

présent¹, *s. m.* present, gift; *faire ~ de* give as a present.

présent², *s.* *m.* present (time); present tense; *— adj.* present, current *à ~* at present; *jusqu'à ~* till now, as yet; *pour le ~* for the time being.

présentation, *s. f.* presentation, introduction.

présenter, *v. a.* present, offer; introduce; *se ~* appear.

préserver, *v. a.* preserve.

président, *s. m.* president.

présomption, *s. f.* presumption; conceit.

presque, *adv.* almost.

pressant, *adj.* pressing.

presse, *s. f.* press; printing-press; haste; crowd.

pressé, *adj.* pressing; *être ~* be in a hurry.

pressentiment, *s. m.* presentiment; misgiving.

pressentir, *v.a.* have a presentiment of.

presser, *v. a.* press, crush; hurry; *pressez-vous!* hurry up!; *se ~* hurry (up).

pression, *s.f.* pressure.

pressurer, *v.a.* press, squeeze; oppress.

prestige, *s.m.* marvel; influence, prestige.

présumer, *v. a.* suppose, expect; presume.

prétendre, *v. a. & n.* pretend, claim; intend.

prétention, *s. f.* pretension, claim.

prêter, *v.a.* lend, attribute; *se ~* lend oneself (*à* to).

prétexte, *s. m.* pretext.

prêtre, *s. m.* priest.

preuve, *s. f.* proof; *faire ~ de* show.

prévaloir, *v.n.* prevail.

prévenir, *v. a.* anticipate, inform, let know.

préventif, **-ive**, *adj.* preventive.

prévention, *s.f.* bias, prejudice.

prévision, *s. f.* prevision, anticipation; forecast.

prévoir, *v.a.* foresee, anticipate, forecast.

prévoyance, *s. f.* foresight.

prier, *v. a.* pray, beg; ask.

prière, *s.f.* prayer; request.

primaire, *adj.* primary.

prime, *adj.* first, early.

primer, *v. a.* surpass, excel; award a prize to.

primeur, *s. f.* early vegetables *(pl.)*.

primitif, **-ive**, *adj.* primitive, original.

prince, *s. m.* prince.

princesse, *s. f.* princess.

principal, *adj.* principal.

principalement, *adv.* principally, mainly.

principe, *s. m.* principle.

printemps, *s. m.* spring-(time); *au ~* in spring.

priorité, *s.f.* priority.
prise, *s.f.* taking; capture, catch; ~ *de courant* (electric) plug.
prisme, *s. m.* prism.
prison, *s. f.* prison.
prisonnier, -ère, *s. m. f.* prisoner.
privation, *s. f.* privation.
privé, *adj.* private.
priver, *v. a.* deprive.
privilège, *s. m.* privilege.
prix, *s. m.* price, cost, charge; prize; *au* ~ *de* at the cost of; ~ *de la course* fare; ~ *par mille* mileage; ~*courant* market-price; ~ *fixe* fixed price.
probabilité, *s. f.* probability.
probable, *adj.* probable.
probablement, *adv.* probably.
problématique, *adj.* problematic(al).
problème, *s. m.* problem.
procédé *s. m.* proceeding.
procéder, *v. n.* proceed.
procédure, *s.f.* procedure.
procès, *s.m.* (law-)suit, trial; *faire un* ~ *u* bring an action against.
procession, *s.f.* procession.
prochain, *adj.* near(est), next. — *s. m.* neighbour
prochainement, *adv.* shortly, soon.
proche, *adj.* near, neighbouring, close at hand.
proclamer, *v. a.* proclaim.
procurer, *v. a.* procure.
procureur, *s. m.* attorney.

prodigieux, -euse, *adj.* wonderful, prodigious.
producteur, -trice, *s. m. f.* producer; — *adj.* producing.
production, *s. f.* production.
produire*, *v. a.* produce, bring forth, yield.
produit, *s. m.* produce; product.
professer, *v. a. & n.* profess; teach.
professeur, *s. m.* teacher; professor; lecturer.
profession, *s.f.* profession.
professionnel, -elle, *adj. & s. m. f.* professional.
profil, *s. m.* profile.
profit, *s. m.* profit, gain.
profitable, *adj.* pro'itable.
profiter, *v. n.* profit (by).
profond, *adj.* deep, profound.
profondeur, *s. f.* depth; *dix pieds de* ~ ten feet deep.
programme, *s. m.* program(me); scheme.
progrès, *s. m.* progress, improvement; *faire des* ~ make progress.
prohiber, *v.a.* prohibit.
projecteur, *s. m.* headlight; searchlight; projector.
projectile, *s. m.* projectile, missile.
projection, *s. f.* projection.
projet, *s. m.* project, plan; scheme; ~ *de loi* bill.
projeter, *v.a.* project throw; scheme, plan.

prolonger, *v.a.* prolong.

promenade, *s.f.* walk; promenade.

promener: se ~ *go for a walk; se ~ en voiture* go for a drive.

promesse, *s. f.* promise.

promettre, *v. a.* promise.

promotion, *s. f.* promotion.

prompt, *adj.* prompt.

pronom, *s. m.* pronoun.

prononcer, *v.a. &n.* pronounce; utter; deliver.

prononciation, *s. f.* pronunciation; delivery.

propagande, *s. f.* propaganda.

propager, *v.a.* propagate.

prophète, *s.m.f.* prophet.

prophétie, *s. f.* prophecy.

proportion, *s. f.* proportion; ratio.

propos, *s. m.* talk, remark; *à ~* in good time; by the way.

proposer, *v.a.* propose, offer.

proposition, *s. f.* proposal, proposition.

propre, *adj* own, peculiar; proper; fit.

propriétaire, *s.m.f.* owner, proprietor; landlord, landlady.

propriété, *s. f.* ownership; property.

propulsion, *s. f.* propulsion; *~ à réaction* jet propulsion.

prosaïque, *adj.* prosaic.

proscrire*, *v. a.* proscribe.

prose, *s. f.* prose.

prospectus, *s.m.* prospectus.

prospère, *adj.* prosperous.

prospérer, *v. n.* prosper, get on (well).

prospérité, *s.f.* prosperity.

protecteur, *s. m.* protector, patron.

protection, *s.f.* protection, support.

protéger, *v.a.* protect; patronize.

protestant, -e, *s. m. f. & adj.* Protestant.

protestation, *s.f.* protest(ation).

protester, *v. n. & a.* protest.

prouver, *v.a.* prove.

provenir, *v.n.* ,come (from), issue, arise.

province, *s. f.* province, country, district.

provincial, *adj.* provincial, country.

provision, *s. f.* provision.

provisoire, *adj.* provisional, temporary.

provoquer, *v. a.* provoke; stir up.

proximité, *s.f.* proximity.

prudence, *s. f.* prudence, caution.

prudent, *adj.* prudent, cautious.

prune, *s. f.* plum.

pruneau, *s. m.* prune.

prunelle, *s.f.* pupil.

psaume, *s. m.* psalm.

psychologie, *s. f.* psychology.

psychologique, *adj.* psychological.

public, publique, *adj.* public, common; *— s. m.* public, audience.

publication, *s.f.* publication.

publicité, *s. f.* publicity.

publier, *v. a.* publish.

puce, *s. f.* flea.

puer, *v. n.* stink.

puéril, *adj.* childish.

puis, *adv.* then, after that.

puiser, *v. a.* draw up, fetch up.

puisque, *conj.* as, since.

puissance, *s.f.* power, might, force.

puissant, *adj.* powerful, strong; *tout* ~ almighty.

puits, *s. m.* well; pit.

punaise, *s. f.* drawing-pin; bug.

punch, *s.m.* punch *(drink)*.

punir, *v. a.* punish.

punition, *s.f.* punishment.

pupille, *s.m.f.* ward, pupil; — *s. f.* pupil (of the eye).

pupitre, *s. m.* desk.

pur, *adj.* pure, clean.

purée, *s. f.* mash, purèe.

purement, *adv.* purely, merely.

pureté, *s.f.* purity.

purgatif, -ive, *adj. & s. m.* purgative.

purger, *v. a.* purge.

purifier, *v.a.* purify, cleanse.

puritain, -e, *adj. & s. m. f.* Puritan.

pyramide, *s. f.* pyramid.

Q

quai, *s. m.* quay; wharf; platform; *billet de* ~ platform ticket.

qualification, *s. f.* qualification.

qualifié, *adj.* qualified.

qualifier, *v.a.* qualify.

qualité, *s.f.* quality.

quand, *adv. & conj.* when; while; ~ *même* all the same.

quant à, *prep.* as for, with regard to.

quantité, *s. f.* quantity; amount; ~ *de* plenty of.

quarante, *adj. & s. m.* forty.

quart, *s.m.* quarter, fourth part; quart.

quartier, *s. m.* quarter; piece, slice; district; ~ *général* headquarters *(pl.)*.

quatorze, *adj. & s.m.* fourteen.

quatre, *adj. &s.m.* four; fourth;

quatre-vingt-dix, *adj. & s. m.* ninety.

quatre-vingts, *adj. & s. m.* eighty.

quatrième, *adj. & s. m.* fourth; fourth floor; — *s. f.* third form.

quatuor, *s. m.* quartet(te).

que, qu', *rel. pron.* whom, which, that; of which, at which; — *adv.* how much, how many; — *conj.* that; than; as; if; as though.

quel, quelle, *adj.* what, which.

quelque, *adj.* some, any; a few; ~ *chose* something, anything; ~ *part* somewhere; ~ *peu*

somewhat — adv. a-
bout, some.

quelquefois, adv. sometimes.

quelqu'un, -e, pron.
somebody; anybody.

querelle, s. f. quarrel.

quereller, v. a. & n. quarrel with.

question, s.f. question;
point, matter, issue.

questionner, v.a. question, interrogate.

queue, s.f. tail; rear;
queue; handle.

qui, rel. pron. who, whom;
which; that; à ~ to
whom.

quille, s. f. keel, skittle.

quincaillerie, s. f. hardware (shop).

quintal, s. m. hundredweight.

quinze, adj. & s. m.
fifteen; fifteenth; ~
jours fortnight.

quittance, s. f. receipt.

quitte, adj. quit, free.

quitter, v. a. leave, give
up, quit.

quoi, rel. pron. what,
which; à propos de ~
what is it about?;
~ qu'il en soit at any
rate.

quoique, conj. (al)though.

quotidien, -enne, adj. &
s. m. daily.

R

rabais, s. m. reduction
in price, rebate.

rabaisser, v. a. lower.

rabattre, v.a. beat down,

pull down; reduce.

raccommoder, v. a. mend,
repair.

raccourcir, v.a. & n.
shorten, abridge.

raccrocher, v.a. hang
up again.

race, s. f. race; stock;
breed.

racine, s. f. root; prendre
~ take root.

raconter, v.a. tell, relate.

radar, s. m. radar.

radiateur, s. m. radiator.

radiation s. f. radiation.

radical, adj. radical.

radieux, -euse, adj. radi-
ant, beaming.

radio, s. f. radio.

radio-actif, -ive, adj. radioactive.

radiodiffuser, v.a. broadcast.

radiodiffusion, s. f. broadcasting.

radiogramme, s. m. X-ray
photograph; radiogram.

radiographie, s. f. X-ray
photograph(y).

radioreportage, s. m. running commentary.

radioscopie, s. f. radio-
scopy.

radioscopique, adj. examen ~ X-ray exami-
nation.

radis, s.m. radish.

raffermir, v.a. strength-
en, fortify.

raffinage, s.m. refining.

raffiné, adj. refined.

raffinement, s. m. refine-
ment.

raffiner, v. a. refine.

rafraîchir, v. a. refresh,

cool; se ~ cool down.

rafraîchissement, *s.m.* refreshment; **~s** refreshments.

rage, *s.f.* rage, fury.

ragoût, *s. m.* ragout, stew.

raide, *adj.* stiff, rigid.

raidir, *v. a.* make stiff.

raifort, *s.m.* horse radish.

rail, *s. m.* rail.

railler, *v.a.* mock, rail at.

raillerie, *s.f.* raillery, mocking.

raisin, *s. m.* grape(s); **~ sec** raisin.

raison, *s.f.* reason; judgement; **à ~ de** at the rate of; **avoir ~** be right.

raisonnable, *adj.* reasonable.

raisonnement, *s. m.* reasoning.

raisonner, *v. n. & a.* reason, argue.

ralentir, *v. a. & n.* slow down.

ramasser, *v.a.* gather up, pick up; take up.

rame, *s. f.* oar; prop.

ramener, *v.a.* bring back, take back.

ramer, *v. n.* row.

rampe, *s.f.* banister; footlights *(pl.).*

ramper, *v.n.* crawl, creep.

rance, *adj.* rancid.

rancune, *s.f.* spite, grudge.

randonneur, -euse, *s. m. f.* excursionist, hiker.

rang, *s.m.* row, line; rank,

rangé, *adj.* tidy.

rangée, *s.f.* row, line, range.

ranger, *v. a.* put in order; arrange; range; se ~ settle down; make room.

ranimer, *v.a.* revive, restore to life, refresh.

râpe, *s.f.* rasp, grater.

râpé, *adj.* shabby.

rapide, *adj.* rapid, fast; steep.

rapidité, *s.f.* rapidity, speed.

rappel, *s.m.* recall.

rappeler, *v. a.* recall, call back; bring back; se ~ remember.

rapport, *s.m.* product, yield; report, account; connection, relation; reference; **sous ce ~** in this respect.

rapporter, *v.a.* bring back; produce; yield; report, state; se ~ relate to, refer to.

rapprochement, *s. m.* drawing closer.

rapprocher, *v. a.* bring closer; se ~ draw nearer.

raquette, *s. f.* racket.

rare, *adj.* rare.

raser, *v. a.* shave, graze; pull down; bore; *v.n.* se ~ shave.

rasoir, *s. m.* razor; **~ électrique** electric razor; **~ de sûreté** safety razor.

rassembler, *v. a.* gather, assemble, collect.

rassis, *adj.* settled; stale.

rassurer, *v.a.* reassure,

comfort.

rat, *s. m.* rat.

râteau, *s. m.* rake.

ratelier, *s. m.* rack; set of false teeth.

rater, *v. n. & a.* miss fire; fail.

ratification, *s. f.* ratification.

ration, *s. f.* ration.

rattacher, *v.a.* tie up again, join.

rattraper, *v.a.* catch again; catch up; overtake.

rauque, *adj.* hoarse.

ravager, *v. a.* ravage, lay waste.

ravir, *v. a.* delight.

ravissant, *adj.* ravishing, charming.

rayer, *v. a.* scratch (out); cross out.

rayon, *s.m.* ray, beam; spoke; radius; shelf.

rayonnement, *s. m.* radiation; radiance.

rayonner, *v.n.* radiate, shine.

razzia, *s. f.* raid.

réacteur, *s.m.* reactor.

réaction, *s.f.* reaction.

réagir, *v.n.* react.

réalisation, *s.f.* realization; carrying out.

réaliser, *v.a.* realize.

réaliste, *adj.* realistic.

réalité, *s. f.* reality; *en ~* in fact.

rebelle, *adj.* rebellious; — *s. m. f.* rebel.

rébellion, *s. f.* rebellion.

rebord, *s.m.* edge, brim.

rébus, *s.m.* riddle.

récemment, *adv.* recently, lately.

récent, *adj.* recent.

récepteur, *s. m.* receiver.

réception, *s. f.* reception, receipt; at-home.

recette, *s.f.* receipt; recipe.

receveur, *s.m.* receiver; conductor *(bus)*.

recevoir*, *v.n.* receive; admit, take in; accept; *v. n.* entertain; *aller ~ qn. à la gare* meet s.o. at the station.

rechange, *s. m. pièces de ~* spare parts.

recharge, *s. f.* refill.

réchaud, *s.m.* dishwarmer.

réchauffer, *v. a.* warm up again.

recherche, *s.f.* research; inquiry.

rechercher, *v. a.* look for, search for; research into.

récipé, *s.m.* recipe.

réciproque, *adj.* reciprocal, mutual.

récit, *s. m.* recital, account.

récital, *s. m.* recital.

récitation, *s. f.* recitation.

réciter, *v.a.* recite.

réclamation, *s. f.* claim, complaint.

réclame, *s. f.* advertisement; *faire de la ~ (pour)* advertise.

réclamer, *v.a.* demand, claim.

recommandation, *s. f.* recommendation.

recommander, *v. a.* recommend; introduce; request; register.

recommencer, *v. a. & n.* begin again.

récompense, *s. f.* reward.

récompenser, *v. a.* reward, repay.

réconcilier, *v. a.* reconcile.

reconnaissance, *s. f.* recognition, gratitude.

reconnaître, *v. a.* recognize, know; acknowledge; explore.

reconstruction, *s. f.* reconstruction.

reconstruire*, *v.a.* rebuild.

record, *s.m.* record *(sport etc.)*.

recourir, *v. n.* ~ *à* have recourse to.

recouvrir, *v.a.* cover again, hide.

récréation, *s. f.* recreation, amusement, pastime.

recrue, *s. f.* recruit.

recteur, *s.m.* rector, chancellor.

rectifier, *v.a.* rectify, correct.

reçu, *s. m.* receipt; *au* ~ *de* on receipt of.

recueil, *s. m.* collection.

recueillir, *v.a.* collect; *se* ~ collect oneself.

reculer, *v.a.* put back; *v. n.* draw back, recoil.

rédacteur, -trice, *s. m. f.* editor; writer.

rédaction, *s. f.* drawing up; composition; editorial staff.

rédemption, *s. f.* redemption.

rédiger, *v.a.* draw up; edit.

redingote, *s.f.* frock-coat.

redire, *v. a.* repeat, say again; *trouver à* ~ *à* find fault with.

redoubler, *v.a.* redouble.

redoutable, *adj.* formidable, dreaded.

redouter, *v.a.* dread, be afraid of.

redresser, *v. a. & se* ~ straighten (up).

réduction, *s.a.* reduction, cut.

réduire*, *v. a.* reduce, cut down.

réduit, *adj.* reduced.

réel, réelle, *adj.* real, actual.

réélection, *s.f.* re-election.

réélire, *v. a.* re-elect.

refaire, *v.a.* do (over) again.

réfectoire, *s. m.* refectory, dining-hall.

référence, *s. f.* reference.

référer, *v. a.* refer; *se* ~ *à* refer to; *nous référant à* referring to.

réfléchir, *v.a.* reflect; consider, think over.

réflecteur, *s. m.* reflector.

reflet, *s. m.* reflection.

refléter, *v. a.* reflect.

réflexe, *adj.* reflex.

réflexion, *s. f.* reflection, consideration.

reflux, *s. m.* ebb.

réformation, *s.f.* reformation.

réforme, *s.f.* reform, improvement.

Réforme, *s. f.* Reformation.

réformer, *v. a.* reform.

refrain, *s. m.* refrain.

refréner, *v. a.* bridle, curb.

réfrigérateur, *s.m.* refrigerator.

réfrigérer, *v. a.* refrigerate.

refroidir, *v. a.* chill, cool.

refuge, *s. m.* refuge; layby.

réfugié, -e, *s. m. f.* refugee.

réfugier: se ~ take shelter, take refuge.

refus, *s. m.* refusal, denial.

refuser, *v. a.* refuse, deny; **~ de connaître** ignore; **être refusé** fail.

regagner, *v.a.* regain, recover; return to.

regard, *s. m.* look.

regarder, *v. a.* look at; concern; regard.

régime, *s. m.* (form of) government; diet.

régiment, *s. m.* regiment.

région, *s. f.* region, area.

régional, *adj.* local.

régir, *v.a.* rule, administer.

régisseur, *s. m.* steward; stage-manager.

registre, *s.m.* register; record.

règle, *s. f.* rule; ruler.

réglé, *adj.* regular; punctual; steady; ruled.

règlement, *a.m.* rule, regulation.

régler, *v. a.* rule; regulate; time; settle.

règne, *s.m.* reign.

régner, *v.a.* reign.

regret, *s. m.* regret.

regretter, *v. a.* regret, be sorry for.

régulariser, *v. a.* regularize.

régularité, *s. f.* regularity.

régulateur, *s. m* regulator.

régulier, -ière, *adj.* regular; correct.

rein, *s.m.* kidney.

reine, *s.f.* queen.

reine-claude, *s. f.* greengage.

rejeter, *v. a.* reject, throw out.

rejoindre, *v.a.* rejoin; overtake, catch up; **se ~** meet.

réjouir, *v. a.* give joy to, cheer up; delight; **se ~** rejoice.

relâche, *s. f.* relaxation; respite.

relâcher, *v.a.* slacken, loosen; relax; **se ~** relax.

relatif, -ive, *adj.* relative; **~ à** relating to.

relation, *s.f.* relation, connection; report; **entrer en ~ avec** get in touch with.

relever, *v. a.* lift, take up; pick up; set off; *v. n.* recover.

relief, *s.m.* relief.

relier, *v. a.* bind (a book); hoop (casks).

religieux, -euse, *adj.* religious; *— s. m.* monk; *s. f.* nun.

religion, *s.f.* religion.

relique, *s.f.* relic.

relire, *v.a.* read (over) again.

remarquable, *adj.* remarkable, noticeable.

remarque, *s. f.* remark, observation, notice.

remarquer, *v. a.* remark,

notice, observe; *faire ~* point out.

rembourser, *v.a.* repay, reimburse.

remède, *s.m.* remedy; medicine.

remerciement, *s.m.* thanks *(pl.).*

remercier, *v.a.* thank *(de* for).

remettre, *v. a.* put back; put on again; postpone; *se ~* recover (oneself).

remilitariser, *v. a.* rearm.

remise, *s. f.* remittance; delivery; allowance; revival, restoration.

remonter, *v. n. & a.* go up, remount; bring up again; set up again.

remords, *s. m.* remorse.

remorque, *s. f.* tow(ing), trailer.

remorqueur, *s. m. (bateau) ~* tug-boat.

remous, *s. m.* eddy(-water), whirl.

remplacer, *v. a.* replace, substitute.

remplir, *v. a.* fill; fill up; fulfil; carry out.

remporter, *v.a.* take away, carry off; get, obtain.

remuer, *v. a. & n.* move, fidget about; *se ~* be busy, move.

rémunération, *s. f.* remuneration.

renaissance, *s. f.* renascence; revival; *la Renaissance* the Renaissance.

renaître, *v.n.* be born again, revive.

renard, *s.m.* fox.

rencontre, *s. f.* meeting, encounter; collision.

rencontrer, *v.a.* meet, meet with; come across; run into; *se ~ avec* meet, be met with.

rendement, *s. m.* output.

rendez-vous, *s. m.* appointment, rendezvous.

rendormir: *se ~* go to sleep again.

rendre, *v.a.* give back, return; yield; render; convey; *~ un arrêt* issue a decree; *~ compte* render an account, realize; *~ visite* pay a visit.

renfermer, *v. a.* lock up again, confine; contain, include.

renfler, *v.a.&n.* swell.

renforcer, *v. a.* strengthen, reinforce.

renfort, *s. m.* reinforcement; help.

renier, *v. a.* deny.

renom, *s.m.* reputation.

renommée, *s. f.* renown.

renoncer, *v.n.&a.* renounce, give up.

renouveler, *v.a.* renew, renovate.

renseignement, *s. m.* information; indication; *bureau des ~s* inquiry office.

renseigner, *v. a.* give information to; *se ~* inquire, ask *(sur* about).

rente, *s. f.* income; rent.

rentrée, *s. f.* return; reopening.

rentrer, *v. n.* reenter, go

in; get back, return home.

renversé, *adj.* reversed, upset.

renverser, *v.a.* upset; overthrow; turn upside down; se ~ be upset, tip over.

renvoi, *s.m.* return; (cross-)reference.

renvoyer, *v.a.* return; dismiss; refer.

réorganiser, *v.a.* reorganize.

répandre, *v.a.* pour; spread, scatter, diffuse.

réparation, *s.f.* repair, amends.

réparer, *v. a.* repair, mend; make up for.

repartir*, *v.a.* answer.

repas, *s. m.* meal.

repasser, *v. n.* pass again.

répéter, *v. a.* repeat; say again; rehearse.

répétition, *s. f.* repetition; rehearsal.

réplique, *s. f.* retort, reply, answer.

répliquer, *v.a. & n.* reply, answer.

répondre, *v. a. & n.* answer, reply; respond to.

réponse *s.m.* answer; response; ~ payée reply paid.

reporter, *v. a.* carry back, take back.

repos, *s. m.* rest; sans ~ restless.

reposer, *v. a.* lay again; *v. n.* rest, lie.

repoussant, *adj.* repulsive.

repousser, *v.a.* push back; repulse; drive back.

reprendre, *v.a. & n.* take back, get back; take up, go on; ~ sa parole go back on one's word.

représentant, -e, *s. m. f.* representative.

représentation, *s. f.* show, production; performance; display; representation.

représenter, *v. a.* represent; show, display.

reprise, *s.f.* renewal.

reproche, *s. m.* reproach, blame.

reprocher, *v. a.* reproach (with); blame for.

reproduction, *s. f.* reproduction.

reproduire*, *v. a.* reproduce.

républicain, -e, *adj. & s. m. f.* republican.

république, *s. f.* republic.

répulsion, *s.f.* repulsion.

réputation, *s. f.* reputation.

requête, *s.f.* request, demand.

réserve, *s.f.* reserve; reservation; caution; de ~ spare; mettre en ~ lay by.

réserver, *v. a.* reserve, lay by; book (in advance).

réservoir, *s.m.* tank (pétrol etc.).

résidence, *s. f.* residence, dwelling.

résident, *s. m.* resident.

résignation, *s. f.* resignation; submission.

résigner, *v. a.* resign; se ~ à resign oneself, make up one's mind.

résistance, *s. f.* resistance.

résister, *v. n.* resist.

résolu, *adj.* resolute.

résolution, *s. f.* resolution.

résonance, *s. f.* resonance.

résonner, *v. n.* resound, ring.

résoudre*, *v.a.* resolve; solve; settle; **se ~** resolve, make up one's mind (to).

respect, *s. m.* respect.

respectable, *adj.* respectable, decent.

respecter *v. a.* respect.

respectif, -ive, *adj.* respective.

respectueux, -euse, *adj.* respectful.

respiration, *s. f.* respiration, breath(ing).

respirer, *v. n. & a.* breathe.

responsabilité, *s. f.* responsibility.

responsable, *adj.* responsible.

ressaisir, *v. a.* seize again.

ressemblance, *s. f.* resemblance, likeness.

ressemblant, *adj.* like, similar.

ressembler, *v* emble.

ressentiment, *s. m.* resentment, grudge.

ressentir, *v.a.* feel; resent; **se ~** be hurt; feel still.

resserrer, *v.a.* tighten; bind.

ressort, *s.m.* spring; energy.

ressortir, *v. n.* come out again; stand out.

ressource, *s. f.* resource.

restaurant, *s. m.* restau-

rant; **~ à libre service** self-service restaurant.

restaurateur, -trice, *s. m. f.* restorer; restaurant keeper.

restauration, *s.f.* restoration.

restaurer, *v. a.* restore.

reste, *s. m.* rest, remainder.

rester, *v. n.* remain, be left; keep; **~ en arrière,** lag behind.

restituer, *v. a.* restore.

restreindre*, *v. a.* restrict.

restriction, *s. f.* restriction.

résultat, *s.m.* result, issue; *avoir pour* **~** result in.

résulter, *v. n.* result (*de* from).

résumé, *s.m.* summing up.

résumer, *v.a.* sum up.

rétablir, *v.a.* restore.

retard, *s. m.* delay; *être en* **~** be late; be overdue.

retarder, *v.a.* delay, retard.

retenir, *v.a.* keep back, hold back; hinder.

retirer, *v.a.* draw back, pull back; extract, get, derive; **se ~** retire.

retomber, *v. n.* fall again, fall back; relapse.

retour, *s. m.* return; *en* **~** homeward bound; *être de* **~** be back.

retourner, *v. n.* turn back; return, go back; **se ~** turn round.

retracer, *v.a.* retrace;

relate, tell.

retraite, s.f. retreat; retirement; *mettre à la* ~ superannuate.

retrancher, v. a. retrench.

rétrécir, v.a. contract; make narrower; shrink.

retrousser, v. a. turn up.

retrouver, v. a. find again, recover.

rétroviseur, s. m. (rear-vision) mirror.

réunion, s.f. reunion.

réunir, v.a. reunite; join again.

réussi, adj. successful.

réussir, v. n. succeed.

réussite, s. f. success.

revanche, s. f. revenge; return match; *en* ~ in return.

rêve, s. m. dream.

réveil, s. m. waking.

réveille-matin s. m. alarm-clock.

réveiller, v.a. & se ~ wake (up).

révéler, v.a. reveal; se ~ come to light.

revenir, v. n. return, come back; recur; cost.

revenu, s. m. income.

rêver, v. n. dream.

révérence, s. f. reverence; curtsey.

révérend, adj. reverend.

rêverie, s.f. reverie, fancy.

revers, s. m. back, reverse, wrong side.

revêtir, v.a. put on; clothe; cover.

révision, s. f. revision.

revivre, v. n. live again; *faire* ~ revive.

revoir, v. n. a. see again,

look over; *au* ~ good-bye (for the present).

révolte, s. f. revolt.

révolter, v. a. revolt; se ~ revolt, rebel.

révolution, s. f. revolution; turn.

révolutionnaire, adj. & s. m. f. revolutionary.

revolver, s. m. revolver.

revue, s. f. review; magazine.

rez-de-chaussé, s. m. ground floor.

rhétorique, s. f. rhetoric.

rhum, s. m. rum.

rhumatisme, s. m. rheumatism.

rhume, s. m. cold (in the head).

ricaner, v. n. sneer, grin.

riche, adj. rich, well off.

richesse, s.f. wealth, riches (pl.).

ride, s. f. wrinkle.

rideau, s. m. curtain.

rider, v. a. wrinkle.

ridicule, adj. ridiculous; — s. m. ridicule.

rien, pron. nothing; not ... anything; trifle.

rigoureux, -euse, adj. rigorous, severe.

rigueur, s. f. rigour.

rime, s. f. rhyme.

rincer, v. a. rinse.

rire*, v. n. laugh; *pour* ~ for fun; — s.m. laugh(ing), laughter.

risque, s. m. risk.

risquer, v.a. risk, run the risk of.

rivage, s. m. beach, shore.

rival, -e, adj. & s. m. f. rival.

rivalité, s. f. rivalry.

rive, *s. f.* bank, shore, beach.

rivière, *s. f.* river, stream.

riz, *s. m.* rice.

robe, *s. f.* gown, dress, frock; robe; ~ *de chambre* dressing-gown.

robinet, *s. m.* tap, cock.

robuste, *adj.* robust; strong, sturdy.

roc, *s. m.* rock.

roche, *s.f.* rock, boulder.

rocher, *s. m.* rock, crag.

roder, *v. a.* run in.

rôder, *v.n.* rove.

rogner, *v. a.* clip, pare.

rognon, *s. m.* kidney.

roi, *s. m.* king.

rôle, *s. m.* roll; part, rôle.

romain, -e (R.), *adj. & s. m. f.* Roman.

roman, *s. m.* novel; ~s fiction.

romançier, -ère, *s. m. f.* novelist.

romanesque, *adj.* romantic.

romantique, *s. m.* romantic.

romantisme, *s. m.* romanticism.

rompre, *v. a. & n.* break.

rond, *adj.* round; — *s. m.* round, circle.

ronde, *s. f.* round; patrol; *à la* ~ round about, around.

rondelle, *s. f.* ring, collar, washer.

ronfler, *v. n.* snore; roar.

ronger, *v.a.* gnaw, eat.

rose, *s. f.* rose; — *adj.* rosy, pink.

roseau, *s. m.* reed.

rosée, *s. f.* dew.

rosier, *s.m.* rose-tree, rose-bush.

rossignol, *s. m.* nightingale.

rôti, *s. m.* roast (meat).

rôtir, *v.a.* roast; toast; *faire* ~ roast, bake.

roucouler, *v. n.* coo.

roue, *s.f.* wheel; ~ *de secours* spare wheel; ~ *dentée* cog-wheel.

rouge, *adj.* red; — *s. m.* red (colour); *bâton de* ~ lipstick.

rougeur, *s.f.* redness, blush.

rougir, *v.n. & a.* turn red, make red; blush.

rouille, *s. f.* rust.

rouiller, *v. n. & a.* rust, get rusty.

roulage, *s.m.* rolling; carriage (of goods); haulage.

rouleau, *s.m.* roll; roller; scroll.

roulement, *s. m.* roll(ing), rotation; ~ *à billes* ball-bearings.

rouler, *v. a. & n.* roll; roll up, wind up; turn, revolve.

roulotte, *s.f.* ~ *(de camping)* caravan.

roumain, -e (R.), *adj. & s. m. f.* Rumanian.

route, *s. f.* road; highway; course; way; en ~ on the way; en ~ *pour* bound for; *code de la* ~ highway code.

routine, *s. f.* routine.

roux, rousse, *adj.* red-(dish).

royal, *adj.* royal.

royaliste, -e, *adj. & s. m. f.* royalist.

royaume, s. m. kingdom.
ruban, s m. ribbon; band.
rubis, s m. ruby.
ruche, s. f. hive.
rude, adj. rough, rude.
rue, s. f. street; ~ *barrée* no thoroughfare; ~ *de traverse* crossroad.
ruée, s. f. rush.
ruelle, s. f. lane.
ruer; se ~ rush, dash.
rugissement, s. m. roar.
ruine, s. f. ruin; wreck.
ruiner, v.a. ruin, destroy.
ruisseau, s. m. stream, brook; gutter.
ruisseler, v.n. stream, run, flow.
rumeur, s. f. noise; rumour.
ruminer, v. a. & n. ruminate, chew (the cud).
rupture, s. f. rupture.
ruse, s. f. craft, cunning.
rusé, adj. cunning, sly.
russe (R.), adj. & s. m. f. Russian.
russien, -enne (R.), adj. & s. m. f. Russian.
rustique, adj. rustic, rural.
rythme, s. m. rhythm.
rythmique, adj. rhytmical.

S

s' see se.
sa, adj. poss. his, her, its.
sable, s. m. sand.
sablonneux, -euse, adj. sandy.
sabre, s. m. sabre.
sac, s. m. bag, sack; ~ *a main* handbag; ~ *de couchage* sleeping-bag.
saccager, v. a. plunder.
sacré, adj. sacred, holy.
sacrement, s. m. sacrament.
sacrifice, s.m. sacrifice.
sacrifier, v.a. sacrifice.
sacristain, s.m. sexton.
sage, adj. wise, well-behaved.
sagesse, s. f. wisdom.
saignant, adj. bleeding; underdone.
saigner, v. a. & n. bleed.
saillant, adj. projecting.
saillir, v. n. stand out, project.
sain, adj. sound; ~ *et sauf* safe and sound.
saint, -e, adj. holy, sacred; — s. m. f. saint.
saisir, v.a. seize.
saison, s. f. season.
salade, s. f. salad.
salaire, s. m. wages (pl.), pay, salary.
sale, adj. dirty, filthy.
saler, v. a. salt.
saleté, s. f. dirt.
salière, s. f. salt-cellar.
salir, v. a. soil, dirty.
salle, s. f. hall; assembly room; house; ~ *d'attente* waiting-room; ~ *de classe* schoolroom; ~ *(de cours)* auditorium; ~ *familiale,* ~ *de séjour* living-room.
salon, s. m. drawing-room; saloon; *petit* ~ sitting-room.
saluer, v. a. & n. bow to; greet.

salut, *s. m.* salvation; bow, greeting.

samedi, *s. m.* Saturday.

sanatorium, *s. m.* sanatorium.

sanction, *s. f.* sanction.

sanctuaire, *s. m.* sanctuary.

sandale, *s. f.* sandal.

sang, *s. m.* blood.

sanglier, *s. m.* wild boar.

sanitaire, *adj.* sanitary.

sans, *prep.* without.

santé, *s. f.* health.

sapin, *s. m.* fir(-tree).

sarcasme, *s. m.* sarcasm.

sarcastique, *adj.* sarcastic.

sardine, *s. f.* sardine.

satellite, *s. m.* satellite.

satire, *s. f.* satire.

satisfaction, *s. f.* satisfaction.

savoir*, *v. n.* know, be aware; be trained in; understand; be able to; — *s. m.* knowledge, learning.

savon, *s. m.* soap.

savourer, *v. a.* taste, relish.

savoureux, -euse, *adj.* savoury, tasty.

scandale, *s. m.* scandal.

scaphandre autonome, *s. m.* skin diver.

scaphandrier, *s. m.* diver.

scarabée, *s. m.* beetle.

sceau, *s. m.* seal.

sceller, *v. a.* seal; fix.

scénario, *s. m.* scenario.

scène, *s. f.* scène; scenery; *fig.* stage; *mettre en ~* produce (a play).

sceptre, *s. m.* sceptre.

scie, *s. f.* saw.

satisfaire, *v. a. & n.* satisfy, please.

satisfaisant, *adj.* satisfactory.

satisfait, *adj.* satisfied.

sauce, *s. f.* sauce.

saucisse, *s. f.* sausage.

sauf, sauve, *adj.* safe; — *prep.* except, save.

saumon, *s. m.* salmon.

saut, *s. m.* jump, leap.

sauter, *v. n.* leap, jump; spring; *faire ~* blow up.

sauvage, *adj.* savage, wild.

sauver, *v. a.* save, rescue; *se ~* run away.

sauveur, *s. m.* Saviour.

savant, -e, *adj.* learned, clever; expert; — *s. m. f.* scholar.

saveur, *s. f.* savour, taste.

science, *s. f.* science, knowledge; *homme de ~* scientist.

scientifique, *adj.* scientific.

scier, *v. a.* saw.

scolaire, *adj.* school; *année ~* school year.

scooter, *s. m.* motorscooter.

scrupule, *s. m.* scruple.

sculpter, *v. a.* carve, sculpture.

sculpteur, *s. m.* sculptor.

sculpture, *s. f.* sculpture.

se, s' *pron.* himself, herself, itself; each other.

séance, *s. f.* sitting, meeting.

seau, *s. m.* pail.

sec, sèche, *adj.* dry dried up.

sécher, *v. a. & n.* dry

(up).

sécheresse, s. f. dryness.

second, adj. second.

secondaire, adj. secondary.

seconde, s. f. second.

seconder, v. a. back.

secouer, v. a. shake.

secourir, v. a. help.

secours, s. m. help, succour, aid; au ~ help!

secousse, s. f. shake, jolt, jerk.

secret, -ète, adj. & s. m. secret.

secrétaire, s. m. f. secretary; — s. m. writing-desk.

secrétariat, s. m. secretariate.

secteur, s. m. sector, section; ~ (de courant) mains.

section, s. f. section

sécurité, s. f. security.

sédatif, -ive, adj. & s.m. sedative.

sédiment, s. m. sediment.

séduire, v. a. seduce.

seigle, s. m. rye.

seigneur, s.m. lord, squire.

seize, adj. & s. m. sixteen; sixteenth.

seizième, adj. sixteenth.

séjour, s. m. stay, visit; (place of) residence.

séjourner, v.n. stay, sojourn.

sel, s. m. salt.

selle, s. f. saddle.

selon, prep. according to; after.

semaine, s. f. week.

semblable, adj. (a)like.

semblant, s. m. semblance; appearance.

sembler, v. n. appear, look, seem.

semelle, s. f. sole (footwear).

semer, v. a. sow.

semestre, s. m. half year; semester.

séminaire, s. m. seminary.

sénat, s. m. senate.

sénateur, s. m. senator.

sens, s. m. sense; judgement, opinion; direction.

sensation, s. f. feeling; sensation.

sensé, adj. sensible, reasonable.

sensibilité, s. f. sensibility, feeling.

sensible, adj. sensible, perceptible; sensitive.

sentence, s. f. sentence.

senteur, s. f. scent, smell.

sentier, s. m. path.

sentiment, s. m. feeling, sense, sentiment.

sentimental, adj. sentimental.

sentinelle, s. f. sentry, sentinel.

sentir*, v. a. feel, perceive; experience; smell; se ~ feel.

séparation, s. f. separation.

séparer, v. a. separate, divide; se ~ part.

sept, adj. & s. m. seven; seventh.

septembre, s. m. September.

septième, adj. seventh.

sérénade, s. f. serenade.

sérénité, s. f. serenity.

sergent, *s. m.* sergeant.

série, *s. f.* series.

sérieux, -euse, *adj.* grave, serious.

serin, -e, *s. m. f.* canary.

seringue, *s. f.* syringe.

serment, *s. m.* oath.

sermon, *s. m.* sermon.

serpent, *s. m.* snake, serpent.

serpenter, *v. n.* wind, meander.

serre, *s. f.* claw; hot-house.

serré, *adj.* tight, close, serried.

serrer, *v. a.* press, crush, jam, tighten.

serre-tête, *s. m.* crash-helmet, headband.

serrure, *s. f.* lock.

serrurier, *s. m.* locksmith.

servante, *s. f.* servant.

service, *s. m.* service, duty; favour; set; *être de* ~ be on duty; *à votre* ~ at your disposal.

serviette, *s. f.* napkin; towel; briefcase.

servir*, *v. a. & n.* serve; be in the service of; ~ *à* be used for; *ne se* ~ *à rien* be of no use; *Mme est servie* dinner is ready; *se* ~ use, make use of, help oneself.

serviteur, *s. m.* servant.

servitude, *s. f.* servitude.

ses, *adj. poss.* his, her, its; one's.

session, *s. f.* session.

seuil, *s. m.* threshold.

seul, *adj.* alone, single, sole, only.

sévère, *adj.* severe, hard.

sévir, *v. n.* punish; rage.

sexe, *s. m.* sex.

sexuel, -elle, *adj.* sexual.

shampooing, *s. m.* shampoo.

si, *conj.* if, whether; — *adv.* so, so much, such.

siècle, *s. m.* century.

siège, *s. m.* seat.

sien, -enne, *poss. adj.* his, hers; its; one's.

siffler, *v. n.* whistle, hiss.

sifflet, *s. m.* whistle.

signal, *s. m.* signal; ~ *d'alarme* communication-cord.

signaler, *v. a.* signal.

signalisation, *s. f.* signals *(pl.); feux de* ~ traffic-lights.

signature, *s. f.* signature.

signe, *s. m.* sign.

signer, *v. a. & n.* sign.

significatif, -ive, *adj.* significant.

signification, *s. f.* signification; meaning.

signifier, *v. a.* signify.

silence, *s. m.* silence.

silencieux, -euse, *adj.* silent.

silhouette, *s. f.* outline, silhouette.

sillon, *s. m.* furrow.

simple, *adj.* simple.

simplicité, *s. f.* simplicity.

simplifier, *v. a.* simplify.

simultané, *adj.* simultaneous.

sincère, *adj.* sincere.

sincérité, *s. f.* sincerity.

singe, *s. m.* monkey.

singulier, -ère, *adj.* singular, strange.

sinon, *conj.* (or) else,

otherwise.

sire, *s. m.* sir, lord.

sirène, *s. f.* siren; hooter, fog-horn.

site, *s. m.* site, place.

sitôt, *adv.* as soon; ~ *que* as soon as; ~ ... ~ no sooner... than.

situation, *s. f.* situation; state; office, position.

situer, *v. a.* place, locate.

six, *adj. & s. m.* six; sixth.

sixième, *adj.* sixth.

ski, *s. m.* ski; *faire du* ~ ski.

skieur, *s. m.* skier, ski-runner.

smoking, *s. m.* dinner-jacket.

sobre, *adj.* sober.

social, *adj.* social.

socialisme, *s. m.* socialism.

socialiste, *adj. & s. m. f.* socialist.

société, *s. f.* society; company; ~ *anonyme* limited liability company.

sœur, *s. f.* sister.

soi, *pron.* oneself; himself, herself; itself.

soi-disant, *adj.* so-called.

soie, *s. f.* silk.

soif, *s. f.* thirst; *avoir* ~ be thirsty.

soigner, *v. a.* take care of, look after.

soigneux, -euse, *adj.* careful.

soin, *s. m.* care; *prendre* ~ *de* take care of; *aux bons* ~s *de* c/o.

soir, *s. m.* evening.

soirée, *s. f.* evening (par-

ty).

soit, *conj.* say; suppose; either ... or; ~ *que* whether.

soixante, *adj. & s. m.* sixty.

soixante-dix, *adj. & s. m.* seventy.

sol, *s. m.* soil; ground.

soldat, *s. m.* soldier.

soleil, *s. m.* sun; *il fait du* ~ the sun is shining.

solennel, -elle, *adj.* solemn.

solennité, *s. f.* solemnity.

solidarité, *s. f.* solidarity.

solide, *adj.* solid.

solidité, *s. f.* solidity.

solitaire, *adj.* solitary.

solitude, *s. f.* solitude.

solliciter, *v. a.* solicit, entreat.

sollicitude, *s. f.* care.

soluble, *adj.* soluble.

solution, *s. f.* solution.

sombre, *adj.* dark; dim.

sombrer, *v. n.* founder, sink.

sommaire, *adj. & s. m.* summary.

somme, *s. f.* sum, amount.

sommeil, *s. m.* sleep; *avoir* ~ be sleepy.

sommeiller, *v. n.* slumber.

sommer, *v. a.* summon.

sommet, *s. m.* top, summit.

sommier, *s. m.* spring mattress.

somnifère, *s. m.* sleeping-pill.

somnolent, *adj.* sleepy.

son¹, sa, *adj. poss. (pl.*

ses) his, her, its; one's.

son², *s. m.* sound.

songe, *s. m.* dream.

songer, *v. n.* dream.

sonner, *v. a.* & *n.* ring, sound; *on sonne (à la porte)* there is a ring at the door.

sonnette, *s. f.* bell.

sonore, *adj.* sonorous.

sorcier, *s. m.* sorcerer, wizard.

sorcière, *s. f.* witch, sorceress.

sornette, *s. f.* nonsense.

sort, *s. m.* fate, lot.

sorte, *s. f.* sort, kind.

sortie, *s. f.* going out; way out, exit; ~ *secours* emergency exit.

sortir*, *v. n.* go out, walk out, leave; *ne pas* ~ keep indoors; *v. a.* take out, bring out.

sot, sotte, *adj.* foolish, silly.

sottise, *s. f.* foolishness, nonsense.

sou, *s. m.* sou, copper, penny.

souci, *s. m.* care, concern.

soucier: se ~ *de* care for.

soucieux, -euse, *adj.* full of care, anxious.

soucoupe, *s. f.* saucer.

soudain, *adj.* sudden; — *adv.* suddenly.

soude, *s. f.* soda *(chemical)*.

souffle, *s. m.* breath.

souffler, *v. a.* & *n.* breathe; blow (out).

soufflet, *s. m.* box (on the ear); bellows *(pl.)*.

souffrance, *s. f.* pain, suffering.

souffrir*, *v. a.* & *n.* suffer, bear.

souhaiter, *v. a.* desire.

soulever, *v. a.* lift, raise; *se* ~ rise (in rebellion).

soulier, *s. m.* shoe.

souligner, *v. a.* underline.

soumettre, *v. a.* submit, subdue; *se* ~ submit.

soumission, *s. f.* submission.

soupçon, *s. m.* suspicion.

soupçonner, *v. a.* suspect.

soupe, *s. f.* soup.

souper, *s. m.* supper; — *v. n.* have supper.

soupir, *s. m.* sigh.

soupirer, *v. n.* sigh; ~ *après* long for.

souple, *adj.* supple, flexible.

source, *s. f.* source, spring.

sourcil, *s. m.* eyebrow.

sourd, *adj.* deaf.

sourd-muet, sourde-muette, *adj.* & *s. m. f.* deaf and dumb (person).

sourire, *v. n.* smile.

souris, *s. f.* mouse.

sous, *prep.* under; beneath; before.

souscripteur, *s. m.* subscriber.

souscription, *s. f.* subscription.

souscrire, *v. a.* & *n.* sign, subscribe (to).

sousdéveloppé, *adj.* under-developed.

sous-marin, *s. m.* submarine.

soussigné, -e, *adj.* & *s. m. f.* undersigned.

sous-sol, *s. m.* basement.

sous-titre, *s. m.* subtitle, caption.

soustraction, *s. f.* subtraction.

soustraire, *v. a.* take away; subtract.

soutenir, *v. a.* support, sustain, maintain.

souterrain, *adj.* underground; — *s. m.* subway.

soutien, *s. m.* support.

soutien-gorge, *s. m.* bra.

souvenir*, *s. m.* remembrance; souvenir; memory; — *v. reflex.* se ~ remember.

souvent, *adv.* often.

souverain, -e, *s. m. f.* sovereign.

spatial, *adj. vaisseau* ~, *véhicule* ~ space-craft, space-vehicle.

speaker, *s. m.* announcer.

speakerine, *s. f.* lady announcer.

spécial, *adj.* special.

spécialement, *adv.* specially, particularly.

spécialiser, *v. a.* specialize.

spécialiste, *s. m. f.* specialist.

spécialité, *s. f.* special(i)ty.

spécifier, *v. a.* specify.

spécifique, *adj.* specific.

spectacle, *s. m.* spectacle, sight.

spectateur, -trice, *s. m. f.* spectator, spectatress, onlooker; bystander.

spéculation, *s. f.* speculation.

spéculer, *v. n.* speculate.

sphère, *s. f.* sphere.

spirale, *adj.* spiral.

spirituel, -elle, *adj.* spiritual; witty.

splendeur, *s. f.* splendour.

splendide, *adj.* splendid.

spontané, *adj.* spontaneous.

sport, *s. m.* sport.

sportif, -ive, *adj.* sporting; sportsmanlike.

squelette, *s. m.* skeleton.

stade, *s. m.* stadium; *fig.* stage.

stalle, *s. f.* stall; box.

station, *s. f.* standing; stay; station, stop; ~ *balnéaire* watering-place, spa.

stationnement, *s. m.* stationing; parking; ~ *interdit* no parking.

stationner, *v. n.* stop; park.

station-service, *s. f.* service-station.

statistique, *s. f.* statistics; — *adj.* statistical.

statue, *s. f.* statue.

statut, *s. m.* statute.

sténographie, *s. f.* shorthand.

stérile, *adj.* sterile.

stimuler, *v. a.* stimulate.

stipuler, *v. a.* stipulate.

store, *s. m.* (Venetian) blind.

strabisme, *s. m.* squint(ing).

stratégie, *s. f.* strategy.

structure, *s. f.* structure.

studieux, -euse, *adj.* studious.

stupéfier, *v. a.* stupefy.

stupide, *adj.* stupid, dull.

stupidité, *s. f.* stupidity.

style, *s. m.* style.

stylo, *s.m.* ~ *à bille* ball(-point) pen.

stylo(graphe), *s. m.* fountain-pen.

suave, *adj.* soft, gentle.

subjonctif, *s.m.* subjunctive.

subjuguer, *v.a.* subjugate, overcome.

submerger, *v. a.* submerge, flood.

subordonné, *adj.* subordinate.

subordonner, *v. a.* subordinate.

subséquent, *adj.* subsequent.

subsistance, *s. f.* subsistence.

subsister, *v. n.* subsist.

substance, *s. f.* substance.

substantiel, **-elle,** *adj.* substantial.

substantif, *s.m.* substantive.

substituer, *v.a.* substitute.

substitution, *s. f.* substitution.

subtil, *adj.* subtle.

subvention, *s. f.* subvention, subsidy.

succéder, *v. n.* succeed (*à* to), follow; *se* ~ follow one another.

succès, *s. m.* success; result.

successif, **-ive,** *adj.* successive.

succession, *s. f.* succession.

sucer, *v. a.* suck (in).

sucre, *s. m.* sugar.

sucré, *adj.* sweet(ened).

sud, *adj. & s. m.* south; *du* ~ southern; *au* ~ southward.

sud-est, *adj. & s.m.* south-east.

sud-ouest, *adj. & s. m.* south-west.

suédois, **-e, (S.),** *adj.* Swedish; — *s. m. f.* Swede; Swedish (language).

suer, *v. n. & a.* sweat.

sueur, *s. f.* sweat.

suffire*, *v.n.* be sufficient, be enough.

suffisamment, *adv.* sufficiently, enough.

suffisant, *adj.* sufficient, enough; conceited.

suffoquer, *v.a. & n.* suffocate, choke.

suggérer, *v.a.* suggest, propose.

suggestion, *s. f.* suggestion, hint.

suicide, *s. m.* suicide.

suisse (S.), *adj. & s. m. (f.* Suissesse) Swiss.

suite, *s. f.* retinue; suite, sequence, result; *à la* ~ after; *tout de* ~ at once, directly; *par* ~ consequently; *par* ~ *de* due to.

suivant, *adj.* following, next; — *prep.* according to.

suivre*, *v.a. & n.* follow; *comme suit* as follows; *ce qui suit* the following.

sujet, **-ette,** *s. m. f.* subject; *s. m.* subject.

superficie, *s. f.* surface, area.

superficiel, **-elle,** *adj.* superficial.

superflu, *adj.* superfluous.

supérieur, *adj.* superior, upper.

supériorité, *s. f.* superiority.

supermarché, *s. m.* supermarket.

supersonique, *adj.* supersonic.

superstitieux, -euse, *adj.* superstitious.

superstition, *s. f.* superstition.

suppléer, *v.a.* supply; substitute, do duty for; *v. n.* make up for.

supplément, *s. m.* supplement; extra charge; excess.

supplémentaire, *adj.* supplementary, extra.

suppliant, -e, *adj.* suppliant; — *s. m. f.* supplicant.

supplier, *v.a.* beseech.

support, *s.m.* prop; support.

supporter, *v.a.* bear, support.

supposer, *v. a.* suppose.

supposition, *s. f.* supposition, conjecture.

suppression, *s. f.* suppression.

supprimer, *v. a.* suppress, abolish, do away with.

suprême, *adj.* supreme.

sur, *prep.* on; over; concerning.

sûr, *adj.* certain, sure; secure, safe; *pour ~!* to be sure!

surcharger, *v.a. & n.* overload; weigh down.

sûrement, *adv.* surely, certainly.

sûreté, *s. f.* safety; security.

surface, *s.f.* surface.

surgir, *v. n.* arise, spring up, emerge.

surmonter, *v.a.* surmount, overcome.

surnaturel, -elle, *adj.* supernatural.

surpasser, *v. a.* surpass, outdo.

surpeuplé, *adj.* overcrowded.

surplus, *s.m.* surplus, excess.

surprendre, *v. a.* surprise.

surprise, *s.f.* surprise.

surseoir*, *v.n. & a.* postpone, delay, put off.

surtaxe, *s. f.* surtax.

surtout, *s. m.* overcoat.

surveillance, *s. f.* supervision.

surveiller, *v.a.* supervise.

survenir, *v. a.* arrive unexpectedly; happen, occur.

survivant, -e, *s.m.f.* survivor.

survivre, *v.n.* survive, outlive.

susceptible, *adj.* susceptible.

suspect, *adj.* suspicious, suspect.

suspendre, *v. a.* hang up; suspend.

suspension, *s. f.* suspension.

svelte, *adj.* slender, slim.

syllabe, *s. f.* syllable.

symbole, *s. m.* symbol.

symétrie, *s. f.* symmetry.

symétrique, *adj.* symmetrical.

sympathie, *s. f.* sympathy.

symphonie, *s. f.* symphony.

symptome, *s. m.* symptom.

synagogue, *s. f.* synagogue.

syndical, *adj.* trade.

syndicat, *s. m.* syndicate; trade-union; ~ *d'initiative* tourist information office.

synthétique, *adj.* synthetic(al).

systématique, *adj.* systematic.

système, *s. m.* system.

T

tabac, *s. m.* tobacco; *bureau de* ~ tobacconist's (shop).

table, *s. f.* table; board; food; ~ *des matières,* table of contents.

tableau, *s. m.* picture; scene; board, panel.

tablette, *s. f.* tablet.

tablier, *s. m.* apron; dash-board.

tabouret, *s. m.* stool.

tache, *s. f.* spot, stain; *sans* ~ spotless.

tâche, *s. f.* task, job.

tacher, *v. a.* spot, stain.

tâcher, *v. n.* try.

tact, *s. m.* touch.

tactique, *s. f.* tactics.

taille, *s. f.* cut; height, stature, size; waist.

tailler, *v. a.* hew, trim; cut.

tailleur, *s. m.* tailor.

taire*, *v. a.* be silent about, conceal; *se* ~ be quiet.

talent, *s. m.* talent, attainment(s).

talon, *s. m.* heel; counterfoil.

talus, *s. m.* slope, bank.

tambour, *s. m.* drum.

tamis, *s. m.* sieve.

tamiser, *v. a.* sift, sieve.

tampon, *s. m.* plug; tampon.

tamponner, *v. a.* plug.

tandis que, *conj.* whereas, while.

tangible, *adj.* tangible.

tant, *adv.* so much, so many, such, so,

tante, *s. f.* aunt.

tantôt, *adv.* shortly, by and by; ~ ... ~ now ... now.

tapage, *s. m.* noise, fuss.

taper, *v. a. & n.* tap, strike, knock; type.

tapis, *s. m.* carpet, rug.

tapisser, *v. a.* upholster.

tapisserie, *s. f.* tapestry.

tapissier, *s. m.* upholsterer.

tard, *adv.* late.

tarder, *v. n.* delay, put off; be long.

tardif, -ive, *adj.* late.

tarif, *s. m.* tariff, rate; price-list; fare.

tarte, *s. f.* tart.

tas, *s. m.* heap, pile; mass; crowd.

tasse, *s. f.* cup.

tâter, *v. a. & n.* feel, taste, handle.

tâtonner, *v. n.* grope.

taureau, *s. m.* bull.

taux, *s. m.* price, rate (of exchange); tax.

taverne, s. f. tavern.

taxe, s. f. tax.

taxer, v. a. tax, rate.

taxi, s. m. taxi; station de ~s taxi-rank.

tchèque (T.), adj. & s. m. f. Czech.

te, pron. you; to you.

technicien, -enne, s. m. f. technician.

technique, adj. technical; s. f. technique, technics.

technologie, s. f. technology.

teindre*, v.a. dye, stain.

teint, s. m. complexion; dye.

teinte, s. f. tint, shade.

teinter, v. a. tint.

teinture, s. f. dye; tincture.

teinturerie, s.f. dye-works, dyer.

tel, telle, adj. such, like, similar.

télécommunication, s.f. telecommunication.

téléférique, s.m. rope-way.

télégramme, s.m. telegram, wire.

télégraphe, s.m. telegraph.

télégraphie, s.f. telegraphy.

télégraphier, v.a. & n. wire.

télégraphique, adj. telegraphic.

télémètre, s.m. range-finder.

téléphone, s.m. telephone.

télescope, s. m. telescope.

téléspectateur, -trice, s. m. f. (tele)viewer.

téléviser, v. a. televise, telecast.

téléviseur, s.m. television-set.

télévison, s. f. television.

télex, s. m. telex.

tellement, adv. so (much).

témoigner, v.a. & n. testify; give evidence.

témoin, s.m. witness; testimony.

tempe, s.f. temple (forehead).

tempérament, s. m. temper(ament), constitution.,

température, s.f. temperature.

tempête, s. f. storm.

temple, s. m. temple, church; chapel; lodge.

temporel, -elle, adj. temporal, transient.

temps[1], s. m. time; opportunity; à ~ in time; pendant ce ~ l in the meantime; en ~ voulu in due time; combien de ~? how long?; la plupart du ~ mostly; de ~ en ~ at times.

temps[2], s.m. weather; prévisions du ~ weather-forecast.

tenaille, s.f. pincers, pliers, tongs (pl.).

tendance, s.f. tendency, trend.

tendon, s.m. tendon, sinew.

tendre[1] adj. tender, soft.

tendre[2], v.a. stretch; strain; bend; hang.

tendresse, s. f. tenderness.

tendu, adj. tense, taut.

ténébreux, -euse, adj.

dark, gloomy, dismal.

tenir*, *v. a. & n.* hold; get hold of; hold on; take, contain; keep; **se ~** stay; remain.

tennis, *s. m.* tennis.

tension, *s.f.* tension.

tentation, *s. f.* temptation.

tentative, *s.f.* attempt.

tente, *s. f.* tent.

tenter, *v.a.* attempt; try; tempt.

ténu, *adj.* thin, slender.

tenue, *s. f.* holding; session; behaviour.

terme, *s. m.* term; expression; goal, aim.

terminer, *v. a.* terminate, end, close; **se ~** (come to an) end.

terminus, *s. m.* terminus.

terne, *adj.* dull, dim.

terrain, *s. m.* soil, earth; site; ground; **~ de jeux** sports-ground.

terrasse, *s.f.* terrace.

terre, *s.f.* earth, land.

terreur, *s.f.* fear.

terrible, *adj.* terrible.

terrifier, *v.a.* terrify, frighten.

territoire, *s. m.* territory.

testament, *s.m.* will, testament.

tête, *s. f.* head.

têtu, *adj.* stubborn.

texte, *s.m.* text; type.

textile, *s.m.* textile.

textuel, **-elle**, *adj.* textual.

texture, *s. f.* texture.

thé, *s. m.* tea.

théâtral, *adj.* theatrical.

théâtre, *s.m.* theatre, stage; drama; *pièce de* **~** play.

théière, *s. f.* tea-pot.

thème, *s. m.* theme, topic; prose.

théologie, *s. f.* theology.

théologique, *adj.* theological.

théorie, *s. f.* theory.

théorique, *adj.* theoretic, theoretical.

thermal, *adj.* thermal.

thermomètre, *s. m.* thermometer.

thermos, *s. m.* thermos.

thèse, *s. f.* thesis.

thon, *s. m.* tunny.

tien, **-enne**, *poss. adj.* yours.

tiers, **tierce**, *adj.* third; — *s.m.* third party.

tige, *s. f.* stem, stalk.

tigre, *s. m.* tiger.

tigresse, *s. f.* tigress.

timbre, *s. m.* bell; sound; (postage-)stamp.

timbre-poste, *s. m.* postage-stamp.

timide, *adj.* timid, shy.

timidité, *s. f.* timidity.

tir, *s.m.* shooting.

tirage, *s.f.* draught, pull(ing); impression; issue.

tire-bouchon *s. m.* corkscrew.

tirer, *v. a. & n.* draw, pull, drag; extract; derive; fire, shoot; print.

tiroir, *s.m.* drawer.

tison, *s.m.* brand.

tisonnier, *s.m.* poker.

tisser, *v.a.* weave.

tisserand, *s.m.* weaver.

tissu, *s. m.* texture, fabric; tissue.

titre, *s. m.* title; heading;

right.

titrer, *v.a.* give a title to.

toast, *s. m.* toast.

toi, *pron.* you.

toile, *s. f.* linen; cloth.

toilette, *s.f.* dress, clothes *(pl.);* dressing-table; *faire sa ~* dress; *cabinet de ~* dressing-room.

toison, *s. f.* fleece.

toit, *s. m.* roof.

tolérance, *s. f.* tolerance, toleration.

tolérer, *v.a.* tolerate, bear.

tomate, *s.f.* tomato.

tombe, *s. f.* tomb, grave.

tombeau, *s. m.* tomb.

tombée, *s.f.* fall.

tomber, *v.n.* fall, fall down; tumble; decay; *~ sur* meet, run into; *faire ~* push down; *laisser ~* drop.

tome, *s. m.* volume.

ton¹, ta, *poss. adj. (pl. tes)* your.

ton², *s. m.* tone; colour; manner.

tondeuse, *s.f.* lawn-mower.

tondre, *v.a.* shear, clip, mow.

tonnage, *s. m.* tonnage.

tonne, *s. f.* barrel, tun; ton.

tonneau, *s.m.* barrel.

tonner, *v.n.* thunder.

tonnerre, *s.m.* thunder-(bolt).

toqué, *adj.* crazy.

torche, *s. f.* torch.

torcher, *v.a.* wipe, rub.

torchon, *s.m.* duster; dish-cloth.

tordre, *v. a.* twist, wring (out).

torpille, *s. f.* torpedo.

torrent, *s. m.* torrent.

tort, *s. m.* wrong, harm, injury; *avoir ~* be wrong.

tortue, *s. f.* tortoise.

torture, *s. f.* torture.

torturer, *v. a.* torture.

tôt, *adv.* soon, quickly; early.

total, *adj.* total, whole.

totalement, *adv.* totally, entirely.

touchant, *prep.* about.

touche, *s. f.* touch; key; hit.

toucher, *v. n. & a.* touch; feel; strike, hit; concern; — *s. m.* touch; feeling.

touffe, *s.f.* tuft.

toujours, *adv.* always, ever; still.

toupet, *s. m.* tuft, lock.

tour¹, *s.f.* tower.

tour², *s.m.* turn; tour, trip; feat, trick; (turning-)lathe; revolution; *~ à ~* in turns; *à son ~* in turn; *faire le ~ de* go round.

tourelle, *s. f.* turret.

tourisme, *s. m.* tourism; touring; *faire du ~ à pied* hike.

touriste, *s. m. f.* tourist, hiker.

tourment, *s. m.* torment, torture.

tourmenter, *v. a.* torment; *se ~* worry.

tournant, *adj.* turning; — *s. m.* turn(ing).

tourné, *adj.* turned; sour.

tournée, *s. f.* tour, walk;

circuit.

tourner, v. a. turn, twist, wind; turn round; v. n. turn, revolve; turn out; turn sour.

tournevis, s.m. screw-driver.

tournoi, s.m. tournament.

tournure, s.f. shape, figure; turn; cast; appearance.

tous see **tout.**

tousser, v.n. cough.

tout, -e, adj. (pl. **tous, toutes)** all, every, any, whole, full; ~ le monde everybody; ~ son possible one's utmost; à ~e force at any cost; — adv. wholly, entirely; ~ coup suddenly; ~ fait thoroughly; ~ de suite directly; ~ à l'heure just now; ~ au moins at least; pas du ~ not at all.

toutefois, adv. yet, nevertheless, however.

tout-puissant, adj. almighty.

toux, s. f. cough.

tracas, s. m. bustle, stir; worry.

tracasser, v. n. & a. worry, bother; fuss; se ~ worry.

trace, s. f. trace, track; footprint.

tracer, v. a. trace, draw; lay out.

tracteur, s. m. tractor.

traction, s.f. traction, pull.

tradition, s. f. tradition.

traditionnel, -elle, adj. traditional.

traducteur, -trice, s. m. f. translator.

traduction, s. f. translation.

traduire*, v. a. translate.

trafic, s. m. traffic; trade, commerce.

trafiquer, v.n. traffic; trade, deal.

tragédie, s. f. tragedy.

tragédien, -enne, s. m. f. tragedien.

tragique, adj. tragic.

trahir, v. a. betray; deceive, mislead.

trahison, s. f. treason, treachery.

train, s.m. pace, rate; train; ~ couloir corridor-train; ~ direct through train; ~ de marchandises goods train.

traîne, s.f. train (of a dress).

traîneau, s. m. sledge.

traîner, v.a. drag, draw; lead (to); delay; v.n. drag; lie about; lag behind.

train-poste, s.m mail-train.

traire*, v.a. milk.

trait, s.m. arrow; dart; flash; line; trait, feature.

traite, s.f. journey; stretch; export; draft, bill.

traité, s. m. treaty.

traitement, s. m. treatment; usage; reception; salary.

traiter, v.a. treat, use,

deal with; call; entertain.

traître, *s. m.* traitor; — *adj.* treacherous.

trajet, *s.m.* passage, journey, course, crossing.

tram, *s.m.* tram(-car).

trammer, *v. a.* weave; plot; devise.

tramway, *s. m.* tram.

tranchant, *adj.* sharp, keen.

tranche, *s. f.* slice, chop, steak.

trancher, *v.a. & n.* cut; cut off; carve; break off.

tranquille, *adj.* quiet, calm; *soyez ~!* don't worry!

tranquilliser, *v. a.* soothe, calm; *se ~* keep calm.

transaction, *s. f.* compromise, transaction.

transalpin, *adj.* transalpine.

transatlantique, *adj.* transatlantic; — *s. f.* deck-chair.

transfert, *s. m.* transfer.

transformation, *s. f.* transformation, change.

transformer, *v.a.* transform, convert.

transfusion, *s.f.* transfusion.

transistor, *s. m.* transistor.

transit, *s.m.* transit.

transition, *s.f.* transition.

transmettre, *v. a.* transmit; forward; pass on.

transmission, *s. f.* transmission.

transparent, *adj.* transparent.

transpiration, *s.f.* perspiration.

transpirer, *v. n.* perspire.

transport, *s. m.* transport, conveyance; *enterprise de ~* forwarding agency.

transporter, *v.a.* transport, convey; transfer; enrapture.

trappe, *s. f.* trap; trap-door.

travail, *s. m.* (*pl.* **-aux**) work, job, employment; task; piece of work; workmanship; *petits travaux* odd jobs; *sans ~* unemployed.

travailler, *v.n. & a.* work, labour; take pains.

travailleur, -euse, *s. m. f.* worker, workman, workwoman.

travers, *s. m.* breadth; *à ~* across, through; *au ~ de* through; *en ~* across.

traverse, *s.f.* traverse; obstacle; crossing.

traversée, *s.f.* crossing, passage.

traverser, *v. a.* traverse, cross, go through; run through.

trayeuse, *s. f.* milking-machine.

trébucher, *v. n.* stumble; turn the scale.

tréfle, *s. m.* clover; club (*cards*).

treille, *s. f.* vine arbour.

treize, *adj. & s.m.* thirteen.

tremblant, *adj.* tembling,

shaky.

tremblement, *s. m.* trembling, shaking; ~ *de terre* earthquake.

trembler, *v. n.* tremble, shake.

tremper, *v. a.* soak, wet; dip; *il est tout trempé* he is wet through.

tremplin, *s.m.* springboard.

trentaine, *s.m.* thirty.

trente, *adj. & s. m.* thirty; thirtieth.

très, *adv.* very, most, very much; ~ *bien* very well; all right.

trésor, *s. m.* treasure.

trésorie, *s. f.* treasury.

trésorier, *s. m.* treasurer.

tresse, *s. f.* plait, tress, braid.

trêve, *s. f.* truce, rest; *faire* ~ stop, cease.

triangle, *s. m.* triangle.

tribu, *s. f.* tribe.

tribunal, *s. m.* tribunal, law-court.

tribune, *s.f.* tribune, platform; grand-stand.

tributaire, *adj.* tributary.

tricher, *v. n. & a.* cheat; trick (s.o. out of).

tricot, *s.m.* (knitted) jersey.

tricoter, *v. a. & n.* knit.

triomphant, *adj.* triumphant.

triomphe, *s. m.* triumph.

triompher, *v. n.* triumph.

triple, *adj.* triple.

tripot, *s.m.* gambling-den.

triste, *adj.* sad.

tristesse, *s. f.* sadness.

trivial, *adj.* trivial.

trois, *adj. & s. m.* three; third.

troisième, *adj. & s. m.* third.

trolley, *s.m.* trolley (-pole).

trolleybus, *s. m.* trolleybus.

trompe, *s.f.* trumpet, horn.

tromper, *v. a.* deceive, cheat, take in; *se* ~ mistake, be mistaken; be wrong; *se* ~ *de train* take the wrong train.

trompette, *s. f.* trumpet; trumpeter.

tronc, *s. m.* trunk; stock; collecting box.

trône, *s.m.* throne.

trop, *adv.* too; too much.

trophée, *s. m.* trophy.

tropical, *adj.* tropical.

tropique, *s. m.* tropic.

trot, *s. m.* trot.

trotter, *v. n.* trot.

trottoir, *s. m.* pavement; footway.

trou, *s.m.* hole; gap; opening.

trouble, *s. m.* disorder; confusion; misunderstanding; dispute; — *adj.* troubled; muddy.

troubler, *v.a.* stir up; disturb; make muddy; muddle; confuse, perplex; upset; trouble.

troué, *s. f.* opening, gap.

trouer, *v. a.* make a hole in; pierce; bore.

troupe, *s. f.* troop, band.

troupeau, *s.m.* herd, drove; flock.

trouvaille, *s. f.* find(ing).

trouver, *v. a.* find, discover; find out; think;

contrive; se ~ be, be found to be, prove; turn out, happen; *je me trouvais là* I happened to be there.

truite, *s. f.* trout.

trust, *s. m.* trust.

T.S.F., *s. f.* (=*télégraphie sans fil*) wireless (set).

tu, toi, *pron.* you.

tube, *s. m.* tube; pipe; ~ *de télévision* TV tube.

tuberculose, *s. f.* tuberculosis.

tuer, *v. a.* kill; slay.

tuile, *s. f.* tile.

tumeur, *s. f.* tumour.

tunnel, *s. m.* tunnel.

turbine, *s. f.* turbine.

turbopropulseur, *s. m.* turbo-prop aircraft.

turboréacteur, *s.m.* turbo-jet engine.

turc, turque (T.), *adj.* Turkish (language), Turk.

tuteur, -trice, *s.m.f.* guardian, trustee.

tutoyer, *v. a.* to 'thee-and thou' s. o.

tuyau, *s. m.* pipe, tube; flue; ~ *d'échappement* exhaust-pipe.

tympan, *s. m.* ear-drum.

type, *s. m.* type.

typique, *adj.* typical.

typographie, *s. f.* typography; printing.

tyran, *s. m.* tyrant.

tyrannie, *s. f.* tyranny.

tyranniser, *v. a.* tyrannize (over); oppress.

U

ulcère, *s. m.* ulcer.

ultérieur, *adj.* ulterior; further.

ultime, *adj.* ultimate, last, final.

ultra-violet-, -ette, *adj.* ulra-violet.

un, une, *art. & pron.* a, an; any; some; one; *l'~ ou l'autre* either one or the other; *ni l'~ ni l'autre* neither one; *l'~ et autre* both; ~*e fois* once; ~ *à* ~ one by one.

unanime, *adj.* unanimous.

uni, *adj.* smooth, even, level; united.

unification, *s. f.* unification.

unifier, *v. a.* unify; unite.

uniforme, *adj.* uniform.

union, *s. f.* union; agreement: match; marriage.

unique, *adj.* unique, sole, only.

uniquement, *adv.* solely, only.

unir, *v.a.* unite; level; smooth; s'~ join.

unité, *s.f.* unity; unit.

univers, *s. m.* universe.

universel, -elle, *adj.* universal; world-wide.

universitaire, *adj.* academic, university.

université, *s.f.* university.

urbain, *adj.* urban.

urgence, *s.f.* urgency; d'~ urgent; *en cas d'~* in case of emergency.

urgent, *adj.* urgent, pressing.

uriner, *v. n. & a.* urinate.

urne, *s. f.* urn.

usage, *s. m.* use, custom;

habit, way; wear; *d'~*
usual, habitual; *en ~*
in use.

usé, *adj.* worn-out,
shabby.

user, *v. n. & a.* use, make
use of; wear out; use
up; — *s.m.* wear,
service, use; *être d'un
bon ~* wear well.

usine, *s. f.* factory, works.

ustensile, *s. m.* utensil;
implement, tool.

usuel, -elle, *adj.* usual,
customary.

usure[1], *s. f.* usury.

usure[2], *s. f.* wear (and
tear).

usurper, *v.a.* usurp.

utile, *adj.* useful, of use,
profitable; *être ~ ( )*
be of use.

utilisation, *s.f.* utiliza-
tion.

utiliser, *v.a.* utilize.

utilité, *s. f.* utility, use.

V

va *int.* agreed!, indeed.

vacance, *s. f.* vacancy;
(pl.), holiday(s), va-
cation; *être en ~s* be
on holiday.

vacant, *adj.* vacant.

vacarme, *s.m.* noise,
uproar.

vaccin, *s.m.* vaccine.

vacciner, *v. a.* vaccinate.

vache, *s.f.* cow.

vaciller, *v.n.* vacillate;
reel; waver.

vacuum, *s. m.* vacuum.

vagabond, *s. m.* trampe.

vague[1], *adj.* vague.

vague[2], *s.f.* wave.

vaillant, *adj.* valiant.

vain, *adj.* vain; empty;
en ~ in vain.

vaincre*, *v. a. & n.*
conquer, defeat.

vainqueur, *s.m.* conquer-
or, victor; — *adj.*
conquering, victorious.

vaisseau, *s. m.* vessel;
ship.

vaisselle, *s. f.* plates and
dishes, table-service;
laver la ~ wash up the
dishes; *lavage de ~*
washing-up.

valet, *s. m.* valet; knave,
jack.

valeur, *s. f.* value, worth;
price; courage; *~s* se-
curities.

valide, *adj.* valid; able-
bodied.

validité, *s.f.* validity.

valise, *s. f.* valise, (travel-
ling-)bag; suitcase; *~
diplomatique* dispatch-
box, diplomatic bag.

vallée, *s. f.* valley.

valoir*, *v.n. & a.* be
worth, be as good as;
deserve; procure; yield.

valse, *s.f.* waltz.

vanille, *s.f.* vanilla.

vanité, *s.f.* vanity.

vaniteux, -euse, *adj.* vain,
conceited.

vanter, *v. a.* extol, cry up;
se ~ boast.

vapeur[1], *s.f.* steam;
vapour.

vapeur[2], *s.m.* steamer.

vaporeux, -euse, *adj.* va-
porous.

vaquer, *v. n.* be vacant.

variable, *adj.* variable,

changeable.

variante, *s.f.* variant.

variation, *s.f.* variation.

varier, *v. n. & a.* vary; ~ *de* ... *à* range from ... to.

variété, *s. f.* variety.

vase, *s. m.* vase; vessel.

vaseline, *s. f.* vaseline.

vassal, *s. m.* vassal.

vaste, *adj.* vast; spacious.

vautour, *s. m.* vulture.

veau, *s. m.* veal; calf.

vedette, *s.f.* mounted sentinel; motor-boat; (film) star.

végétal, *s. m.* vegetable; plant.

végétation, *s. f.* vegetation.

végéter, *v. n.* vegetate.

véhémence, *s. f.* vehemence.

véhément, *adj.* vehement.

véhicule, *s. m.* vehicle.

véhiculer, *v. a.* transport.

veille, *s. f.* waking; vigil; eve.

veiller, *v. n.* sit up, keep watch; *v.a.* watch.

veine, *s. f.* vein; luck.

vélo, *s.m.* bike.

vélocité, *s.f.* velocity.

velours, *s.m.* velvet.

velouté, *adj.* velvety, soft.

velu, *adj.* hairy.

venaison, *s.f.* venison.

vendange, *s.f.* vintage, grape-harvest.

vendeur, -euse *s. m. f.* salesman, shop assistant; saleswoman.

vendre, *v. a.* sell; *à* ~ for sale.

vendredi, *s. m.* Friday; *le* ~ *saint* Good Friday.

vénéneux, -euse, *adj.* poisonous.

vénérable, *adj.* venerable.

vengeance, *s. f.* vengeance, revenge.

venger, *v.a.* avenge, revenge; *se* ~ avenge oneself.

venin, *s.m.* poison.

venir*, *v. n.* come, arrive; grow; occur; arise; ~ *de* come from; ~ *à bout de* manage.

vent, *s. m.* wind; *grand* ~ gale; ~ *alizé* trade-wind.

vente, *s. f.* sale; auction; *en* ~ for sale.

venteux, -euse, *adj.* windy.

ventilateur, *s. m.* ventilator.

ventilation, *s. f.* ventilation.

ventre, *s. m.* belly.

venue, *s.f.* coming, arrival.

ver, *s.m.* worm.

verbal, *adj.* verbal, oral.

verbe, *s.m.* verb.

verdeur, *s.f.* greenness; harshness.

verdict, *s.m.* verdict.

verdure, *s.f.* verdure; greenness.

verger, *s.m.* orchard.

vergue, *s.f.* yard.

vérification, *s.f.* verification; check(ing).

vérifier, *v.a.* verify; check; confirm.

vérité, *s.f.* truth.

vermicelle, *s.m.* vermicelli.

vernir, *v. a.* varnish; polish.

vernis, *s.m.* varnish; polish.

verre, *s.m.* glass.

verrou, *s.m.* bolt.

verrouiller, *v.a.* bolt.

vers[1], *s.m.* line; verse.

vers[2], *prep.* towards, to; about.

verser, *v. a.* pour (out) spill, upset; *v. n.* overturn.

version, *s. f.* translation; version.

vert, *adj.* green; hearty; sharp.

vertical, *adj.* vertical, upright.

vertige, *s. m.* dizziness.

vertu, *s.f.* virtue.

vessie, *s.f.* bladder.

veste, *s. f.* coat, jacket.

vestiaire, *s. m.* cloakroom.

vestibule, *s.m.* lobby, hall; **grand ~** lounge.

veston, *s. m.* coat; **complet ~** lounge-suit.

vêtement, *s.m.* clothes *(pl.);* **~s de dessous** underwear, underclothes.

vétéran, *s.m.* veteran.

vétérinaire, *s. m.* veterinary surgeon, vet.

vêtir*, *v. a.* clothe, dress.

véto, *s.m.* veto.

veuf, *s.m.* widower.

veuve, *s.f.* widow.

vexer, *v. a.* vex, annoy.

via, *prep.* via.

viaduc, *s. m.* viaduct.

viande, *s. m.* meat; **~ réfrigérée** chilled meat.

vibration, *s. f.* vibration.

vibrer, *v. n.* vibrate.

vicaire, *s.m.* curate.

vice, *s.m.* vice, evil.

vice-, *prefix* vice-

vicieux, -euse, *adj.* vicious; faulty.

vicomte, *s. m.* viscount.

victime, *s.f.* victim.

victoire, *s.f.* victory.

victorieux, -euse, *adj.* victorious.

victuailles, *s. f. pl.* victuals.

vide, *adj.* empty; void; vacant; **—** *s.m.* space.

vider, *v. a.* empty; drain.

vie, *s.f.* life.

vieillard, *s.m.* old man.

vieillesse, *s. f.* old age.

vieillir, *v.n.* grow old.

vierge, *s. f.* virgin, maid.

vieux, vieil, vieille, *adj.* old.

vif, vive, *adj.* live; quick; lively; full of life; bright, vivid; fiery, ardent.

vigilant, *adj.* watchful.

vigne, *s.f.* vine; vineyard.

vignoble, *s.m.* vineyard.

vigoureux, -euse, *adj.* vigorous.

vigueur, *s.f.* vigour force.

vilain, *s. m.* villain, ca⟨⟩

village, *s.m.* village.

ville, *s. f.* town, city; **hôtel de ~** town hall.

vin, *s. m.* wine.

vinaigre, *s. m.* vinegar.

vingt, *adj. & s.m.* twenty; twentieth.

vingtième, *adj.* twentieth.

violation, *s.f.* violation.

violence, *s.f.* violence.

violent, *adj.* violent; excessive.

violer, *v. a.* violate, ravish.

violette, *s.f.* violet.

violon, *s.m.* violin.

violoncelle, *s. m.* (violon-)cello.

violoniste, *s. m f.* violinist.

vipère, *s.f.* viper.

virgule, *s.f.* comma; *point et* ~ semicolon.

virtuose, *s. m. f.* virtuoso.

vis, *s. f.* screw.

visa, *s.m.* visa, visé.

visage, *s. m.* face.

vis-à-vis, *prep.* opposite; facing.

viser, *v.a.* aim (at); aspire to.

viseur, *s. m.* view-finder.

visibilité, *s. f.* visibility.

visible, *adj.* visible.

vision, *s.f.* sight.

visite, *s. f.* visit; *faire* ~ *à* pay a visit to, call on.

visiter, *v. a.* visit; ~ *les curiosités* go sightseeing.

visiteur, **-euse**, *s. m. f.* visitor.

visser, *v. a.* screw (down, in).

visuel, **-elle**, *adj.* visual.

vital, *adj.* vital.

vitalité, *s.f.* vitality.

vitamine, *s. f.* vitamin.

vite, *adj.* fast; swift; — *adv.* fast, rapidly.

vitesse, *s. f.* speed; rate (of speed); gear; *à toute* ~ at top speed; *boîte de* ~ gearbox; ~ *de croisière* cruising speed.

vitrail *s. m.* church window.

vitre, *s. f.* pane.

vitrier, *s.m.* glazier.

vivant, *adj.* alive, living: full of life; *de mon* ~ in my lifetime.

vivement, *adv.* quickly, fast.

vivre*, *v. n.* live, be alive.

vocabulaire, *s. m.* vocabulary.

vocation, *s.f.* vocation, calling.

vœu, *s. m.* (pl. -x) wish, desire; vow.

vogue, *s. f.* vogue, fashion; *avoir la* ~ be in vogue.

voici, *prep.* here (is); *le* ~! here he is!

voie, *s.f.* way, road; route; line, track; means, channel.

voilà, *prep.* there (is).

voile[1], *s.m.* veil.

voile[2], *s.f.* sail.

voiler, *v.a.* veil, cover, hide.

voilier, *s. m.* sailing-ship.

voir*, *v. a.* see; look at; view; *faire* ~ show; *ne pas* ~ miss.

voire, *adv.* even.

voisin, *adj.* neighbouring, adjoining, next (door).

voisinage, *s.m.* neighbourhood.

voiture, *s.f.* vehicle, conveyance; carriage; car; coach; van; wagon; *aller en* ~ drive.

voiture-ambulance, *s. f.* ambulance(-car).

voix, *s. f.* voice; sound; *à haute* ~ aloud.

vol[1], *s. m.* flying, flight.

vol[2], *s. m.* theft, robbery.

volaille, *s.f.* poultry, fowl.

volant, *s.m.* steering-wheel.

volcan, *s.m.* volcano.

volée, *s.f.* flight.

voler[1], *v. n.* fly; run at top speed.

voler[2], *v. a. &* st. steal, rob.

volet, *s.m.* shutter.

voleur, *s. m.* thief, robber.

volontaire, *adj.* voluntary. — *s. m. f.* volunteer.

volonté, *s. f.* will; *à* ~ at will.

volontiers, *adv.* willingly.

volt, *s.m.* volt.

voltiger. *v.n.* flutter about, fly about.

volume, *s. m.* volume; bulk.

voluptueux, -euse, *adj.* voluptuous.

vomir, *v. a. & n.* vomit, be sick.

vos, *adj. poss.* your.

vote, *s. m.* vote; voting.

voter, *v. n.* ~ *& a.* vote.

votre, *adj.* yours.

vouer, *v. a.* vow; dedicate.

vouloir*, *v. a.* want, require, demand; ~ *bien* be willing; *je voudrais* + *inf.* I should like to; *comme vous voulez* as you please.

vous, *pron.* you; to you.

vous-même, *pron.* yourself.

voûte, *s.f.* vault, arch.

voyage, *s.m.* journey; voyage; *bon* ~*l* a pleasant journey (to

you)!; *partir en* ~ set off on a journey; *faire un* ~ make a journey.

voyager, *v.n.* travel, make a trip.

voyageur, -euse, *s. m. f.* traveller, passenger.

voyelle, *s.f.* vowel.

voyou, *s.m.* hooligan.

vrai, *adj.* real, true, right; *être* ~ hold (good); — *s. m.* truth; *être dans le* ~ be right.

vraiment, *adv.* truly, really; indeed.

vraisemblable, *adj.* likely, credible, probable.

vu, *prep.* considering.

vue, *s. f.* sight; vision; view; *à* ~ at sight; *en* ~ *de* with a view to; *point de* ~ point of view; *avoir la* ~ *courte* be short-sighted; *être en* ~ be in the limelight.

vulgaire, *adj.* vulgar; common; coarse.

W

wagon, *s. m.* coach, carriage, car.

wagon-lit, *s. m.* sleeping-car.

wagonnet, *s. m.* tub; truck.

wagon-poste, *s. m.* mail-van.

wagon-restaurant, *s. m.* dining-car.

water-closet, *s. m.* W. C.

water-polo, *s. m.* water-polo.

wattman, *s.m.* tram-driver.

week-end, *s.m.* weekend.

whisky, *s.m.* whisky.

yeux *see* œil.

yogourt, yoghourt, *s. m.* yoghourt, yaourt.

yougoslave, *adj.* Yugoslav.

youyou, *s.m.* dinghy.

X

xérès, *s. m.* sherry.

xylographie, *s. f.* xylography.

xylophages, *s.m.* *pl.* xylophages.

Z

zèbre, *s.m.* zebra.

zébrer, *v.a.* stripe.

zèle, *s.m.* zeal.

zélé, *adj.* zealous.

zénith, *s.m* zenith.

zéro, *s.m.* zero.

zézayer, *v.n.* lisp.

zigzag, *s.m.* zigzag.

zinc, *s.m.* zinc.

zone, *s.f.* zone, belt.

zoo, *s.m.* zoo.

zoologie, *s.f.* zoology.

zoologique, *adj.* zoological.

zut, *int.* ~! damn it!

Y

y, *adv.* here, there; *il* ~ *a* there is, there exists; *s'*~ *connaître* well informed.

yacht, *s. m.* yacht.